YOUNG MR PEPYS

SAMUEL PEPYS
holding his song, 'Beauty Retire'

by J. Hales

JOHN E. N. HEARSEY

YOUNG
MR PEPYS

———✦———

HISTORY BOOK CLUB

This edition published by
The History Book Club
St. Giles House, 49/50 Poland Street,
London W1A 2LG
by arrangement with Constable & Company Ltd.
Copyright © 1973 by John Hearsey

ISBN 0 09 459140 7

Set in 'Monotype' Ehrhardt
Printed in Great Britain
by Ebenezer Baylis and Son Ltd.
The Trinity Press, Worcester, and London

IN MEMORY OF MY MOTHER
WHO MADE IT POSSIBLE
FOR ME TO BECOME A WRITER

Contents

Illustrations

A*

Illustrations

Acknowledgements

I should like to express my thanks to the following for permission to use reproductions of paintings and prints as illustrations: the Dean and Chapter of Westminster; the Trustees and Directors of the British Museum; the National Portrait Gallery; the London Museum; the National Maritime Museum, London; and the Guildhall Library.

I should also like to thank all those who have helped bring the book itself into being.

J.E.N.H.

Introduction

IF the Diary of Samuel Pepys chronicles a decade in the life of a
man, it is also the odyssey of an individual who stands almost
outside time, for in the many facets of his being there is something
of everyone who has ever lived, hoped, feared, striven and succeeded. By its very nature a diary must lack conscious over-all shape,
and yet that is a quality Samuel Pepys gave to his writing. What is
more, the Diary exists on several levels at once: the psychology of
his mind laid bare—by his own unbelievable truthfulness—as completely as it could have been done by the lengthy probings of a skilled
analyst, the wealth of detail about everyday life, which is, after all,
the basis of everyone's existence, however exalted he may be.
Everything is there, from the grossness of a few notorious passages
(which merely distort but do not deepen the picture), through the
sometimes perilous seas of his married life, his work at the Navy
Office, his encounters with people of all degrees, glimpses of life at
Court and the great world on whose fringes he moved, and perhaps
above all the great events which he witnessed and participated in,
and which have long since become part of a nation's history.

A day-to-day journal ought to lack shape, yet it is just one of the
Diary's unique qualities that it has a beginning, a most dramatic
middle, and an end which is both inevitable and valedictory. Had
Samuel Pepys continued the Diary for another six months it would
have ended not only with his fear of blindness, but with the death of
Elizabeth, his child-like wife.

Paradoxically, it is the fact that there is no deliberate literary style
that gives the Diary its unique flavour: there is no conscious searching for the right word, the right phrase. Pepys could sum up a person
and their characteristics in a line or two that can be mordant or
heart-warmingly endearing. Perhaps it would not be unfair or
inaccurate to suggest that the sections of the Diary which come

I

nearest to possessing literary style are those dealing at length with the political scene, when in Dr Johnson's phrase 'the attention retires'.

The contemporary Bohemian artist Wenceslaus Hollar engraved an incredibly detailed panorama of London before and after the Great Fire, and with his pen Pepys performed the same service for later generations. Covering as it does nearly a million and a quarter words, it is not so much a matter for regret that the Diary ends when it does, but gratitude that he continued it for so long. As Clerk of the Acts to the Navy he was an exceedingly busy man, who in the years to come after he had regretfully closed his beloved journal for the last time would not only reform the administration of the Navy, but even lay the foundations of the Civil Service itself. In that Diary is a gallery of characters perhaps only rivalled by Dickens himself, except that these really existed. For nine and a half years a window was opened on to a world that three hundred years later is still almost tangible: a world of sunshine and dirt; of corruption and little kindnesses; of great happenings and the ordinariness of every-day life; of good music and the trials of keeping house; of loving; of friends and enemies; of the pleasures of the flesh and of getting money: the sum total of human existence in fact. And then suddenly that window is closed, not only on a man's whole life, but on all the people he knew and loved and hated. We all know what happened to James, Duke of York—so plain in his nightgown—or 'pretty witty Nell', but what of Mrs Pierce the surgeon's wife, or Tom Edwards who married Jane the maid: did he turn out better than Pepys expected? What of Mrs Bagwell, the carpenter's wife?

It would be idle to pretend that the Diary is all straightforward reading: at times it is complex, and the very number of names involved makes it confusing, while its sheer length calls for con-siderable perseverance. Not only could Samuel Pepys charm, and in his turn be charmed by his fellow men, but he could communicate his immense enthusiasm for life; and perhaps what sustains him so unflaggingly in the Diary is the fact that he was never bored by the world about him, and least of all by the people in it. That so observant an individual should have been afflicted with defective sight is the supreme irony. When the first mutilated and truncated edition of the transcribed Diary appeared in 1825 Pepys was, per-haps, regarded with good-humoured amusement. But over the intervening years he has come to be appreciated not only as an observer of life, and a great administrator; but in an age which seems corroded with bitterness, hatred and cruelty, as a most uncommon ordinary man who was touched with the priceless gifts of humanity and of a love for his fellow men.

Chapter 1

Early Years
1633–59

ALTOGETHER eleven children were born to John and Margaret Pepys in their house in Salisbury Court, in the shadow of St Bride's Church, just off Fleet Street. But of those eleven children only four were to survive childhood; the other seven being buried in the adjoining churchyard. In that particularly crowded and un-hygienic area of the City it was perhaps something of an achievement to bring up even four. John Pepys, born in 1601, had left his native village of Cottenham in Cambridgeshire at the age of fourteen, to become a tailor's apprentice in London. After serving his apprentice-ship he wished to branch out on his own, but he was a 'foreigner': neither a Londoner by birth nor a member of the Merchant Taylors' Guild. As a result he was subjected to restrictions, and could only carry on his craft in the Liberties outside the walls of London, though within the jurisdiction of the City itself. So he settled in Salisbury Court, a few hundred yards inside the City's western boundary at Temple Bar, with Alsatia, that thieves' kitchen of tene-ments which was a haven for criminals and which few outsiders dared enter, as a near neighbour.

John Pepys was descended from many generations of fenmen, among whom were bailiffs to the great Abbey of Crowland, which in the Middle Ages was a bastion of Christianity in those remote flood-swept pasture lands; but his wife Margaret Kite was a Londoner through and through. Her brother was a butcher, while a sister was also married to one of the same trade, and another to a blacksmith named Fenner. They were to become the aunts of the future Samuel Pepys, who would usually refer to the former as 'Aunt Kite' (despite her married name of Clarke), and the latter as 'Aunt Fenner'.

John Pepys was not the only member of the family to come to London. There was his half-brother Thomas by his father's first marriage, who in his turn had a son, Thomas the Turner, the owner of a shop close to Paul's Churchyard. All these Pepyses and their relations by marriage were steeped in Puritanism, but none more so than the one referred to as 'Aunt James'. Her religious zeal was that of the fanatic. The fifth child of John Pepys, born on 23 February 1633 and christened Samuel, naturally absorbed the precepts of his elders, who regarded the Court of Charles I and his Popish Queen Henrietta Maria as at best frivolous and at worst damned. But Samuel Pepys was a friendly child, with a knack of making friends, infinitely curious and with a great liking for the pleasures of the world, such as Bartholomew Fair and above all the theatre; and so he remained, both as a man, and as a man of consequence. But there was one pleasure John Pepys indulged in without any qualms, and that was music. He himself played the bass viol, and at an early age Samuel showed both a love and an aptitude for music, and all through his life he would find time to play the bass viol, the violin, the lute, or to sing. Even in the flush of excitement on the mission to bring Charles II back to England at the start of the Restoration, he could find time to make music with congenial companions on board the warship *Naseby*, the pride of the English fleet.

By and large it was a reasonably happy childhood, little affected by the momentous events going on in London and throughout the country. Of much more immediate interest must have been the relations who also lived in Salisbury Court. There was another John Pepys, descended from the Norfolk branch of that widely scattered family, and a figure of importance in the legal world. From time to time he invited Samuel, his brothers Tom and John (died 1641) and sister Pall (Paulina) to stay at his country house at Ashstead, near Epsom. Those visits must have been a welcome escape from the teeming and congested alleys around Salisbury Court, some of which were so narrow that even a handcart could not pass up or down. Evidently John Pepys was anxious to perpetuate his own christian name, for when Samuel's eldest surviving brother of that name died at the age of eight, another son born soon after was also given the name of John. With the death of the eldest girl, Mary, the number of children in the house was reduced to four: Samuel, who was now the eldest; Thomas, who would follow in his father's footsteps and become a tailor; Paulina; and John, who would enter the Church.

All his life Pepys was tormented by ill-health, and especially as a child. He suffered when it was excessively hot, and quite equally from the cold. But above all he was afflicted by the stone, and in 1658 he could count himself lucky to recover completely from a major surgical operation for the removal of a large stone. It would seem to have been inherited from his mother's side of the family, for she too suffered from it, and eventually it was to kill poor fanatical 'Aunt James'.

When he was ten, Samuel Pepys was sent into the country, perhaps for his health, but whatever the reason he went to the Grammar School at Huntingdon, where some twenty-five years before Oliver Cromwell had been a pupil. Here he was watched over by his elderly great-uncle Talbot Pepys, squire of Impington, near the village of Cottenham. At Hinchingbrooke, just outside Huntingdon, lived some distant, but very grand cousins. A sister of Talbot Pepys had married the squire there who resided in a house once owned by Sir Oliver Cromwell (until lavish living forced him to sell), who was the future Protector of England's uncle. Now it was the home of the Montagu family. Curiously enough Edward Montagu was also related to Oliver Cromwell. Seventeen years later, Sir Edward, as he then was, was to become his young kinsman's friend and patron, and to set the course of his life by obtaining for him the position of Clerk of the Acts to the Navy Board. Close to Huntingdon was yet another relative: Uncle Robert, half-brother to Samuel's father, who lived at Brampton where he owned a house and lands. His wife was a widow, with children by her first marriage, who later, after he had inherited his uncle's estate in 1661, were to prove a thorn in Samuel's flesh.

From 1642 the Civil War was raging throughout England, though apart perhaps from the excitement of a visit to Huntingdon by Cromwell seeking recruits for his New Model Army, it did not concern him personally. The young Pepys would have been no more than a schoolboy with Roundhead and republican sympathies who was an onlooker to events unparalleled in the history of England. Those events had their beginnings in the attitudes of the first two Stuart kings towards subjects who were no longer prepared to accept a passive and subservient role.

James I and Charles I both believed that the power and will of the laws of the land stemmed from them, via *their* judges; while judicial leaders such as Sir Edward Coke were beginning to argue that English Common Law was above everyone, including the

King. English Common Law went back to the Middle Ages, but the Prerogative Courts dated only from the time of the Tudors at their most absolute. To make an already inflamed situation worse the two men who wielded the greatest power in Charles I's name were out of touch with the changing times.

One was Archbishop Laud, whose inflexibility led in the end to his execution in 1642, and the abolition of the Bishops. From the 1580s onwards, Puritanism had been a growing force, both in the religious and political spheres, yet Laud was High Church and in spiritual matters nothing short of a dictator. The Church had its own courts; and many resented the fact that the Queen's co-religionists, the Catholics, were not persecuted, while Puritans were. Political dissenters like William Prynne were sentenced by the hated Star Chamber Court, which dealt out royal justice independently of the established courts of law.

If Laud was the spiritual supporter of the royal coat of arms of Charles I, Thomas Wentworth, Earl of Strafford, filled the same function in the political field. The Irish were the first to feel his heavy hand, and after antagonising Catholic and Protestant alike, Strafford returned to England, when what was to become the Long Parliament was called in 1640. It was destined to break the power of the sovereign, take the ruling of the country into its own hands and even direct the Army during the Civil War. On one side were the King himself, Laud and Strafford; and for Parliament not only the Puritans but men of more moderate opinions. Men like Pym and John Hampden: it was the latter who made legal history when he defied the King by refusing to pay Ship Money when the tax was illegally imposed.

Much was to come out of the Long Parliament, starting with the overthrow of Strafford, the abolition of the hated Star Chamber and the impeachment of Laud. The imposition of Ship Money, without the authority of Parliament, was declared illegal. Strafford was too powerful, and in his way too clever, to be allowed to live, and like Laud he was consigned to the Tower to await trial. Under pressure, Charles I signed the Act of Attainder which meant the death of his friend. Then he had to put his signature to a Bill by which Parliament could be dissolved only with its own consent. Next came the Grand Remonstrance, a Puritan-inspired demand that the King's councillors should be men acceptable to Parliament, and the Root and Branch Bill for the abolition of the bishops. After that it was the vital question who should control the Army, the King or Parliament. But now, in January 1642, Charles I had had enough, and went to Westminster to arrest Pym, Hampden, Hazelrigg, Holles and Strode; only to find that the birds had flown to the safety of the anti-royalist City. Civil war was now only a matter of months away.

When it came it was not a struggle that divided the country along clear social class lines. Any division was not horizontal, but vertical. Among the Parliamentarians were a number of peers, such as the Earls of Essex and Manchester, who were to be followed into the camp of the Roundheads by young men like Edward Montagu. The High Church followers, as well as Catholics and many more moderate Anglicans were Royalists almost to a man. It was the Presbyterians, Puritans and sectarians who became the Roundheads. If Charles I had the good-will of the Royalists, and such money as they could raise, the Roundheads had the wealth of the City which was Puritan and republican at heart.

To counter the King's forces Cromwell set about raising his New Model Army, with its backbone of Ironsides, mostly recruited from East Anglia, and the conflict swayed first one way and then the other. Marston Moor was a victory for the Roundheads and their Scottish allies in 1644, but soon afterwards Lostwithiel in Cornwall was taken by the Royalists, and the Earl of Essex made prisoner. This proved the occasion for Cromwell to come to the fore both in Parliament and on the battlefield. Then the Royalist armies took to plundering, to try to fill the King's coffers, and lost more in good-will than they gained in hard cash. Under General Fairfax the King's army sustained a decisive defeat at Naseby in 1645, and a year later the Royalist capital at Oxford surrendered. By now the war was almost over, at least for the time being, and most of those who had been caught up in it willy-nilly were longing for peace and a stable government regardless of where it came from. Had the Long Parliament handled the situation with tact in 1646–7, the Civil War might never have flared up again; but the righteous Presbyterians who dominated Parliament would tolerate no spiritual deviation and persecuted Anglicans on the one hand and the extreme sectarians on the other with equal zeal, and all in the name of the Lord. Also Parliament went in for mass expropriation of Royalists' property, and punitive fines, as a convenient way of refilling the exchequer (much as Henry VIII had done over a century before with the wealth of the despoiled abbeys). The extreme elements in the Long Parliament even demanded the expulsion from the New Model Army of the Independent officers: men who had done as much as anyone to put and keep them in power.

War broke out again, and Cromwell inflicted two crushing defeats on the Royalists, at Preston and the siege of Colchester (1648). Charles I was tried as a traitor to the laws of England, and among those who saw the last act 'in the street at Whitehall' on that frosty day in January 1649 was the fifteen-year-old Samuel Pepys, by then a staunch supporter of the Roundheads.

The stay at Huntingdon Grammar School had not been long for Samuel Pepys, probably not more than three or four years. It was to be the prelude to more rigorous academic studies at St Paul's School, just across the road from the cathedral. There the eleven- or twelve-year-old boy learnt Latin, Greek and Hebrew—the three pillars of a classical education—so that, with all the precosity of the educated child of the seventeenth century, he could make orations in Latin and Greek and read Virgil and Aeschylus in the original. Whether it was a good all-round education or not might be open to question, but it was the springboard which would send him to Cambridge on a scholarship (called an Exhibition) provided by the Mercers' Company. He was fortunate, and in June 1651 he set out for Cambridge; first to Trinity Hall, but soon he transferred to Magdalene, whose new Master John Sadler was in fact a neighbour in Salisbury Court. They must have been pleasant years, away from the mainstream of turbulent politics.

England might be a Republic and a Commonwealth after 1649, but away in the north young Charles II was crowned as King of Scotland at Scone. Royalist hopes were however again shattered: the royal armies were defeated on 3 September 1650 at Dunbar, and exactly a year later at Worcester. Charles II fled abroad, to remain in exile for nine years. When he did return the mission would be under the command of Sir Edward Montagu who would have with him Samuel Pepys acting as his secretary. In the ten years both men would come a long way from their republicanism of the 1640s.

Early in the Civil War the Roundheads had gained control of a large part of the Navy (the remainder was under the command of Prince Rupert), and during the Commonwealth they built it up into a fine fighting force, which was a match even for the very able

Dutch fleet during the Dutch War of 1652-4. It was under the command of Robert Blake, and ironically it was his creation that was bequeathed to Charles II at the Restoration. Blake showed the Commonwealth flag as far away as the Mediterranean, soundly beating the Barbary pirates who preyed on English merchantmen, and by so doing greatly enhanced the prestige of the new rulers of England.

At home Cromwell dismissed the Rump, the disarrayed remnants of the Long Parliament, referring contemptuously to the mace as a bauble, and became Protector. Now there was the rule of the Major Generals, but before his death in 1658 Cromwell was starting to feel his way back towards constitutional government, while at the same time becoming ever more regal in his daily life and attitudes. After his death, as England was swept by the greatest storm in living memory, an onlooker might well have feared that the country would lapse into anarchy, and even another civil war. But after a great deal of tension General Monk came forward as a strong man, if not the leader of the nation, and where he led others were prepared to follow.

During the years of the Commonwealth, Samuel Pepys pursued his studies at Cambridge, which he left as a Bachelor of Arts, and the idyll was over. Back he went to London, where for a while he probably worked in his father's shop, making himself useful in whatever way presented itself. His father's fortunes had by now slightly improved. For years it must have been a source of insecurity for him that he was not a member of the Guild of Merchant Taylors, and thus carried on his business only on sufferance. In the past there had been talk of depriving all interlopers—or 'foreigners'—of the right to work in the City and the Liberties. But in 1653 he became a member of the Guild, and thus gained an equal footing with the other London tailors.

Another member of the Pepys family became Lord Chief Justice of Ireland, while Edward Montagu became a member of Cromwell's Council of State and a Commissioner of the Treasury. Close contact with the Protector required his constant attendance at Whitehall Palace, where Cromwell, his wife and daughters lived in ever-increasing splendour, so he had lodgings nearby, probably in King Street, backing on to the Palace garden. After two years he was appointed Joint-Commander of the English Navy, with Robert Blake, and while he was at sea he asked his young kinsman Samuel

Pepys to keep an eye on his affairs. Pepys agreed, and before long he was living in the rooms over the gateway which spanned the public right of way through the Palace to Whitehall Stairs. The gatehouse was just to the left of Inigo Jones's Banqueting House, as seen from modern Whitehall. There he showed his gifts as an administrator, keeping Edward Montagu's financial affairs in excellent order, as well as undertaking tasks for his wife at Hinchingbrooke, and seeing all was well with their children at school at Twickenham. It was the foundation of a friendship which in time would ripen until he was like a member of the family, and almost an uncle to the children.

At Whitehall Pepys met Edward Montagu's elder sister, Lady Pickering, the wife of a fire-breathing Cromwellian who became the Protector's Lord Chamberlain. Lady Pickering was kind to Pepys, giving him good advice. Just how much fortunes were to change could be gauged by the fact that within five years she was giving Pepys £5 to encourage him to put in a good word with her own brother, now a King's man.

Pepys already showed that talent he had for making friends with all kinds of people. Among those he came to know were Shepley, the steward at Hinchingbrooke, and Robert Barnwell, the agent. Another was John Creed, Edward Montagu's secretary, though Pepys was never quite sure whether he really liked him, finding him somewhat cunning, much as he enjoyed his company. Also, he could claim acquaintanceship with Edward Montagu's father-in-law, John Crewe, who from time to time invited him to his house in Lincoln's Inn Fields.

That Samuel Pepys was very different from his relations perhaps first manifested itself when at the age of twenty-two he fell head-over-heels in love with the fifteen-year-old daughter of an impoverished French Huguenot who had come to England at the same time as Queen Henrietta Maria. She was Elizabeth le Marchant de St Michel, and only half French, for her mother had been the daughter of an Anglo-Irish knight. With her pale complexion and face framed with curls she looked little more than a child. What was more, neither she nor Pepys had a penny to their names. But on 10 October 1655, they married at St Margaret's, Westminster, and went on to the City to have their wedding breakfast at a tavern on Fish Street Hill.

In addition to his own numerous relations Samuel Pepys now had a father- and mother-in-law, and a brother-in-law named Balthazar, known as Balty, who, while charming, was also shiftless and good-for-nothing. While genuinely fond of each other, the young couple had their differences: there was no denying that Elizabeth was nowhere near Samuel's intellectual level. He tried to improve her mind by reading what he considered suitable books in the evening, but she was happier with a sentimental French romance, and not being nagged about her untidyness. These were difficult years, and it was some time before each came to terms with the other's nature: but there was a very real love, if at times clouded with jealousy, and each deep down was afraid of losing the other.

By this time Pepys's old affliction, the stone, had become so acute that if possible something had to be done about it. Among his father's neighbours in Salisbury Court was Thomas Hollier, a surgeon at St Thomas's Hospital. He was prepared to operate, and it was decided this should be done in the house of Mrs Turner, a kindly neighbour, who was also yet another cousin. To have the operation, without any form of anaesthetic of course, was a serious not to say solemn decision, for the chances of survival were no more than fifty-fifty, with death from sepsis as the greatest risk. All the family assembled to watch, as though they were bidding someone goodbye before a perilous voyage to the New World or the East Indies, and in their presence the operation was successfully carried out on 26 March 1658 and a stone as big as a tennis ball removed. For years afterwards Pepys regarded the day as one of thanksgiving and an occasion for celebration, and if possible he would entertain all those who had been present.

If the operation for the removal of a stone was the most important event for Pepys in the year 1658, the second most important, and one which would set him on the ladder of his career, came later that summer. Pepys became a Clerk of the Exchequer, which would be the equivalent to being a junior clerk in the Department of Inland Revenue. From the Middle Ages onwards it had been the custom for the nation's taxes to be received at a table covered with a chequered cloth, hence its name. Pepys worked in one of the Exchequer offices at Westminster, a duty he combined with looking after Edward Montagu's affairs, as it may have been through the latter's influence that he had received his new appointment.

His employer was George Downing, an unscrupulous man who in future years would see the inside of the Tower for a short while, for disobeying an order of Charles II. But for the present he was a loud and loyal servant of the Commonwealth. Also in the office was Hawley, Pepys's equal at the bottom of the promotion ladder, while above them was William Bowyer. Bowyer was a kind-hearted man, some years older than Pepys, who took an interest in the young man and his girl-wife, to the point of letting Elizabeth stay with his father in the country when Samuel's changing fortunes took him abroad. Pepys enjoyed the company of his fellow clerks: drinking, chatting, and making music whenever possible, though few were to remain members of his circle when he moved onwards and upwards. Indeed, there were occasions when Elizabeth must have felt neglected. It was not as though he only had the mean little rooms over the gateway to come home to now. They had a house of their own on lease in Axe Yard, which stood back from King Street, about halfway between Whitehall and Westminster, on the same side as St James's Park. Axe Yard formed a small community not unlike that in which Pepys had grown up in Salisbury Court. Although small the house included such luxuries as a study Pepys could call his own, a dressing-room, a cellar and a back yard. Elizabeth even had a maid to help with the work: Jane Wayneman, who was to prove a faithful servant, and become almost one of the family. All this was maintained on £50 a year, the salary Pepys received from his job at the Exchequer Office, plus the extra he was paid by Edward Montagu. There were more friends to be made, like their neighbour Mrs Crisp, who could play the harpsichord, and whose pretty daughter, Diana, Pepys would come to know rather too well; and Mr and Mrs Hunt with whom Elizabeth wiled away many evenings when Pepys was elsewhere. Usually he was socialising with the other clerks, or in the company of the friends he was making as a result of his contact with Edward Montagu. Among these was Henry Moore, a lawyer who would one day join him as a fellow Clerk of the Privy Seal, yet another appointment obtained by his generous patron.

That September Cromwell died, and though on the face of it England pursued the same course, the wind was already starting to shift, and the Protector's son—Tumbledown Dick—was not the one to prevent a change in men's hearts and minds. More and more Pepys was becoming interested in the Anglican form of religion, even to the point of skipping Presbyterian services in favour of furtive visits to houses where the Anglican religion was kept alive, despite official disapproval, not to say prosecution if caught. With Richard Cromwell's disappearance from the scene such government as there was passed into the hands of the Army, and that travesty of Parliament, the Rump, which now consisted of no more than fifty members who had trimmed their sails sufficiently dexterously to avoid expulsion for one reason or another. Many, including Sir Edward Montagu, as he now had become, had been prepared to follow a man as great as Cromwell. But if all that could be offered in his place was first his son Richard, and then a group of self-seekers who themselves were unsure in which direction they wanted to go, they now began to feel that the country could do worse than be ruled once again by a king.

Sir Edward was in fact out of the country, helping to negotiate a peace between Sweden and Denmark, from the warship *Naseby*, riding in the Ore Sund. This was in May 1659, and one can only regret that Pepys had not already started to keep his diary, for he was sent on official business to Sir Edward, crossing the North Sea in the ketch *Hind*. The only contemporary reference to Pepys's visit is in Sir Edward's journal, though in later years Pepys was to make passing references to the mission. If his official reason for going was important, whatever he told his kinsman in private was of greater consequence, because after that time Sir Edward threw in his lot with the exiled Charles II, and started what in the light of his allegiance to the Commonwealth was a highly treasonable correspondence with the Stuart king. Something of this change in loyalty must have filtered back to the wrong ears at Whitehall and Westminster, for he returned to find himself under suspicion, and wisely took himself off into the country, to his estates at Hinchingbrooke. There he remained until the following February, when on Pepys's advice he returned to London, and to high office in the Navy. Pepys had kept him meticulously informed of everything that could be of the slightest interest to him.

The beginning of the end for the Commonwealth came when the apprentices in London demanded that the City's ancient liberties should be restored: liberties that had been whittled away by the very people whom the City had so staunchly supported since long before the outbreak of the Civil War in 1642. Where parliamentary democracy had gone can be gathered by the fact that such rule as there was came from a Committee of Public Safety. Now even the soldiers were being attacked in broad daylight by the citizens. As things were, who could be sure of his place tomorrow? Pepys would not have been human if he had not felt anxious for himself. His was a government job at the Exchequer Office, and he had the responsibility of providing for Elizabeth, and their home in Axe Yard.

Chapter 2

The London of Samuel Pepys

THE years of Pepys's youth saw little change in the outward appearance of either the City or Westminster. As the country drifted towards civil war no one had the money or the inclination for lavish building work, and if some Londoner who had known the City well in 1600 had climbed the tower of St Mary Overy (now Southwark Cathedral) some fifty years later and looked across the panorama spread out on the opposite bank of the Thames, he would have found surprisingly little had altered. Still, there was the multitude of church towers rising above the tiled roofs of the three- and four-storeyed half-timber houses, and dominating everything at the west end of the City the massive bulk of Old St Paul's. There had in fact been alterations to the cathedral which the observer might have spotted. The Norman nave and transepts had been remodelled in the Renaissance style by Inigo Jones. And below, almost at his feet, the observer would have noticed that much of the northern end of Old London Bridge was bare of houses. They had been burnt off in a fire in February 1633, just twelve days before the birth of Pepys.

For more than a century London had been steadily overflowing its walls, and by 1660 only about one-third of its inhabitants lived within the confines of the City. Now the houses stretched to Hoxton and Whitechapel on the eastern side, though to the north of the walls Moorfields was still a 'moorish place', and also a rubbish dump. Beyond that it was a pleasant walk across the fields on a summer's evening to hamlets such as Islington and Newington. It was to the west that the growth had been greatest. Originally Westminster had been a small royal village containing the palace and burial place of the English monarchs. The great hall rebuilt by Richard II rose like some medieval reliquary, and close by was Henry III's French Gothic abbey church, as yet without its west towers. Round it clustered a number of surprisingly mean looking houses, as can be seen in the engravings done in the first half of the seventeenth century by the Bohemian artist Wenceslaus Hollar. Close to the Abbey was, and still is, the parish church of St Margaret's; the entrance to Palace Yard was through a gatehouse tower, containing a prison, but only really remembered in the engravings of Hollar. Not only was Westminster Hall the heart of the Palace, and the setting for great events such as the trial of Charles I, but it also housed various offices connected with the processes of the Law; while just inside the main door were little wooden booths and shops for booksellers, and even sellers of linen. It was a recognised place for hearing the latest news, and if there was something in particular that Pepys wanted to find out, like as not one of his acquaintances among the vendors would know.

But by the time of the Civil War, Westminster was no longer isolated from the City. Houses stretched all the length of King Street not already taken up by the huge and rambling Whitehall Palace. Further on at Charing Cross the thoroughfare changed direction to join the Strand, which by then was particularly densely built up on its north side. Charing Cross stood where Le Sueur's beautiful statue of Charles I on horseback now looks down Whitehall, towards the Banqueting House outside which he was beheaded.

The old cross marked the last resting place of the cortège that bore the body of Edward I's beloved Queen Eleanor from the Midlands, and the name Charing is in fact a corruption of *Chère Reine*. Another Eleanor Cross was in the City itself: in Cheapside, but it too has vanished, destroyed in 1644 by order of the Long Parliament.

Beyond Charing Cross was the site of what is now Trafalgar Square, and where the National Gallery stands were the royal Mews, to which Pepys made a brief reference in 1661. 'Meeting Sir R. Slingsby in St Martin's Lane, he and I in his coach through the Mewes, which is the way that now all coaches are forced to go, because of a stop at Charing Cross, by reason of digging a drain there to clear the streets.' Some aspects of the London scene are still very much as they were over three centuries ago.

All the way to the City between the Strand and the river were the great town houses occupied by various nobles: such as Somerset House originally built by the Duke of Somerset in Edward VI's reign; and Worcester House, visited by Pepys at the outset of his career when it contained the office of the Lord Chancellor. Beyond Temple Bar was the Temple itself. Although the church had to be almost rebuilt after the Second World War, it would be familiar to Pepys, and so would the Middle Temple Hall close by. On the other side of the Strand was Drury Lane with its Theatre Royal. It was in that same thoroughfare that Pepys would first see in June 1665 houses marked with a red cross and the words 'Lord have mercy upon us', on their doors. It was the start of the Plague.

Restoration London had sprouted theatres at a truly remarkable rate as old ones reopened and new ones opened their doors for the first time. Pepys was an avid playgoer, particularly during 1661, when on occasions he went three times in a week. As far back as Elizabeth's reign the City had adopted a strongly Puritan stand, and forced the theatres within the City to move across the river to Southwark, into London's 'red light' district. So the theatres Pepys visited ranged from the shabby and indifferent Red Bull in Clerken-well, when there 'were not above ten more than myself' in the pit, to the theatre in Lincoln's Inn Fields or the Cockpit Theatre in Whitehall Palace itself, where there was an excellent chance of finding the King, the delectable Barbara Villiers and the Duke of York among the audience. After the Restoration there was even a theatre in Salisbury Court, but from an historical point of view the most interesting of all must have been the Blackfriars. Blackfriars Priory was dissolved in Henry VIII's reign, and in the time of Elizabeth the actor-manager Burbage had taken over part of it for his theatre. By an almost freakish coincidence the room he used and where Shakespeare's *Henry VIII* was performed was the actual chamber in which Henry's divorce petition from Katharine of Aragon was heard before Cardinal Campeggio.

In Pepys's day London still possessed at least the lower parts of the walls built by the Romans, except along the Thames. To the west the walls and bastions with their later additions overlooked Old Bailey, and were pierced by two gateways: to the south Ludgate, and several hundred yards north, Newgate. Both were fitted up as prisons, and of the two Newgate was by far the more substantial, being the principal jail for London's criminals. State prisoners were still confined in the Tower. From Newgate the road ran nearly straight to Tyburn, the place of execution for most condemned malefactors. Tyburn was close to where Marble Arch now stands, but was then on the extreme western edge of London, and it was that journey from Newgate or the Tower which gave rise to the saying 'to go west'.

At the bottom of Ludgate Hill was perhaps the most squalid area in all London; a veritable shanty-town along the banks of the Fleet Ditch (a small river now running underground which at that time was little more than an open sewer). At its mouth was Bridewell, originally built as a royal palace in Henry VIII's reign, but which soon became a house of correction. Up the hill through Ludgate the street led to Old St Paul's, dwarfing everything by its sheer size. Once the largest cathedral in Europe it had in Pepys's day an overall length of about 635 feet. Begun in 1087, the year of the Conqueror's death, it had a massive Norman nave and transepts, with a comparatively light and airy choir added in the middle of the thirteenth century. Until its destruction by lightning in Elizabeth I's reign the great central tower possessed a spire about 459 feet high, but when Pepys knew it it had only a low pyramid-shaped roof. While Westminster Abbey could claim the kings and queens of England, Old St Paul's could boast the graves and monuments of John of Gaunt, Sir Philip Sidney, Elizabeth I's favourite Sir Christopher Hatton, John Donne, and Sir Anthony Van Dyck. In the Middle Ages, the cathedral had been one of the great pilgrimage centres of Europe, where the faithful came to pray and make offerings at the huge bejewelled shrine of the almost forgotten St Erkenwald, a seventh-century Bishop of London. But much as the Londoner's might love their cathedral, that fact did not stop them abusing it. By the beginning of the seventeenth century, the nave was a meeting place for half London. There lawyers met their clients, and those in search of a servant would go to Paul's Walk in search of a man to hire. It was somewhere dry if not warm for the unemployed, and even a favourite place for assignations. During the Civil War, Old St Paul's suffered every possible indignity: the choir was walled off to make a 'preaching house', at one time 800 cavalry horses were stabled in the nave, and during a severe winter their dung was sold as fuel.

Around Paul's Churchyard were the booksellers, including Kirton, patronised by Pepys. He would go there to buy new books, seek out old and rare editions, and take books of his own to be bound most handsomely in leather. Unwittingly it was the booksellers who contributed to the destruction of the cathedral during the Great

ELIZABETH PEPYS

Engraving by Thomson, after J. Hales

S. Magnes   Gray church   S. Dunstan in the East

Costomhowse

Billings gatt

Lyon key

THE BRIDGE

THE CITY, ABOUT 1635 *by Hollar*

Fire. As the flames approached they stacked as many books as they could in the crypt, which was also the parish church of St Faith's, and the remainder against the walls of the choir, so enabling the flames to get a hold and to spread down into the crypt through windows at ground level.*

Hard by the south-east corner of the cathedral was St Paul's School, where Pepys would be a pupil. On the river side the walls had long since vanished to be replaced by wharves, warehouses and narrow alleys and several Halls of the Livery Companies, including that of the Fishmongers near Old London Bridge. Altogether there were more than fifty such halls in the City, many in the one-time town houses of nobles who had chosen to move out to the light and air of the Strand. If the Tower was the great fortress guarding London and the Thames at the south-eastern corner, there was another and smaller waterside castle near the south-western edge of the City; the massive Baynard's Castle, itself nearly as old as the Tower, with historical associations which included Richard III and Mary Tudor.

Perhaps London's real high street was the Thames, and most who could afford the boatman's fare found it far quicker and cleaner to travel by water, but the main thoroughfare on land would have been Cheapside. Lined with fine merchants' houses it was the setting in the Middle Ages for jousts, and at the Standard, like a market cross, proclamations were read and in times of insurrection rough justice was meted out to hated officials such as tax gatherers. With its open-air market stalls it was the popular heart of the City, while the medieval Guildhall a few hundred yards away to the north was the administrative centre revolving around the Lord Mayor. To the east stood the Royal Exchange, one of the handsomest buildings Pepys would have known in the London of his day. Built by Sir Thomas Gresham in Elizabeth I's reign as a place for merchants to meet, it had an arcaded courtyard, which contained the best shops in London, specialising in luxury goods, spices and rarities from the East Indies as well as fine linen and haberdashery. It was a place where hours could be spent window shopping, or hearing news from home and abroad. For Pepys it rivalled Westminster Hall as a place where information could be gathered. What the booksellers and other

---

* Nearly three centuries later history failed to repeat itself during the terrible fire-raid of December 1940, when the booksellers in Ave Maria Lane and Paternoster Row lost no less than six million volumes, but St Paul's survived.

vendors at Westminster Hall and the merchants on the 'Change did not know about Parliament and the royal circle was not worth knowing.

Pepys, who had spent his childhood and adolescence in Salisbury Court on the western edge of the City, lived out his young manhood near its centre, in the house which went with his job at the Navy Office in Seething Lane, in the triangle between Fenchurch Street and Tower Street. At the top end of Seething Lane (a corruption of Sidon Lane) was St Olave, Hart Street, Pepys's parish church, where he and Elizabeth would be buried. Also near at hand was the Dolphin, the tavern frequented by the members of the Navy Board. On the other side of Thames Street was Trinity House and the Customs House, while at the bottom of the steep Fish Street Hill was that wonder of bygone England, Old London Bridge. There had been a wooden bridge thereabouts since Roman times, forming London's only link with the south-east, but in 1209 a stone replacement was completed. It was King John who suggested that it should help pay for its own upkeep by the rents from houses which could be built along its length. Old London Bridge was surprisingly narrow, only twenty feet wide, which because of the houses (most of which projected over the river and were supported on massive beams) was reduced to twelve feet. At the southern end was a stone gateway, forming part of the defences of the City, and a drawbridge which had long ago ceased to move. In the fourteenth century there were about 180 shops along its length, as well as a chapel, and a tavern at either end. At the City end was the Bear, which Pepys visited on a number of occasions to drink sack.

Thus the London Pepys grew up in and which he was to see vanish in 'a bloody malicious flame' was a medieval city of narrow twisting streets and alleys overhung by half-timber houses. It was a city of warehouses, small factories, numerous breweries and fine old houses, all cheek-by-jowl. To call the City a square mile is not strictly true: the area is about twice as long as it is broad, and into that space were crowded no less than 109 parishes, each with its own church. And what a cascade of names they had: St James-Garlikhythe; St Benet Buda; St Nicholas ad Bladum; St Nicholas-flee-Shambles (destroyed in Henry VIII's reign); St Peter-le-Quern (in Blow-bladder Street); St Peter-le-Poore, St Michael Paternoster Royal (Dick Whittington's church); and St Benet Sherehog, to mention only a few.

The City was Pepys's real home. But over the years Whitehall Palace was to become a second one. As Clerk of the Acts in the administration of Charles II's Navy he was not only to deal with the Navy Office, which was in the City, but also with the Admiralty, which was at Whitehall. And the fact that Sir Edward Montagu continued to keep lodgings near the Palace would not only take Pepys there frequently, but also bring him into contact with everyone from the King downwards.

Whitehall Palace straddled both sides of the thoroughfare that ran from Westminster to the City. Most of the royal apartments were on the south side fronting on to the river, while behind was the part built by Cardinal Wolsey not long before his fall, and confiscated by Henry VIII who made it his principal residence in London. That part included the Great Hall, the Chapel, the Privy Gallery and the Stone Gallery with its ceiling painted by Holbein. Inigo Jones's Banqueting House (all that now remains above ground of Whitehall Palace) was built by James I, and beside it was the gateway above which Pepys once lived, which led to the river at Whitehall Stairs. Beyond the passageway were the 'offices', the wood yard, bakery, brewery, scalding-house and the like. Also there was the part called Scotland Yard, where in Saxon times Scottish kings had a palace, used when they had to come south to swear oaths of loyalty to the English rulers. In the early nineteenth century it gave its name to the headquarters of the Metropolitan Police, which occupied the site. Two gates spanned what is now Parliament Street and Whitehall: to the west was the King Street Gate, while the other (the Holbein Gate) was in fact a bridge connecting the two halves of the Palace. On the north side were more apartments; Henry VIII's Covered Tennis Court (looking more like a chapel), and the Cockpit, by then converted into a theatre, and the Tilt-yard (adjoining the as-yet unbuilt Horse Guards). Behind was St James's Park, where Pepys was first to encounter the King after his return to London. That occasion arose less than six months after he had started to keep his Diary.

Chapter 3

The Auspicious Year
1660

IF there were a change in the governing of England there would be many who would regret it, and if he openly supported the monarchy Pepys wondered whether he would be allowed to retain his job at the Exchequer Office. It showed promise of reasonable prospects, and at least he was 'esteemed rich, but indeed very poor'. He had the good opinion of his neighbours in Axe Yard, and the days in the gatehouse, when he had to pawn his beloved lute, and Elizabeth did all the washing, should by right belong firmly to the past. What was more, at the beginning of 1660 he was free from pain resulting from the operation for the stone, carried out nearly two years before.

It was the beginning not only of a new year but also of a new decade, and to his methodical and logical mind it was an excellent occasion on which to start to keep a diary. It may have been at the Exchequer Office that he had been taught to use a cypher, a form of shorthand invented by one Thomas Shelton. Now, if he used this method at home he could record exactly what he thought, did and saw without the risk of giving offence, or causing unhappiness to Elizabeth should she discover the diary. So it began ordinarily enough, as thousands of others before and since have begun, except that Samuel Pepys would keep it up for nearly ten years, witnessing some of the most famous events in history, and standing closer to the heart of the nation's affairs than perhaps he ever realised. The 1 January 1660 was a Sunday. 'This morning (we living lately in the garret) I rose, put on my suit with great skirts, having not lately worn any other clothes but them. Went to Mr Gunning's Chapel at Exeter House, where he made a very fine sermon upon these words: "That in the fullness of time God sent His Son, made of woman", etc: showing that by "made under the law" is meant circumcision, which is solemnised this day. Dined at home in the garret, where my wife dressed the remains of a turkey, and in the doing of it burnt her hand. I stayed at home the whole afternoon, looking over my accounts: then with my wife to my father's, and in going observed the great posts which the City workmen set up at the Conduit in Fleet Street.'

The Diary had begun modestly enough, but before it was abandoned ten years later because of the strain it caused to his defective sight, future generations would be able to know more about one man and his times than almost any other in English history.

At Westminster Hall Pepys found there was much in the air, as he walked to and fro listening to the conversations of others, or talking with the booksellers and stallholders. General John Lambert was on his way to London; Lord Fairfax was of uncertain loyalty; and it was rumoured that the members who over the last years had been excluded might be allowed to return and take their places in Parliament. All the news Pepys could gather was soon on its way to Sir Edward at Hinchingbrooke. Among the pieces of information passed on was the news that writs for the replacement of those members discharged from Parliament in 1648–9 should soon be sent out, and that General Monk had been summoned to London, along with Fairfax.

Letter writing and entering up the Diary kept Pepys busy in the evenings, though at the Exchequer Office work was slack. 'From thence to the office, where nothing to do; but Mr Downing came and found me all alone, and did mention to me his going back into Holland, and did ask me whether I would go or no, but gave me little encouragement, but bade me consider of it; and asked me whether I did not think that Mr Hawley could perform the work of my office alone. I confess I was at a great loss all the day after to bethink myself how to carry on this business. I stayed up till the bell-man came by with his bell just under my window as I was writing this very line, and cried, "Past one of the clock, and a cold, frosty, windy morning." '

Pepys had reason to be worried by Downing's offer. Was he sincere in asking if he would like to go to Holland, or was it a trap to discover whether he justified his position in the Exchequer Office? If he agreed that his colleague could do all his work as well as his own, it was an admission he was not essential. He must tread carefully. Early on the morning of 19 January, Pepys was summoned to his employer's home. 'This morning I was sent for to Mr Downing, and at his bedside he told me, that he had a kindness for me, and that he thought that he had done me one, and that was, that he had got me to be one of the Clerks of the Council; at which I was a little stumbled, and could not tell what to do, whether to thank him or no; but by and by I did; but not very heartily, for I feared that his doing of it was only to ease himself of the salary which he gives me.' His head full of questions Pepys went off to Whitehall, to seek out the other Clerks of the Council and discover what he could. There he was in for a disappointment, for they told him that the evening before his name had in fact been mentioned, but that that was as far as it had gone.

The rest of the month slipped away with routine business at the office, rumours and speculations about the course General Monk might take: would he declare in favour of the restoration of Charles II, or wouldn't he? Pepys was bored by a 'lazy, poor sermon', started to put buckles on his shoes, and fell into a ditch in the dark in the grounds of Whitehall Palace. On 24 January he and Elizabeth were invited to a party at the house of Mr Pierce, the surgeon on the *Naseby*. It was a smart occasion, and Elizabeth had bought herself new shoes, with raised soles and heels to keep the wearer out of the mud: '. . . and she in her way being exceedingly troubled with a pair of new patterns, and I vexed to go so slow, it being late.' After dinner a couple pretended to be newly married, and the party indulged in the bawdy ritual which followed seventeenth-century nuptials. Although now a monarchist at heart Pepys was still enough of a Puritan to be shocked. 'There was a pulling off Mrs bride's and Mr bridegroom's ribbons, and a great deal of fooling among them that I and my wife did not like. Mr Lucy [the pretended groom] and several other gentlemen coming in after dinner, swearing and singing as if they were mad, only he singing very handsomely.' But all around the young couple events were happening which would culminate in the return of Charles II from exile. 'Coming home, heard that in Cheapside there had been but a little while before a gibbet set up, and the picture of Huson hung upon it in the middle of the street.' John Hewson was a colonel in the Parliamentarian Army, and one of those who had sentenced Charles I to death. Now it was his own picture dangling from the gallows.

In return for watching over his affairs in London, and sending regular reports to Huntingdonshire of what was happening in the nation's affairs, Sir Edward allowed his kinsman to use his lodgings at Whitehall Palace for entertaining his own relations. 'Home from my office to my Lord's lodgings, where my wife had got ready a very fine dinner—viz. a dish of marrow-bones; a leg of mutton; a loin of veal; a dish of fowl, three pullets, and a dozen larks all in a dish; a great tart, a neat's tongue, a dish of anchovies; a dish of prawns and cheese. My company was my father, my uncle Fenner, his two sons, Mr Pierce [whose party Samuel and Elizabeth had found so unseemly only two nights before], and all their wives, and my brother Tom.'

Pepys was still suspicious of George Downing's motives for asking if he would like to go to Holland and whether he thought Hawley could manage the work for both of them in the office. He was no less so the following day [28 January] when Downing announced that that very morning he was leaving for Holland, and already his baggage was being loaded on to a barge at Charing Cross Stairs. Pepys was surprised at the civility of his leave-taking, still fearing he would be told his services were no longer required. 'But he did not, but [said] that he would do me any service that lay in his power.'

Eleven years before, on 30 January 1649, a very republican Pepys had stood among the crowd to watch the execution of Charles I. Now, on that anniversary, he started the day—before even getting out of bed—by singing his own setting of Montrose's verses on the event:

> 'Great, good and just, could I but rate
> My grief and thy too rigid fate,
> I'd weep the world to such a strain
> That it would deluge once again.'

It was as though all England was waiting to take its cue from General Monk. If he gave a lead, the nation would follow. His long journey from Scotland was nearly over, and on 6 February Pepys stood on the steps in Palace Yard to see the General go by, as he did so acknowledging the presence of the Judges with a salutation. Since the beginning of the century the City had been strongly Puritan and anti-royalist: now it looked as though it would be prepared to stand out against Monk. If the Common Council were defiant, Parliament was in no mood for opposition, and sent Monk and his troops to draw their teeth, or rather to smash down the gates and portcullises of the City. Events were happening fast, and Pepys heard that Parliament should, before long, have its full number of members, including the return to the Commons of those discharged from the Long Parliament up to ten years previously. He hurried the few hundred yards from Axe Yard to Westminster Hall to see for himself how the news was being received: 'and it was very strange how the countenance of men in the Hall was all changed with joy in half an hour's time. So I went up to the lobby, where I saw the Speaker reading of the letter [from Monk], and after it was read, Sir A. Hazelrigge [one of the Five Members] came out very angry, and Billing [a Puritan member] standing at the door, took him by the arm, and cried, "Thou man, will thy beast carry thee no longer? Thou must fall!"' Determined to see the reaction at the other end of London, Pepys took himself off in a coach to the Guildhall, which he found full of people awaiting the arrival of Monk and the Lord Mayor. 'Met Monk coming out of the chamber where he had been with the Mayor and Aldermen, but such a shout I never heard in all my life, crying out, "God bless your Excellence!"' Although he could not of course know it, Pepys had in fact just witnessed the prologue to the Restoration. While at the Guildhall he ran into Matthew Locke, the composer whose music would be played some eighteen months hence in the King's coronation procession. What Locke had to tell Pepys was of great interest. It was the contents of Monk's letter to Parliament. It complained that many members of the House were 'of the late tyranical Committee of Safety', and went on to criticise that epitome of the Commonwealth at its most self-righteous, Praise-God Barebones, for insisting that Parliament should force yet another oath on the long-suffering public. But most important of all was Monk's demand, no less, that 'all writs for the filling up of the House be issued by Friday next, and that in the meantime he would retire into the City, and only leave them guards for the security of the House and Council.'

The Londoners were quick to sense that the tide had turned, and was running against the Parliamentarians and their Puritan attitudes. In the streets the inhabitants were calling out 'God bless you' to Monk's troops and giving them drink and money. The next day they would be breaking Praise-God Barebones's windows. Pepys remained in the City till evening. 'In Cheapside there was a great many bonfires, and Bow bells and all the bells in all the churches as we went home were a-ringing. Hence we went homewards, it being about ten at night. But the common joy that was everywhere to be seen! The number of bonfires, there being fourteen between St Dunstan's and the Temple Bar, and at Strand Bridge I could at one time tell thirty-one fires. In King Street seven or eight, and all along, burning, and roasting, and drinking for rumps [in derision of the Rump Parliament]. There being Rumps tied upon sticks and carried up and down. The butchers at the May Pole in the Strand rang a peal with their knives when they were going to sacrifice their rump. On Ludgate Hill there was one turning of the spit that had a rump tied upon it, and another basting of it. Indeed it was past imagination, both the greatness and the suddenness of it. At one end of the street you would think there was a whole lane of fire, and so hot that we were fain to keep on the further side.'

Work at the office must have suffered at this time. Judging from the entries in the Diary Pepys was more out of it than in. But who could blame him when there was so much to see? On 21 February there was the spectacle of about twenty of the members who had for so long been excluded returning to Parliament. Among them was William Prynne, the old adversary of Archbishop Laud during the years before the Civil War. In 1633 Prynne had published an attack on the theatre and masques, which were a favourite diversion of the Queen. This the ultra-royalist Laud took to be a personal attack on Henrietta Maria, and on his orders the lawyer was punished by suffering personal disfigurement, and being branded on the forehead and placed in the pillory. Twenty-seven years later the hideously mutilated Prynne was taking his place in a Parliament which would shortly vote for the restoration of a king. 'Mr Prin came in with an old basket-hilt sword on, and had a great many shouts upon his going into the Hall.' While he was watching Pepys was joined by Mr Crewe, Sir Edward Montagu's father-in-law, who invited him home to dinner, and told him that Monk had been made General of all the forces in England, Scotland and Ireland. What was more, he advised Pepys to tell Sir Edward it was a pro-pitious moment for him to return to London. After dinner Pepys hurried back to Westminster Hall again, fearful lest he should miss anything. There he met Matthew Locke and Henry Purcell, the father of a one-year-old boy who would one day do much for the reputation of English music. Music was almost an overwhelming passion with Pepys, and even at that time he was prepared to go off with his companions 'to the Coffee House, into a room next the water. Here we had variety of brave Italian and Spanish songs, and a canon for eight voices, which Mr Locke had lately made on these words: "Domine salvum fac Regem." Here out of the windows it was a most pleasant sight to see the City from one end to the other with a glory about it, so high was the light of the bonfires, so thick round the City, and the bells rang everywhere.'

The 23 February was Pepys's twenty-seventh birthday, and the day on which he heard that 'my Lord' (his way of referring to Sir Edward, long before he became Earl of Sandwich) had been elected one of the Council of State, along with his father-in-law Mr Crewe. At once he wrote to inform him of the news. Then Pepys set out, but not for Hinchingbrooke. Like himself his younger brother John had been a scholar at St Paul's School, and had won a scholarship to Cambridge. The previous day John had ridden to Cambridge, and now Samuel was following. With him went Mr Pierce the surgeon, to join a regiment stationed there. Near Cambridge they parted, and Pierce went towards Hinchingbrooke. For Pepys it was a pleasant reunion with old friends and fellow scholars from his days at Magdalene. 'To the Three Tuns, where we drank pretty hard and many healths to the King and etc:' The next day came the reason for the visit: 'My father, brother and I to Mr Widdington [his brother's tutor-to-be], at Christ's College, who received us very civilly, and caused my brother to be admitted.' But soon after John changed to Magdalene, whose Master was a neighbour in Salisbury Court. The following day Pepys was rejoined by Pierce, who informed him that Sir Edward Montagu had already left Hinchingbrooke for London. Long before dawn next morning Pepys was up and on his way back to London and the Exchequer Office. This time he travelled through Saffron Walden, where he broke his journey to visit Audley End, where 'the housekeeper showed us all the house, in which the stateliness of the ceilings, chimney-pieces and the form of the whole was exceedingly worth seeing. He took us into the cellar, where we drank the most admirable drink, a health to the King. Here I played on my flageolet, there being an excellent echo. He showed us excellent pictures, two especially, those of the Four Evangelists and Henry VIII.'

The journey back to London took two days, and on arrival Pepys went straight to Mr Crewe's house, where he found Sir Edward. Not only was he a member of the Council, but Sir Edward had been chosen to act as one of two Generals-at-Sea. Their fortunes were entwined, and with any luck Pepys could rise along with his distant cousin. He was about to reach one of the turning points in his life, which would bring him into close and fruitful contact with the Navy. 'He [Sir Edward] bid me look out now at this turn some good place, and he would use all his own, and all the interests of his friends that he had in England, to do me good, and asked me whether I could, without too much inconvenience, go to sea as his secretary, and bid me think of it. He also began to talk of things of state, and told me that he should want one in that capacity at sea, that he might trust in, and therefore he would have me go.' When Pepys finally made up his mind to accept the offer, he was changing not only the course of his own life, but perhaps that of England itself, for it was he who would lay the foundations of the modern Navy.

With his head full of Sir Edward's offer Pepys went to visit 'Mrs Jem', his patron's young and as yet unmarried daughter Jemimah. It was Shrove Tuesday, and the whole household was in carnival mood. 'To see Mrs Jem, at whose chamber door I found a couple of ladies, but she not being there, we hunted her out, and found that she and another had hid themselves behind a door. Well, they all went down into the dining-room, where it was full of tag, rag and bobtail, dancing, singing, and drinking, of which I was ashamed, and after I had stayed a dance or two, I went away.' Poor Samuel Pepys: the Puritan in him was dying hard. Only a few weeks before he had been shocked by the conduct and talk of his fellow guests at Surgeon Pierce's house, and now he was shocked by the pre-Lenten rampage of Jem and her young friends.

Everything seemed to be happening at once. Only the day after being offered the post of secretary to one of England's new Generals-at-Sea, Pepys heard unofficially from Washington, who also worked in the Exchequer Office, that Sir Edward's cousin George was to become Custos Rotulorum for Westminster, and if Pepys knew what was good for him he would apply for the position of Clerk of the Peace. He did not know what to do for the best. If he turned down the job of Secretary and nothing came of his application to become a Clerk of the Peace he would be like the dog with the bone in the fable. The best course would be to ask Sir Edward's advice outright. He did so, and the idea of becoming Clerk of the Peace for Westminster vanished instantly. 'My Lord he believes Mr Montagu had already promised it, and that it was given him only that he might

gratify one person with the place I look for.' Whatever influence was
at work, it would not be in favour of Pepys, so he abandoned the
idea. But the day was not yet over, and there was more news to come
for Pepys. His father had just returned from a visit to Uncle Robert
at Brampton. Uncle Robert had a bad leg, and in the opinion of
Samuel's father he could not be expected to last much longer. 'My
uncle did acquaint him, that he did intend to make me his heir, and
give my brother Tom something, [and] something to raise portions
for John and Pall. I pray God he may be as good as his word! This
news and my Lord's great kindness makes me very cheerful within.'
Sixteen months later the old man died, having made Pepys his heir,
as he said he would.

The prospect of a small income of his own did much towards
making up Pepys's mind, and it was completely made up for him
when he had a chance encounter with a naval officer in the Dog
tavern. It was still an age when honesty was what you chose to make
of the word, and if you did not look after your own interests, you
were considered a fool. The advice Captain Philip Holland gave
him was simple and to the point. He told Pepys 'to have five or six
servants entered on board as dead men, and I to give them what
wages I pleased, and so their pay be mine; he also urged me to take
the Secretary's place that my Lord did proffer me.' After that all
which remained to be done was to go and tell Sir Edward he
accepted his offer, and write and ask George Downing to release
him from his position in the Exchequer Office and to arrange, for a
consideration, for two other clerks to take on his duties. But there
was still something to worry Pepys. While he was away, who would
keep an eye on Elizabeth? Even now she was not yet twenty, and
far from worldly. Surely she could not remain alone in the house in
Axe Yard, with only Jane Wayneman as companion? Off he went
into the City to see his father at Salisbury Court, where he found
him at work in his cutting room. They discussed Samuel's plans for
going to sea, and what should happen to Elizabeth. It was Will
Bowyer, the senior clerk at the Exchequer Office, who came to the
rescue. Elizabeth could go and stay with his father in Buckinghamshire. Elizabeth was a little put out to hear of the arrangements
made for her without her knowledge; but Pepys's mind was made
up, and in the end she accepted the situation. Both she and Jane fell
to knitting comforts for the new secretary, a woollen cap and stockings. On 12 March, Pepys rode to Huntsmore in Buckinghamshire,

despite a heavy cold. 'To Mr Bowyer's, where I found him well, and all well, and willing to have my wife come and board with them while I was at sea. Here I lay, and took a spoonful of honey and a nutmeg, scraped for my cold by Mr Bowyer's direction.'

Becoming a Clerk of the Exchequer had been the first step in Pepys's career, but accepting the position of secretary to Sir Edward was a far larger step. By 14 March he had plunged into his work as 'my Lord's' new secretary. One of his first tasks did not concern the Navy, but Sir Edward's attempts to prepare the ground for having his relatives elected as Members of Parliament for the town of Huntingdon at some future date. 'I went to St James's to speak with Mr Clerke, Monk's secretary, about getting some soldiers removed out of Huntingdon to Oundle, which my Lord told me he did to do a courtesy to the town, that he might have the greater interest in them, in the choice of the next Parliament. Not that he intends to be chosen himself, but that he might have Mr G. Montagu and my Lord Mandeville [both relatives], chose there in spite of the Bernards [a prominent Huntingdon family]. This done, I saw General Monk, and methought he seemed a dull heavy man.'

There was so much to be done before Sir Edward could put to sea: an 'infinity of business to do, which makes my head full', was how Pepys described the third week in March. Much was happening as well at a national level. First the Commons had voted that all the Rump's actions against the House of Lords were void, and the town was full of talk that the Commons would shortly come out in favour of the King. Parliament had dissolved itself, while in the City someone had climbed a ladder in the courtyard of the one-time Royal Exchange, and obliterated the inscription 'Exit Tyrannus Regum Ultimus', added at the start of the Commonwealth to the defaced statue of Charles I. Not only that, but a huge bonfire was lit in the courtyard and the citizens were openly calling out 'God bless King Charles II'.

Pepys discovered with satisfaction that he was now a man of some importance. 'I gave Captain Williamson his commission to be Captain of the *Harp*, and he gave me a piece of gold, and 20s in silver [18 March 1660].' On 22 March he recorded: 'To Westminster, and received my warrant of Mr Blackburne, to be secretary to the two Generals of the Fleet. Strange how these people do now promise me anything; one a rapier, the other a vessel of wine, or a gun, and one offered me a silver hatband to do him a courtesy. I pray

God to keep me from being proud, or too much lifted up hereby.'
Also there were his own private affairs to be set in order. First he
made his will, leaving everything but his books to Elizabeth. She
was to have his books in French, while the remainder of his library
went to John, now at Magdalene. Sir Edward had had the same idea,
and put his will in a black box which he gave to Pepys to take to
yet another cousin for safe-keeping. Heavy rains followed by a
strong easterly wind caused flooding in the low-lying area about
Whitehall, where the Palace was subject to periodic inundations,
and it even flooded Axe Yard and Pepys's house on the other side of
King Street. Whether or not all the water about the house seemed
like a solemn premonition, he was in poor spirits when he said goodbye to his father and mother. Elizabeth had been seen off into the
country, and at last Sir Edward, Captain Isham (related by marriage to my Lord), John Crew (yet another relative), one Mr
Thomas, Will Howe (to wait on Sir Edward), and Pepys were on
their way to Tower Wharf. Pepys was wearing a sword, and he had
with him a boy of his own, called Eliezer, to dance attendance on
him. Barges took the party down-river to Long Reach, to join the
Swiftsure. As they went on board, a salute was fired by the other
ships, welcoming the General-at-Sea to his new command. Soon
after they were joined by Vice-Admiral Lawson and the commanders
of the other frigates which made up the little fleet. It did Pepys's
heart good to see with what respect his kinsman and patron was
treated. But soon he had to get down to work in his cabin, which
though small 'was the best that any had that belonged to my Lord'.
All went well until 'the boy Eliezer flung down a can of beer upon my
papers, which made me give him a box on the ear, it having cost me a
great deal of work'. Letters arrived from London for Sir Edward,
including papers for the nomination of members for the Cinque
Ports, which was of concern to the Navy. Also there was one from the
Secretary to the Admiralty addressed to Pepys personally: 'who with
his own hand superscribes it to S. P. Esq. of which God knows I was
not a little proud. Mr Ibbott prayed, and preached a good sermon.
At dinner, I took place of all but the Captain. After that, sermon, at
which I slept, God forgive me!'

Even at such a time Pepys could remember to be grateful for past
good fortune. The 26 March was the second anniversary of the
operation at Mrs Turner's house in Salisbury Court. In his Diary he
blessed God for the fact he was now in as good health as he had ever

known. Then he fell to work again, making a list of all the ships in the whole Fleet, and the number of their guns and crew. At the end of a long and tiring day he must have felt that all his efforts were worthwhile when Captain Cuttance came to his cabin, and stayed drinking till eleven o'clock, an honour which as Pepys happily observed 'he does not often do the greatest officer in the ship'.

Passing the Vice-Admiral's ship was not without hazard to the *Swiftsure*, for the salute fired in honour of the General-at-Sea broke all the windows in Pepys's cabin. But any discomfort would have been more than made up for by the pleasure of supping at the same table as my Lord and Captain Cuttance. Not only that, but there was the intellectual satisfaction of discoursing far into the night in Latin and French with a 'gentleman very well bred', who in his cups while leaving Gravesend for Flushing had shouted for the King, and let it be known that he and all his family were out-and-out Royalists. He had been brought on board the *Swiftsure*, lying off the town, as a suspected person, but had been freed on Sir Edward's orders.

If Pepys enjoyed the Cavalier's conversation, his kinsman was feeling slightly less pleased. All his machinations to get his relatives nominated for Huntingdon had come to nothing. John Bernard and Nicholas Pedley would be the new members for the next Parliament.

The little fleet was still at anchor off Gravesend when on 30 March the *Naseby* dropped anchor nearby while Sir Edward and Pepys were at dinner. The great ship was familiar to both of them from the time it had been Sir Edward's flagship during his mission to the Ore Sund, and he had been visited on board by Pepys. But there was still much to be done before they could transfer to the *Naseby*. Among other things, Sir Edward gave Pepys a list of ships commanded by Anabaptists, whose loyalty to himself with his Royalist sympathies he doubted. For his part Pepys drew satisfaction from the gifts of money he received from time to time. 'I made a commission for Captain Wilgness of the *Bear*, tonight, which got me 30s.' Next morning, Samuel and his boy Eliezer were up very early to pack their possessions ready to transfer to the *Naseby*. 'My cabin is little, but very convenient, with two windows and a good bed.'

All the time reports were reaching the *Naseby* that it was only a matter of time before the King would 'come in'. Certainly General Monk had not yet declared openly in favour of restoration, but equally he had not said he would oppose such a move. If everyone was waiting to see how he would react, he was waiting to see what everyone else would do. It was rumoured that the Council was making preparations for some kind of treaty with the King. Even Robert Blackburne, the Puritan-to-the-core Secretary of the Admiralty (who had addressed Pepys as Esquire) and was now himself on the *Naseby*, was speaking in praise of Charles II.

At last, on 5 April, the flagship set sail with all the other vessels, keeping close to the Kent shore. The great adventure might have begun, but 'the wind grew high, and we, being among the sands, lay at anchor; I began to be dizzy and squeamish'. But evidently Pepys soon recovered, and twenty-four hours later he was borrowing Lieutenant Lambert's telescope to look at two fine merchantmen, 'and at the women on board them, being pretty handsome'. Next day they were off the Forelands, and for the first time Pepys could glimpse Elizabeth's native land, if only at a distance. Small craft still kept coming out to the Fleet with news of the happenings ashore, and one detail which Pepys considered of special significance was that when the Skinners' Company entertained General Monk in their Hall they had replaced the Commonwealth Arms (the Irish Harp and the Cross of St George) with the Royal Arms. For weeks there had been a wind from the east which could blow the King to his Fleet, but first there must be a wind to blow that Fleet to Holland to invite him to return to his father's kingdom.

Pepys soon found his sea-legs, though at times the wind mounted to gale force. Life on the *Naseby* was pleasant as the Fleet waited for the wind to change. Those on board were not slow to realise that Sir Edward's little secretary, not much over five feet tall, was a most remarkable and charming individual. Not only was he invited to join the officers amusing themselves playing at nine-pins, but he was invited by the Vice-Admiral on board the *London*, and the day after that he was the guest of the Captain of the *Speaker*. 'After dinner home, not a little contented to see how I am treated, and with what respect made a fellow to the best commander in the Fleet.' After several anxious days because he had received no word from Elizabeth, his mind was put at rest by two letters from her, and his happiness was complete. There was even time for music, and he and Will Howe would sing together. Sir Edward, his steward Edward Shepley from Hinchingbrooke, and Lieutenant Lambert were all musical. Sir Edward, like Will Howe and Pepys, was a string player, and the three made music together in his cabin after the day's work was finished.

On 1 May, when the inhabitants of Deal set the royal flag on their maypoles and drank the King's health on their knees in the streets, Charles II's letter from Breda was read to the House of Commons. He was prepared to return to England, and as Pepys noted in his Diary, it was 'the happiest May-day that hath been many a year in England'. Even that stronghold of republicanism, the City, did an about-face, disclaiming that it had ever acknowledged any other government than that of the King, Lords and Commons. The enthusiasm spread to the Fleet where it did not escape Pepys's notice that Commanders who a week before had been unwilling to commit themselves, now spoke out openly in favour of the King. As for the seamen: 'as many as had money or credit for drink, did nothing else this evening [2 May]'. The next day Sir Edward received a copy of the King's letter, as well as the sovereign's own letter to him and the other General-at-Sea.

Now the pace was quickening after the weeks of waiting. A Council of War was called to meet in the Council Chamber of the *Naseby*, referred to by Pepys as 'the coach', at which all the Commanders were present. As Sir Edward's secretary it fell to Pepys to read the King's letter to them, after which they voted. 'Not one man seemed to say No to it, though I am confident many in their hearts were against it. After this was done, I went to the quarter-deck with my Lord and the Commanders, and there read both the papers and the vote; which done, and demanding their opinion, the seamen did all of them cry out, "God bless King Charles!" with the greatest joy imaginable.'

Then it fell to Pepys to visit every ship in the Fleet and read what the officers and crew of the *Naseby* had already heard. It took the rest of the day, and on all the ships Pepys found himself received with respect and honour. In the evening when he was boarding the Vice-Admiral's ship Sir Edward ordered the *Naseby* to fire a salute, which was taken up by all the other warships in the Fleet. 'Which was very gallant, and to hear the bullets go hissing over our heads as we were in the boat.' On returning to the *Naseby*, Pepys found Sir Edward in the highest spirits, and he now showed him a clandestine correspondence which he had been carrying on in the past months not only with the King but also with his brother James, Duke of York. The King asked from where he could take ship to return to England, while the Duke of York wanted Sir Edward to teach him seamanship. Pepys marvelled at the tone of the letters. They were so friendly: 'in such familiar words as if Jack Cole and I had writ them'. Jack Cole was a school friend from his days at St Paul's. Not only had Pepys a kinsman who was a good friend, but now he turned out to be on quite intimate terms with royalty. What prospects it opened up; nothing was impossible, and nothing need be unattainable. The next morning Pepys was instructed to write a letter to be sent unofficially to Charles II telling him of the Fleet's reaction. At the same time Sir Edward had written to Parliament saying it was for them to inform the King of the Fleet's answer. In the private letter it was also agreed that the King should take ship from Scheveningen, and that Sir Edward's greatest desire was to attend His Majesty on that voyage. The question of money had not been overlooked, and a minister who came on board the *Naseby* repeated that Parliament had ordered the City to provide the King with £50,000, while twelve City Companies were to contribute £1,000 each. That night the ship's parson prayed for 'the long life and happiness of our King and dread Sovereign, that may last as long as the sun and moon endureth'.

Pepys had acquitted himself well in the eyes of Sir Edward, who had written to his employer George Downing at the Exchequer Office commending his ability and personal diligence. On the evening of 6 May, Sunday, Pepys took Sir Edward's private letter across to the *Assistance*, and after drinking the King's health he returned to the *Naseby*, while the *Assistance* set sail for Breda. He had reason to feel confident. 'I find that all my debts paid and my preparations to sea, I have £40 clear in my purse, and so to bed.' A few days later he lost 9s. to Sir Edward while playing nine-pins, a large sum to wager in those days. But now he was writing off for silk flags, scarlet waistcloths for the officers, a barge, trumpets and even fiddlers. When Charles II returned to England it would be in a style befitting a king. The comings and goings aboard the *Naseby* grew more frequent; among the arrivals was Sir Edward's son, also called Edward. 'The child was sick,' noted Pepys laconically. In London Charles II had been officially proclaimed, and a copy of the proclamation sent to the Fleet. Sir Edward also received a letter from the Lords requesting him to meet the Commissioners at Dover and take them over to Holland to the King. So the Arms of the Commonwealth were taken down and replaced with the Royal Arms, and the Fleet set sail for Dover to be saluted with thirty guns from the Castle, while Sir Edward sent ashore to inquire whether or not the Commissioners were on their way. But now came word that the Commissioners were not to cross the North Sea, but to await the King's arrival at Dover.

The provisions had already been taken aboard, 'so my Lord did give order for weighing of anchor, which we did, and sailed all day'.

When Pepys came on deck next morning, Sunday, he found the ship's tailors and painters already hard at work. The tailors were cutting out a crown and CR from yellow cloth, which were sewed to a 'fine sheet', and then inserted into the flag in place of the Commonwealth Arms. In the afternoon there was another council of war, but it was only to inform the Commanders of the other vessels that they must follow the *Naseby*'s lead, and remove the Harp from their flags: 'it being very offensive to the King'.

After an uneventful voyage the Fleet anchored off the Dutch coast, within sight of The Hague, and 'some nasty Dutchmen' came alongside offering to take passengers and baggage ashore, no doubt at a greatly inflated price. Of his own admission Pepys was as anxious to go ashore as 'my boy', his expression for young Edward Montagu, who had been given into his care. He let Edward go ashore with the party which landed to pay their respects to the Queen of Bohemia (the Winter Queen, and daughter of James I) on behalf of Sir Edward. In the afternoon the same party returned to The Hague, this time to kiss hands with the Prince of Orange, and Pepys was given leave to accompany them, along with Edward and the Judge Advocate of the Fleet. Pepys's pleasure was increased when he found they would share a carriage with 'two very pretty ladies, very fashionable, and with black patches, who very merrily sang all the way, and that very well, and were very free to kiss two blades that were with them'. He found The Hague a most attractive town, and he and the Judge Advocate and Edward fell in with an Englishman who showed them the sights, and explained the maypoles set up in front of the houses of citizens of consequence: 'of different greatness according to the quality of the person'. They had to wait till ten at night to greet the young Prince of Orange, since he did not return to his residence till then. 'His attendance very inconsiderable as for a Prince, but yet handsome, and his tutor a fine man, and himself a very pretty boy.' After that they returned to their lodgings where the ten of them in the party made a disappointing supper off a salad and two or three bones of mutton. Pepys and the Judge Advocate shared one bed, while Edward slept on a bench by Pepys's side. Such was their desire to see all they could that they were up again at three. A schoolmaster acted as their guide on the second day. 'Everybody of Fashion speaks French or Latin, or both. The women, many of them very pretty and in good habits, fashionable, and black spots. We bought a couple of baskets for Mrs Pierce and my wife. The Judge and I to the Grande Salle, where the States sits in Council. The Hall is a great place, where the flags that they take from their enemies are all hung up; and things to be sold, as in Westminster Hall, and not much unlike it, but that not so big. To a booksellers, and bought for the love of the bindings three books.' When they returned to Scheveningen the wind was still high. Two small boats were overturned, pitching the finely dressed gallants into the surf.

Back on board Pepys had a long private discussion with Sir Edward on many topics, including religion and the need for some degree of uniformity, and at supper he noticed Captain Cuttance was more deferential to him than ever. But after the meal was over the *Naseby* was rolling so much that Sir Edward advised Pepys, who could hardly stand, to take himself off to bed.

The next morning Pepys met for the first time Peter Pett, one of a long line of eminent shipbuilders, and himself a Commissioner of the Navy. Back in London Pepys would have frequent dealings with him at the Navy Office and in the dockyards. Now Commissioner Pett was on board the *Naseby* to make sure everything was as it should be for the King's return.

Pepys was told by one who had just seen him how overjoyed the King was when brought money. 'So joyful, that he called the Princess Royal and the Duke of York to look upon it, as it lay in the portmanteau, before it was taken out.' One day John Wilmot, Earl of Rochester, would dub his tolerant sovereign as 'scandalous and poor'. All through his exile Charles II had known penury (and for that matter would continue to do so on and off for the whole of his reign).

Also there was the news that the Duke of York had just been made Lord Admiral, and would therefore be Sir Edward's commander. Pepys must have remembered the friendly letters he had been shown.

For the third day running he went ashore, in the hope of seeing the King. With him was Edward. They were lucky, thanks to a captain who had just brought Charles II a letter from the Lord Mayor of London; and also to Doctor Cade, a 'merry mad parson of the King's'. Through their good offices Pepys and the boy were shown into the King's presence. Charles kissed Edward, and Pepys kissed hands with his King, the Duke of York and the Princess Royal. In his opinion Charles was a very sober man; an opinion he was to revise drastically in the future. Also, they were received by the Lord Chancellor (Clarendon, and father-in-law of the Duke of York), who was in bed with gout, but received his guests cheerfully enough. Before the day was over there was more royalty to be visited. First the Queen of Bohemia and then the Queen Dowager, whose house Pepys found to contain 'one of the most beautiful rooms for pictures in the whole world'.

Still the wind blew. It had started in March, and here in the middle of May it was at gale force. In fact it was so strong that Pepys and Edward were prevented from returning to the *Naseby*. Off the boy went on his own sightseeing in Delft, followed by Pepys. There they found a blacksmith's boy who acted as guide, and showed them the tomb in a church of Admiral Van Tromp, that scourge of the seas during the Commonwealth who tied a broom to his masthead to indicate what he intended to do to the English fleet. Pepys loved Delft. 'It is a most sweet town, with bridges and a river in every street. In every house of entertainment there hangs in every room a poor man's box, it being their custom to confirm all bargains by putting something into the box, and that binds as fast as anything. We also saw the Guest-house, where it was pleasant to see what neat preparation there is for the poor. We saw one poor man dying there. Back by water, where a pretty, sober, Dutch lass sat reading all the way, and I could not fasten any discourse upon her.'

Another day passed before Pepys and his companions could return to the *Naseby*, and even then it was a hazardous journey in a small boat. News came from England that Parliament had ordered the arrest of all those who acted as judges at Charles I's trial, together with all the court officials. Since Sir Edward had passed over all his powers to the Duke of York, as the new Lord High Admiral, Pepys suddenly found himself at a loose end. As his duties dwindled, so the final preparations for the voyage back to England were put in hand. On 22 May the Duke of York and his younger brother the Duke of Gloucester were escorted on board by Sir Edward. Standing by the entry port were Captain Cuttance, Pepys and others. Now Pepys really could count himself among the elect: 'upon the quarterdeck table, under the awning, the Duke of York and my Lord, Mr Coventry [the Duke's secretary], and I, spent an hour allotting to every ship their service, in their return to England, which being done, they went to dinner, where the table was very full.'

Later that same day word reached the *Naseby* that the King was on

the shore, and Sir Edward ordered a salute to be fired. In his enthusiasm Pepys asked to be allowed to touch off the cannon nearest
his cabin: 'but holding my head too much over the gun, I had almost
spoiled my right eye.' Already the King's entourage was starting to
board the *Naseby*, where Pepys found himself moved into the carpenter's cabin, which he would share with Clerke, a doctor of
medicine.

At last it was happening: after nine years of wandering exile
Charles II really was about to return to his own country. Thousands
stood on the shore to watch him being taken out to the *Naseby*, where
Pepys was among those waiting to kiss hands with him and his relatives. Though there was confusion on the flagship, it was a noble
confusion in Pepys's eyes, and the sight of the royal family at dinner
in 'the coach' was a 'blessed sight to see'. A few days before, the ship's
tailors had been altering the flag: now Charles II rechristened a number
of the ships in the Fleet whose names he was hardly likely to appreciate. The *Naseby*, named after the Royalist defeat in the Civil War,
became the *Charles*; the *Lambert*, so called in honour of the Parliamentarian general, was changed to the *Henrietta*; while the *Richard*
(Cromwell) became the *James*. If the easterly wind had kept the
Fleet bottled up in the Thames Estuary for several days in March,
it now sent them bowling across the North Sea back to England. It
was too good to be true. There on the quarterdeck the King talked to
Pepys, telling him at great length of his escape after the Battle of
Worcester on 3 September 1651. 'It made me weep to hear the stories
that he told me of his difficulties that he had passed through, every
step up to his knees in dirt, with nothing but a green coat and a pair
of country breeches on, and a pair of country shoes that made him so
sore all over his feet, that he could scarce stir. Yet he was forced to
run away from a miller and other company, that took them for
rogues. His sitting at table at one place, where the master of the
house, that had not seen him in eight years, did know him, but kept it
private; when at the same table there was one, that had been of his
own regiment at Worcester, could not know him, but made him
drink the King's health, and said that the King was some five fingers
higher than he. At another place, he was by some servants of the
house made to drink, that they might know that he was not a Roundhead, which they swore he was. In another place, at his inn, the master
of the house, as the King was standing with his hands on the back of a
chair by the fireside, kneeled down and kissed his hand, saying that

42

he would not ask him who he was, but bid God bless him whither he was going. Then the difficulties in getting a boat to get into France, where he was fain to plot with the master thereof to keep his design from the foreman and a boy (which was all the ship's company), and so to get to Fécamp, in France. At Rouen he looked so poorly, that the people went into the rooms before he went away, to see whether he had not stole something or other.' Years later, at Newmarket, Pepys would take down the full story of Charles II's escape.

There was a holiday atmosphere aboard the *Charles* the next day when they were out of sight of land, 'and most glorious weather'. To walk about the decks was like being at Court, with everyone either a noble lord or some gentleman of consequence, and Pepys even had business which took him in to the King. 'I was called to write a pass for my Lord Mandeville, to take up horses to London, which I wrote in the King's name, and carried it to him to sign, which was the first and only that ever he signed in the ship *Charles*. To bed, coming in sight of land before night.'

Amid all the preparations to go ashore at Dover at noon, 25 May, Charles II remembered to give £50 to be divided among Sir Edward's servants, and £500 for the officers and crew of the *Charles*. In all Pepys's share came to £60, for Sir Edward generously gave him £20 of the £50. Again he was close to the centre of events, going ashore in a barge accompanying the King and his brothers, Sir Edward and Captain Cuttance. Even in exile Charles II was inseparable from his dogs, and one was now in the barge with Pepys. It could not wait to reach dry land, which set him reflecting 'that a King and all that do belong to him, are but just as others are'. On the shore was General Monk and the Mayor of Dover, who presented the King with a fine Bible, which he received graciously, remarking with doubtful sincerity that it was the object he loved above all things in this world. There was a canopy for him to stand under while talking to General Monk; and then he was away in a coach, first to Canterbury and then on to London. Sir Edward had not come ashore, so Pepys rejoined him in his barge and together they returned to the *Charles*.

Sir Edward was in a jubilant mood; partly because all had gone off smoothly, and partly because he was anticipating the honours and decorations that surely would come his way. He did not have long to wait. Two days later the King at Arms came aboard the *Charles* as she lay at anchor. Sir Edward was invested with the Order of the Garter then and there in the presence of all the Commanders of the

Fleet. The ceremony took place in the Council Chamber, with Pepys among the spectators. It was a great honour, the only other to receive it at this time being General Monk, and as Pepys noted in his Diary it was rarely given to those who had not the rank of Earl. Since the ship was so crowded Pepys had to dine in his cabin: 'where Mr Drum brought me a lobster and a bottle of oil, instead of vinegar, whereby I spoiled my dinner. Late to Sermon.'

The King entered London on 29 May, his thirtieth birthday, to receive the reception of a lifetime, but Pepys and Sir Edward stayed on at Dover. They went riding, and had a wager which was the higher —the cliffs or the tower of Old St Paul's. On looking up the latter in a book of Shepley's when back on board the *Charles*, they found that the cathedral was the higher by a good 150 feet. They played nine-pins, Captain Cuttance returned decidedly fuddled after a hard day's drinking, and Sir Edward went fishing with the Vice-Admiral. There was some work to be done though: calculating a month's pay for the thirty ships which crossed over to Holland to bring back the King. The sum required would amount to £6,538. 'I wish we had the money,' wrote Pepys. And there would be many times in the future when he would make that same observation at the Navy Office. When he thanked his kinsman for his share of the money given by the King, Sir Edward remarked: 'We must have a little patience, and we will rise together; in the meantime, I will do yet all the good jobs I can [for you].' It was a generous promise of help, and on 8 June they really were riding towards London. Pepys, the musician, was clutching the King's guitar.

Chapter 4

Clerk of the Acts
1660 (continued)

PEPYS returned to London on 8 June, having been away since 23 March. He went straight to Whitehall with Sir Edward and his young son. When he left London the Palace had been forlorn, but now Charles II was once again King in his own domain, and it was walking in St James's Park that Pepys first caught sight of his restored monarch. 'Found the King in the Park. There walked, gallantly great.'

It was not until the following day that he made his way to the City and to his father's house in Salisbury Court. There he found Elizabeth had already returned from the Bowyers at Huntsmore, and together they walked in Lincoln's Inn Fields; no doubt Samuel told her of all his adventures, his increase in fortune, 'my Lord's' promises, and above all his long conversation with the King on the quarterdeck of the *Charles*. For a fortnight they remained in Salisbury Court, until their own house in Axe Yard was ready for reoccupation. Since it had been shut up immediately after being flooded in March, it must have been very musty and damp.

Soon all those who lived in Salisbury Court would have been aware how well John Pepys's son was doing. Dorset House, once owned by the Bishops of Salisbury from whom the Court took its name, was also the residence of the Lord Chancellor, and Samuel was to be seen the very next day accompanying Sir Edward on a visit to the great man. He also accompanied his patron on a visit to the Duke of Gloucester: while Sir Edward dined with the King's younger brother Pepys found a place for himself with the pages.

The King had not forgotten Sir Edward, who was created an Earl, taking his title from Portsmouth, though it was almost immediately changed to Sandwich. Also he became a Master of the Great Wardrobe and a Commissioner of the Treasury. Business took Pepys to the Admiralty, situated at Whitehall: 'where I wrote some letters.

45

Here Col. Thompson told me, as a great secret, that the *Naseby* was on fire when the King was there, but that it is not known; when God knows it is quite false. Got a piece of gold from Major Holmes for the horse I brought to town.' Seven years later Robin Holmes would be directly responsible for the most shameful episode in English naval history when the Dutch sailed up the Medway, burnt the dockyard at Chatham, together with a number of warships, and towed the *Charles* in triumph back to Holland. It was tit-for-tat for 'Holmes's bonfire', when he played havoc ashore and afloat on the islands of Vlieland and Terschelling.

In less than three months fortune had raised Pepys to undreamed-of heights, but now the time had come when he must consolidate his position if he were to remain a person of consequence. He would have been justified in thinking himself already exalted when no less than Sir Edward's own sister came to him, with a present of £5 wrapped up in paper, asking him to use his influence on behalf of her husband Sir Gilbert Pickering. During the Commonwealth this Anabaptist had gone out of his way to persecute Anglican clergy, and now his star had set.

While Sir Edward, or Lord Sandwich as he was soon to become, dined with Charles II at Baynard's Castle, Pepys went home to his house in Axe Yard for the first time since his return. 'My wife and the girl and the dog came home today. I found a quantity of chocolate left for me, I know not who from.' The dog, a little black bitch, had been a present from Elizabeth's brother Balty, but Pepys's liking for her suffered a setback when he discovered she lacked even the rudiments of house-training.

Not only had Pepys £5 in his pocket, and a present of chocolate, but now hardly a day passed without his receiving something for past favours or hopes of favours to come.

'18 June. [Captain] Murford showed me five pieces to get a business done for him, and I am resolved to do it.'

'21 June. At the *Dog Tavern* Captain Curle, late of the *Maria*, gave me five pieces in gold and a silver can for my wife, for the commission I did give him this day for his ship, dated April 20, 1660.'

Nor did the new Lord Sandwich turn away from a windfall when it was offered. 'Mr Hill (who for these two or three days hath constantly attended my Lord) told me of an offer of £500 for a baronet's dignity, which I told my Lord of, and he said he would think of it.'

But someone else was claiming an almost virtual monopoly of 'commissions' for positions obtained under the Crown. She was the Duchess of Albemarle, the Army farrier's daughter who had been General Monk's mistress and then his wife. Now she lived with her husband in apartments near the Cockpit. If there were a position vacant or a commission to be granted she expected the application to be made through her, for a consideration. Even the accredited coach-maker had to enlist Pepys's aid to get his old position back: 'who gave me a case of good julep, and told me how my Lady Monk deals with him and others for their places, asked £500, though he was formerly the King's coach-maker, and sworn to it'. Lord Sandwich was soon to come into conflict with the Duchess of Albemarle over this question of 'commissions', and on behalf of Pepys himself.

Perhaps the most important action in Lord Sandwich's life—for the future of the English Navy if not for himself—came on 18 June. 'Back again to the Admiralty, and so to my Lord's lodgings, where he told me that he did look after the place of Clerk of the Acts for me.' It was an important position in the Navy Office, and its holder was responsible for the sea- and battle-worthiness of the Fleet, for keeping the dockyards in efficient working order, and seeing the sailors were properly looked after.

Lord Sandwich had promised Pepys the post, the most worthwhile office that had yet come his way, but Lady Albemarle had offered it elsewhere, and if that were not enough to worry him, Mr Turner of the Navy Office was said to be after the position for himself. Lady Albemarle proved to be the lesser obstacle. Lord Sandwich pointed out that no doubt her husband would take it amiss if he, a General-at-Sea, were to nominate officers in her husband's army: 'and therefore he desired to have the naming of one officer in the Fleet'. But Turner caused Pepys considerable worry. 'Thence to the Admiralty, where I met Mr Turner of the Navy Office, who did look after the place of Clerk of the Acts. He was very civil to me, and I to him, and shall be so.' One can almost see them, like two stiff-legged dogs circling each other before a fight. At least Pepys had an ally in Mr Coventry, the Duke of York's secretary, whose aid he had already been to Whitehall Palace to enlist. The next day it must have been brought home to him just what the Clerkship might be worth; 'Mr Watt, a merchant, offered me £500 if I would desist from the Clerk of the Acts place. I pray God direct me in what I should do herein.' It was a worrying time, not less so because people were already congratulating him: 'With my Lord to the Duke, where he spoke to Mr Coventry to dispatch my business of the Acts, in which place everybody gives me joy, as if I were in it, which God send.'

But there comes a time in everybody's life when he or she must be prepared to stake everything, and now Pepys was doing that. He resigned his position at the Exchequer Office. 'To Sir George Downing, the first visit I have made him since he come [from abroad]. He is so stingy a fellow I care not to see him; I quite cleared myself of his office, and did give him liberty to take anybody in. After this to my Lord, who lay abed till eleven o'clock; it being almost five before he went to bed, they supped so late last night with the King. This morning I saw poor Bishop Wren going to Chapel, it being a thanksgiving day for the King's return.' (Already the Bishop's nephew Christopher had made a name for himself in academic circles as an astronomer, and soon he would come before a wider public as an architect.) Pepys had more to say on the subject of the hours kept by the King, who even after a late night which would keep his brother the Duke of York or Lord Sandwich in bed till noon, was in the habit of rising early. 'The King do tire all his people that are about him with early rising since he come.'

The next day the anxious Pepys received his warrant from the Duke of York to become Clerk of the Acts. But even now he was not out of the wood. Lord Sandwich had dealt with the Duchess of Albemarle, and Pepys thought he had bested Turner. Now unexpectedly a new obstacle appeared: '. . . to Whitehall, where I was told by Mr Hutchinson at the Admiralty, that Mr Barlow, my predecessor, Clerk of the Acts, is yet alive, and coming to town to look after his place, which made my heart sad a little.' Off he went in search of Lord Sandwich, who advised him to get hold of his patent as quickly as possible, and have it registered; then no one could claim the Clerkship from him. In the midst of his own affairs he was also busy preparing 'my Lord's' Patent of Nobility, which had to be drawn up with a preamble in Latin, and submitted together with his pedigree. Turner had not quite given up hope, and wrote offering Pepys £150 to have his name included in the patent for the Clerkship, and also offering advice how to keep Barlow out of the picture. Pepys had actually gone so far as to buy an expensive outfit suitable for his new position. 'This morning come home my fine camlet cloak, with gold buttons and a silk suit, and I pray God to make me able to pay for it.' If he were counting his chickens, at least he knew it. Some comfort came when those newly appointed to the Navy Board were empowered to take up their jobs without waiting for their patents to be accepted. The four Principal Officers would be Sir George Carteret, Treasurer; Sir William Batten, Surveyor; Comptroller (not yet appointed); and Clerk of the Acts, Samuel Pepys. Also there would be three Commissioners, not employed full-time at the Navy Office. They would be Sir William Penn, General-at-Sea during the Commonwealth; Lord Berkley of Stratton, a Cavalier soldier; and Peter Pett of the famous family of shipbuilders.

What must have made Pepys more anxious than ever to have the job was the discovery that the salary had just been increased to £350, a considerable sum for those days. Moreover, on 9 July he went to the Navy Office in Seething Lane: 'and there I begun to sign bills in the office the first time'. To lose everything now would be too cruel, and the next day he sought out Lord Sandwich in the gardens of Whitehall Palace, and urged him to ask the Secretary of State to obtain the King's signature on his bill as soon as possible, so he could have his patent registered. 'Up early and by coach to Whitehall with Commissioner Pett, where after we had talked with my Lord, I went to the Privy Seal, and got my bill perfected there, and at the Signet.' After that he hurried to the House of Lords and was told to apply to one Mr Beale to get his patent engrossed, but Mr Beale was too busy to do it himself in 'Chancery-hand', and off Pepys went 'to run up and down Chancery Lane and the Six Clerks' Office, but could find none that could write the hand that were at leisure'. Finally, the next day, he found a friend who could make out the document in the required style. Armed with it he returned to Mr Beale: 'but he was very angry, and unwilling to give it [the required docket], because he said it was ill-writ, because I had got it writ by another hand, and not by him'. Finally Pepys gave him two pieces of gold: 'after which it was strange how civil and tractable he was to me'. Now he had to hurry to Worcester House, and by using Lord Sandwich's name soon found himself in the Chancellor's office. The patent was passed, he was granted a seal, and at last he could breathe again—and call himself Clerk of the Acts.

Elizabeth was waiting in a coach, and proudly Pepys showed her his new patent: 'at which she was overjoyed', and together they went to the Navy Office, in Seething Lane, no great distance from

Tower Hill. A century before it had been the large and probably rambling town house of Sir Francis Walsingham. The bigger part had been transformed into the Navy Office itself, while the remainder was divided up into houses for about six of the officials connected with the administration of the Navy. In front there was evidently a courtyard, with a wall between it and the street, and a gateway.

If the course of his domestic life had been set, so had that of his sovereign. Already Charles II had on several occasions kept Lord Sandwich up till after dawn with his parties, and now Pepys could see for himself how he enjoyed his leisure. 'Late writing letters [in Lord Sandwich's lodgings in King Street]; and great doings of music at the next house, which was Whally's; the King and Dukes there with Madam Palmer, a pretty woman that they had a fancy to, to make her husband a cuckold. Here at the old door that did go into his Lodgings, my Lord, I and Will Howe, did stand listening a great while to the music.' A nice picture of the three eavesdropping on their King. 'Madam Palmer' was in fact Barbara Villiers, the most notorious of Charles II's mistresses, who became Lady Castlemaine on the ennoblement of her complacent husband, and later Duchess of Cleveland.

While Pepys had been worrying whether he would ever obtain the post of Clerk of the Acts, life had continued as usual at home. The maid Jane, who went with Elizabeth into the country during his absence abroad, had evidently met with an accident, and Pepys considered that Elizabeth must have more help in the house. 'This day come Will, my boy, to me: the maid continuing lame, so that my wife could no longer be without help.' A few days later, 9 July, Pepys put on his new silk suit for the first time to attend the wedding of a Dutchman, which took place at Goring House, where Buckingham Palace now stands: 'with very great state, cost and noble company. But among all the beauties there, my wife was thought the greatest.'

Ever since he first saw the house in Seething Lane Pepys had been on tenterhooks, lest everything should be snatched away at the last minute. On 4 July he had been 'up very early, and with Commissioner Pett to view the houses in Seething Lane belonging to the Navy, where I find the worst very good, and had great fears that they will shuffle me out of them, which troubles me'. But a fortnight later the little house in Axe Yard was empty and shut up and Pepys's *ménage*, including Elizabeth, Jane, the boy Will and the dog, had moved to their part of the old Tudor house in the City. Also, Pepys had made a satisfactory treaty with his rival Barlow for the Clerkship of the Acts. Pepys found him 'an old consumptive man, and fair conditioned. After much talk, I did grant him what he asked, viz, £50 per annum if my salary was not to be increased, and £100 per annum in case it be £350, at which he was very well pleased to be paid as I received my money, and not otherwise, so I brought him to my Lord's bedside, and he and I did agree together.' Also at this time Pepys took into his household Will Hewer, the nephew of Robert Blackburne, the Secretary of the Admiralty who had gladdened his heart by addressing him on a letter as Esquire. The seventeen-year-old boy was to act as his clerk at the office and make himself useful at home where he would live with the family. 'Will,' wrote Pepys on the day he moved house, 'Mr Blackburne's nephew, is so obedient, that I am greatly glad to have him.' As time passed Will was to become one of Pepys's staunchest friends, remaining loyal in bad times as well as in good, and forty-three years later it would be in his house at Clapham that Pepys would die.

Pepys's new fortunes were now so consolidated that there was no reason for them to slip from his grasp. His personal savings he now recorded at £100; he had a salary of £350, of which £100 would have to go to Barlow, but no doubt the deficit could be made up in pickings. He now worked for the Navy as Clerk of the Acts; and Lord Sandwich had also passed on to him a Clerkship of the Privy Seal, one of the honours and offices granted by the King to the man who made his return possible. Only a few days before Pepys had been desperate to get his patent accepted and his seal passed by the Chancellor. Now, together with Henry Moore, the friend from the Exchequer Office, he would be in for an exceedingly busy and lucrative time at the Office of the Privy Seal, signing commissions and patents, and collecting the fees himself. He had a fine house in Seething Lane, a household that had swollen to five, clothes such as he would never have dreamed of owning only a few months before, and most important of all the good-will and kindness of his patron, the Earl of Sandwich. Further, he had the good opinion of the Duke of York, the Lord High Admiral. The Restoration had brought many low, and he had every reason to be thankful to find himself on his knees alongside my Lord before Sir William Morris, the Secretary of State, taking the Oath of Allegiance and Supremacy.

Fortune was certainly smiling. In addition to being Clerk of the
Acts and a Clerk of the Privy Seal, he remained also secretary to
Lord Sandwich, his duties being those connected with the Navy,
while the Earl's other affairs were in the hands of John Creed, a
capable man whose company Pepys enjoyed readily enough either
in the tavern or at the playhouse, although he did not altogether
trust him. 'This afternoon [30 July] I got my £50, due to me for my
first quarter's salary as Secretary to my Lord, paid by Thomas
Hayter for me, of which I felt glad. At the Rhenish wine-house,
drinking. The Sword-bearer of London (Mr Man) came to ask for
us, with whom we sat late, discoursing about the worth of my office
of Clerk of the Acts, which he hath a mind to buy, and I asked four
year's purchase.'

Pepys attended Lord Sandwich and the principal officers of the
Navy Board at Whitehall when the subject under discussion was
how to raise money for the Navy: 'which is in a very sad condition,
and money must be raised for it'. All afternoon Pepys was calculating what was owing. A couple of days later he was back at the
Admiralty, together with Sir William Batten and Sir William Penn;
along with my Lord, they spent the morning racking their brains:
'about ordering of money for the victuallers, and advising how to
get a sum of money to carry on the business of the Navy'. The
afternoon he spent at the Privy Seal where he found signing commissions and bills brought in £40 in two days. He confided to his
Diary: 'my heart rejoiced for God's blessing to me'. It was time, he
decided, to dispose of the lease of the house in Axe Yard, though
there were occasions when he wondered if it would be wise to do so
in case his fortunes were suddenly reversed. 'Many people look after
my house in Axe Yard to hire it, so that I am troubled with them.'
Among their number was John Lord Claypole, whose marriage to
Elizabeth Cromwell had made him the Protector's son-in-law, and,
curiously, his 'Master of the Horse' and a 'Lord of the Bedchamber'.
In the end Pepys sold the lease of the house to one of the King's
wine-sellers, and received £41 for it.

In the middle of August, life began to become less hectic. Lord
Sandwich departed for Hinchingbrooke, together with his father-
in-law Mr Crewe, and daughter 'Lady Jem'. Pepys had been buying
more expensive clothes for himself, including a velvet coat and cap:
'the first that ever I had'. He did not forget Elizabeth: 'I landed my
wife at Whitefriars [he was on his way to Westminster by water],

EDWARD MONTAGU, 1ST EARL OF SANDWICH
by De Critz, after Lely

WILL HEWER

by Kneller

with £5 to buy her a petticoat, and my father persuaded her to buy a most fine cloth, of 26s a yard, and a rich lace, that the petticoat will come to £5; but she doing it so innocently, I could not be angry.' What was more, when she wore it next day, Sunday, it did not even *look* expensive. 'Home to dinner, where my wife had on her new petticoat that she bought yesterday, which is indeed a very fine cloth and a fine lace; but that being of a light colour, and the lace all silver, it makes no great show.' But no matter, the next day when he went to the Office of the Privy Seal he found there £100 waiting for him in fees. Later the Lord Chancellor gave him not only his time, but also some good advice. 'Before he would begin any business, he took my papers of the state of the debts of the Fleet, and there viewed them before all the people, and did give me his advice privately how to order things to get as much money as we can of the Parliament.'

When the summer nights were warm Samuel and Elizabeth could enjoy walking in their garden, or else taking the air on the leads, through the door Pepys had had cut leading to the roof. When he told my Lord of the City Sword-bearer's offer of £1,000 for the Clerkship of the Acts, Lord Sandwich pointed out it was not so much the salary that was worth having as what would come his way unofficially. In a small way Pepys was already discovering the truth of that worldly observation. 'Come a vessel of Northdown ale from Mr Pierce, the purser [not to be confused with Mr Pierce the surgeon: they both served on the *Charles*, and both were friendly with Pepys], and a brave Turkey-carpet and a jar of olives from Captain Cuttance, and a pair of fine turtle-doves from John Burr [a clerk in Pepys's employ] to my wife.'

There was much to occupy Pepys at the end of August, especially since Lord Sandwich had returned from Hinchingbrooke on the 30th, with orders from the Duke of York to go to sea. This time Pepys was not to accompany him, but to make the necessary preparations, including informing the Fleet to prepare to sail. At home there was trouble: the boy Will had proved to be a thief and a liar, and on 5 September 'I put away my boy, and tore his indentures.' Fine though the house was in Seething Lane Pepys had plans of his own for its improvement, including having the dining-room floor relaid. 'Looking after my workmen, whose laziness do much trouble me.' Also there were difficulties between those who belonged to a Guild and those who did not.

Now Pepys felt himself to be of consequence in the affairs of state, and if he reflected the joys and celebrations of royal circles, he must also respect their griefs. After a brief illness the young Duke of Gloucester, whom he had first met on the mission to Holland, died at Whitehall Palace from smallpox. Off went Pepys to his father, to order a suit of mourning clothes, and he gave Elizabeth £15 to do the same for herself.

For neighbours in Seething Lane Pepys had Sir William Penn, his wife and a daughter, Margaret. One of their sons, also christened William, would one day become a founding father in the New World, with a name that still lives on in Pennsylvania. The other neighbour was Sir William Batten, his wife and two daughters. Of the two Pepys found Penn the more approachable, and at the beginning of September he had an opportunity to assess his character: 'drinking a glass of wine late and discoursing with Sir William Penn. I find him a very sociable man, and an able man, and very cunning.' Frequently all three members of the Navy Board could be found at the Dolphin tavern, near Seething Lane, where Penn no doubt entertained them with the 'very bawdy songs' mentioned by Pepys. The Dolphin would see many gatherings in the years ahead, and in March the following year the occasion would be a family affair for the three neighbours. 'To the *Dolphin* to a dinner of Mr Harris's [a sail-maker, who would wish to cultivate the members of the Navy Board], where Sir Williams both and my Lady Batten, and her two daughters, and other company, where a great deal of mirth, and there stayed till eleven o'clock at night; and in our mirth, I sang and sometimes fiddled, and at last we fell to dancing, the first time that I ever did in my life, which I did wonder to see myself do. At last, we made Mingo, Sir W. Batten's black, and Jack, Sir W. Penn's, dance, and it was strange how the first did dance with a great deal of seeming skill.'

If Pepys found they were now living in a good neighbourhood, he also realised that entertaining was likely to prove both expensive and exhausting. Disastrous would be an accurate description of the morning after he and several companions had wined well at the Hope Tavern, and between them eaten no less than two hundred walnuts. Whilst about my Lord's business at Whitehall he was extremely sick. It was the blot on an otherwise most satisfactory day. Still his advancement continued, and in chambers at the Temple he and Sir William Batten were sworn in before the

Solicitor-General and the Recorder of London as Justices of the Peace for Middlesex, Essex, Kent and Southampton (an appointment connected with the Naval Dockyards). 'Which honour I did find mightily pleased, though I am wholly ignorant in the duties of a Justice of the Peace.'

Now Lord Sandwich had returned from Holland, bringing over the Princess Royal (like the Duke of Gloucester she would soon die of smallpox at Whitehall) to stay with her brother the King. He had much to tell Pepys, who for his part could have told him an interesting piece of social history—'I did send for a cup of tee, a China drink of which I never had drank before.' Later Lord Sandwich took Pepys into his confidence after dining alone with him, when 'he did treat me with a great deal of respect'. It was he who wanted his secretary's advice, how to obtain sufficient money to clear his debts. What Pepys's advice was he did not record.

All the while he was improving his house, encouraging the workmen with a drink and being merry with them. An advantage of living so near the Navy Office was that he could come home for meals and see 'my painters now at work upon my house'. Also he would call in at his father's to change his long black cloak for a shorter one: 'the long cloaks being quite out'. The erstwhile Puritan was fast becoming a Man of Mode, and even requesting his father's help to get hangings of gilded leather for his dining-room walls. He had seen a portrait he coveted, in my Lord's rooms at Whitehall: '. . . and saw in his chamber his picture, very well done; and am with child till I get it copied out, which I hope to do when he is at sea.' The painting was by Lely, and the day before Lord Sandwich set sail Pepys asked if he could have it copied, while his kinsman was away bringing to England Queen Henrietta Maria. He had hardly left the Palace before Pepys was bearing off the painting to have it copied by a Mr de Cretz. Together with its frame it would cost him £3 10s.

That my Lord was now to be numbered among the most important men in the country was brought home to Pepys when his friend Henry Moore came to tell him that those who had judged and condemned Charles I had appeared at the Sessions House in Old Bailey: 'there being upon the bench the Lord Mayor, General Monk, my Lord of Sandwich and etc; such a bench of noblemen as had not been ever seen in England!' The next day the regicides made their defence, for what it was worth, and two days later Pepys recorded: 'I went to Charing Cross, to see Major-General Harrison hanged, drawn and quartered; which was done, he looking as cheerful as any man could do in that condition. He was presently cut down, and his head and heart shown to the people, at which there were great shouts of joy. Thus it was my chance to see the King beheaded at Whitehall, and to see the first blood shed in revenge for the King at Charing Cross. Setting up shelves in my study.'

In fairness to Pepys, who was far from being hard-hearted, he soon sickened of the punishments being meted out to the regicides. 'I saw the limbs of some of our new traitors set up upon Aldersgate, which was a sad sight to see; and a bloody week this and the last hath been, there being ten hanged, drawn, and quartered.' And it was around this time that his own republican youth returned to haunt him in a most unexpected situation. He and Sir William Penn had ridden to Sir William Batten's substantial house at Waltham-stow, and among the guests round the dinner table that 1 November was an old school-fellow from St Paul's. 'He did remember that I was a great Roundhead when I was a boy, and that I was much afraid he would have remembered the words that I said the day that the King was beheaded, that, were I to preach upon him, my text should be—The memory of the wicked shall rot; but I found afterwards that he did go away from the school before that time.'

Perhaps the person least disturbed by the week's events (though Pepys heard that he would have liked to have commuted the sentences on the regicides) was Charles II himself. Pepys was ever ready for an opportunity to be in Whitehall, so, having the right to a place in the Chapel through his official position at the Privy Seal Office: 'To Whitehall Chapel, where one Dr Crofts made an indifferent sermon, and after it an anthem; ill-sung, which made the King laugh. Here I first did see the Princess Royal since she came into England. Here I also observed, how the Duke of York and Mrs Palmer did talk to one another through the hangings that parts the King's closet where the ladies sit.' The pleasures of church-going reached new heights a week later when Lady Sandwich, 'Lady Jem' and Pepys were allowed to sit in the King's closet during the service: their sovereign had gone to greet his mother, being brought to England by Lord Sandwich.

Church-going was certainly different from what it had been only a year before, with the return of the Book of Common Prayer, which thoroughly confused the congregation at St Olave, Hart Street, Pepys's own parish church in the City, and the sound of organs and the sight of the choir in surplices at Whitehall and in Westminster Abbey. But best of all was the gallery, especially built in St Olave's for the use of the officials at the Navy Office and their families. Seated there above the rest of the congregation Pepys really did feel high and mighty, and it began to show. 'We sat in the foremost pew, and behind [us] our servants, and I hope it will not always be so, it not being handsome for our servants to sit so equal to us.' What was more, he was now ready to put his own family in its place. There was a discussion with his father whether his sister Pall (Paulina) should come to live with them in Seething Lane. 'I told her plainly my mind was to have her come not as my sister but as a servant, which she promised me that she would, and with many thanks did weep for joy.' What was more he meant what he said, and when Pall came to take up residence on 2 January 1661 he kept her to that promise. 'Home to dinner, where I found Pall was come; but I do not let her sit down at table with me, which I do at first that she may not expect it hereafter from me.'

If Pepys was having his head turned, his friend, patron and kinsman was not altogether free from snobbishness either. When Lady Sandwich remarked that she could get a good merchant for Lady Jem (who may not have been considered very marriageable owing to a slight deformity of the neck), her husband retorted that he would rather see her with a pedlar's pack on her back than marry a citizen: it must be a gentleman or nothing. On a number of occasions Pepys had had to conduct his business at my Lord's bed-side after a late night at one of the King's parties, and once when he seemed unduly depressed Pepys was told afterwards by Will Howe that Lord Sandwich had recently lost a great deal of money at cards, to which he was obviously becoming over-addicted. Now he wanted a French chef, and one day Elizabeth arrived at his lodgings to find Lady Sandwich trying to interview a French maid. Neither could understand the other, so Elizabeth acted as interpreter. What was more, when Pepys had to go about his business, Lord Sandwich invited Elizabeth to stay and dine with him: 'the first time he did ever take notice of her as my wife, and did seem to have a just esteem for her'. From Whitehall Pepys returned to Seething Lane only to go out again in the evening, to his neighbour Sir William Batten, who was giving a dinner to celebrate the wedding of two of his servants, which was attended by 'a great number of merchants, and others of good quality'. In the middle of the seventeenth century the social barriers were on occasions far less rigidly maintained than in the nineteenth century, and without any suggestion of being patronising. After dinner the guests gave money to the couple. 'I did give 10 shillings and no more, though I believe most of the rest did give more, and did believe that I did so too.' At the end of the month Lady Batten paid a social call on Elizabeth: 'the first that ever she made her, which pleased me exceedingly'.

With all the activity of carrying out Lord Sandwich's business, working at the Navy Office, leading a full social life, including frequent visits to the theatre ('to the Cockpit to see "The Moor of Venice", which was well done. A very pretty lady that sat by me called out, to see Desdemona smothered'), perhaps he was, without knowing it, thoroughly overtired. Whatever the underlying reason, he was at this time less than his usual endearing self. 'December 1st. This morning, observing some things to be laid up not as they should be by my girl, I took a broom and basted her till she cried extremely, which made me vexed; but, before I went out, I left her appeased.' The next day it was Elizabeth who was in the wrong. 'My wife and I all alone to a leg of mutton, the sauce of which being made sweet, I was angry at it, and eat none, but only dined upon the marrow-bone that we had beside.'

The spirit of the Restoration had reached out, beckoning to Pepys, and willingly he followed. 'Went to the *Sun Tavern*, on Fish Street Hill . . . where we had a very fine dinner, good music, and a great deal of wine. I very merry. Went to bed: my head aching all night.' Further temptation lay near at hand; next door in fact, to a party at Sir William Batten's. 'About the middle of the night I was very ill— I think with eating and drinking too much—and so I was forced to call the maid who pleased my wife and I in her running up and down stairs so innocently in her smock, and vomited in the basin, and so to sleep.' But the new life had not completely swamped Pepys's old loves, reading and above all music, and so there were at least some evenings spent by his own hearth. 'I fell a-reading Fuller's *History of Abbeys*, and my wife in *Great Cyrus* (a French romance) till twelve at night, and so to bed.' A few nights later he was to record: 'Home and to bed reading myself asleep, while the wench [Jane] sat mending my breeches at my bedside.'

For one so musical it is remarkable that five months passed without music in the house in Seething Lane. Then on 21 November: 'At night to my violin (the first time that I have played on it since I come to this house) in my dining-room, and afterwards to my lute there, and I took much pleasure to have the neighbours come forth into the yard to hear me.'

Elizabeth too had her troubles, but they were of a minor nature. 'Found my wife making of pies and tarts to try her oven with, but not knowing the nature of it, did heat it too hot, and so a little over-baked her things, but knows how to do better another time.' It is entries like that, of no consequence in themselves, that annihilate the centuries and make Pepys and his circle almost painfully alive.

From time to time work did intrude as the year ran to its close. The Treasurer of the Navy, Sir George Carteret, told him that his secretary had a plan to put before Parliament by which discharged seamen would not be paid in cash (for the simple reason that there was no money, and official policy was to reduce the size of the Navy as soon as possible), but with tickets, which could be exchanged at some future date, and until that time would bear an interest rate of eight per cent. It was a monstrous suggestion, especially for men who had not a penny in the world. But it was taken up, and in the future tickets would be a cause of much hardship and even rioting among the seamen.

A few days later, Pepys was called early in the morning to Sir William Batten's house. News had just come from Woolwich that the ship *Assurance* had been blown over by a gust of wind and sunk with the loss of twenty lives. While 'both Sir Williams' went by barge to Woolwich to see the disaster for themselves, Pepys went to inform the Duke of York, who was still in bed having 'sat up late last night, and lay long this morning'. Two days later, Pepys went down-river with Elizabeth and Lady Batten, together with the latter's maid, to see the *Assurance*, lying with only her masts and upper deck above water. The captain seemed more worried about his loss of clothes and money than of a ship and twenty lives. Pepys was acting in his official capacity now as a Justice of the Peace, and questioned a seaman about the disaster, 'but could find no reason to commit him'. A week later better news came than could be expected. The *Assurance* had been raised without damage to the hull, which as Pepys reasoned 'argues her to be a strong, good ship'.

Christmas was nearly upon them, and acceptable presents came to the house in Seething Lane, such as a large chine of beef and six tongues sent by an old friend who was a parson in Huntingdonshire. Christmas Day was a religious festival, and not a holiday as such. In the morning Pepys went to church, where the Admiralty pew had been decorated with rosemary and baize, and home to dine off chicken and mutton. Then back he went to church again in the afternoon, where he dropped off to sleep during a dull sermon by a visiting preacher.

As the year ran out most of London was talking of the Duke of York. One rumour had it that he had married Anne Hyde, the Lord Chancellor's daughter; another that he would marry her, and a third that he had got her with child. The truth was that while still in exile in Holland he had seduced Anne Hyde while she was a Maid of Honour to his sister, the Princess of Orange. Then he married her in secret, and only when she became pregnant, admitted to the union (in September 1660).

On the last day of the year, the most auspicious year of Pepys's life, he bought a copy of one of the parts of Shakespeare's *Henry IV*, before going to see the play performed at Tom Killigrew's new theatre, the King's Playhouse. Afterwards, Pepys regretted having read it first: 'I believe it did spoil it a little.' Plays had started in London again only since October, though they had never been entirely banished during the Commonwealth. In 1656, Sir William Davenant had given what were deceptively described as entertainments at Rutland House, including *The Siege of Rhodes*, which could claim to be the first English opera, though its music has disappeared. The libretto was by Sir William Davenant, while the music came from several pens: those of Matthew Locke, Henry Lawes, Edward Coleman (who together with his wife sang in the first production of 1656) and George Hudson. In style *The Siege of Rhodes* probably more resembled the masque-like works of Henry Purcell, such as *The Fairy Queen* and *King Arthur*, than the conventional Italian operas of the period. Over the years Pepys would hear it on a number of occasions, and himself would try his hand as a composer by setting the lines beginning *Beauty Retire*.

The year ended with a new addition to the household in Seething Lane. Pepys had gone to my Lord's lodgings in King Street to greet his patron, and found him at cards with 'some persons of honour'. Evidently he had with him the boy he had taken into his employment after sacking Will—he was another Will, and brother to the maid Jane. On hearing that the house in Seething Lane was over-run with mice, the Earl's housekeeper Sarah gave Will a cat to take home.

On the return journey they shared a coach with a one-eyed Frenchman. 'Strange,' wrote Pepys, who after all was married to a half-French girl, 'how the fellow, without asking, did tell me all that he was, and how that he had run away from his father, and come into England to serve the King, and now was going back again.' But of course, the fellow wasn't English, after all.

Chapter 5

'So glorious was the show'
1661

THE turn of the year was a time to pause and take stock in the Diary. 'At the end of the last and the beginning of this year, I do live in one of the houses belonging to the Navy Office, as one of the principal officers, and have done now about half-a-year: my family being myself, my wife, Jane, Will Hewer, and [Will] Wayneman, my girl's brother. Myself in constant good health, and in a most thriving and handsome condition. Blessed be Almighty God for it! As to things of state—the King settled, and loved of all. The Duke of York matched to my Lord Chancellor's daughter, which do not please many. The Queen upon her return to France with the Princess Henrietta [widow and daughter of Charles I respectively]. The Princess of Orange [another daughter] lately dead, and we in new mourning for her. We have been lately frighted with a great plot, and many taken up on it, and the fright not quite over.' This was a fierce but pathetic rising attempted by the anti-monarchy Venner and the Fifth Monarchy men. Rumours of an armed rising had spread through London at top speed, and since it was reported that the dockyards would be seized at the beginning of January, it concerned the Navy Office. There the vacant post of Comptroller had been given to Colonel Slingsby, whose father had held the same office. He must have been a man of exceptional stature; and Pepys who came to value his friendship was genuinely distressed at his death less than a year later. Since he had a house of his own in Lime Street, Colonel (afterwards Sir Robert) Slingsby did not occupy one of the official residences in Seething Lane.

In addition to 'both Sir Williams' as neighbours the Pepyses had on one side Mr and Mrs Davis, and on the other Mr and Mrs Turner. The first was Storekeeper at Deptford, while Turner was the one-time contender for the Clerkship of the Acts. Soon after their arrival in Seething Lane Mrs Davis locked the door on to the leads, to Pepys's annoyance, but they evidently did not stay long before moving to Deptford, or so it would appear. If there were any animosity on Mr Turner's part because he failed to become Clerk of the Acts, it did not show, though relations were strained for a few days when Pepys discovered that the contents of the Turners' over-full privy were leaking into his cellar. But taking it all round there was harmony among the occupiers of the Navy Office houses in Seething Lane, strengthened that January by a common bond of apprehension caused by Venner's rising.

On the way home from a Twelfth Night party (held on 7 January, presumably because the 6th was a Sunday) Samuel and Elizabeth were stopped and questioned in the street several times. The previous night six or seven people had been killed by the Fifth Monarchy men, led by Venner, the hell-fire preacher from Colman Street. Now the Train-bands (Home Guard) were out, and everyone more jumpy than he cared to admit. Two days later Pepys was awakened by the sound of people in the street. Rumour had it that the Fanatics, as he called them, were in arms in the City. He went back into his house: 'though with no good courage at all, but that I might not seem to be afraid, and got my sword and pistol, which, however, I had no powder to charge; and went to the door, where I found Sir R. Ford [later Lord Mayor], and with him I walked up and down as far as the Exchange, and there I left him. In our way, the streets full of train-bands, and great stir. What mischief these rogues have done! and I think near a dozen had been killed this morning on both sides. The shops shut, and all things in trouble.'

The Fanatics, who were instantly expecting the Second Coming of Christ, were taken very seriously by the authorities, and on 12 January Pepys went with Colonel Slingsby to Deptford to ensure the safety of the Dockyard. For the first time Pepys realised just what it meant to be Clerk of the Acts. 'Never till now did I see the great authority of my place. All the captains of the Fleet coming cap in hand to us.' Then he went to Mr Davis's house: 'and there was most prince-like lodged, with so much respect and honour, that I was at a loss how to behave myself.' There he met another colleague from the Navy Office, Peter Pett, who was now living at Deptford while supervising the building of the King's yacht. After two days arms arrived from the Tower of London and were handed out to the seamen. Pepys also encountered an old acquaintance, Lieutenant Lambert, who had been on the voyage to Holland.

Together they inspected the yards. Then in a coach lent by Mrs Pett the Clerk of the Acts and the Comptroller were off again, to Woolwich. 'Up and down the Yard all morning, and seeing the seamen exercise [i.e. drilling], which they do already very handsomely.' After dinner he and Col. Slingsby inspected the rope-yard and the tar-houses. It was the first of many such inspections Pepys would make in His Majesty's Dockyards, to the exasperation of the incompetent, and the fear of the dishonest.

Already the turmoil caused by Venner's uprising was starting to die down, and when Pepys returned to Whitehall to report to Mr Coventry, the Duke of York's secretary, he found that Lady Sandwich had gone to Chatham, thinking to find him there. Pepys set out in pursuit, and the whole episode petered out in a pleasant two days with Lady Sandwich, 'Lady Jem' and others, visiting the ships of the Fleet, where they were treated as honoured guests, especially aboard the *Charles*. Lord Sandwich was still at sea at this time, after taking Queen Henrietta Maria and her daughter back to France. Sir William and Lady Batten were also at Chatham: 'who I knew were here, and did endeavour to avoid'. He never really liked the couple in the way he did Colonel Slingsby. Malicious tongues could have started a scandal, though it was all innocent enough, for Lady Sandwich and her party and Pepys spent the first night at an inn in Rochester, and the second at Dartford.

Sometimes it was by design, sometimes fortuitous, but so often Pepys saw the beginning, middle and end of the events of the day. So it was with the rising by the Fifth Monarchy men: on 19 January he and Colonel Slingsby were on their way to Whitehall: 'in our way meeting Venner and Prichard upon a sledge with two more of the Fifth Monarchy men were hanged today, and first two drawn and quartered'. The entry for that day continues: 'went to the theatre where I saw *The Lost Lady*, which did not please me much. Here I was troubled to be seen by four of our office clerks, which sat in the half-crown box, and I in the 1s. From hence home by link [a guide with a torch] and bought two mouse-traps from Thomas Pepys the Turner.' A few days later he returned to the theatre to see the same play again: 'which do now please me better than before; and here I sitting behind in a dark place, a lady spit backwards upon me by mistake, not seeing me, but after seeing her to be a very pretty lady, I was not troubled at it at all.'

From the moment he had heard about it from the Comptroller,

Pepys had been troubled by the thought that discharged seamen would be paid with tickets. On the 24 January he (and presumably Colonel Slingsby) had to appear in Westminster Hall before the Commissioners sitting to discuss the whole question of paying the Army and Navy. '. . . we sat with our hats on, and did discourse about paying off the ships, and do find that will much displease the poor seamen, and so we are glad to have no hand in it.' Just a month later the Commissioners began their work, which as Pepys had foreseen, caused very bad feeling. On 27 February Pepys wrote: 'This day the Commissioners of Parliament begin to pay off the Fleet, beginning with the *Hampshire*, and do it at Guildhall, for fear of going out of the town, into the power of the seamen, who are highly incensed against them.'

Since Lady Batten, as First Lady in Seething Lane, had called socially on his wife Pepys felt it was time to invite a few friends and neighbours to dinner. The cost came to £5, but this was money well spent: the first real entertaining Samuel and Elizabeth had done in the house. Seated round the dining-room table were Sir William and Lady Batten and their not very enticing daughter Martha; Sir William Penn; Captain Cuttance; and Mr Fox. The last was in Pepys's estimation 'a fine gentleman', first encountered on the *Charles*, who later became Paymaster to the Forces. Even if the chimney did smoke, it was a highly successful evening's entertaining, though evidently something of a nervous strain: 'To bed, being glad that the trouble is over.'

Pepys was in the midst of a round of entertaining. Two days later Captain Cuttance was again a guest at dinner, along with Lieutenant Lambert and both the Pierces from the *Charles*, together with their wives. Already his father had come to see the house, and marvel at his son's neatness, and on 2 February a number of the Pepys family came to be handsomely entertained for most of the day by the up-and-coming young Clerk of the Acts. His father and mother, uncle and aunt, brother Tom, the rector of St Olave's and his wife were among the guests. They were 'very well pleased, and I too; it being the last dinner I intend to make a great while. Three dinners within a fortnight.' Life was good. Pepys evidently enjoyed Lady Sandwich's company, finding her gracious and friendly, and whenever possible he went to see her and 'Lady Jem' in their lodgings at Whitehall when business took him to the Palace or to Westminster. Also, pleasant afternoons were wiled away listening to the tales of sea captains telling of Algiers, and what it was like to be sold into slavery. Pepys always loved the theatre, which for him now had an added attraction: female parts were for the first time played not by boys but by women: 'which makes the play much better than ever it did to me'.

Samuel and Elizabeth had been quite accepted by the other members of the Navy Board (with some reservations in the case of the Battens), and nowhere was it more evident than on St Valentine's Day. To his satisfaction Elizabeth chose her own husband to be her Valentine, while he tactfully selected Martha Batten: 'which I do only for complacency'. A few days later he went with her to the fine shops at the Royal Exchange and spent 40s. buying the traditional present, in this case seven pairs of gloves. For his part Sir William Batten chose Elizabeth, while Sir William Penn selected Lady Batten. It was a day off work for everyone. They all scrambled into the office barge and sailed downstream to Deptford to see how Commissioner Pett was getting on with building the King's new yacht. Even included was young Will Wayneman, who was referred to as Pepys's boy, while Sir William Penn's attendant was referred to as Penn's boy. Then it was back into the barge and on to Woolwich to dine on board the *Rose-bush*, commanded by Lady Batten's brother. It was a special occasion for Elizabeth, as Pepys noted: 'the first time I ever carried my wife a-ship-board'. What was more when he made up his accounts soon after he found he had saved £350, quite apart from what he owned in the way of furniture and other possessions. Life was good, there was no mistake about that.

All London, or so it seemed, was talking of whom Charles II would marry, and there was even a rumour that he was already married and the father of two sons. 'Whilst sorry if it should be so,' wrote Pepys, 'but yet am gladder that it should be so, than that the Duke of York and his family should come to the Crown, be being a professed friend to the Catholics.' It is ironic that he should have made such a comment. Twenty-eight years later the birth of a son and heir to the Catholic James and Mary of Modena precipitated the revolution which forced them from the throne, and also ended Pepys's public career, because whilst accepting William and Mary as his lawful sovereigns, loyalty to James prevented him from accepting their offer of continued office.

Marriage or no marriage, the King's coronation was fixed for 23 April. Already Pepys had observed the stands going up in the

City for spectators. But his interest in the coronation was that of an onlooker. It was more personal for Lord Sandwich, who would be an active participant, and thus needed coronation robes costing a great deal of money. In the strictest confidence he asked Pepys if he would arrange a loan of £1,000. Pepys was successful, the lender being his own well-to-do cousin Thomas Pepys who lived near Deptford (not to be confused with Thomas the Turner). When his birthday came round on 23 February, he was able to write: 'This is now 28 years that I am born. And blessed be to God, in a state of full content, and a great hope to be a happy man in all respects, both to myself and friends.'

Lent was early that year, but it made little difference to Pepys's life-style. For one thing the Puritans had looked on it as a Popish thing, and had been almost aggressive in their meat-eating at that time. But on Ash Wednesday he resolved to eat 'as little as I can'. Nor was there any abatement in his theatre-going, which was becoming almost obsessive. Pepys was now visiting the play-house two and three times a week. But as well as a critic of the theatre he was also something of a connoisseur of sermons, and sometimes on Sunday would visit several City churches in succession, sampling the quality of the preaching, and more often than not recording his opinion. 'A dull sermon of a stranger, which made me sleep'; 'A good sermon there was'; 'An indifferent sermon'; 'A good, honest and painful sermon'; 'A poor dry sermon'; 'A tedious long sermon'; 'A cold sermon'; 'A great flattering sermon (before the King).' One sermon he had to sit through in his own church riled not only Pepys: 'A most tedious, unreasonable and impertinent sermon, by an Irish doctor. His text was "Scatter them, O Lord, that delight in war". Sir W. Batten and I very much angry with the parson.'

Only a few weeks before Pepys had complained to his old acquaintance the surgeon who had operated for the stone, saying that his memory was not all it should be. The surgeon advised him to cut down on heavy drinking. When Mr Mills, the rector of St Olave's, preached against drunkenness Pepys rated it the best sermon he had ever heard in his life. But just over a week later the homily would seem to have been quite forgotten when he found himself drinking level in distinguished company in a notable setting. 'At noon, Sir William Batten, Colonel Slingsby, and I by coach to the Tower, to Sir John Robinson's [the Lieutenant] to dinner; where great good cheer. High company; among others the Duchess of

Albemarle, who is ever a plain homely dowdy. After dinner, to drink all the afternoon. Towards night the Duchess and ladies went away. Then we set to it again till it was very late. I was much contented to ride in such state into the Tower, and be received by such high company, while Mr Mount, my Lady Duchess's gentleman usher, stood waiting at table, whom I ever thought a man so much above me in all respects, also to hear the discourse of so many high Cavaliers of things past. It was a great content and joy to me.'

Everything could be said to have interested Pepys: architecture in the shape of fine houses and such cathedrals as Canterbury and Rochester; sculpture, painting and of course music. Among his acquaintances he numbered Henry Purcell, senior, and Matthew Locke; then there was Thomas Fuller, the antiquarian and divine, and Mr Salisbury, a painter he regarded very highly. The return of Charles II had meant the reintroduction of organs into the services, which met with his approval, though the splendid sound of trumpets and drums was not to his liking: 'To Whitehall; where I stayed to hear the trumpets and kettle-drums, and then the other drums, which are much cried up, though I think it dull, vulgar music.' Subjects of much comment were the King's twenty-four string players, considered by many to be too French and fantastical, particularly for use in the Chapel. And Charles, who could be a master of tact when he chose, managed to make them the centre of some ill-feeling during a play in the Cockpit Theatre. Not satisfied with the incidental music provided by one of the Court musicians, 'the King did put a great affront upon Singleton's music, he bidding them stop, and made the French music play, which my Lord says, do much outdo ours'.

Salisbury was something of a miniaturist, for he copied portraits of both Charles II and Lord Sandwich. Like many others, including Cardinal Wolsey and Dr Johnson, nothing would induce him to 'shoot' Old London Bridge in a small boat. At certain states of the tide it could be dangerous, not to say fatal, to take a boat through the mill-race which boiled between the arches. The difference in water level on either side could be as much as five feet, because the openings had with the passing of the centuries become so constricted by the huge piles, known as starlings, driven into the river bed to protect the piers from the force of the current. 'I took him [Salisbury] to Whitehall with me by water, but he could not go through the bridge, and we were fain to go round by the *Old Swan*.'

Pepys had no such qualms, and on one occasion mentions how he stepped out on to the starlings, and walked under the bridge while his boat was being hauled through by hand. In an entry for August 1662, he could not resist having a dig at the French. The story had been told him by Mr Falconer, Clerk of the Ropeyard. 'He told me of the passage of a Frenchman through London Bridge. Where, when he saw the great fall, he begun to cross himself, and say his prayers in the greatest fear in the world; and as soon as it was over he swore, "*Morbleu, c'est le plus grand plaisir du monde*", being the most like a French humour in the world.'

Life for the moment had ceased to be momentous: ahead lay the excitement of the Coronation, but for the present day-to-day existence was pleasant enough. As noted earlier, social drinking featured largely in Pepys's life-style at this time, especially at the Dolphin with 'both Sir Williams', which resulted in his head aching the whole of the next day, despite his colleagues giving him 'two good drafts of sack today, to cure me of my last night's disease, which I thought strange, but I think to find it true'. Perhaps he summed up life in a sentence: 'Then home, and at night to Sir W. Batten's, and there very merry with a good barrel of oysters, and this is the present life I lead.'

When he did go about the Navy's business it was more like a family outing for the neighbours in Seething Lane. On one such occasion he visited Chatham to inspect the Dockyard. Elizabeth did not accompany the Navy Office officials this time, but Lady Batten and Mrs Turner did. In Chatham their stay was more like a house-party, and Pepys pretended he was frightened out of his wits because he would occupy the room in which a former Treasurer died and whose ghost was said to walk. 'Lay and slept well till three in the morning, and then wakening, and by the light of the moon I saw my pillow (which overnight I flung from me) stand upright, but, not bethinking what it might be, I was a little afraid, but sleep overcame all.' Now Pepys was becoming more sure of himself, as he candidly admitted in the privacy of the Diary. 'It was a great pleasure all the time I stayed here to see how I am respected and honoured by all people; and I find that I begin to know now how to receive such reverence, which, at the beginning, I could not tell how to do.'

He and Sir William Batten first inspected the store-houses, where there were goods to be sold as part of the official policy of running down the Navy. These were sold by the candle, a method of auction

Pepys had already seen used at the Navy Office when two ships were sold by the inch. The last person to make a bid as the candle reached a certain mark was successful. Two ships, the *Indian* and the *Half-moon*, were sold for £1,300 and £850 respectively in this way: 'and we have much to do to tell who did cry last'. Among the items being auctioned at Chatham were coats of arms: whether Commonwealth or Royalist Pepys did not say, but since Sir William Batten wanted several to adorn his garden, and others to use for a bonfire on Coronation night, one assumes they were from the time of the late unlamented Commonwealth. After the sale they all took to the office barge to go on board the *Sovereign*, one of the great warships. 'We went to see the *Sovereign*, which we did, taking great pleasure therein, singing all the way, and among other pleasures, I put my Lady [Batten], Mrs Turner, Mrs Hempson, and the two Mrs Allen [a sea captain's daughters], into the lanthorn, and I went in and kissed them, demanding it as a fee due to a principal officer, with all which we were exceeding merry, and drunk some bottles of wine, and neat's tongues and etc, and after much mirth, to bed.' Even Sir William Batten's African servant Mingo was with them, and when Commissioner Pett gave Lady Batten the finest looking parrot Pepys had ever seen, the bird at once recognised Mingo, so presumably he was once in Pett's employment. Lady Batten went round the house and gardens eyeing everything in a most covetous fashion, for once it had belonged to the Surveyor of the Navy, and wasn't that her husband's position? What was more, she said outright she meant to have it all. Undoubtedly the best part of the visit for Pepys was the mutual interest he and Rebecca Allen had in each other. Not only did she seem anxious to have his good opinion, but asked him to sing, which he found flattering. In fact he and Mrs Turner stayed at the Captain's house talking and singing till two o'clock in the morning: 'and was most exceeding merry, and I had the opportunity of kissing Mrs Rebecca, for which God forgive me'. It was one of those rare occasions, that come from time to time, when Pepys was conscious of the happiness of it all as it was happening, and not just in retrospect. 'Of all the journeys that ever I made, this was the merriest, and I was in a strange mood for mirth.'

Pepys had the blessed gift of falling into conversation and getting on well with whoever he came into contact: like the boy with a lantern who lighted his way home through the dirty and uneven streets of the City a few weeks before. When he first saw him the boy had been looking for rags, and as they walked he talked to Pepys, telling him how sometimes he could get three or four bushels of rags a day, at three pence a bushel: 'and many other discourses, what and how many ways there are for poor children to get their livings honestly'. So it was as they returned to London. First the party encountered two schoolboys taking end of term pitchers of ale to their schoolmaster, and Pepys gave one 2*d.* to drink some of it. Then they came upon two girls minding cows. It was Pepys's humour to request one, the prettier, to ask his blessing, telling the naïve girl he was her godfather. She asked then was he Ned Wardling, and he answered yes, he was. So she kneeled down and asked his blessing. Like the boys with the ale she was given 2*d.* Yet as in a painting by Breughel, death and the macabre in seventeenth-century England were never very far away. 'Mrs Anne [Lady Batten's maid] and I rode under the man that hangs upon Shooter's Hill, and a filthy sight it was to see how his flesh is shrunk to his bones. So home, and I found all well, and a good deal of work done [alterations] since I went. So to bed very sleepy for the last night's work, concluding that it is the pleasantest journey in all respects that ever I had in my life.'

From time to time business took him to Whitehall, to Mr Coventry or the Duke of York himself. On one occasion he found the latter not yet dressed: 'and in his night-habit he is a very plain man'. So for that matter he found Anne Hyde, now Duchess of York, a very plain woman when he saw her at the Cockpit Theatre. However, there were others who pleased him better. 'Many great beauties, but, above all, Mrs Palmer, with whom the King doth discover a great deal of familiarity.'

Preparations were now well advanced for the Coronation: triumphal arches were going up in the City, while outside East India House a large picture of ships 'and other things' had been set up. Near Whitehall the streets were so encumbered with lengths of timber to be used as crush-barriers that on one occasion Pepys could not get back home to the City. On 21 April there was heavy rain, which did not deter the crowds from so filling the streets to see the arches and decorations that he could hardly push his way through them. In the entry for that day he made one of the few direct references to the Diary itself. 'Home, people being at church, and I got home unseen, and so up to my chamber, and sat down these last five or six days Diaries.'

Although he could not know it, Charles II was to go down in history as the last sovereign to make the journey through the City on the eve of his coronation. From the time of the boy-king Richard II it had been the custom for the new sovereign to go from the palace-fortress-state prison of the Tower to Westminster in a procession of recognition, which was in fact an opportunity for the Londoners to have a good look at their new ruler. '22nd. The King's going from the Tower to Whitehall. Up early, and made myself as fine as I could, and put on my velvet coat, the first day that I put it on, though made half a year ago.' The household did not watch the procession together. Elizabeth went to view it from the window of an old acquaintance in Fleet Street: Jane the maid took up her station at the house of Thomas the Turner by Paul's Churchyard, while her brother Will saw it go by on Tower Hill. For his part Pepys was with his colleagues from the Navy Office in the house of Mr Young, the flag-maker, on Cornhill. There they had a room to themselves, with wine and 'good cake' for refreshments.

The almost medieval pageantry made a brave sight, and the air was full of the sounds of cornets, sackbuts, kettledrums and side-drums—some of the music was provided by Pepys's friend Matthew Locke. For him there was the additional pleasure and satisfaction of knowing personally some of those riding under the window. Now he could see why his kinsman and patron had wanted £1,000 for his coronation robes. 'Among others, my Lord Sandwich's embroidery and diamonds were not ordinary among them.' That evening, when Pepys made his way to my Lord's lodgings at White-hall Lord Sandwich confided that his richly embroidered suit, which had been made in France, cost £200. 'The Knights of the Bath was a brave sight of itself. Remarkable were the two men that represent the two Dukes of Normandy and Aquataine. The King, in a most rich embroidered suit and cloak, looked most noble. The streets all gravelled, and the houses hung with carpets before them, made a brave show, and the ladies at the windows. So glorious was the show with gold and silver, that we were not able to look at it, our eyes at last being so much overcome. Both the King and the Duke of York took notice of us, as they saw us at the window.' After the procession had finally gone its way towards Cheapside and on to Ludgate the party was entertained to dinner by Mr Young.

It was 23 April; St George's Day and Shakespeare's birthday, as well as Charles II's coronation day. Pepys was up by 4 a.m., and off to Westminster. There Sir John Denham, Surveyor-General, poet and courtier, was showing a party into the Abbey. Unnoticed Pepys joined them, and soon he was sitting on a stand in the North Transept, faced with a seven-hour wait. But there was much to see, for he had an excellent view of the 'theatre', the raised area with its stool which would be occupied by the King for part of the ceremony, before he moved into the Sanctuary for the actual crowning. At last they came: the great ones of England bearing the regalia before the King and the Duke of York. Lord Sandwich was carrying the St Edward Staff. After a service, the bare-headed monarch moved into the Sanctuary: 'which to my great grief I and most in the Abbey could not see'. All those present, whether they could see or not, knew the exact moment of crowning by the great shout that went up. Then the King returned to the theatre, and back again into Pepys's range of vision. There the Bishop of London administered the oaths to his sovereign. (The ceremony should of course have been performed by the Archbishop of Canterbury, but age and infirmity had made it impossible for Juxon, who had attended Charles I on the scaffold, to do so.) The Challenge was made by the King at Arms on three sides of the theatre, to anyone who thought they had reason to oppose Charles II's right to the crown to come forward. Silver medals were flung among the onlookers, but Pepys was unable to come by one, and because of the noise it was impossible to hear the music provided by the royal musicians in their red vests.

By now Pepys had had enough, and slipped away before the end of the ceremony. Outside, he set off boldly along the blue carpet within barriers which stretched from the Abbey to Westminster Hall, and would soon be trodden by the King himself. He estimated the crowd at about 10,000 people. Into Westminster Hall he went, to find that now two large stands ran the length of each side, from which privileged spectators would soon be able to watch the banquet, which included rituals that would continue to the time of George IV. Among the 'scaffolds one upon another full of brave ladies' was Elizabeth, and shortly before Charles II entered Pepys found a place for himself. 'And the King come in with his crown on, and his sceptre in his hand, under a canopy borne up by six silver staves, carried by Barons of the Cinque Ports, and little bells at every end.' How amazed Pepys would have been could he have known that twenty-four years later, at the coronation of James II, *he* would be one of those supporting the canopy over the new king. But for the

73

present he was feasting his eyes on the pageantry and ritual, and the Knights of the Bath carrying in the first course of the banquet, after it had been tasted in the kitchens by the Duke of Albemarle. As each of the succeeding courses was brought in three peers on horseback, Northumberland, Suffolk and Ormond, led the way. Finally, the King's Champion entered on horseback, in armour, to throw down the gauntlet and challenge anyone to doubt Charles II's claim to the throne. Then he rode right up to the King, who pledged him from a golden goblet, which he passed across to Sir Edward Dymock to drink his health. The knight was by tradition allowed to keep the goblet when he withdrew.

Now all the official guests were dining, and Pepys went with many others to watch them. What was more, Will Howe, Lord Sandwich's personal attendant, scrounged four rabbits and a pullet, while Pepys and John Creed asked for bread, and so themselves had a meal. 'I took a great deal of pleasure to go up and down, and look upon the ladies, and to hear the music of all sorts, but above all the 24 violins.' The dinner over, Pepys went up to join Elizabeth on her stand. The banquet had finished, and with it the official ceremonies of the day. As the King left Westminster Hall the skies opened up: 'it fell a-raining and thundering and lightning as I have not seen it do for some years'.

Off he went to the house of Mr Bowyer, the senior clerk in the Exchequer Office, where they went on to the leads to watch for the fireworks, but there were none that rain-swept April evening. Then he made his way with Elizabeth to visit their old neighbours in Axe Yard. There they found three bonfires, and a large number of 'gallants, men and women', who insisted that Samuel and Elizabeth should drink the King's health on their knees, which they did, 'and I wondered to see how the ladies did tipple'. Elizabeth spent the night there with a one-time neighbour, while Pepys went off again, to my Lord's lodgings. 'But no sooner a-bed with Mr Shepley but my head began to turn, and I to vomit, and if ever I was foxed, it was now.' There was the inevitable price to be paid. 'Waked in the morning, with my head in a sad taking through last night's drink, which I am very sorry for. So rose, and went out with Mr Creed to drink our morning draft, which he did give me in chocolate, to settle my stomach.' Off he went through a City that was also nursing its head back home to write up his Diary for the past three days, while in the distance he could hear the crackle of exploding fireworks: 'which are now playing upon the Thames before the King; and I wish myself with them, being sorry not to see them'.

What might be called social drinking was something of a problem to Pepys. If the company were agreeable it was difficult to stop without seeming churlish, and he was honest enough to recognise his inability to take a firm line with himself. Not only were there hangovers, but he feared it was affecting his memory, and he even found 'my head grows weak nowerdays, if I come to drink wine, and therefore hope that I shall leave it off of myself, which I pray God I could do'. But temptation was everywhere, even on his own roof. 'I took my flageolet, and played it on the leads in the garden, where Sir W. Penn come out in his shirt into his leads, and there we stayed talking and singing and drinking great drafts of claret, and eating botargo [a sausage made from eggs and the blood of mullet], and bread and butter till nearly twelve at night, it being moon-shine; and so to bed, very near fuddled. 6th June. My head ached all night, and all this morning, with my last night's debauch.' For Pepys, as for Oscar Wilde, the one thing he couldn't resist was temptation.

Before that crowded April was out Pepys was planning another journey, to inspect the dockyards at Portsmouth. It would be another family affair, with Elizabeth, John Creed, Thomas Hayter (an official in the Navy Office) and his wife. Pepys was in for a pleasant surprise regarding Mrs Hayter: 'who, through her mask, seemed at first to be an old woman, but afterwards I found her to be a very pretty, modest black [haired] woman'. It was another pleasant excursion, nearly as enjoyable as the visit to Chatham, though Pepys could not but regret leaving the metropolitan delights, even for a few days. 'I am sorry I am not in London, to be at Hyde Park tomorrow [May day], among the great gallants and ladies, which will be very fine.' But there were other pleasures to be enjoyed, like staying at the inns recently used by the King when he accompanied his mother to Portsmouth on the first stage of her return journey to France. He found Portsmouth a pleasant and strong place, and together with Creed made the circuit of the town along the top of the walls. The officers of the Dockyard treated him with gratifying respect, and he made a thorough inspection of the stores, and sold off surplus provisions. The return journey was equally uneventful. At Guildford they put up at the Red Lion, in the room occupied by the King, and went to see Archbishop Abbot's hospital, and were civilly treated by the Master of the Free School. They stayed over Sunday, hearing a better sermon by the red-faced parson of the town than Pepys had expected, and before dinner of his own admission played the fool with Creed, seeing who could jump the better over an old well-head. Pepys won the wager, a quart of sack. Ever since he had first seen her Pepys had been taken with Mrs Pierce, the surgeon's wife, and now over dinner he quarrelled with Elizabeth about her merits. Elizabeth declared Mrs Pierce was no beauty, while Samuel stoutly defended her, 'till we were both angry'.

Back once again in London there was news to interest Pepys. The son born to the Duke of York and Anne Hyde had not survived: 'and I hear that the Duke and his Lady themselves are not much troubled at it'.

Life went on as before in Seething Lane. Pepys's younger brother John had come from Cambridge to see the Coronation, and now he was returning. 'I did give him some good council, and 20s in money, and so he went away. At night comes my wife not well, from my father's, having had a foretooth drawn out today, which did trouble me.'

When Charles II created Lord Sandwich Master of the Great Wardrobe (St Andrew by the Wardrobe takes its name from the long-vanished Wardrobe Tower which was the repository for the royal robes and clothing), he also was given the use of a house, which now became his official residence. Pepys at first had not been impressed by the place, but now it had been decorated, and was fine enough for any man. Pepys was sent for by his kinsman, who would shortly be setting out on a mission, because one of the officers of the Wardrobe was in failing health. 'He did instruct me as to the business of the Wardrobe, in case in his absence, Mr Townsend should die, and told him that he did intend to join me and Mr Moore with him as to the other business, now he is going to sea, and spoke to me many other things, as one that he do put the greatest confidence in, of which I am proud.'

Although he seldom mentioned it in the Diary, it must have been a disappointment to him and Elizabeth that they never had any children, for he obviously loved them. Perhaps the nearest he came to having a family of his own were my Lord's children: Edward, who became Lord Hinchingbrooke, Sidney, Oliver, John, Jemimah and Paulina. The affection was mutual. On one occasion when about to dine with Lady Sandwich 'after we were set, comes some persons of condition, and so the children and I rose and dined by ourselves all. The children and I were very merry, and they mightly fond of me.'

Lord Sandwich was about to set off on his longest mission yet: he was to take possession of the town of Tangier, which would be ceded to England by Portugal as part of the dowry of Charles II's future Queen, Catharine of Braganza* (he would be bringing her back on the return voyage); and he was to attack the Barbary pirates who were still making a pest of themselves, preying on merchant shipping. Pepys as usual helped his kinsman prepare for the voyage. He and Sir George Carteret had drawn up a letter for the Duke of York pointing out that work at the Navy Office had almost been brought to a stop for want of funds, and that they were in the humiliating position that 'none will sell us anything without our personal security given for the same'. And now Lord Sandwich had come to Pepys saying he must have £300 to buy cloth to give as presents to the Turks on the Barbary coast.

The expedition sailed on 13 June, and Pepys accompanied the Earl in his barge as far as Deptford, where they inspected the King's new yacht, now nearly finished, and were delayed by Will Howe's late arrival with his master's personal baggage. At last they set sail, with Pepys still on board. But soon it was time for him to sing one last duet with Will Howe, and climb over the side into the wherry waiting alongside: 'and my Lord did give me five guns, all they had charged, which was the greatest respect my Lord could do me, and of which I was not a little proud. So with a sad and merry heart I left them sailing presently from Erith, hoping to be in the Downs tomorrow early.' With him was Captain Ferrers, attached to Lord Sandwich's household, and something of a cross between Tybalt and Bardolph. Quick tempered, on two occasions he was involved in quarrels when blood was spilt, in the second of which he lost several fingers when one of my Lord's footmen slashed at him with a sword. 'We towards London in our boat. Pulled off our stockings, and bathed our legs a great while in the river, which I had not done [for] some years before ... at Woolwich went on shore: and home, with wine enough in my head, went to bed.'

* Over the years Tangier became an exceptionally costly drain on the Navy's already overstretched and sometimes non-existent financial resources, until in the end it was abandoned and the harbour installations destroyed. Among those on that expedition in 1683 would be Pepys himself, accompanying Lord Dartmouth at the King's own request.

Just a year before Pepys had been told that his Uncle Robert at Brampton had made him his heir. On 2 July 1661, he heard from his father that 'my uncle is by fits stupid, and like a man that is drunk, and sometimes speechless'. On 6 July, came news early in the morning that the old man was dead. Pepys set out for Brampton, sad and glad all at the same time, and reached the Huntingdonshire village at nine at night. 'My uncle's corpse in a coffin standing upon joynt-stools in the chimney in the hall; but it begin to smell, and so I caused it to be set forth in the yard all night, and watched by my Aunt. My father and I lay together tonight, I greedy to see the will, but did not ask to see it till tomorrow.' And a great deal of trouble and worry it would cause him too. If Pepys had hoped for a windfall which would just require picking up, he was in for a disappointment.

The day after his arrival his father read him the will. The old man had kept his promise, and made Pepys his ultimate heir, though his father had the estate for his life. But now there was the funeral to attend to: gloves and ribbons to be procured for distribution to the mourners according to custom. It was Sunday, and a large number of friends and neighbours followed the coffin to the church where the parson was evidently at a loss what to say about Robert Pepys. 'Mr Turner preached a funeral sermon where he spoke not particularly of him anything, but that he was one well known for his honesty: that it spoke for itself above all that he could say for it.'

Uncle Robert might not have been a man of great wealth, but his affairs would take some unravelling. To add to the complications Samuel's aunt, Anne Pepys, had been previously married, and there was trouble from that quarter. 'Much troubled with my Aunt's base, ugly rumours. We had news of Tom Trice [stepson to Robert Pepys] putting in a caveat against us, in behalf of his mother, to whom my uncle had not given anything.' What with family quarrels, missing papers and the confusion of those that were found, the inferior quality of the meat and drink, being bitten at night by gnats, and not returning to London within a week, it was one long catalogue of woe for Pepys. But he could not resist taking a day off to visit Cambridge and old friends, and was annoyed to find his brother John still in bed at eight o'clock in the morning. Then on to look up his elderly great-uncle Talbot Pepys, the squire of Impington. Five days later he was on his way back to London, breaking his journey at Hatfield House where a friendly gardener showed him both the house and the gardens. It was the latter in particular that impressed Pepys: 'such as I never saw in all my life; nor so good flowers, nor so great goosberries, as big as nutmegs'. His troubles were only just beginning, however. At the start of August he was once again in Impington, to ask the advice of Talbot Pepys's son about the estate at Brampton. Now yet another uncle, Thomas Pepys, was going to contest the will, which necessitated further visits to Brampton and Impington as certain copyhold documents relating to some of the land were missing, and Thomas Pepys had been declared heir-at-law, at least as far as the copyhold land was concerned.

If Pepys were worried, he did not show it at the Navy Office, but gave quite a different impression. 'I give it out among them that the estate left me is £200 a year in land, besides mortgages, because I would put an esteem on myself.' Finally he heard on 7 October that he had been admitted as heir-at-law, and that the will would go in his favour. It had been decided that his father, quite elderly now, should go and live together with his mother at Brampton. Brother Tom would take over the shop in Salisbury Court, though whether he had it in him to make a success of the business was another matter. For some time Pepys had found his mother increasingly difficult and unreasonable, and as for his sister Pall—when he returned from his first visit to Brampton that summer he was 'troubled to hear how proud and idle Pall is grown, that I am re-solved not to keep her'. Now they were both off to the country, with no regrets on Pepys's part. '5th September. Put my mother and Pall into the waggon, and saw them going presently, Pall crying exceedingly.'

Uncle Robert of Brampton was not the only relative to die that summer: two aunts on his mother's side also died. One was Aunt Fenner, wife of the blacksmith, and the other Aunt Kite. Several of his mother's relations were more than Pepys could bear without his gorge rising. '15th [September]: with my wife to the burial of my Aunt Kite [her maiden name], where, besides us and my Uncle Fenner's family, there was none of any quality, but poor and rascally people. So we went to church with the corpse, and there the service read at the grave, and back again with Peg Kite [daughter], who will be, I doubt, a troublesome carrion to us executors, and if she will not be ruled, I shall fling up my executorship.' Cousin Peg proved to be a troublesome carrion, and determined to make what was considered an unsatisfactory marriage. 'Peg Kite now hath declared she will have the beggarly rogue the weaver, and so we are resolved neither to meddle nor make with her.' And with that she disappears from the Diary. As for Uncle Fenner, it was obvious he would not remain a widower for long. 'With my mind full of trouble, to my Uncle Fenner's, where at the ale-house I found him drinking, and very jolly and youthsome, and as one that I believe will in a little time get him a wife.'

Before five months had passed Uncle Fenner had remarried, and Pepys's account of the wedding reveals all his undisguised loathing for his mother's squalid relations. '23rd [January 1662]. By invitation to my Uncle Fenner's, where I found his new wife, a pitiful, old, ugly, ill-bred woman, in a hat, a midwife. Here were many of his, and as many of her relations, sorry, mean people; and after choosing our gloves, we all went over to the Three Cranes Tavern, and though the best room in the house, in such a narrow dog-hole we were crammed, and I believe we were near forty, that it made me loathe my company and victuals; and a sorry, poor dinner it was too.'

Illness and death also took their toll among his friends and acquaintances. Not only was Lady Sandwich seriously ill shortly before the birth of a daughter (both survived), but letters came from the Mediterranean saying that Lord Sandwich was ill with fever ashore in Alicante. These filled Pepys with foreboding, and he kept the news from Lady Sandwich. Even the son Edward fell ill, and was in great fear lest he had contracted smallpox. For safety's sake the other sons were sent to stay in Seething Lane. But after a few days good news came from Alicante, my Lord had recovered, and for the first time Pepys told Lady Sandwich of his illness. Also, every day Edward grew better: whatever it was he had been suffering from, it was not smallpox. Then it was the Duke of Albemarle's turn to be ill, and Thomas Fuller, author of *Fuller's Worthies*, as well as the Dean of St Paul's, died. 'It is a sickly time both in the City and country everywhere, of a sort of fever, that never was heard of almost, unless it was in a plague-time.' That same morning Pepys and all the staff of the Navy Office had been at the burial of one of the Comptroller's clerks, whom he had thought to be in the best of health. In October Sir Robert Slingsby, the Comptroller himself, died after a week's illness, leaving a widow. Pepys was personally affected by the death: 'which put me into so great a trouble of mind, that all night I could not sleep, he being a man that loved me, and had many qualities that made me to love him, above all the officers and commissioners in the Navy'. The new Comptroller would be Sir John Minnes, whom Pepys found to be a 'fine gentleman and a very good scholar'.

Day-to-day life had its incidents, faithfully recorded: such as the occasion when Will Hewer left the street door unlocked and a thief slipped in and stole a fine silver tankard, which prompted the normally easy-going Pepys to note spitefully: 'I hear that my man Will hath lost his clock with my tankard, at which I am very glad.' Perhaps it was the theft which gave Sir William Batten the idea for a silly practical joke which in the end misfired. Evidently he took a tankard from Sir William Penn's house, pretending it too had been stolen, and got Pepys to write a letter, as though from the thief. 'After dinner we were very merry with Sir W. Penn about the loss of his tankard, though all be but a cheat, and he do not yet understand it; but the tankard was stolen by Sir W. Batten, and the letter, as from the thief, wrote by me, which makes very good sport.' Apparently Pepys had put in the letter that Penn could have the tankard back at a price. 'To the *Dolphin*, to drink the 30s that we got the other day of Sir W. Penn about his tankard.' Most of the neighbours from Seething Lane, as well as others including Captain Allen and Robin Holmes, were present when they decided to let him in on their joke. 'We begun to tell Sir W. Penn the business, but he had been drinking today, and so is almost gone, that we could not make him understand it, which caused us more sport.' Two days later came the sequel. 'Called at Sir W. Batten's, and there heard that Sir W. Penn do take our jest of the tankard very ill, which I am sorry for.'

Quite apart from the strain put upon neighbourly relations between 'both Sir Williams' by the episode of the tankard, there was also a cooling of relations between Elizabeth and Lady Batten. Pepys was quick to notice that Lady Batten and Martha were looking sideways at Elizabeth 'because my wife do not buckle to them, and is not solicitous for their acquaintance'. Uppishness would seem to be in the air, and even to have affected steady, reliable Will Hewer, which troubled Pepys, who recognised his good qualities. 'Much offended in mind at a proud trick my man Will hath got, to keep his hat on in the house, but I will not speak of it to him today, but I fear I shall be troubled with his pride and laziness, though in other things he is good enough.' A few days later he could stand it no longer: 'I did give my man Will a sound lesson about his fore-bearing to give us the respect due to a master and mistress.'

Additional help came to the house in Seething Lane in the form of a second servant. 'This morning come the maid that my wife hath lately hired for a chamber maid. She is very ugly, so that I cannot care for her, but otherwise she seems very good.' A few Sundays later Pepys again referred to the girl: 'To church, and coming home again found our new maid Doll asleep, that she could not hear us to let us in, so that we were fain to send a boy in at a window to open the door to us.'

Pepys may have found poor Doll plain, but there were others, and his interest did not stop at looking, which was the case with the daughter of his one-time neighbour Mrs Crisp in Axe Yard. Shortly before he sold the lease he invited the girl into the empty house one afternoon. Even in a diary kept in cypher the Puritan in him made Pepys lapse into Latin (in later years French, Spanish and Italian were added to record his success): 'Nulla puella negat'—the girl denies (me) nothing. Fond though he was of Elizabeth it did not stop him from straying, either in thought or in deed. If Pepys could never resist the company of a pretty lady, it did not stop him from being jealous of Elizabeth: such as the occasion when he encountered 'a French footman with feathers' who wanted to speak privately with her: 'but I could not tell what it was, only my wife promised to go to some place tomorrow morning, which did trouble my mind how to know whither it was'. The picture of Pepys biting his nails with apprehension and curiosity is not without its humour, and evidently he never did find out what it was all about.

But the one who fascinated him above all others was Mrs Palmer, the future Lady Castlemaine. On several occasions he was gratified to find she too was in the theatre. 'I sat before Mrs Palmer, the king's mistress, and filled my eyes with her, which much pleased me.' Another time the King, the Duke of York and Mrs Palmer were present: 'which was great content; and, indeed, I can never enough admire her beauty.'

Even Pepys had qualms about the extent of his theatre-going—two and three times a week—and he resolved only to go in company with his wife. But like his resolution not to eat meat during Lent it was soon broken. Twice they went to see *Bartholomew Fair*, acted with puppets, and twice to *Hamlet*, with Betterton, the greatest actor of his day, as the Prince. Among the plays seen at this time was *The White Devil*, *'Tis pity she's a Whore*, *The Silent Woman*, as well as others which have long since disappeared into the limbo of theatrical history. One play that tempted him to break his vow not to enter a theatre without Elizabeth can certainly be said to have lived on. 'Walking through Lincoln's Inn Fields, observed that the Opera, a new play, *Twelfth Night*, was acted there, and the King being there: so I, against my own mind and resolution could not forebare to go in, which did make the play seem a burden to me, and I took no pleasure in it; and so, after it was done, went home with my mind troubled for my going thither, after my swearing to my wife that I would never go to a play without her.' That women's parts were now played by women and not by boys was in itself an attraction, and an even greater one was the sight of a woman playing a man's part: 'having the best legs that ever I saw, and I was very well pleased with it'. Davenant's *The Wits* drew him back to the theatre three times in less than a fortnight, and he wrote: 'Troubled in mind that I cannot bring myself to mind my business, but to be so much in love of plays.' Most of Jacobean drama was too sombre for his liking, such as Beaumont and Fletcher's *The Maid's Tragedy*: 'Which I never saw before, and methinks it is too sad and melancholy.' He liked *The White Devil* of Webster even less: 'Methinks, a very poor play.' But perhaps the play to get the worst notice from Pepys was *Romeo and Juliet*, given at the Opera, with the much admired Betterton and his wife in the lead. 'It is a play of itself the worst that ever I heard, and the worst acted that ever I saw these people do, and I am resolved to go no more the first time of acting for they were all of them out more or less.'

Drinking more than he could carry was still a source of worry, especially when it was noticed by his father during a visit to Brampton, and not long after he nearly disgraced himself in front of everyone at home, and on a Sunday too. 'What at dinner and supper I drink, I know not how, of my own accord, so much wine, that I was even almost foxed, and my head ached all night; so home to bed, without prayers, which I never did yet, since I came to the house, of a Sunday night; I being now so out of order that I durst not read prayers, for fear of being perceived by my servants in what case I was.'

Pepys's wardrobe continued to grow, with a gold lace waistcoat

and a beaver hat, together with a coat cut in the latest fashion. Whatever else a gentleman chose to do without, he noted down, he should
not stint his clothes. If 'both Sir Williams' encouraged him to spend
too much time at the Dolphin, the one most likely to lead the
twenty-eight-year-old Clerk of the Acts astray was Captain Ferrers.
He took Pepys to a gaming-house in Lincoln's Inn Fields, but what
he saw did not appeal: 'strange the folly of men to lay and lose so
much money, and very glad I was to see the manner of a gamester's
life, which I see is very miserable, and poor, and unmanly'. More
to his liking was the dancing school they visited next, which had a
company of young girls. But his life, like that of so many others in
London in the morning of the Restoration, was only a pale reflection
of life at Court. Already people's good opinion of Charles II was
beginning to wane. 'At Court things are in a very ill condition, there
being so much emulation, poverty, and the vices of drinking, swearing and loose amours that I know not what will be the end of it, but
confusion. And the Clergy so high, that all people that I meet with
do protest against their practice. In short, I see no content or
satisfaction anywhere, in any sort of people.'

Some eighteen months before a respectful Parliament had listened
to the reading of Charles II's letter from Breda which was the
prelude to his return to England. But already its mood was altering.
What was more the Lords and Commons were far from being in
accord. As far back as July that year Pepys had heard rumours: 'I
found the two Houses at a great difference, about the Lords chal-
lenging their privileges not to have their houses searched, which
makes them to deny to pass the House of Commons' Bill for searching for pamphlets and seditious books.' By October the Commons
was in a mood to ask questions, and they wanted to know where all
the money already received by the King had gone. But when
Parliament reassembled on 19 October it was with the addition of
the Bishops sitting once again in the Lords, and they voted the huge
sum of £1,200,000 to be raised to pay the King's debts.

The return of Parliament had its effect on the Navy Office away
on the far side of the City, for so long as it was sitting the members
of the Navy Board would have to work in the afternoons as well as
in the mornings. Shortage of money was making itself felt, and it
had to be brought to the attention of the Duke of York in person.
'This morning Sir W. Batten, and Sir W. Penn and I, waited upon
the Duke of York in his chamber, to give him an account of the

condition of the Navy for lack of money, and how our bills are offered on the Exchange, to be sold at 20 in the 100 less.' Even Pepys, usually quite loyal to Charles II, now wrote candidly: 'The want of money puts all things, and above all, the Navy, out of order; and yet I do not see that the King takes care to bring in any money, but think of new designs to lay out money.' It was all very worrying, at least for someone as conscientious as Pepys, and at the year's end when he came to add up the Navy's debts he found they amounted to no less than £374,000, nearly a third of the sum voted to the King by Parliament.

He was also engaged in a little historical research, started when the Duke of York asked what he knew of the custom by which foreign vessels were supposed to strike their flags when passing English ships. Pepys, to his chagrin, knew nothing about it, but that did not stop him making up a cock-and-bull story for Mr Coventry about having read that in Henry VII's time the King had instructed his captains to make Danish ships in the Baltic strike their flags to English vessels. Originally the question had been raised by Captain Robin Holmes, and before long Pepys found himself following it up in all seriousness, so that he could present a report to the King and Council. He even asked an old acquaintance at the Exchequer Office to look up in Domesday Book and see if there were any reference to it there. When he came to sum up the year he made mention of what he was about: not that it ever came to anything, apart from arousing his interest in naval history. 'I am upon writing a little treatise to present to the Duke, about our privilege in the seas, as to other nations striking their flags to us.'

If he found little cause for satisfaction in the state of the Navy's finances on 31 December 1661, there was reason for some degree of complacency in his own life. 'So home, and after supper and my barber had trimmed me, I sat down to end my journal for this year, and my condition at this time, by God's blessing, is that my health is very good, and so my wife's, in all respects: my servants, W. Hewer, Sarah [in place of Jane Wayneman], Nell and Will Wayneman: my house at the Navy Office. I suppose myself to be worth about £500 clear in the world, and my goods, and what is coming to me from Brampton, when my father dies, which God defer.' Further on he inspects the debit side of his balance sheet, with a long hard look at himself. 'But my greatest trouble is, that I have for this last half year been afraid to cast up my accounts, though I hope I am worth what I say above. But I will cast them up very shortly. I have newly taken a solemn oath about abstaining from plays and wine, which I am resolved to keep, according to the letter of the oath which I keep by me.'

Chapter 6

Hard Work
1662

I F work at the Navy Office had come a bad second to the other side of Pepys's life during 1661, a truly remarkable change was to come over him in the year just beginning. He had had his fling, and whilst not prepared to put aside all pleasures, Pepys was now prepared to make the Navy Office his life, and not merely a means to a salary. He vowed to cut down on both drinking and play-going: his greater success was with the former. During 1661 he must have visited the theatre between sixty and seventy times, while in 1662 it was not above twenty, though he and Elizabeth were to go three nights running in one week. 'Both Sir Williams' were drinking hard, and amused themselves by stupefying their companions at the Dolphin, and it must have taken considerable moral courage for their young colleague to drop out of their drinking bouts whenever possible. If Pepys's reformation were to prove pure gain for the Navy Office it was at times at the expense of Elizabeth, who at least for the first few months of 1662 found herself almost neglected at home. For her the New Year began rather inauspiciously: '1st January. Waking this morning out of my sleep on a sudden, I did with my elbow hit my wife a great blow over her face and neck, and waked her with pain, at which I was sorry, and to sleep again.'

There was one luxury which Pepys was indulging in at this time which gave great pleasure to them both. They were sitting for an artist in Cheapside named Savill who was painting two separate portraits. At first Pepys was doubtful, for after the first sitting he feared it would not be like him. But a further visit, when Savill started on Elizabeth's portrait, was more enjoyable. 'With my wife to the painter's, and there she sat the first time to be drawn, while I all the while stood looking on a pretty lady's picture, whose face did please me extremely. At last, he having done, I found that the dead colour of my wife is good, above what I expected, which

87

pleased me exceedingly.' Either Mr Savill was not an outstanding artist or else Pepys was something of a back-seat driver when it came to portraiture. 'My wife and I to the painter's, and there she sat the last time, and I stood by, and did tell him some little things to do, that now her picture I think will please me very well; and after her, her little black dog sat in her lap, and was drawn, which made us very merry; so home to dinner.' The two portraits cost £6, and another 36s. for the frames; but Pepys was not quite satisfied yet, and wanted alterations to Elizabeth's. On 24 January, after dining at the Wardrobe with Lady Sandwich they went to Cheapside together to see the portraits: '. . . and in her opinion, that it do much wrong her; but I will have it altered'. Back he and Elizabeth went a few days later: 'To have her picture mended, which at last is come to be very like her, and I think it well done; but the painter, though a very honest man, I found to be very silly as to matter of skill in shadows.'

The portraits were to hang in the dining-room which Pepys was transforming into a handsome chamber, and he wanted its improvement to come as a surprise to Elizabeth. It was St Valentine's Day, and this year Will Bowyer from the Exchequer Office was her Valentine, which would be useful in keeping her out of the way. Will Bowyer 'held her hands all the morning, that she might not see the painters that were at work in gilding my chimney-piece and pictures in my dining-room'. Already Pepys had bought several paintings in the City and on 22 February in came 'Mr Savill with the pictures, and we hung them up in our dining-room. It comes now to appear very handsome with all my pictures.' Soon the portraits were varnished, and Pepys had a room in which he would be proud to entertain the most eminent of his acquaintances.

An artist of greater fame whose studio he visited—though only to admire—was Lely. '18th June. I walked to Lely's, the painter's, where I saw, among other rare things, the Duchess of York, her whole body, sitting in state in a chair; in white satin, and another of the King, that is not finished; most rare things. I did give the fellow something that showed them us, and promised to come some other time, and he would show me Lady Castlemaine's, which I could not then see, it being locked up! Thence to Wright's, the painter's: but Lord! the difference that is between their two works.'

The previous year Pepys had taken singing lessons. Now he decided to branch out even further, and have lessons in composition from a Mr Berkenshaw, for it was his particular desire 'to compose some airs', though he felt it was an expensive diversion. 'Long with Mr Berkenshaw in the morning at my music practice, finishing my song of "Gaze not on Swans", in two parts, which pleases me well, and I did give him £5 for this month or five weeks that he hath taught me, which is a great deal of money, and troubled me to part with it.' Pepys may have learnt all he could from his music-master, but the latter thought otherwise, and a few days later 'come Mr Berkenshaw, and in our discourse we fell to angry words, so that in a pet he flung out of my chamber, and I never stopped him'.

Compared with a few years earlier, Pepys's health had improved, as he noted down on his twenty-ninth birthday (23 February 1662), despite being kept at home by a heavy cold, 'and like to live and get an estate'. Just as determinedly as he had resolved to keep a diary, so he maintained his tradition of giving a dinner on the anniversary of his operation for the removal of a stone. Among the guests were Mrs Turner and her daughter, who had lent her house for the opera-tion. It was in his own words 'a pretty dinner'; the first course consisting of two stewed carp, six roast chicken, and salmon. For the second there were two calves' tongues, cheese and tanzy: the last a pudding made from eggs and cream, flavoured with the herb tansy.

Blood-letting was the physician's answer to most ailments in the seventeenth and eighteenth centuries, and in that spring of 1662 'Mr Holliard come to me, and let me blood, about 16 ounces, I being exceeding full of blood, and very good. I begun to be sick; but lying on my back, I was presently well again, and did give him 5s for his pains. After dinner, my arm tied up with black ribbon, I walked with my wife to my brother Tom's.'

A result of Pepys now taking a very real interest in the Navy Office was the effect not only on his professional relationships, but also his friendship with 'both Sir Williams'. The more he became immersed in his work the more disillusioned he became with his two colleagues' casual approach, to say nothing of the way most afternoons were spent at the Dolphin. Also, both he and Elizabeth were starting to find Lady Batten just a little patronising, which neither was prepared to accept willingly. The year started amicably enough, with wedding anniversaries. Sir William Penn had been married eighteen years, and for his guests there was a dish containing as many mince pies. At dinner it did not escape Pepys's notice that

gallant Major (or Captain in the Navy) Holmes was trying to become
very friendly with Elizabeth: 'but I shall prevent it, and she herself
hath also a defiance against him'. Sir William Batten had been
married three years (obviously a second marriage for him), so there
were only three large pies, one more like an open tart, which a
fellow-guest topped up with a pint and a half of white wine which
she then drank off as a health to the couple: 'it being the greatest
draught that ever I did see a woman drink in my life'.

The previous year Pepys had been Martha Batten's Valentine,
but not in 1662. He was keeping away from their house: 'there
being no great friendship between us now, as formerly'. In Pepys's
world the balance of power was shifting away from Penn and Batten
towards Sir George Carteret, the Comptroller. Just as much as he
had found Sir Robert Slingsby a congenial companion, till the
latter's untimely death ended the friendship, so he now found he
had more in common with Sir George, who was undoubtedly made
of finer clay than either the Surveyor or the Commissioner to the
Navy Board. Also the Comptroller shared his enthusiasm for work.
Pepys's resolution to do well at his job can be dated exactly: '6th
[February]. After dinner, my barber trimmed me, and so to the
office, where I do begin to be exact in my duty there, and exacting
my privileges.' Before long he found that hard work agreed with
him, and gave such satisfaction, that he wished he could maintain
the pace every day. At the office he found all the paper-work relating to his mission to Holland with Sir Edward Montagu, as he then
was: '5th March. To my office, and there sat looking over my papers
of my voyage, when we fetched over the King, and tore so many of
these that were worth nothing, as filled my closet as high as my
knees.' By then he had already been sworn in as a Younger Brother
of Trinity House, and received the satisfaction of having all the
Elder Brethren come to shake his hand.

For years there had been what amounted to corrupt practices
between the Navy Office and City merchants who provided supplies
of one kind or another, and now Sir George Carteret and Pepys had
caught red-handed 'one Colonel Appesly, whom we had taken
counterfeiting of bills with all our hands and the officers of the
yards, so well that I should never had mistrusted them'. It took until
ten in the evening to straighten out the matter, and then a constable marched the Colonel off to the Compter Prison in Poultry.
The more work Pepys did the more he enjoyed it. 'I find great

pleasure in it, and a growing content.' But it was not only such as 'both Sir Williams' and certain merchants who would have reason to regret his zeal. Now Pepys had an office of his own, and he intended to keep his clerks up to the mark. 'To my office, where I fell upon boring holes for me to see from my closet into the great office, without going forth, wherein I please myself much.' And this was the Samuel Pepys who only a few months before would have been up and out of the office at the drop of a hat if anything of interest were taking place anywhere in London.

One day a German came to the Navy Office with a secret weapon designed to blow up ships: but it was so secret that he would only tell the King, who in his turn must only tell his heirs. Pepys and his colleagues were not all that impressed, remarking that it had been known in the time of the Commonwealth, but there had been the question of the device's safety on board ship. And so Dr Knuffler departed with an unfulfilled promise to discuss his invention with the Duke of York.

Money was as big a problem as ever it had been, and the crew of the small vessel *Guernsey* had not been paid since before Charles II's return, nearly two years before, with the result that the men had been forced to borrow money at a rate of interest, so that when at last they did receive their wages there was very little left they could call their own.

The withdrawal of Pepys's friendship from Batten and Penn was beginning to make itself felt at home, where rivalry between the families was coming into the open. First Pepys dressed his boy Will in a smart new livery. Then he went one better. 'ist May. Our boy waiting on us with his sword, which this day he begun to wear, to outdo Sir W. Penn's boy, who do this day, and Sir W. Batten's, do begin to wear new liveries; but I do take mine to be the neatest of them all.' Even St Olave, Hart Street, witnessed the social struggle. There it took the form of fighting for precedence in the office pew. To his pleasure Pepys had discovered that Lady Batten before becoming a wife had been a mistress, and now he encouraged Elizabeth to upstage her whenever possible. 'My wife and I to church in the afternoon, and seated ourselves, she below me, and by that means takes the precedence of our pew, which my Lady Batten and her daughter takes, is confounded.' Since they were bent on antagonising their neighbours Samuel and Elizabeth were thoroughly suspicious when that same Sunday evening they were sent a crab and a lobster by the Penns. 'The reason of which we cannot think, but something there is of plot or design in it; for we have a little while carried ourselves pretty strange to them.' Obviously Lady Batten had been trying to deceive the Clerk of the Acts and his wife. With relish Pepys recorded on 26 May that the Brethren of Trinity House had chosen Sir John Minnes as a new Master, and not Sir William Batten: 'at which I am not a little pleased, because of his proud lady'. Later, in June, Penn incurred Pepys's undying dislike by trying to take away his right to prepare contracts, and give it to Mr Coventry, who had just joined the Navy Board as an additional Commissioner. Pepys was furious, there was a heated argument, and in the end he won the day. 'Sir W. Penn did it like a base rascal, and so I shall remember him while I live.'

Before the breach with 'both Sir Williams' became complete there was another visit to Portsmouth. Evidently it became something of a test case for Pepys, who insisted that if one of their wives came, all could. Elizabeth would have liked to come with them, but had to be disappointed, which led to bad feeling, and they parted coldly from each other. The party consisted of Pepys and Will Hewer, Penn with two clerks; and Sir George Carteret who had with him Dr Clerke, a physician known to Pepys since they first met on the *Charles*. Evidently Sir William Batten was following separately, but a message was sent to stop him because he intended to come with his wife, contrary to what had been agreed. As a result it seems he did not join them on the trip to Portsmouth. Apart from that—or in Pepys's case, because of it—it was a pleasant excursion. At Guildford 'there passed our time in the garden, cutting up asparagus for supper—the best that ever I eat in my life but in the house last year'. In Portsmouth Pepys's eye was gladdened by the sight of their host's wife. He and Dr Clerke shared a room, and Pepys declared they were cousins because of the doctor's name and his position. 'We lay very well, and merrily; in the morning, concluding him to be the eldest blood of the house of the Clerkes, because that all the fleas come to him and not to me.'

First there were the account-books at the Pay-house to be inspected, which took an afternoon and the whole of the following day. But it was not all work, and there were convivial evenings: 'but I was much troubled in my eyes, by reason of the healths I have this day been forced to drink'. After that he and Sir George Carteret went on to Southampton, which Pepys considered a fine town and well worth seeing. The good impression was enhanced by the Mayor feasting them on sturgeon, 'which had not been caught hereabouts for twenty years'. But he found the caviare disappointing: 'for they had neither given it salt enough, nor are the seeds of the roe broke, but are all in berries'. Back in Portsmouth preparations were well in hand for the arrival from Lisbon of Catharine of Braganza, somewhere at sea with Lord Sandwich. Pepys saw the rooms she would occupy, and the Lord Mayor also showed him the present Portsmouth would give: a silver salt cellar with crystal sides, surmounted by four eagles and four greyhounds holding up a dish.

Two good pieces of fortune were waiting for Pepys. The first was an offer by Dr Clerke to introduce him to Lord Brouncker, the first President of the Royal Society. Later Pepys would come to know him quite well, when he became a Commissioner of the Navy, and later still Pepys would himself become President of the Royal Society. The other piece of good fortune was a visit from a burgess requesting him to accept a burgess-ship of Portsmouth: in fact at that very moment the Mayor was awaiting his arrival. 'So I went, and there they were all ready, and did with much civility give me my oath, and after the oath, did by custom shake me all by the hand; so I took them to a tavern and made them drink, and paying the reckoning, went away. It cost me a piece in gold to the Town Clerk, and 10s to the Bailiffs, and spent 5s.'

The journey back to London was uneventful, apart from hearing at Petersfield that the Duchess of York had given birth to a girl. 'At which I found nobody pleased.' That girl was to grow up to become Queen Mary. The day after his return Pepys took a letter from Dr Clerke to his wife, and after his easy comradeship with him suddenly felt abashed to find how grand Mrs Clerke and her friends were. 'I was much out of countenance, and could hardly carry myself like a man among them; but, however, I stayed till my courage was up again, and talked to them, and viewed his house, which is most pleasant, and so drank and good night.'

If Pepys had made two enemies at the Navy Office in 'both Sir Williams', he also had his allies: Sir George Carteret and now Mr Coventry, the Duke of York's secretary. At first he was not sure whether he liked the idea of Coventry becoming a Commissioner, and his apprehension was not diminished by the row he had with Penn on 3 June over who should make out the contracts, which he regarded as his duty by right of his position as Clerk of the Acts.

But soon his opinion of the Duke's secretary improved: 'I find Mr Coventry is resolved to do much good, and inquire into all the miscarriages of the office.' Pepys, it seems, liked Coventry rather better than Sir George did. The latter was very quick to inform him that in the past the new Commissioner had feathered his own nest by selling positions. Pepys was astute enough to see how the wind blew—for himself—and wrote in his diary: 'Upon the whole, I do find that he [Sir George] do much esteem me, and is my friend, and I may make good use of him.'

Day by day, week by week, Pepys became more deeply immersed in the workings of the Navy Office, and he was to be seen there between four and five on those fine sunny mornings of 1662; like as not poring over Speede's maps of the Forest of Dean, from which came much of the timber for the Navy's ships. Now he began to take a personal interest in the supplies purchased by his office, which was to prove not unlike stirring up a hornet's nest as far as corrupt practices were concerned. Complaints about the quality of the yarn supplied had been made by the ropemaker Hughes, and Pepys was shocked to discover 'that some of it had old stuff that had been tarred, covered over with new hemp, which is such a cheat as hath not been heard of. I was glad of this discovery, because I would not have the King's workmen discouraged (as Sir W. Batten do most basely do) from representing the faults of merchants' goods, when there is any.' Less than a month later, on 25 June, he was comparing prices with different merchants: 'Into Thames Street, and there enquire among the ships' [chandlers] the price of tar and oil, and do find great content in it, and hope to save the King money by this practice.'

It was indeed time someone showed concern for the maintenance of the Navy, and during the first half of 1662 Pepys had made a remarkable start, and all on his own initiative. For his part he drew satisfaction from what he was doing. 'For my business is a delight to me, and brings me great credit, and my purse increases too.' And if the rumours were true, England was going to need an efficient Navy. There was talk of conflict with Holland: it would be another trade war, and while twenty ships were to be mobilised, in Pepys's eyes not more than five could be prepared to put to sea.

If Pepys had the drive and organising ability to undertake what would amount to the reformation of the way the Navy was run, Sir George Carteret had the social position and influence to be able to gain the ear of those who mattered at Court. For his part Pepys realised the advantages of such an association, which was ripening into friendship. He dined with Sir George and Lady Carteret at Whitehall. 'All their discourse, which was very much, was upon their sufferings and services to the King.' On the last day of June he had the infinite satisfaction of inviting Lady Carteret home to Seething Lane, before going on to Greenwich with her. Once he had been gratified when Lady Batten called on Elizabeth, but this was not to be compared. 'I took great pride to lead her through the court by the hand, she being very fine, and her page carrying up her train, she staying a little at my house, and then walked through the garden, and then took water, and first went on board the King's pleasure-boat, which pleased her much.' Then to Greenwich Park: 'and with much ado she was able to walk up to the top of the hill, and so down again'. Evidently Elizabeth accompanied them on the outing, for the entry ends: 'So we supped with her, and then walked home to bed.'

All the while there had been another, though at this time invisible thread running through Pepys's life: Lord Sandwich on his voyage to the Mediterranean. For weeks at the beginning of the year there had been no news of the Fleet, which by then should have been on its way to Portugal. But on 20 February letters came at last, telling that after the Portuguese had defeated the Moors my Lord had been able to put ashore 300 armed men into Tangier, and so at last take possession of the port which was part of Catharine of Braganza's dowry. At the end of the month the Fleet was in the Tagus, opposite Lisbon, and on 8 May, after an absence of nearly a year, in home waters. 'The Queen and the Fleet were in Mount's Bay on Monday last; and that the Queen endures her sickness pretty well.'

A week later all the bells in London started to ring, to announce the arrival of Charles II's future queen at Portsmouth. 'But I did not see much true joy', noted Pepys, 'but only an indifferent one, in the hearts of people, who are much discontented at the pride and luxury of the Court, and running into debt.'

Indeed, the Court was a source of fascinating gossip, such as how Frances Stuart had fallen out with Lady Castlemaine and likened her to Jane Shore, and hoped she would come to the same end. That was quite an insult. Jane Shore, by all accounts a very pleasant woman, had been the wife of a prominent goldsmith in the City, and the mistress first of Edward IV and then of the ill-fated Lord

Hastings, and according to tradition after her death her body had been thrown upon a dung-hill. Now there was much speculation about Lady Castlemaine's future at Court once the Queen arrived. If there was one woman above all others that Pepys found irresistibly attractive it was Barbara Villiers. '21st May. My wife and I to my Lord's lodgings; where she and I stayed walking in Whitehall Garden. And in the Privy-garden saw the finest smocks and linen petticoats of my Lady Castlemaine's, laced with rich lace at the bottom, that ever I saw; and did me good to look at them.' And it did not stop at looking: Pepys would even dream he was sporting with the King's mistress, little imagining that one day his particular love-goddess would take the celebrated rope-dancer Hall from Bartholomew Fair as her lover. But now she was the unofficial queen of Whitehall, and it was from my Lord's housekeeper Sarah that Pepys heard: 'how the King dined at my Lady Castlemaine's, and supped, every day and night, last week; and that the night that the bonfires were made for joy of the Queen's arrival, the King was there; but made no fire at her door, though at all the rest of the doors almost in the street; which was much observed: and that the King and she did send for a pair of scales and weighed one another; and she, being with child [the future Duke of Southampton], was said to be the heaviest.'

It was not a very good augury for the future Queen brought up in a palace which in some ways must have resembled a secular convent. But at last Lord Sandwich was back, safe and sound, having left Catharine at Portsmouth where the King and Duke of York had gone to meet her. During his absence Pepys had acted as a friend and counsellor to Lady Sandwich and her children, the two eldest of whom were now in France, learning to become polished gentlemen, and no doubt a great deal else besides. On a number of occasions Pepys dined with Lady Sandwich, and admired the strange presents sent from time to time by her husband, including a civet cat, a parrot, apes and exotic fruits. One excursion he made with her, her children and those of her sister-in-law was to the Tower. Since the time of Henry III the fortress had contained a royal menagerie (in 1835 it was removed to Regent's Park to become the nucleus of the London Zoo). 'I took them and all my Ladys to the Tower, and showed them the lions, and all that was to be shown; Sir Thomas Crewe's children being as pretty, and the best behaved that ever I saw of their age.' On another occasion he took the

Montagu children by water to Greenwich to show them 'the King's yacht, the house, and the park, all very pleasant; and so to the tavern, and had the music of the house, and so merrily home again'.

Lord Sandwich's homecoming was not entirely free from worry, for he was in debt to the tune of £7,000, but likely to receive at least £6,000 from the King. Also, he had been given a bag containing £1,400 in gold by Catharine at the end of the voyage, though some eyebrows were raised that she did not give a sum to be distributed among the captain and officers. According to my Lord the chosen Queen was a very agreeable lady who painted well, but had acted like a recluse: 'and all the voyage never come upon the deck, nor put her head out of her cabin; but did love my Lord's music, and would send for it down to the state-room, and she sit in her cabin within hearing of it'. Pleasant though she may have been the new Queen had made a bad impression on the worldly and cynical courtiers about Charles II from the moment they first set eyes on her. The Portuguese Court was not exactly fashion-conscious, and she and her ladies were wearing farthingales, which would have been familiar to Elizabeth I some seventy years before. Also it was reputed that some of the ladies-in-waiting were such old maids they would not sleep in a bed in which a man had lain, which makes one suspect that a story recorded by Pepys may well have been a malicious invention. 'This day I am told of a Portugal lady, at Hampton Court, that hath dropped a child since the Queen's coming, and the King would not have them searched whose it is; and so it is not commonly known yet.' However, another report told that those who had seen her found Catharine of Braganza a fine, handsome lady, and discreet. 'And that the King is pleased enough with her: which, I fear, will put Madame Castlemaine's nose out of joint.'

Behind all the diplomatic courtesies Lord Sandwich had had some hard bargaining with the Portuguese Council over the dowry: it would consist of Tangier, free trading rights to the East Indies, and two million crowns. Most of the latter arrived in the form of goods or bills of exchange. What money there was was brought ashore at Tower Wharf by John Creed and Edward Shepley and taken to Pepys's house for safe keeping. There three chests of crusados, totalling about £6,000, were put in his cellar. It was quite a responsibility. 'Home and to bed, my mind troubled about the charge of money that is in my house, which I had forgot, but I made the maids to rise and light a candle, and set it in the dining-room, to scare away thieves.' To his relief the money was soon removed to a City merchant's, where it was weighed and its value assessed exactly.

Only two years had passed since the return of Charles II, but already the goodwill was evaporating, and Parliament had grown exceedingly touchy. When the Lord Chancellor suggested it might be advisable to revive the Army (with the Duke of York as its General), using Venner's rising as an excuse, he was told outright that Parliament had grown too wise to be fooled again, because anyone who commanded the Army could also become a king. Then, in March, a new levy was proposed, and agreed to by Parliament, that there should be a tax of 2s. on every chimney in the country. Two months after that the terms of the Act of Uniformity were published: 'which it is thought, will make mad work among the Presbyterian ministers'. In its way the Act would be the instrument of every bit as much persecution and intolerance as anything thought up during the Commonwealth. But what shocked thinking people was the trial and execution of Sir Harry Vane. Once he had been almost a rival to the Earl of Strafford, and had brought about his downfall. But at the Restoration he had been promised 'a merciful indemnity' by Charles II, as he had not been directly involved in his father's death: but that did not save him, and on 14 June Pepys and his colleagues from the Navy Office went to a room overlooking Tower Hill to watch the last act. For centuries it had been the custom for house owners with windows overlooking Tower Hill to hire their rooms to spectators when there was an execution: in Henry VIII's reign it must have amounted to an additional income. When Sir Harry tried to address the crowd, protesting against the illegality of the whole proceeding, trumpets were hurriedly sent for to drown his words. After that he confined his speech of justification for his actions to those around him, but after continual interruptions he gave up, and died bravely but in a temper. It was the first of the many foolish things that Charles II was to do during his reign of a quarter of a century.

For Pepys hard work was not only its own reward: his finances continued to improve. After putting it off he at last on 1 March audited his accounts, and whilst he found he was £500 in hand, during the previous half year he had spent no less than £250. It was better than he had dared hope, but not as good as he would have wished. But it did not stop him building castles in the air as he lay in bed with Elizabeth: 'proposing to her what I could and would do, if I were worth £2,000: that is, be a knight, and keep my coach, which pleased her'. By the end of June he found he was worth £650. Diligence was beginning to pay off, though their life was not altogether frugal. Clothes were bought: riding clothes for Samuel and such items as new-fashioned petticoats trimmed with black lace for Elizabeth, as well as a new outfit for the boy Will. Evidently the young man had a mind of his own. 'Called Will up, and chid him before my wife, for refusing to go to church with the maids yesterday, and telling his mistress that he would not be made a slave of.' But a talking-to was not sufficient, and a few days later, when Will had called him late in the morning, Pepys decided to take action. 'I reckoned all his faults, and whipped him soundly, but the rods was so small that I fear they did not much hurt to him, but only to my arm, which I am already, within a quarter of an hour, not able to stir almost.'

Pepys was no hard task-master, and his temper seems to have been better than the previous year when he was drinking to excess. 'After some merry discourse in the kitchen with my wife and maids, as I now-a-days often do, I being well pleased with both maids, to bed.' Also, on the spur of the moment, he on one occasion suggested that Elizabeth and the maids should go with him on an outing. 'Took boat to Fox-hall [Vauxhall], where I had not been a great while. To the old Spring Garden, and there walked along, and the wenches gathered pinks. Thence to the New one . . . and here we also walked, and the boy crept through the hedge, and gathered abundance of roses.'

At the beginning of the year, Pepys had the honesty to admit in the privacy of his Diary what he knew to be his principal failing. '26th January. Thanks be to God, since my leaving drinking of wine, I do find myself much better, and do mind my business better and do spend less money, and less time lost in idle company.' What was more, now that he was no longer so friendly with the hard-drinking Sir Williams, it was easier to refuse to drink all the healths that they downed, and when he did go into a tavern with friends about all he drank was small beer. Not only had he written out the vows he intended to keep, and made a practice of reading them over each Sunday, but he had bought a pewter poor-box to put his forfeits in every time he broke a resolution.

From time to time the lure of the theatre proved irresistible, though not on the scale of the previous year. Back he and Elizabeth went to the Red Bull in Clerkenwell, which must have been the worst theatre in London, and were again disappointed. 'To the Red Bull, where we saw *Doctor Faustus*, but so wretchedly and poorly done, that we were sick of it.' After going to the theatre three nights running Pepys remembered his vows and decided it was time to give the playhouse a miss—at least until next time. Going from church to church, 'hearing a bit here and a bit there', continued as a Sunday diversion. But one sermon at the Temple Church suffered a sudden interruption: 'a boy being asleep, fell down from a high seat to the ground, ready to break his neck, but got no hurt'.

If listening to sermons was an edifying way to spend Sunday, Pepys also witnessed a favourite diversion of the Court in St James's Park. 'Here the King and Duke come to see their fowl play.' And in March there would be no shortage of procreant water-birds skimming over the lake to disappear in a cloud of spray. That such conduct was also commonplace at the Court itself was general knowledge, and in a brief summing-up of the state of the country Pepys noted in his Diary on 30 June 1662, under the heading 'Observations': 'This I take to be as bad a juncture as ever I observed. The King and his new Queen minding their pleasures at Hampton Court. All people discontented; some that the King do not gratify them enough; and the others, Fanatics and all sorts, that the King do take away their liberty of conscience; and the height of the Bishops, who I fear will ruin all again. They do much cry up the manner of Sir H. Vane's death, and he deserves it. Much clamour against the chimney-money; and the people say they will not pay it without force. And in the mean time, like to have war abroad; and Portugal to assist, when we have not money to pay for an ordinary layings-out at home.'

If the world about him was going from bad to worse in his eyes, Pepys was determined to continue on the course he had mapped out for himself, both in his professional and private life. Most mornings he was up 'while the chimes went four', to put in several hours work at the office before the others arrived. The harder Pepys worked, the more likely he was to be scornful of those who did not measure up to his standards: such as his ex-neighbour Mr Davis who, because a relation had just died, was not available when he went to inspect the Store-house at Deptford. 'He do trouble himself most ridiculously

as if there was never another woman in the world.' In his opinion
the clerks were doing only about a third of the work they should perform, and was gratified that Mr Coventry shared his opinion. That
same evening (2 July) a major abuse was revealed to him by one Mr
Lewis, who asked if he had ever looked into the running of the Chatham Chest, a fund for disabled seamen started in Elizabeth I's reign,
towards which the men were supposed to contribute 6d. a month from
their pay. It was not until November that an inquiry was held, and
among those who did not come out of it too well was Commissioner
Pett.

The surest way to catch out dishonest merchants would be to
meet them on their own ground, by being able to recognise poor
quality materials, such as rope, and to calculate exactly how much
timber was actually supplied as against how much had been charged
for. The first fish to be caught was of considerable size and importance: no less than the merchant Sir Richard Ford. It was his old
yarn, covered with tar and hemp that had so scandalised Pepys at
Woolwich Dockyard. As a result of Pepys's revelations his contract
was cancelled. But if only a short study of rope-making were necessary to tell whether the King was being cheated in that matter or
not, it would take close study and hard work before he could be in
a position to catch out dishonest timber merchants. At this point
the disadvantage of a severely classical education made itself felt.
For all his organising ability his knowledge of mathematics was
severely limited. He recognised the fact and asked the one-time
mate of the *Charles* to come to the office early in the morning to give
him lessons. 'After an hour's being with him at arithmetic, my first
attempt being to learn the multiplication-table.' For most of July
he was up early, to learn his tables by heart, which he found the
only difficult part of his lessons. Later he was to reward Cooper by
obtaining for him the position of Captain on a vessel under the
overall command of Major Holmes.

Pepys now had a very low regard for both Batten and Penn,
especially when the former was found to be involved in the fraudu-
lent sale of old ropes, but instinct told him it would be unwise to
break openly with Penn. He had powerful allies of his own, so on
the surface all appeared as before. 'At noon [5 July], had Sir W.
Penn, who I hate with all my heart, for his base treacherous tricks,
but yet I think it not policy to declare it yet, and his son William
[the future coloniser of the New World], to my house to dinner. We

were very merry as I could be in that company.' A few days later Penn left on a private visit to Ireland, and before he went he asked his neighbour to keep an eye on alterations about to be made to his house, which like Pepys's was to have an additional storey added. 'I did, God forgive me! promise him all my service and love, though the rogue knows he deserves none from me, nor do I intend to show him any; but as he dissembles with me, so must I with him.'

Next it was Mr Mills, the rector of St Olave's, about whom Pepys now revised his opinion. 'Come Mr Mills, the minister, to see me, which he hath rarely done to me, though every day almost to others of us, but he is a cunning fellow, and knows where the good victuals is, and the good drink, at Sir W. Batten's. However, I use him civilly, though I love him as I do the rest of his cloth.' From now on the rector could do nothing right, in or out of his church. 'There saw the first time Mr Mills in a surplice: but it seemed absurd for him to pull it over his ears in the reading-pew, after he had done, before all the church, to go up into the pulpit, to preach without it.'

If Pepys were having his patience tried, there was worse to come. The addition of an extra storey meant the house would be dirty and uncomfortable for some time, and with a certain lack of foresight the roof was stripped off on St Swithin's Day, and of course the weather broke. Gales lashed the Channel so that the Duke of York and Lord Sandwich could not cross to bring Queen Henrietta Maria over, and the Duke's ship lost its sails, ropes and even masts. It was nearly as bad in London. The rain was so heavy that Pepys abandoned a boat taking him along the Thames to shelter ashore, and saw Charles II pass by in his barge. Acidly he recorded: 'But methought it lessened my esteem of a king, that he should not be able to command the rain.'

Considerable damage had been done to his house. 'I found all my ceilings spoiled with rain last night, so I fear they must be all new whited when the work is done.'

But even though the King could not command the elements, his work must still be done, and Pepys revisited the Woolwich Dockyard to continue his study of the various types of hemp used in rope-making. He called it his 'great survey', and intended to hand his findings to the Duke of York when he returned from France. Another visit was paid to the Dockyard to see for himself how cords were made and tarred. No one could be sure when he would appear, or what he would insist on seeing, and nothing escaped his notice.

'To Deptford, and there surprised the Yard, and called them to a muster, and discovered many abuses.'

If the rope-makers were the first to suffer from his inquisition, it was soon the turn of the flag-makers and the timber merchants. Only a few weeks earlier he had considered the fraud perpetrated by the rope merchant 'the greatest cheat': now he used exactly the same words about the flag-makers, who claimed their contract allowed them 8*d*. a yard, when in fact it should only have been 5*d*. Nothing if not thorough, Pepys felt that a knowledge of timber should begin with a standing tree, and he rode out to Waltham Forest to see for himself how it was cut, measured and transported. With him went Anthony Deane, the Assistant Shipwright at Woolwich, who would one day become MP for Harwich, a Commissioner of the Navy and receive a knighthood. Full of enthusiasm, Pepys increased his knowledge *en route*, at Ilford. 'While dinner was getting ready, he and I practiced measuring of the tables and other things, till I did understand measuring of timber and board very well.' In his Diary Pepys judged Deane rather harshly, thinking he was more ambitious for himself than genuinely concerned for the well-being of the dockyard. It could have been jealousy at finding someone as enthusiastic as himself, but later Pepys was genuinely taken aback at his kindness. '29th September. Home, where I find Mr Deane, of Woolwich, hath sent me the model he hath promised me; but it so far exceeds my expectation, that I am sorry almost he should make such a present to no greater person, but I am exceedingly glad of it, and shall study to do him a courtesy for it.' Whether the model was for Pepys instruction or delight seems vague, but there was another which served to teach him the parts of a ship. A large chest stood in his office, locked, and one day when a smith was there they forced it open: inside was a fine model of a vessel. Pepys was still at the office late one August Saturday evening, having a mathematical lesson from the mate Cooper: 'and he and I by candle-light at my model, being willing to learn as much of him as possible before he goes'.

Yet again would Pepys have reason to be grateful to Lord Sandwich. A commission was set up in August, the seed of the Tangier Office, and my Lord put forward Pepys's name as one of the officers to serve on it: 'which is a very great honour to me, and may be of good concernment to me'. He had never stood higher in Lord Sandwich's estimation, and his patron was genuinely gratified to see his confidence in Pepys so well justified, and he told him that William Coventry 'spoke of me to him to great advantage; wherein I am much pleased'. But that was nothing to his elation on 8 October when Lord Sandwich told him of the Duke of York's good opinion of him, going so far as to thank Lord Sandwich for having brought Pepys into the Navy's service: 'which is the greatest comfort and encouragement that ever I had in my life, and do owe it all to Mr Coventry's goodness and ingenuity'.

When Pepys saw the list of names on the commission for Tangier he had justification for feeling a little proud. Among them were the Duke of York, Prince Rupert, the Duke of Albemarle, Lord Sandwich, Sir George Carteret, Mr Coventry and Captain Cuttance. Oddly enough another name was that of Sir Richard Ford, the rope merchant whose dishonest practices Pepys had helped to expose. The Commission met for the first time in William Coventry's rooms in St James's Palace, when the questions under discussion included supplying the garrison with victuals, and the matter of building a mole to protect the harbour.

Another commission with which Pepys was concerned (and its setting up was at his instigation), was to look into the running of the Chatham Chest, and on 3 December he went through Commissioner Pett's accounts: 'in which I did see things which did not please me; as his allowing himself £300 for one year's looking to the business of the Chest, and £150 per annum for the rest of the years. But I found no fault to him himself, but shall when they come to be read at the Board.'

The finances of the Chatham Chest were not Pepys's only concern: there was the ever-present worry of finding the money to pay the seamen's wages, and for the running of the Navy itself. '12th December. Mr Creed dined with me, and we sat all afternoon together, discoursing of ways to get money, which I am now giving myself wholly up to.' That October Charles II had sold Dunkirk to Louis XIV, to the disgust of many people, including Pepys, and on 21 November 'come the King's pleasure-boats from Calais with the Dunkirk money, being 400,000 pistolles'. It was taken to the Tower where Charles II and his brother went to view it. At the news of the visit Pepys and his colleagues crossed Tower Hill to have a look at the royal party. 'But methought it was but a poor discourse and frothy that the King's companions, young Killigrew among the rest, had with him.' Perhaps some of the money might be used for the Navy, Pepys hoped. It was wishful thinking, but at the end of the year he heard in Westminster Hall from one of his old Exchequer Office colleagues that £200,000 would be allotted, which was quite a reasonable sum.

Money of his own was also in Pepys's thoughts, and he regularly made up his accounts. Slowly the amount he saved was creeping upwards. At the end of August it stood at £680 19s. 2½d.: but two months later it had dropped slightly to £660, as a result of a levy imposed by Parliament to assist needy Cavaliers who had lost all during the Civil War and Commonwealth. Pepys had had to find £30, a considerable sum. The next time he sat down after supper to do accounts he found 'by my expense in bands and clothes this month, abated a little of my last, and that I am worth £679 still; for which God be praised'. In one month alone alterations to the house, together with the housekeeping money, came to £50. What with having the house flooded when the roof was off, and the bad feeling the extra storey caused with his neighbour Sir John Minnes, there must have been times when Pepys must have wished he had never had such an idea. The Comptroller complained his view had been spoilt, as well as having his use of the leads restricted, and in retaliation he claimed the use of one of Pepys's bedrooms. But after a great deal of worry for Pepys, Sir John failed to make good his claim.

In the kitchen a law was starting to operate by which the more they had, the more they needed. Elizabeth was either extravagant or not a very good housewife. One week alone, Pepys discovered, her housekeeping bill for food, wine, fuel, candles, soap and 'many other things' came to about 30s., which he considered more than enough, and now she wanted to emulate the world of fashion by having a young woman as companion, to keep her company and go out and about with her. In the past he had tolerated her desire for the new-fangled perruques, but only because she used her own hair, and it was Major Holmes who had introduced her to them. Despite her extravagances, their relationship was at that time perhaps better than it had ever been, as he admitted in the Diary. '2nd November. Talking with my wife, in whom I never had greater content, blessed be God! than now—she continuing with the same care and thrift and innocence, so long as I keep her from occasions of being otherwise, as ever she was in her life, and keeps the house as well.'

But this desire for a *dame de compagnie* could be expensive. No, insisted Elizabeth, only the cost of her food. It was her ne'er-do-well brother Balty who introduced them to the Misses Gosnell. The younger in particular appealed to both Samuel and Elizabeth, though for differing reasons. No doubt Pepys found her most accomplished and attractive, and though he also feared she might put expensive notions in Elizabeth's head, wrote 'I am rightly pleased with her humour and singing.' He went so far as to buy a book of instructions for country dancing against her arrival, and even before she moved into the house in Seething Lane Samuel and Elizabeth had nicknamed her Marmotte. But she came on the fifth of December, and left on the ninth. It was all Balty's fault. He had led the little Marmotte to believe that life at the Pepyses would be one long round of attendances at Court alternating with visits to the theatre, and after accompanying Elizabeth to church on Sunday 'which was very graceful', she made up a story about needing considerable time to attend to her mother's affairs. She went, leaving Pepys feeling relieved at the expense that had been saved. 'I am somewhat contented therewith, and shall make my wife so, poor wretch, I know will consider of things.'

Theatre-going was not altogether missing from Pepys's life in the autumn and winter of 1662. He saw a play on 29 September—the very day his vows lapsed—which irritated him nearly as much as *Romeo and Juliet*. 'To the King's Theatre, where we saw *A Mid-Summer Night's Dream*, which I had never seen before, nor shall ever again, for it is the most insipid, ridiculous play that ever I saw in my life.' He had better luck the next day with Mr and Mrs Betterton in *The Duchess of Malfi*, which was well performed, in his opinion. But already his conscience was starting to prick: 'strange to see how easily my mind do revert to its former practice of loving plays and wine, but this night I have again bound myself to Christmas next'. Two nights later he was at the Cockpit Theatre, but it was all Lord Sandwich's fault. He went, and Pepys followed. He sneaked into a box next to that occupied by the King and Queen by following four or five gentlemen, where even if he could not see Charles II and Catharine of Braganza, at least he could look at the ladies in the audience, though he decided they were not so much beautiful as well dressed. In this case the play was a tragi-comedy called *The Cardinal*, by Shirley, but it was his companions in the box who fascinated him most. 'The company that come in with me into the box were all Frenchmen, that could speak no English; but, Lord!

what sport they made to ask a pretty lady that they got among them, that understood both French and English, to make her tell them what the actors said.'

Like a bad tooth the lawsuit over his Uncle Robert's estate had nagged at Pepys for months: what with action being taken against him by the old man's stepsons, as well as legal action by his cousin Thomas Turner, it was enough to take the edge off what enjoyment he might have had in his spare time. There was yet another visit to Brampton, where the case was heard by the Lord of the Manor at his Court. For a while it looked as though it would go in favour of Thomas Pepys: and the hearing went on all day, but eventually the decision was made in favour of John Pepys and his son Samuel. 'I did with the most complete joy of mind go from the Court with my father home.' At last it was, if not over, at least only a matter of settling the details with his relations. The visit confirmed his bad opinion of Pall: 'to whom I did give 10s, but have shown no kind of kindness since I come, for I find her so very ill-natured, that I cannot love her, and she so cruel an hypocrite, that she can cry when she please.'

A treasure hunt at the Tower turned out to be abortive. For a time during the Commonwealth the Governor had been yet another regicide, Barkstead. The previous March he and others had been arrested at Delft by Pepys's old employer Sir George Downing, acting as the King's agent. They were shipped back to England, tried and sentenced to death. Almost inevitably their path crossed that of Pepys. 'I went to Aldgate, and at the corner shop, a draper's, I stood, and did see Barkstead, Okey and Corbet drawn towards the gallows at Tyburn; and there they were hanged and quartered.' Now a Mr Wade, who lived in Axe Yard, had come to Lord Sandwich with a tale that during his time at the Tower Barkstead had hidden away some £7,000. The King issued a warrant for a search to be made by Pepys, acting for Lord Sandwich. If they were lucky Wade would receive £2,000, Lord Sandwich the same sum, and the King the remainder. The place where the treasure was reputed to be hidden was in the Cold Harbour, a long-vanished gate-tower which gave access to the innermost part of the Tower when it still contained Henry III's royal palace (south of the White Tower, and mostly demolished during the Commonwealth). They had a guide who claimed to know the exact whereabouts of the treasure. 'He went into several little cellars, and then went out-a-doors to view, and to the Cole-harbour . . . to digging we went till almost eight o'clock at night, but could find nothing.' They locked up for the night and went off to the Lieutenant and the Deputy Governor, presumably in the Queen's House. 'But, Lord! to see what a young simple fantastic coxcomb is made Deputy Governor, would make me mad; and how he called out for his nightgown of silk, only to make a show to us: and yet for half an hour I did not think he was the Deputy Governor, and so spoke not to him about the business, but waited for another man.'

Back they all went on 1 November: 'to the Tower cellars, and made one trial more; where we stayed two or three hours, and dug a great deal all under the arches . . . but we missed of all: and so we went away the second time like fools'. A week later the search was resumed, this time armed with information given by a woman who had been 'Barkstead's great confidante'. According to her she had helped the ex-Governor put £7,000 in butter barrels just before he fled the country, adding that if she helped his escape she could have the money for herself. Pepys and his companions went to work again, digging over the cellar floor: 'At noon we sent for a dinner, and upon the head of a barrel dined very merrily, and to work again.' But their search was no more rewarding than before, so another was made, this time in the open, on a bitterly cold day: 'and I did sit all the day till three o'clock by the fire in the Governor's House; I reading a play of Fletcher's, being *A Wife for a Month*, wherein no great wit or language.' But again the diggers had drawn blank. 'I bid them give over, and so all our hopes ended. Home, a little displeased with my wife, who, poor wretch, is troubled with her lonely life, which I know not how, without great charge, to help as yet, but I will study how to do it.'

An enterprise of a family nature which took up a considerable amount of Pepys's time was trying to marry off his brother Tom, now in charge of their father's shop in Salisbury Court. He was not the most dashing of prospective bridegrooms, and made wild statements about money which could only be made good with difficulty. Already his prospective mother-in-law was making objections. While finding Mrs Butler a discreet, sober woman, Pepys wondered if he and she would ever agree. 'She finds fault with Tom's house, and his bad imperfection in his speech.' To make matters worse Tom showed a marked preference for another young woman, described as his mistress.

In Seething Lane, war with the Battens had now reached the point when the servants joined in. 'My Lady Batten did send to speak with me, and told me very civilly that she did not desire, nor hoped I did, that anything should pass between us but what was civil, though there was not the neighbourliness between her and my wife that was fit to be, and so complained of my maid's mocking of her. When she called "Nan" to her maid within her own house, my maid Jane in the garden overheard her, and mocked her, and of my wife's speaking unhandsomely of her. But I promised to avoid such words and passages for the future. At night I called up my maids, and schooled Jane, who did answer me so humbly and drolly about it, that, though I seemed angry, I was much pleased with her and [my] wife also.'

Not only had Lady Carteret visited his house and garden, but William Coventry now invited himself to dinner unexpectedly. It should have been a proud occasion for Pepys, but was marred by the fact that the leg of mutton and two chicken were under-cooked, as he pointed out after his distinguished guest had departed. 'When he was gone, very angry with my wife and people.' But Christmas was coming, and already there had been an early fall of snow, the first for three years, and hard frost. There was a new diversion in London that winter, which had been brought over from Holland by the Cavaliers who had shared the King's exile: 'over the Park, where I first in my life, it being a great frost, did see people sliding with their skates, which is a very pretty art'. A few days later Pepys was again at Whitehall. 'To the Duke, and followed him into the Park, where though the ice was broken and dangerous, yet he would go slide upon his skates, which I did not like, but he slides very well.' Christmas brought its almost obligatory gifts of food: a great chine of beef and no less than three dozen tongues. On the 25th Pepys enjoyed a pleasant walk to Whitehall, but was too late to receive communion in the Chapel. So he wandered into the Palace itself to look at the pictures (the ease with which well-dressed people could enter the public rooms to see the King and his Court pass to and fro both at Whitehall and Versailles is almost unbelievable by present-day standards), before returning to hear a sermon by the Bishop of Winchester castigating the follies of the Court. 'It was worth observing how far they are come from taking the reprehensions of a bishop seriously, that they all laugh in the chapel when he reflected their ill actions and courses.' Elizabeth had been unwell, and after walking home with great pleasure he dined at her bedside: 'having a mess of brave plum-porridge and a roasted pullet for dinner, and I sent for a mince-pie abroad, my wife not being well, to make herself any yet.'

The Court may have laughed at the bishop's sermon, but among ordinary citizens disappointment with Charles II was still growing. Whilst tolerating—and probably secretly envying him—such a mistress as Lady Castlemaine, many were now shocked at the blatant way he openly flaunted the relationship in front of his long-suffering wife. Catharine had been very quickly advised who and what Lady Castlemaine was. According to Lord Sandwich's housekeeper Sarah, there had been a row between Lady Castlemaine and her husband, over the christening of her infant, sired by the King. Pepys saw the couple on 23 August while awaiting the arrival of the King and Queen at Whitehall from Hampton Court, travelling by water. Whilst the Puritan in him might find much that was reprehensible, Lady Castlemaine was still beyond compare. He was intrigued to notice how she and her husband ignored each other, apart from greetings when they first arrived at the water-side: 'but both of them now and then would take their child, which the nurse held in her arms, and dandle it'. A stand full of spectators suddenly collapsed: 'but she of all the great ladies only run down among the common rabble to see what hurt was done, and did take care of a child that received some little hurt, which methought was so noble'. Everything became her in Pepys's eyes, even borrowing a man's hat: 'which was but an ordinary one, to keep the wind off; but it become her mightly, as everything else do'.

At last he was able to gratify his ambition to see Lely's portrait of Lady Castlemaine: 'here among other pictures, saw the so much desired by me picture of my Lady Castlemaine, which is a most blessed picture; and one that I must have a copy of'. Although not to be placed in the same category, Pepys was attracted by Mrs Pierce, *la belle* Pierce he called her in the Diary, and he was scandalised when the surgeon told him that Sir Charles Berkley, of the Privy Purse, had offered her £300 a year to become his mistress.

To add to the gossip about the King was the story repeated by Mr Creed that 'young Crofts' (the future ill-starred Duke of Monmouth), a weakly handsome youth and darling of the Court, was indeed the King's legitimate son, by his reputed marriage to Lucy Waters during the Commonwealth. She was of good family, and her attachment to the exiled King earned her a spell in the Tower. Later she was supposed to have become a prostitute and died from venereal disease.

While Charles II's Court diminished popular respect for him, his policies did little to redress the balance. The sale of Dunkirk for hard cash was resented, and then there was the Act of Uniformity, passed in 1662, which whilst bringing back the Book of Common Prayer also forced about 2,000 Presbyterian ministers out of their livings, leaving many of them destitute. Charles II's opinion was that Presbyterianism was no religion for a gentleman, but it was felt that this was no reason for him to behave badly. The expulsions caused particularly bad feeling in the City, and it was reported that the new Prayer Book was being removed from the churches and torn up. There were even murmurs of revolt, by the Fanatics, as Pepys called them.

But for Pepys, disapproval of so much that went on either at Court or in the King's name continually dissolved in the sheer pleasure of finding himself actually moving on the fringes of that exalted world. Thanks to Mr Povy, one of his fellow-Commissioners for Tangier, he was able to see the New Year's Eve ball at Whitehall: they were all there, the King and Queen, the Duke and Duchess of York, 'Young Crofts', and 'all the finest ladies, the greatest of the Court'. Among them was of course Lady Castlemaine. Before Pepys's delighted gaze the King led out the Duchess of York (the Queen seldom danced, but like everyone else she stood when her husband took the floor), and then out came all the lords and ladies. Charles II had an undeniable charm, which he knew how to use in the face of justifiable indignation, and also a dry wit. 'Then to country dances; the King leading the first, which he called for; which was, says he, " 'Cuckolds all awry', the old dance of England".' It was a wonderful, glittering evening: 'of the ladies that danced, the Duke of Monmouth's mistress, and my Lady Castlemaine, and a daughter of Sir Harry de Vicke's, were the best'. Eventually Pepys tore himself away, filled with an infinite content, and returned to my Lord's lodgings, to bring his Diary up to date.

'Thus ends this year, with great mirth to me and my wife. Our condition being thus:—we are at present spending a night or two at my Lord's lodgings at White Hall. Our home at the Navy Office, which is and hath a pretty while been in good condition, finished and made very convenient. By my last year's diligence in my office, blessed be God! I am come to a good degree of knowledge therein; and am acknowledged so by all the world, even the Duke himself, to whom I have a good access: and by that, and by my being Commissioner for Tangier, he takes much notice of me; and I doubt not but, by the continuance of the same endeavours, I shall in a little time come to be a man much taken notice of in the world, specially being come to so great an esteem with Mr Coventry.'

Chapter 7

Growing Confidence
1663

IN the space of two years Pepys was already a changing man: now
his position as Clerk of the Acts was moulding him. It had ceased
to be simply a job and had become a vocation. Many of those around
him were corrupt or lax: in the Navy Office, the City and at the
Dockyards. So, he would be diligent, work long hours, learn all he
could about the Navy, both ashore and afloat, and make an all-out
effort to overcome what he regarded as his failings. If at times he
fell short of his ideals and vows, still repeated weekly, he was after
all only human. Such conscious striving after perfection led to a
certain undercurrent of priggishness in some of the Diary's entries
during 1661: a censoriousness about the failings of others. But as
the new and consciously sought character became merged into his
whole personality, so in 1662 the righteous note started to diminish.
Also, he was becoming used to the new and exalted world in which
he now moved. From the pleasure with which he recorded tributes
paid by such as Mr Coventry or the Duke of York himself, they
obviously meant much more than mere financial and worldly
success. So often they were accompanied by the hope that such good
fortune would not turn his head. Pepys never took that good fortune for granted. In addition to gratitude for what the world had
given him, there was now a growing awareness that as time passed
he was better able to meet his new world on more or less equal
terms. The first entry for 1663 is evidence. 'January 1st. To White
Hall, where I spent a little time walking among the courtiers, which
I perceive I shall be able to do with great confidence, being now
beginning to be pretty well known among them.' At Court he never
seems to have been subjected to the type of jeer or sneer about being
a tailor's son which sooner or later would undoubtedly have come his
way at the French court, with its inward-looking obsession with
ancestry and the straitjacket of etiquette.

Sir William Penn had returned from visiting his estates in Ireland, but could not be rated an active member of the Navy Office, being frequently laid up with gout. He and Pepys were on terms of exchanging social courtesies, while his on-off relationship with the Battens was entering a slightly more cordial phase. At the Navy Office Pepys's strongest ally was William Coventry, who was as enthusiastic for reform as he himself. Also he was on friendly terms with Sir George Carteret, though his initial good opinion of Sir John Minnes was fast evaporating. The Comptroller had claimed he understood his duties as easily as cracking a nut between his teeth. Pepys pointed out in the privacy of the Diary that the old man was toothless.

Pepys's all-embracing enthusiasm for things naval had inspired him to compile a book of notes and correspondence for his own reference. On 14 January he wrote: 'Examining part of my sea-manuscript with great pleasure, my wife sitting working by me.' A few days later he took it to his bookseller. 'My manuscript is brought home handsomely bound, to my full content; and now I think I have a better collection in reference to the Navy, and shall have by the time I have filled it, than any of my predecessors.'

The previous year Pepys had made the acquaintance of the timber merchant William Warren, or, rather, had been sought out by him. Up till then he had found it impossible to obtain contracts from the Navy Office because his rival, Sir William Wood, had made it worth Batten's while to give him all the contracts. But now in the City merchants were starting to speak with respect about the thirty-year-old Clerk of the Acts. Obviously he was a capable young man, and not enmeshed in the corruption of his elders. But for all that it was still the seventeenth century, and William Warren used traditional methods to ingratiate himself with Pepys. First he showed him his timber yards, and then invited him home. After a lapse of several months he followed up the opening. '10th February. W. Warren come himself to the door, and left a letter and a box for me, and went his way. His letter mentions giving me and my wife a pair of gloves; but, opening the box, we found a pair of plain white gloves for my hand, and a fair state-dish of silver, and cup, about £18, which is a very noble present, and the best I ever had yet. So, after some contentful talk with my wife, she to bed and I to rest.'

Perhaps word of Warren's move reached other ears, but two days later: 'Mr Cole, our timber-merchant, sent me four couple of ducks.' Together with his head clerk, Tom Hayter, Pepys went over the accounts of the Navy—it took till eleven at night—and they found expenses were running at the rate of £374,743 a year. The next day Pepys made a sad entry in the Diary. 'February 19th. My eyes begin to fail me, lying so long by candle-light upon white paper.' Six years later defective sight would force him to give up the Diary.

Pepys's shining example, however, did not necessarily galvanise others in the King's service, let alone endear him to his colleagues, and in an unusual mood of near-defeat he admitted to himself that he was vexed some people did not share his devotion to business, after he had gone to such lengths to find out at the shipyards just what was needed for the fitting-out of vessels. One who did have cause for satisfaction was William Warren. He received a contract worth £3,000 to provide masts. Evidently Pepys resisted temptation, at least on that occasion, for he recorded: 'but, good God! to see what a man might do, were I a knave'.

Though the cost of the Navy came to £375,000 per annum, by June Parliament had proposed it should be limited in future to £200,000.

In Sir Philip Warwick at the Treasury, however, Pepys considered he was dealing with a government official he could respect. During their first meeting at Whitehall, Sir Philip informed him that their accounts had been settled to within £50,000, and that up to Michaelmas 1663, so that day (12 September) Pepys returned home feeling more contented with the King's business than he had done for many months. 'I have thus begun an acquaintance with him, who is a great man, and a man of as much business as any man in England, which I will endeavour to deserve and keep.' At a meeting on 3 December, Sir George Carteret informed his fellow-officers that with the exception of current work at the dockyards and a few small bills the Navy was out of debt. 'Which is extraordinary good news, and upon the 'Change to hear how our credit goes as good as any merchants' upon the 'Change is a joyful thing to consider, which God continue! I am sure the King will have the benefit of it, as well as we some peace and credit.' But it was a false dawn. In the new year merchants at the Exchange would again be refusing to accept the bills of exchange presented by the Navy Office.

William Coventry now found himself in trouble: like all who wielded power he had his enemies, and they put it about that he sold places for personal profit. The rumours reached his own ears, and he brought the matter up at a meeting at which the Duke of York was present. He appealed to the Duke, asking whether he did anything which was not done by his predecessors. Sir George Carteret told him that the selling of places was something that never had been, and never should be, condoned. At this Coventry rounded on him, saying he was one of the first to do it: 'and he believed he made £7,000'. Sir George denied the allegation, and then added that he might have made, say, £2,500 in the first year. In self defence Coventry handed the Duke a list of 250 appointments which he had made, claiming that he had not received a farthing more for them than was allowed in the scale of fees drawn up by the Duke himself. Then Lord Berkley cut in to suggest that Coventry had come by £50,000 from selling places. The matter closed with the Duke of York commenting that he wished they had all made more out of their jobs than they had done, because all together it would not equal what Sir George Lane (a Clerk of the Privy Council) had made for himself, 'below stairs at Court'.

Pepys knew where to go to obtain stores such as tar and oil at competitive prices; could tell good rope from bad; knew how to measure timber and had learnt mathematics. What was more he continued his unexpected visits to the dockyards, keeping everyone on their toes, and no doubt making himself cordially disliked in certain quarters. In July he paid another visit to Chatham to inspect the *Prince*, which had been undergoing repairs in dry dock, and 'went in her, and was launched in her'. Commissioner Pett had designed a new wet dock: it would cost £10,000, but Pepys considered it money well spent, which the King could well afford. On an earlier visit Pepys had caught the guards napping—literally—so at eleven at night he took a boat and was rowed down-river to where the guard ships lay at anchor: 'it being a most pleasant moonshine evening that ever I saw almost'. Their captain was ashore, and Pepys spent the rest of the night rowing from one vessel to the next: 'in which I found, for the most part, neither officer aboard, nor any men so much as awake, which I was aggrieved to find'. When he returned to London he would have something to say to the Duke.

In addition to the duties of the Navy Office there was now the Tangier Commission, which from time to time brought Pepys to Whitehall. True to the age, it was not long before he received his first bribe. A Captain Grove wanted to hire ships to trade with Tangier, and it was Pepys—emulating those around him—who made the first move. 'I did hint to him my desire that I could make some lawful profit thereof, which he promises.' A few days later he was given a letter by the Captain. 'I discerned money in it, and took it, knowing as I found it to be, the proceed for the place I have got him to be, the taking up of vessels for Tangier. But I did not open it till I come home—not looking into it till all the money was out, that I might say I saw no money in the paper, if ever I should be questioned about it. There was a piece of gold and £4 in silver.' With the letter in his pocket Pepys went on to a meeting of the Tangier Committee where finances were discussed. The maintenance of the garrison at the lowest estimate would come to £53,000; while that year's work on the mole would take another £13,000. Then there was £1,000 a year for the Governor, as well as other expenses: which puts us to a great stand.' Pepys considered the plan of the mole, which he saw on a later occasion, a brave draft, thought Tangier the most considerable of the King's overseas possessions. But it was to prove an excessively expensive foothold in the Mediterranean, which in the end would have to be abandoned.

Pepys was correct when he considered life at Court was not doing Lord Sandwich much good. An upright man, steadfast, though he did not give his friendship easily, he had a fine career and a charming wife and family, and should perhaps have been content; but fashion decreed otherwise. Before 1663 was out, Pepys would feel compelled, though in some trepidation, to take his friend and patron, an Earl and Garter Knight, to task. Only after a period of coolness would he be forgiven for having told the truth.

The trouble all started after Lord Sandwich had been ill in March (it could have been a recurrence of malaria), when he decided to go into the country, to Chelsea, to recuperate. There he became smitten with Betty, the daughter of Mrs Becke, a merchant's wife, in whose house he was staying. Pepys visited him there, and heard how everything met with my Lord's approval: 'mightily extolling the manner of his retirement, and the goodness of his diet; the mistress of the house, Mrs Becke, having been a woman of good condition heretofore, a merchant's wife, hath all things most excellently dressed; among others, her cakes admirable, and so good, that my Lord's words were they were fit to present to my Lady Castlemaine.' But his satisfaction did not stop at cakes and country air. Lord Sandwich did return to his duties at Whitehall, but his visits there became fewer and fewer that summer. On one occasion he was actually sent for, to join Charles II and Lady Castlemaine at cards, and lost £50. Soon his absence from Court was noticed, and in a society which thrived on gossip it was not long before the cause was known.

Will Howe knew what was afoot, and confided in Pepys. Now Pepys was likely to fall in love with women he had never even spoken to, like Lady Castlemaine, but his feelings for Lady Sandwich were genuinely fond and not of an amorous nature, so he was inclined to disapprove of her husband's dalliance at Chelsea. But at first he was understanding. 'Though I do not wonder at it, being a man amorous enough, and now begins to allow himself the liberty that he sees everybody else at Court takes.' Only in September, after Ned Pickering (a brother of the Earl's brother-in-law Sir Gilbert Pickering) had told him all, did he begin to express his indignation in his Diary. '. . . I am ashamed to see my Lord so grossly play the fool, to the flinging off of all his honour, friends, servants, and everything and person that is good, and only will have his private lust undisturbed with this common whore, his sitting up night after night alone, suffering nobody to come to them. With his carrying her abroad, and playing on his lute under her window, and forty poor sordid things, which I am grieved to hear.' Still Pepys felt it was not for him to meddle, but to wait for God and his conscience to bring his patron to a reasonable frame of mind. But he paid a special visit to Chelsea after Mr Pierce the surgeon had told him that the King was expressing surprise at the Earl's absence from Court—only to find that when the time came he could not bring himself to broach the subject. So he decided to write a letter, which the boy Will took to Chelsea. It was a letter within a letter, for in the outer envelope was a note requesting Sandwich to read it only when alone and not pressed for time.

It was either a very officious or a very brave letter for Pepys to have written, for he must have realised that there was a chance Lord Sandwich would never speak to him again. It began with a convoluted paragraph saying that he owed everything to his Lordship, and in return was anxious for his good name. He touched on the comment caused by the Earl's absence from Whitehall and from his place at the Council, and reported that it was being suggested that after being well rewarded by the King he had abandoned his duties at Court, as well as to the Navy.

'Another sort [of people], and those the most, insist upon the bad report of the house wherein your Lordship, now observed in perfect health again, continues to sojourn, and by name have charged one of the daughters for a common courtisan, alleging both places and persons where and with whom she hath been too well known, and how much her wantonness occasions, though unjustly, scandal to your Lordship, and that as well to gratifying some enemies, as to the wounding of more friends I am not able to tell.

'Lastly, my Lord, I find a general coldness in all persons towards your Lordship, such as, from my first dependance on you, I never knew, wherein I shall not offer to interpose any thoughts or advice of mine, well knowing your Lordship needs not any. But with a most faithful assurance, that no person nor papers under Heaven is privy to what I here write, besides myself and this, which I shall be careful to have put into your own hands, I rest confident of your Lordship's just construction of my dutiful intentions herein, and in all humility take my leave. May it please your Lordship,

Your Lordship's most obedient Servant,
S.P.'

Twenty-four hours later Pepys went to the Earl's lodgings, where he met his patron about to go to the service in the Chapel. Gravely Lord Sandwich thanked him for his concern, and then asked for the names of the informants. Pepys had to tell him they were Mr Pierce, Ned Pickering and Mr Hunt, his one-time neighbour in Axe Yard. Obviously he knew about the letter from another source: Will Howe. Pepys was in tears, and perhaps to put him at his ease the Earl changed the subject and talked about the paintings in the gallery.

If Lord Sandwich had wanted to speak plainly to Samuel Pepys he must have felt restrained by the fact that his kinsman had lent him £700. The parting, though reserved, was quite friendly. A few days later Pepys heard from Mr Pierce that Lord Sandwich had resolved not to go again to Chelsea. But Will Howe was in disgrace for having discussed his employer's affairs behind his back.

Ruefully Pepys wrote in his Diary: 'Methinks, by my Lord's looks upon me today [30 November], my Lord is not very well pleased, nor, it may be, will be a good while, which vexes me; but I hope all will be over in time, or else I am but ill-rewarded for my good service.' By 14 December it had nearly blown over. Will Howe told him that my Lord had been very, very angry: 'but when I did hear how he had come to himself, and hath wholly left Chelsea, and the slut, and that I see he do follow his business, and becomes in better repute than before, I am rejoiced to see it, though it cost me some disfavour for a time'. At the end of the year Lord Sandwich went out of his way to ask how Elizabeth was. 'The first time he hath done so since his being offended, and in his conscience he would be glad to be free with me again, but he knows not how to begin.' Pepys was vindicated, but it had been a near thing whether he lost the friendship and good-will of the man to whom he owed all worldly success.

Earlier in 1663 Pepys had had much to worry him as a result of an action for false imprisonment brought against him and his fellow JP's at the Navy Office by one Field, who had been committed to prison for slandering the Navy Office. Pepys and his colleagues had not realised that while their jurisdiction covered Middlesex, it did not hold good in the City of London, where their action had been illegal. Field sued for damages of £30 against each of them, and won his case. Pepys unwisely thought the law, or at least the King, should be on their side, and ignored what was happening. He was shattered when a writ was served on him in the Office on 21 February. The server informed Pepys he was 'his prisoner in Field's business: which, methought, did strike me to the heart, to think we could not sit in the middle of the King's business'. Pepys told him to go away as he was busy, but soon the man was back with four bailiffs, asking what Pepys was doing about the matter. Pepys said he was waiting to hear from the King: in fact Sir John Minnes had gone post haste in a coach to Whitehall to try to clear up the situation. The server and the bailiffs talked among themselves, and as it was time for a meal asked Pepys if he was prepared to stay where he was till they came back. Yes, said Pepys, and promptly went home. Before long they were back at the Navy Office, this time with the parish constable.

A few houses along Seething Lane, Pepys was being invited by Mingo, Sir William Batten's African servant, to come through Sir John Minnes's house to safety in theirs. Pepys used a ladder to get over the fence at the back. Meanwhile, 'the fellows stayed in the yard, swearing, with one or two constables, and some time we locked them in the yard, and by and by let them out again, and so kept them all the afternoon, not letting them see me or know where

I was'. Later Sir John Minnes returned from Whitehall, saying there was nothing he could do, and that the Lord Chancellor had wondered why they did not set some of the seamen on the bailiffs: 'which we wished we could have done without our being seen in it'. Captain Grove, who had been given a commission by Pepys to take ships to Tangier, was all for attacking them, and even drew his sword, and afterwards one of the men claimed he had been slightly wounded in the chest.

Finally the solicitor for the Navy Office arrived to say that the Court's fees had been settled: 'so he showed them this release, and they seemed satisfied, and went away with him to their attorney to be paid by him'. So Pepys breathed more freely, and 'by advice took occasion to go abroad, and walked through the street to show myself among the neighbours, that they might not think worse than the business is'. Back came the solicitor, having paid the court the fees for the commission (presumably for serving the warrant), but having refused to give the bailiffs the £5 they demanded for their day's work, he advised Pepys to stay at home over the weekend. Whilst annoyed at this turn of events Pepys was gratified to see everybody: 'man, woman and child, my Lady [Batten] and Mrs Turner especially for me'.

On Monday business forced Pepys to go to Whitehall, and on his return for fear of the bailiffs, he landed on Tower Wharf, near the Iron Gate, and went home by going right round the fortress and over Tower Hill, reflecting as he went how terrible it must be to be a debtor in continual fear of arrest. Safely back home he found a note left by the solicitor to say Pepys was a free man: that all matters had been stopped in court (though the case would still have to be heard at a future date).

Up to that point it could not have been much of a birthday for him, his thirtieth, but in a sudden surge of happiness and relief he suggested that he, John Creed and Elizabeth should all go to the theatre. Off they went to the Duke's Theatre to see *The Slighted Maid*: 'being most pleased to see the little girl dance in boy's apparel, she having very fine legs, only bends in the hams, as I perceive all women do'. After that they went on to the Court Theatre, where he was disappointed with *The Wild Gallant*. 'The King did not seem pleased at all, the whole play, nor anybody else.' Yet another Shakespeare play disappointed: *Twelfth Night*, 'well acted, though it be but a silly play, and not relating at all to the name or day'. But taking it all round, it was a pleasant conclusion to a nerve-racking three days.

As time passed so something of the character of the Diary altered. Many of the entries were no longer personal, but were sober, lengthy reflections on events of importance, or accounts of what he had heard about happenings or customs in places as far apart as Leghorn and Königsberg. For Pepys life was nothing without curiosity. With astonishment he wrote of someone up from the country: 'I never could have thought there had been upon earth a man so little curious in the world as he is.'

A never-ending source of curiosity to most people was the Court, and especially the King's relationships with the Queen and Lady Castlemaine. If anyone had expected the latter's eclipse, he was underestimating her powers of survival—and attraction. At the beginning of January 1663, the King was supping and staying at her lodgings four nights a week, but soon there was the pleasure for those in the know of watching the power struggle between the favourite and a new rival, Mrs Stuart. La Belle Stuart* may have merited the comment: 'It is hardly possible for a woman to have less wit and more beauty', but such was her attractiveness that even Pepys started to transfer his distant adoration from Lady Castlemaine to her, an almost unbelievable piece of treachery. Perhaps it was simply a case of 'How happy could I be with either, were t'other dear charmer away'.

At least at first she and Lady Castlemaine were amiable enough to each other, and Pepys recorded an event which could only have happened in the second half of the seventeenth century, and might have come from a play such as Wycherley's *The Country Wife*. Lady Castlemaine had invited Frances Stuart to a party: 'and at night begun a frolic that they two must be married—and married they were, with ring and all other ceremonies of church service, and ribbons and a sack posset in bed, and flinging the stocking; but in the close, it is said that my Lady Castlemaine, who was the bridegroom, rose, and the King come and took her place.' A medal was made for and of La Belle Stuart, while others were prepared at the Tower Mint of Lady Castlemaine and the Duchess of Portsmouth, but they were never actually struck. When age caught up with Frances Stuart, Duchess of Richmond, she made provision of

* For three hundred years she reigned supreme as Britannia, first on the halfpennies and then on the pennies of the realm.

annuities for her cats, which moved Pope to comment: 'Die and endow a college, or a cat.'

As Pepys became more and more enamoured of Frances Stuart, so his opinion of Lady Castlemaine waned, until the day came when he could write in his Diary: 'In our way we saw my Lady Castlemaine, who, I fear, is not so handsome as I have taken her for, and now she begins to decay something. This is my wife's opinion also, for which I am sorry.'

The one who deserved the sympathy, however, was the Queen, behaving with dignity in a difficult situation. According to Pepys, Charles never supped with her for three months on end, being engaged elsewhere. Finally Lady Castlemaine did the obvious thing: 'they say [she] is removed as to her bed from her own home to a chamber in Whitehall, next to the King's own; which I am sorry to hear, though I love her much.' But even Charles received a sharp jolt when Catharine fell ill in October. It was serious: 'the spotted fever; that she was as full of spots as a leopard'. Indeed she was expected to die and her head was shaved and she received extreme unction. 'The King, they all say, is most fondly disconsolate for her, and weeps by her, which makes her weep.' But she recovered, and the King returned to his old ways.

In London on the anniversary of the Coronation Pepys was shocked if not altogether surprised to find that there were not more than ten people in some of the churches he visited during the services of thanksgiving. And on the Continent too public opinion was turning against the sovereign. 'I am told how in Holland publicly they have pictured our King with reproach; one way, is with his pockets turned the wrong side outward, hanging out empty; another with two courtiers, picking of his pockets; and a third, leading two ladies, while others abuse him; which amounts to great contempt.' Of course there was the serious side to the King, as typified by his interest in architecture and science, including medicine. But the ribald was never far away: Ned Pickering, obviously a snapper-up of unconsidered trifles, told Pepys 'the story is very true of a child that being dropped at the ball at Court; and that the King had it in his closet a week after, and did dissect it; and making a great sport of it, said that, in his opinion it must have been a month and three hours old'. Later he and Dr Clerke dissected the bodies of a man and a woman, though not, one hopes, in his closet.

Of his own admission Pepys was curious about everything. He and

Commissioner Pett had been invited to a lecture and then to dine at the Surgeons' Hall. After dining, and drinking a health to the King from the goblet presented by Henry VIII, and admiring Holbein's portrait of the same monarch, a doctor had something to show a group of friends. Pepys joined the party. 'I went with them, to see the body of a lusty fellow, a seaman, that was hanged for a robbery. I did touch the dead body with my bare hand: it felt cold, but me-thought it was a very unpleasant sight.'

On two occasions Elizabeth suffered loss of possessions: once by Samuel's carelessness and once by theft. On the first they were returning home in a coach, and she had given him her outer garments to take care of, but he left them behind. Pepys tried to shift the responsibility by saying she should have reminded him: 'though, I confess, she did give them to me to look after. It might be as good as 25s loss.' The theft reduced Elizabeth to tears. Then it happened she was in a coach in Cheapside, bringing home a fine new petticoat. A man thrust his head in at one window and asked the way to the Tower, and as she spoke a second man reached in at the other and snatched the bundle from her lap and ran off: 'Which vexes me cruelly, but it cannot be helped.'

Pepys was as fashion-conscious as ever, spending a good part of his income on clothes, and also giving spending money to Elizabeth. At the end of October he found that in that one month alone he had given her £12 for herself, and laid out no less than £55 on his own wardrobe: a velvet cloak, two new cloth shirts, a new gown trimmed with gold buttons, a new hat, silk tops for his legs and much else besides. If he wanted to keep abreast of fashion, he was anxious that Elizabeth should do so too, and after seeing Lady Falconbridge—Cromwell's daughter Mary—wearing a mask at the theatre, they went straight to the shops at the Exchange to buy one for Elizabeth.

After all the buying of furniture and pictures the year before there was a letting-up in that direction, though Pepys did acquire 'a fine table for my dining-room, cost me 50s'. A few days later he christened it with a dinner party, when he found it 'very proper' and able to seat nine or ten people. Among the guests were Dr Clerke, his wife, sister and cousin, as well as the Pierces and others. How proud Pepys was of his house in Seething Lane, and what satisfaction it gave him to entertain his friends in fine surroundings. 'I had for them, after oysters, at first course, a hash of rabbits and lamb, and a rare chine of beef. Next, a great dish of roasted fowl, cost me about

30s, and a tart, and then fruit and cheese. My dinner was noble, and enough. I had my house mighty clean and neat; my room below with a good fire in it; my dining-room above, my chamber made a with-drawing chamber, and my wife's a good fire, also.' The day before he had been next door with an ulterior motive. 'To my Lady Batten's, and sat with her a while, but I did it out of design to get some oranges for my feast tomorrow, which I did.'

And visiting could be no less pleasing than entertaining. After a visit to Mrs Clerke at Whitehall, he and Elizabeth returned: 'talking much of what we had observed today of the poor household stuff of Mrs Clerke, and her show and flutter that she makes in the world; and pleasing myself in my own house and manner of living more than ever I did, by seeing how much better and more substantially I live than others do'.

1663 was an important year in the fashion world: the periwig arrived, and of course Pepys was determined to be modish. The year before he had shaved off his moustache, and decided to keep his face smooth with pumicestone, but this new fashion was a major undertaking requiring not a little courage. On 2 November he heard that the King and Duke of York were about to adopt the new fashion, and noted: 'I never till this day observed that the King is mighty grey.' He was in fact already the owner of two periwigs, costing £3 and 40s., but he had put off appearing in them. But now he would delay no longer. What was good enough for the King was good enough for him. The barber came to the house and cut off all his hair, though he was loth to see it go, carried off to make him yet another wig. 'And I, by and by, went abroad, after I had caused all my maids to look upon it; and they conclude it do become me; though Jane was mighty troubled for my parting of my own hair, and so was Besse.' At the office he was relieved to find his colleagues did not pull his leg, while at Whitehall Lord Sandwich was mildly curious: 'and wondered first to see me in my perrique, and I am glad it is over'. Pepys was convinced that no one in church on Sunday would be able to keep his eyes off it: 'but I found no such thing'. There was one more person he would have to face, and then all his friends and acquaintances would have seen the transforma-tion. 'To the Duke, where, when we come into his closet, he told us that Mr Pepys was so altered with his new perriwig that he did not know him.' With that pleasantry it ceased to be a novelty.

Slowly his private fortune was creeping upwards: at the end of

July it amounted to £726; at the end of September it was £760, though only a month later he found to his great sorrow it was down to £717, thanks to all the clothes he had been buying. That year Elizabeth had again returned to the attack over her desire to have a companion. There was talk of Pall returning from Brampton: not that Pepys wanted to have her in the house, but she could not cost as much as a stranger. Eventually he agreed they should have a girl named Mary Ashwell, straight from a school for young ladies at Chelsea. She endeared herself to Pepys from the start by her musical ability, and after hearing her play the harpsichord at Lord Sandwich's lodgings (this was months before the episode of the letter) he stopped on the way home to buy her a book of pieces for the virginals at the Temple. Also she liked dancing, and was good at it: 'which makes my wife almost ashamed of herself to see herself so outdone, but tomorrow she begins to learn to dance for a month or so'.

And so began Pepys's worries. Mr Pembleton might be 'a pretty neat black [haired] man', but he would also be the apple of discord in the household in Seething Lane. '25th April. In the evening, merrily practising the dance which my wife hath begun to learn this day of Mr Pembleton, but I fear will hardly do any good at it, because she is conceited that she do well already, though I think no such thing.' A few days later Pembleton arrived—in time for supper—and afterwards 'we all up dancing till late. They say I am like to make a dancer. I think I shall come to do something in a little time.' Soon the whole household was dancing, and it was getting out of hand. 'A little angry with my wife minding nothing now but the dancing-master, having him come twice a day.' Soon petty irritation turned to fear and jealousy, and Pepys himself admitted he had a jealous nature. Was there anything between them? First he found them alone talking, not dancing. Then he caught the odious Pembleton making sheep's-eyes at Elizabeth from the body of the church when she was sitting up in the Admiralty pew at St Olave's. No doubt drawing on personal experience of his own furtive, illicit pleasures he was consumed with worry, coming home from the Office unexpectedly, and even hastening upstairs to have a quick look at the smoothness of the bed. He was nearly out of his mind, as he confided to the Diary, and Elizabeth was not slow to spot what was wrong. Pointedly she asked if he would rather she postponed her lesson until he returned from the Office. When the time came Pepys deliberately returned late, trying to appear casual, which was the last thing he felt. At the end of the month Pembleton would go, and as far as Pepys was concerned he would never set foot inside the house again.

The day after Elizabeth had paid him off there was a curious coincidence. Samuel, Elizabeth and the trouble-making Ashwell had gone to the Duke's Theatre, to see *Hamlet*. Betterton was in the lead, but who should have a walking-on part but Gosnell, Elizabeth's ambitious companion for a few days the previous year. Back they went the next day, and there she was again in *The Slighted Maid*. 'Wherein Gosnell acted Pyramena, a great part, and did it very well, and I believe will do it better, and prove a good actor.'

There was no disguising the fact, Mary Ashwell was a thoroughly disruptive influence in the life of the family: urging Elizabeth to extravagances, taking her side against Samuel, almost inciting her to rebellion. The best thing would be to send them both off to Brampton, to vegetate among the cows and the gnats for a while. Pepys saw them off in the coach: 'where I am troubled to see her forced to sit in the back of the coach, though pleased to see her company none but women and one parson, and so kissing her often, and Ashwell once, I bid them adieu.'

Although the Manorial Court at Brampton had found in favour of John and Samuel Pepys, that did not mean an end to the affair. In October a settlement was made between Samuel and his Uncle Thomas for the £200 claimed as interest on a bond by Uncle Robert's stepsons the Trices. Pepys offered £80, and eventually settled for £100. It was a relief to have ended the affair, even at such a sum.

Hard work at the office and re-reading his vows did not stop Pepys's mind from wandering, and more and more his thoughts turned during Elizabeth's absence to the possibility of conquests among some of his acquaintances, particularly in Westminster Hall. One was Betty Lane. He took her to the Rheinish wine-house in Cannon Row, and while seated near a window so far forgot himself in an ecstasy of fondling that a passer-by threw a stone at the glass, and shouted at him to stop it. Suddenly brought down to earth Pepys made off through the back entrance, feeling ashamed of himself and sweating with fright. There were other fondlings and kissings, but to his obvious disappointment it never went beyond that. Sometimes it was inhibition on his own part which acted as the check: the Puritan within was still alive.

Ever since she had come to the Navy Office Pepys had also been attracted by Mrs Bagwell, the wife of a carpenter at the Deptford Dockyard. He wished to further the acquaintance, and went so far during a visit as to order a muster of all the workers. Bagwell was among them, and he struck up an acquaintance. He was invited to their house, where he again met Mrs Bagwell, and no doubt expressed suitable surprise. It was a carefully planned campaign, and far from creditable, which could have wrecked a perfectly happy marriage. But it was not until the following year that the carpenter's wife surrendered to Pepys's clandestine siege.

That summer there was another diversion. Pepys went to the Epsom races. '25th July. Having intended this day to go to Banstead Downs to see a famous race, I sent Will to get himself ready to go with me; but I hear it is put off, because the Lords do sit in Parliament today.' The next day, a Sunday, found him at Epsom, where he viewed the town and the strollers: 'which was very pleasant to see how they are there, without knowing what to do, but only in the morning to drink waters'. Evidently the place had something of the look of a modern Derby Day. 'But, Lord, to see how I met there of citizens, that I could not have thought to have seen there; that they had even had it in their heads or purses to go down thither.' On the return he and Will looked through the gates at Nonsuch, built by Henry VIII, and by all accounts a magnificent country house. But its days were numbered: all too soon Charles II would give it to Lady Castlemaine, who had it demolished for the price of its building materials.

Apart from the enforced celibacy which caused Pepys to stray in thought, word and very nearly in deed, the temporary separation from Elizabeth was probably good for both of them. But in the middle of August the stay at Brampton came to a heated end when Elizabeth quarrelled with Samuel's father. Ashwell was quite out of hand, and when Elizabeth cuffed her, she returned the blow. Having, indirectly, nearly wrecked the marriage, she left soon after returning to London, and disappeared from the pages of the Diary. Taking it all round, 1663 was an unsettled year for the Pepys's household: servants left, including good, reliable Jane Wayneman, while her brother Will later ran away. Like Mary Ashwell, young Will showed himself ready to hit out, quarrelling with John Creed's boy. 'Mine had struck down Creed's boy in the dirt, with his new suit on, and the boy taken by a gentlewoman into a house to make clean, but the poor boy was in a pitiful taking and pickle, but I basted my rogue soundly.'

The maid Susan returned temporarily, but for a while Elizabeth was having to manage the house unaided, and on 1 October Pepys recorded despairingly: 'I am troubled to see that my servants and others should be the greatest trouble I have in the world.' But a pleasant interlude that autumn was a visit to Brampton with Elizabeth. On the way, at Buntingford, Pepys received a fright. Whilst still hot from travelling, Elizabeth drank cold beer. Soon after she was sick: 'and become so pale, and I alone with her in a great chamber there, that I thought she would have died, and so in great horror, and having a great trial of my true love and passion for her, called the maids and mistress of the house, and so with some strong water, she come to be pretty well again.'

Family business took him into the heart of the Fens. 'Over most sad fens, all the way observing the sad life which the people of the place do live, sometimes rowing from one spot to another, and then wading.' It was an enjoyable visit to Brampton, despite the gnats. For the first time Pepys really felt he had entered into his inheritance. And Elizabeth's brief sickness had a salutary effect on Samuel, making him more appreciative of the good things of life. On their return he really was grateful for his wife and home: 'and having got a good fowl ready for supper against her coming [by coach], we ate heartily, and so with great content and ease to our own bed, there nothing appearing so to our content, as to be at our own home after being abroad awhile'. Perhaps it is in these tiny details that the Diary's unique charm lies—quite apart from its value as a social and historical mirror of its time. 'This morning, about two or three o'clock, knocked up in our own back yard, and rising to the window, being moonshine, I found it was the constable and his watch, who had found our back yard door open, and so come in to see what the matter was. So I desired them to shut the door, and bid them goodnight.'

Life in Seething Lane resumed its domestic course: Pepys had broadened his horizons and increased his knowledge immeasurably, largely through his own efforts, and now he wanted to pass on some of his knowledge to Elizabeth. He would teach her geography and mathematics. 'My wife and I all the afternoon at arithmetic, and she is come to do Addition, Subtraction, and Multiplication very well.' He was even talking of crossing the Channel to Calais or some such place in France the following summer, which mightily pleased Elizabeth. The two maids they now had (27 November), Jane Gentleman and Besse, were invited as well: 'and it makes good sport that my maid Jane dares not go; and Besse is wild to go, and is mad for joy, but yet will be willing to stay, if Jane hath a mind.'

Though the year 1663 was ending for Pepys in an atmosphere of domestic harmony, the same could not be said for the nation as a whole. On the horizon was a war-cloud, then no bigger than a man's hand, but presaging conflict with Holland. Largely as a result of pressure by still-resentful Anglican Cavaliers who had suffered in the past, there would be no Indulgence for the Presbyterians: the Conventicle Act made their places of worship illegal, and there were years of prosecution and persecution ahead for them. For his part the King had declared in his speech to Parliament that the Papists would never be admitted to office under the Crown, and the Commons wanted the Act of Uniformity rigorously enforced, with no leniency either to Catholics or Presbyterians. Pepys himself had had some lingering sympathies with the Presbyterians, but he also showed the national distrust of the Papists and wrote that 'the King hath sent to the House his concurrence wholly with them against the Popish priests, Jesuits and etc. which gives great content, and I am glad of it'.

In two further entries coming events could be said already to have cast their shadows before them. 'The plague is got to Amsterdam, brought by a ship from Algiers; and it is also carried to Hamburg.' By the end of November, an Order in Council was made for quarantine regulations. 'The plague it seems, grows more and more at Amsterdam; and we are making of all ships coming from thence and Hamburg, or any other infected places, to perform their Quarantine, for thirty days.'

The end of the year was darkened by the death of a cousin, Edward Pepys. Inwardly, at any rate, Pepys must have had one eye drooping and one in mirth, for Lord Sandwich had agreed to lend him his coach and six horses for the funeral. He was, he felt, restored to favour. New Year's Eve was spent quietly by his own fireside. 'To dinner, my wife, and I, a fine turkey and a minced pie, and dined in state, poor wretch, she and I, and have thus kept our Christmas together all alone almost, having not once been out.' As was now his custom at the end of each year in the Diary, he assessed the situation in the world in general as well as in his own family circle. 'I do live at my lodgings in the Navy Office, my family being, besides my wife and I, Jane Gentleman, Besse, our good-natured cook-maid, and Susan, a little girl, having neither man nor boy. [Will Hewer had gone to lodge elsewhere, and Will Wayneman, after being beaten once too often, had run away.] At the office I am well, though envied to the devil by Sir William Batten, who hates me to the death, but cannot hurt me. The rest either love me, or at least do not show otherwise, though I know Sir William Penn to be a false knave touching me, though he seems fair. My father and mother well in the country; and at this time the young ladies of Hinchingbrooke with them—their house having the smallpox in it. My wife's brother [Balty] come to great unhappiness by the ill disposition, my wife says, of his wife, and her poverty which she now professes, after all her husband's pretence of a great portion. My brother Tom I know not what to think of; for I cannot hear whether he minds his business or not; and my brother John at Cambridge, with as little hopes of doing good there; for when he was here, he did give me great cause of dissatisfaction with his manner of life. Pall with my father; and God knows what she do there; or what will become of her; for I have not yet anything to spare her, and she grows now old, and must be disposed of, one way or other. The Turk very far entered into Germany, and all that part of the world at a loss what to expect from his proceeding. Myself, blessed be God! in a good way, and design and resolution of sticking to my business to get a little money with, doing the best service I can to the King also; which God continue! So ends the old year.'

Chapter 8

Pleasure and Profit
1664

HALF a year had passed since Pepys last visited the playhouse, for he had again made and kept a vow. Now, on the 1 January 1664, he went with a clear conscience to the Duke's Theatre. For him Shakespeare was not England's greatest dramatist, but one playwright among many, and he did not like *Henry VIII* any better than he had *Twelfth Night*, *A Midsummer Night's Dream* or *Romeo and Juliet*. 'Though I went with a resolution to like it, it is so simple a thing, made up of a great many patches, that, besides the shows and processions in it, there is nothing in the world good or well done.' At the very end of 1668 he did in fact see the play again, when he was 'mightily pleased, better than I ever expected, with the history and shows of it'.

The year opened well: Lord Sandwich's coolness towards Pepys had all but disappeared, so that their relationship was nearly back to what it had been before Betty Becke had attracted the Earl's attention; and there seemed some prospect of getting rid of further embarrassments. To Pepys's disgust Elizabeth's father and mother lived in Long Acre, a district well known for its brothels, and he was not anxious that his wife should visit them there more often than necessary. Nor were they encouraged to visit Seething Lane: Balty was quite enough—in Pepys's eyes he was feckless, and too ready to take advantage of the Clerk of the Act's prosperity and useful acquaintances. Now Elizabeth's father, something of a Don Quixote, and much affected by talk of a Turkish invasion of Western Europe, set off for Germany, to fight the infidel. Whilst the news saddened Elizabeth, Pepys gave the impression he wished Balty would go too. 'He is so idle, and out of all capacity, I think, to earn his bread.' A few weeks later Balty did in fact decide to go to Holland to seek his fortune there, and Pepys wished him godspeed in a practical manner, giving him ten shillings and an old coat trimmed with lace which had once adorned one of Elizabeth's petticoats.

But the year was also to bring its misfortunes. Mournfully Pepys had noted in his Diary after the deaths in rapid succession of several cousins that the family of Pepys was contracting, there being no corresponding number of births to redress the balance. And 1664 would bring a further share of mortality. Two members to depart were his 'she-cousin Scott', and Uncle Fenner the blacksmith. In the past he had had little contact with the old man's two sons-in-law, Anthony and William Joyce, but after this time Pepys saw something of Will—not that he really liked him, but he found his company entertaining. He was a man with an amusing not to say wicked tongue, of which Pepys was just a little afraid. Death was also to come to Tom Pepys, Samuel's younger brother. Running their father's shop was beyond his capabilities, and now he was slowly dying of tuberculosis. Tom had irritated his capable and ambitious brother, and for a while in the early part of 1664 Samuel was unaware just how ill he was. But at the end of January he heard that he had been given not more than two months to live. It was in fact to be only two weeks. On 14 February Tom was delirious, and did not even recognise his brother when he visited him, and so reduced Samuel to tears. The next evening he coughed his life away: 'which put me into a present very great transport of grief and cries, and indeed it was a most sad sight to see the poor wretch lie now so still and dead, and pale like a stone. I left my wife to see him laid out, and I by coach home, carrying my brother's papers, all I could find, with me.' At first it had been Samuel's intention to have Tom buried alongside their other brothers and sisters in St Bride's churchyard, but he changed his mind, deciding that he should be interred in the nave of the church, at an extra cost of 20s.

Before the funeral Pepys had an encounter with the sexton worthy of Hamlet's meeting with the gravediggers at Elsinore. 'But to see how a man's tombs are at the mercy of such a fellow, that for six-pence he would, as his own words were, "I will jostle them together but I will make room for him"; speaking of the fullness of the middle aisle, where he was to lie; and that he would, for my father's sake, do my brother, that is dead, all the civility he can; which was to disturb other corpses that are not quite rotten, to make room for him; and methought his manner of speaking it was very remarkable; as a thing that now was in his power to do a man a courtesy or not.'

Tom Pepys could not have complained of lack of mourners when the time came: one hundred and twenty had been invited, but Pepys thought nearer one hundred and fifty were present. Each received 'six biscuits apiece, and what they pleased of burnt claret'. That night Pepys mused in his Diary: 'But, Lord! to see how the world makes nothing of the memory of a man, an hour after he is dead! And, indeed, I must blame myself; for, though at the sight of him dead and dying, I had real grief for awhile, while he was in my sight, yet presently after, and ever since, I have had very little grief indeed for him.'

Tom might be buried, but his past lived on. He had run the business in a most slap-dash manner, letting his employees do all the cutting-out, while a glance at his accounts showed he owed £290, with only £200 due to him. There was worse to come. The previous year two attempts had been made to marry him off. The first came to nothing because the girl's mother raised objections, complaining about the smallness of the house and even about an impediment he had in his speech. The other venture failed quite simply because, in Pepys's own words, the girl did not fancy Tom. Unfortunately, the same could not be said about Tom's maid-servant Margaret, 'an ugly jade'.

It was a one-time servant of Pepys's father who revealed the skeleton in Tom's cupboard, and a great deal of trouble it would cause Samuel. Margaret had given birth to twins, of which one girl survived. Tom had tried to farm her out 'on one Cave, a poor pensioner in St Bride's parish, to take it, giving him £5, he thereby promising to keep it for ever without more charge'. But there was trouble from the parish, which eventually found itself responsible for the baby girl, and Cave was sent to the Compter Prison. Eventually he was freed, and the wretched child consigned to one John Taylor, for a consideration, a bond of £100. Now the old servant came to Pepys saying he was the one who had lent Tom the money, and that he would like to have it back. Samuel had himself lent Tom £87, which had vanished into thin air, and it transpired also that his cousin, Dr Thomas Pepys, had also lent a sum, which he too was now demanding from Samuel. Little wonder there was not much brotherly love on Samuel's part.

The death of Samuel's cousin Edward Pepys the previous December had caused Elizabeth to ask what would happen to her in in the event of *his* demise, so he decided to make a new will (he had made one before sailing to Holland with Lord Sandwich in 1660).

The copy was drafted one evening at the Office, and on 30 January: 'in the evening signed and sealed my last will and testament, which is to my mind, and I hope to the liking of God Almighty. This evening I tore some old papers; among others, a romance which, under the title of "Love a Cheat", I begun ten years ago at Cambridge; and, reading it over tonight, I liked it very well, and wondered a little at myself, at my vein at that time when I wrote it, doubting that I cannot do so well now if I should try.' And the way Pepys's fortunes were prospering he would soon have an estate worth leaving Elizabeth. When he reckoned it all up he found that he was worth £858: 'which is the greatest sum I ever yet was master of'. At the end of July that sum had reached the infinitely satisfying round figure of £1,000, at which he was overjoyed; and by the end of the year £1,349, of which £500 had come to him in that one year alone.

Although he felt restored to favour with Lord Sandwich, who had gone so far as to speak of Elizabeth as his cousin (by marriage), Pepys was not quite sure yet how warmly he would be received. But the change in the Earl was not personal; others had noticed that he was now more reserved than in the past. It was Henry Moore who told him how the Earl had 'grown very high and stately, and do not admit of any to come into his chamber to him as heretofore, and that I must not think of his strangeness to me, for it is the same he do to everybody'. Even so, Pepys judged that the time had come when he could risk inviting Lord Sandwich to dinner. Since he reckoned it would cost £10 or £12, however, he decided to think carefully before laying out so much money. Moreover, he did not wish Lord Sandwich to think he was running after him; and decided eventually 'by grave and humble, though high deportment, to make him think I do not want him, and that will make him the readier to admit me to his friendship again'. Pepys had seen the way others thrust themselves at 'my Lord', and he was not going to be guilty of the same conduct. At the back of Pepys's mind too was a suspicion of resentment, because he had had to act as security for the loan of £1,000 Lord Sandwich had borrowed from Thomas Pepys of Deptford to pay for his Coronation robes. 'I do not like his being angry and in debt together to me; and, besides, I do not perceive he looks after paying his debts, but runs farther and farther in.'

So relations between Pepys and his patron had become somewhat strained. But he was still very welcome with Lady Sandwich and the children. When he went to visit them at their new house in Lincoln's Inn Fields—which he considered fine but deadly dear—it was he who was a little reserved. But he thawed when Lady Jemimah and Paulina came to see him one evening soon after at Seething Lane. The visit was unexpected, and 'my wife would not be seen, being unready. Very merry with them; they mightily talking of their thrifty living for a fortnight before their mother come to town, and other such simple talk, and of their merry life at Brampton, at my father's, this winter.' Obviously he loved children, though he could write in the Diary that he was glad he and Elizabeth had none of their own.

One who was interested in the likelihood of a family was Uncle Wright, who even dropped hints to Elizabeth that if necessary he was prepared to deputise for Samuel: 'and is mightily inquisitive to know whether she is with child or no, which makes me wonder what his meaning is, and after all my thoughts, I cannot think, unless it be in order to the making his will; and I would to God my wife had told him that she was!' At the same time Elizabeth received a message from her mother, asking her to return an old morning gown: 'which was almost past wearing; and I used to call it her kingdom, from the ease and content she used to have in the wearing of it. I am glad I do not hear of her begging any thing of more value.'

Whilst Pepys had a liking and compassion for animals, judging by the Diary, they did not stir his feelings very deeply. Elizabeth had the little black bitch, which merited two or three entries, and there was the cat to keep down the mice. A carpenter from Deptford dockyard presented him with a blackbird, which enchanted him by its ability to whistle snatches of tunes, though never able to get very far with any of them, and in February that year there was a new occupant in the house in Seething Lane. '17th. Home, and dined, where I found an excellent mastiff—his name Towser—sent me by a surgeon.' Presumably he was the first of many dogs to bear that endearingly silly-sounding name.

Although not obsessed by his health, from time to time it caused both worry and pain during 1664. When at times he could not pass water he feared a recurrence of his old trouble, the stone, though that does not seem to have been the cause. In January he wrote: 'my eyes begin to fail me, and to be in pain, which I never felt to now-a-days'. Five months later he recorded: 'My eyes, beginning every day to grow less and less able to bear with long reading or writing, though it be by daylight: which I never observed till now.'

Missing from the Diary were references to the struggle he once had to resist social drinking: when Lady Carteret offered wine he settled for coffee, not very well made, with sugar. Another beverage he liked was 'Jocolatte'. Once in a while he went to the theatre; as he did on Mr Pierce's advice to see *The Indian Queen*, of which one of the authors had been Dryden, whom he had known slightly at Cambridge. He found it 'a most pleasant show, and beyond my expectation'. Later the son of his old acquaintance Henry Purcell would write incidental music, which has survived, while the play itself has all but vanished into oblivion. Another acquaintance from a very different sphere was Sir John Robinson, the Governor of the Tower. But whilst Pepys enjoyed dining at the Queen's House, he did not have any very high opinion of his host, especially when he became Lord Mayor of London as well. He found him 'a-talking, bragging, buffleheaded fellow'. At this time Pepys's favourite pejorative noun was coxcomb, and Sir John did not escape. 'I observe him to be as very a coxcomb as I could have thought had been in the City.' His successor turned out to be an equal disappointment, at least so far as the Lord Mayor's Banquet was concerned. Costing between seven and eight hundred pounds, it was not the food with which Pepys found fault: 'but it was very unpleasing that we had no napkins nor change of trenchers, and drunk out of earthen pitchers, and wooden dishes. I expected music, but there was none but only trumpets and drums, which displeased me. Being wearied with looking upon a company of ugly women, Creed and I went away, and took coach, and through Cheapside, and there saw the pageants [Lord Mayor's Show], which were very silly.'

A public spectacle that Pepys, like most of his fellow citizens, did not go out of his way to avoid was an execution. Early in the year 'Colonel Turner, a mad, swearing, confident fellow, well known by all, and by me', had gagged and bound an elderly merchant and his maid in Lime Street, and stolen £1,050 in cash and £4,000 in jewels. He was arrested on 10 January, tried, and hanged on the 21st. 'I to the 'Change; and seeing people flock in the City, I enquired, and found that Turner was not yet hanged. So I went among them to Leadenhall Street, at the end of Lime Street, near where the robbery was done; and to St Mary Axe, where he lived. And there I got for a shilling to stand upon the wheel of a cart, in great pain, above an hour before the execution was done; he delaying the time by long discourse and prayers, one after another, in hopes of a reprieve; but none come, and at last he was flung off the ladder in his cloak. A comely-looked man he was, and kept his countenance to the end. I was sorry to see him. It was believed there were at least 12 to 14,000 people in the street.'

The year before there had been talk of the inevitability of a trade war with Holland, and step by step it was coming nearer. 'Great talk of the Dutch proclaiming themselves, in India, Lords of the Southern Seas, and denying traffic to all ships but their own, upon pain of confiscation; which makes our merchants mad.' That was on 9 February 1664: only a few days later letters were brought to Pepys at the Navy Office recounting how scornful the Dutch were of the English on the west coast of India. At Surat they had beaten up several employees at the English factory and hung the flag of St George below their own standard. Of such actions were wars made. By April few people had any illusions about the inevitable outcome of events. 'To the 'Change, where everybody expects a war. Thence to dinner, where my wife got me a pleasant French fricasée of veal.' And only four years earlier Charles II had been an exile among the Dutch.

The change in events meant a busy time for Pepys: that same month he was up by four in the morning to go by boat in a foggy dawn to Greenwich, and from there to walk on to Woolwich, stopping several times to listen to the nightingales. Later, when he saw William Coventry, he found him full of talk about the probability of a war with Holland. Both Houses were in favour of a conflict, and he had been requested by the King to inquire what stores would be needed for the Navy, and buy whatever was necessary. 'Home to dinner, where I and my wife much troubled about my money that is in my Lord Sandwich's hand, for fear of his going to sea, and being killed: but I will get what out of it I can.'

Much as it went against his humanitarian instincts Pepys felt that the press-gang was the only way to obtain the required number of seamen to man the Fleet, which since 1660 had in the name of economy been allowed to run down. He expressed his views to the Duke about using extreme measures: 'without which we cannot really raise men for the Fleet of twelve sail, besides that it will assert to the King's power of pressing, which at present is somewhat doubted, and will make the Duke believe that we are in earnest'.

Pepys had been interested in naval history ever since he drew up a memorandum on foreign vessels striking their flags in the narrow

seas to English ships, and now as the war-clouds gathered he turned
to old Navy books, noting that in the past things had been much
better run than now. Within a matter of months England would
certainly be involved in another conflict, and Mr Coventry told
Pepys he thought of asking him to write a history of the previous
Dutch War: 'which I am glad to hear, it being a thing I much desire,
and sorts mightily with my genius; and, if well done, may recom-
mend me much'.

Not only was the Exchange a place for news, but also for inaccurate
rumour, as Pepys discovered when 200 men had been discharged
after refitting vessels for the Fleet. 'The town do talk that the King
discharges all his men—200 yesterday, and 800 today—and that now
he hath got £100,000 in his hand, he values not a Dutch war. But I
undeceived a great many, telling them how it was.'

Pepys's worry at the unpreparedness of the Fleet, however, was
from time to time sweetened in the time-honoured way by merchants wishing to benefit from his good-will. This was particularly
true of William Warren, now a Knight, who at this time provided
one of the most unintentionally funny entries in the Diary. 'He did
give me a pair of gloves for my wife wrapt up in a paper, which I did
not open, feeling it hard; but did tell him that my wife should thank
him, and so went on in discourse. When I come home, Lord! in
what pain I was to get my wife out of the room without bidding her
go, that I might see what these gloves were; and, by and by, she
being gone, it proves a pair of white gloves for her, and forty pieces
in good gold, which did so cheer my heart, that I could eat no victuals almost for dinner.' That might have been a present meant for
his eyes alone, but Mr Falconer, Clerk of the Rope Yard, visited
Elizabeth at home, and gave her a silver cup with a cover, which
when Pepys changed it for a 'fair tankard' at the goldsmith Alderman Backwell's shop, was found to be worth £5 16s. Another source
of private gain was the Tangier board, where Pepys was becoming
increasingly exasperated with his fellow-Commissioner Mr Povy.
Whilst he admired his cellar where all the bottles had paper labels,
and his bath at the top of the house, he nonetheless considered him
an absolute fool. In fact he used his favourite expression to describe
him: a coxcomb. A merchant who had benefited by a contract even
showed his gratitude at the office: 'whither comes Mr Bland, and
paid me the debt he acknowledged he owed me for my service in his
business of the Tangier merchant—twenty pieces of gold, a pleasant

sight. It cheered my heart; and, he being gone, I home to supper, and showed them to my wife; and she, poor wretch, would fain have kept them to look on, without any other design but a simple love to them; but I thought it not convenient, and so took them into my own hand.' But that was nothing to the present from Denis Gauden, the Victualler. He offered to let Pepys choose plate to the value of £100. Pepys decided the merchant should make the selection instead: 'so at noon I find brought home in fine leather cases a pair of the noblest flagons that ever I saw all the days of my life; whether I shall keep them or no I cannot tell; for it is to oblige me to him in the business of the Tangier Victualling; so, with a merry heart, I looked upon them, and locked them up.' Even unofficially Pepys was prepared to show gratitude for what he received, and when he heard that Falconer had died quite suddenly his compassion was stirred. 'We went to his widow, who is sick in bed also. The poor woman in great sorrow, and entreats our friendship; which we shall, I think, in everything do for her. I am sure I will.'

Pepys took his work as seriously with the Tangier Commission as he did at the Navy Office, and could record: 'To a Committee of Tangier about providing provisions, money, and men; but it is strange to see how poorly and brokenly things are done of the greatest consequence.' Eventually the contract for victualling the Tangier garrison went not to Gauden but to Plymouth merchants. They were to receive 3s. 2d. a week from the government, while for his part in securing the contract Pepys was to receive £300 a year: a very pleasant addition to his income. Indeed Pepys himself wrote: '26th September. I have looked a little too much after Tangier and the Fishery [yet another Commission on which he served], and that in the sight of Mr Coventry; but I have good reason to love myself for serving Tangier, for it is one of the best flowers in my garden.'

He may have been feathering his own nest under the gaze of William Coventry, but there was nothing self-seeking in his endeavours to set at least twelve vessels of the Fleet on a war footing. Overseas the situation was rapidly deteriorating, as much through Major Holmes's conduct, as through that of the Dutch, who had detained an English ship, the *Leopard*, and interfered with the Guinea Company. For his part Holmes, on his own initiative, had captured two forts and an island. Both Samuel and Elizabeth had been worried at the thought of Lord Sandwich going to sea against the Dutch, and now Pepys heard he intended to sail with the fleet of twelve vessels he was busy preparing. Not only did Pepys stand to lose a friend and patron, but also a very considerable sum of money lent personally, quite apart from acting as surety for the £1,000 lent by his cousin. Now Lady Sandwich had caught measles, and fearful lest it should turn out to be smallpox her daughters were moved out of the house, but not this time to Seething Lane. Their father decided they could go to Chelsea, to stay with Mrs Becke. 'With Creed talking of many things, among others of my Lord's going so often to Chelsea, and he do tell me that his daughters do perceive all, and do hate the place, and the young woman, Mrs Betty Becke; for my Lord who sent them thither only for a disguise for his going thither, will come under a pretence to see them, and pack them out of doors to the Park, and stay behind with her.' A few days later, when Pepys was visiting Lady Sandwich, by then convalescing at Kensington, who should he find among the other visitors but Betty Becke. First he was fascinated, and then almost won over, even if he found her 'one that hath not one good feature in her face, and yet is a fine lady, of a fine taille, and very well carriaged, and mighty discreet. I took all the occasion I could to discourse with the young ladies in her company to give occasion to her to talk, which now and then she did, and that mighty finely, and is, I perceive, a woman of such an air, as I wonder less at my Lord's favour of her, and I dare warrant him she hath brains enough to entangle him. After much mirth, discoursing to the ladies in defence of the city against the country or court, and giving them occasion to invite themselves tomorrow to me to dinner to my venison pasty, I got their mother's leave, and so good-night, very well pleased with my day's work, and, above all, that I have seen my Lord's mistress.'

The next day was another of the pleasant interludes which punctuate the course of the Diary. An unexpected guest was Creed. 'Very merry we were with our pasty, very well baked; and a good dish of roasted chickens; pease, lobsters, strawberries.' After dinner they all played cards till 5 p.m. when they went by boat to Greenwich. There they walked up the hill, and at the top sat down to yet another game of cards. 'And so to the Cherry Garden [at Rotherhide], and then by water singing finely to the Bridge and there landed.' Paulina was another of those who feared to shoot Old London Bridge: 'such a troublesome passage, in regard of my Lady

Paulina's fearfulness, that in all my life I never did see any poor wretch in that condition'.

But all was not well with his patron, as Pepys heard from Henry Moore. The estate was not thriving as it should, and the Earl was getting deeper and deeper into debt: not surprisingly Pepys worried over what was owing to him and his cousin Thomas. Before long Lady Sandwich confided openly to him her own fears and worries. 'My Lady and I sat two hours alone talking of the condition of her family's being greatly in debt, and many children now coming up and to provide for. I did give her my sense very plainly of it, which she took well, and carried further than myself, to the bemoaning their condition, and remembering how finely things were ordered about six years ago, when I lived there, and my Lord at sea every year.'

It really was a case of someone led astray by the extravagance and promiscuity of the Court, and it was the innocent who suffered. Despite her rival in Mrs Stuart it was still Lady Castlemaine who was the first lady, and Lord Sandwich had received the curious present of her portrait, painted by Lely, which Pepys could not help but admire. The day was Sunday, when he and Lady Sandwich had their heart-to-heart talk, and afterwards he went with her, Lady Jemimah and her brother Sidney, to hear a long, poor sermon at St Giles's Church. 'Thence set them down, and in their coach to Kate Joyce's christening, where much company and good service of sweetmeats; and, after a hour's stay, left them, and in my Lord's coach—his noble, rich coach—home.' How Pepys envied that coach (one day he would have one of his own), no doubt emblazoned with Lord Sandwich's coat of arms. Another coach which aroused his all-embracing interest was that of the Duke of Monmouth, seen the day after the young man's marriage. At Court and in the City there were whispers that Charles intended to make his son his heir, an unheard of step. 'I observed his coat [of arms] at the tail of his coach: he gives the arms of England, Scotland and France, quartered upon some other fields; but what it is that speaks his being a bastard I know not.'

That the King doted on his mistresses, as well as on his darling son, was common knowledge. About Frances Stuart, the Diary records: 'He values not who sees him, or stands by him while he dallies with her openly; and then privately in her chamber below, where the very sentries observe him going in and out, and that so commonly, that the Duke, or any of the Nobles, when they would ask where the King is, they will ordinarily say, "Is the King above or below".' It was the witty, wicked John Wilmot, Earl of Rochester, who hit on the idea of dressing up paid informers as sentries and posting them outside doors behind which he thought there might be happenings of interest to his fetid mind. As for Monmouth, he swore he would kill any man who said the King was not married to his mother: 'though Alsopp [the King's brewer] says, it is well known that she was a common strumpet before the King was acquainted with her. But it seems, he says, that the King is mighty kind to these his bastard children; and at this day will go at midnight to my Lady Castlemaine's nurses, and take the child and dance it in his arms.' For most people the Queen was fast becoming an object of pity: neglected and with a husband who, though witty and charming to some, was reputed to be sullen towards her. And now it was widely circulated that she was incapable of childbearing. (In the next few years she conceived more than once, but all the offspring were premature and stillborn.)

Thanks to Mr Pierce, the surgeon, Pepys saw the inside of both the Queen's and the King's private rooms. 'Mr Pierce showed me the Queen's bed-chamber, and her closet, where she had nothing but some pretty pious pictures, and books of devotion; and her holy water stoup at her head as she sleeps, with a clock by her bed-side, wherein a lamp burns that tells her the time of night at any time.' It was very different with the King: 'Where such a variety of pictures, and other things of value and rarity, that I was properly confounded, and enjoyed no pleasure in the sight of them; which is the only time in my life that I was so at a loss for pleasure, in the greatest plenty of objects to give it me.' For Pepys a glimpse of the home life of the Duke of York was a more edifying spectacle. 'With the Duke, and saw him with great pleasure play with his little girl, like an ordinary private father of a child.' The girl was the future Queen Mary.

That summer of 1664 was stormy, presaging the conflict to come, and in fact there had not been such thunderstorms in living memory. 'At noon, to dinner, where the remains of yesterday's venison, and a couple of brave green geese, which we are fain to eat alone, because they will not keep, which troubled us.' The preparations for war had one funny outcome, if not for Pepys. Timber was being chosen from the royal estates for the King's ships, and he sent

Anthony Deane, now the Assistant Shipwright at Woolwich, to mark oaks in Clarendon Park, near Salisbury, not realising that this particular royal property was now in the hands of Lord Clarendon himself. Recently this man of granite had had a stiff encounter with his enemy Lord Bristol, who tried to have him impeached on various trumped-up charges. In the end it was Bristol who turned and literally fled, having met more than his match in the Duke of York's father-in-law. Now Pepys had incurred his wrath by trying to cut down *his* trees. In a state of great anxiety therefore Pepys went to Lord Sandwich, who had already received the full blast of Clarendon's wrath for being the patron of Mr Pepys. Pepys received the impression that what worried his kinsman was the fear that he too might fall under the Lord Chancellor's displeasure. So Pepys asked for an interview with Clarendon, and was granted one that same evening: 'telling him that I was the unhappy Pepys that had fallen into his high displeasure'. Lord Clarendon was pleasant, saying that Lord Sandwich had given him an excellent character, and after that the little Clerk of the Acts and the gouty Lord Chancellor walked and talked in the garden for more than an hour. 'He told me by name that he was more angry with Sir George Carteret than with me, and also with the whole body of the Board. Lord! to see how we poor wretches dare not do the King good service for fear of the greatness of these men.' At least he had the satisfaction of noticing that Sir George Carteret, who had called too, was kept waiting for more than an hour while they talked, and that the great man 'would have me walk with my hat on'.

August was as hot as July, and on the 16th Pepys saw a Dutch giant, and the next night was really frightened by a thunderstorm. The tall foreigner was encountered at Charing Cross: 'and there saw the great Dutchman that is come over, under whose arm I went with my hat on, and could not reach higher than his eyebrows with the tip of my fingers'. What followed the next night was a foretaste of September 1666. 'Wakened about 2 o'clock this morning with a noise of thunder, which lasted for an hour, with such continued lightnings, not flashes, but flames, that all the sky and air was light; and that for a great while, not a minute's space between new flames all the time; such a thing as I never did see, nor could have believed had even been in nature. And being put into a great sweat with it, could not sleep till all was over. And that accompanied with such a storm of rain as I never heard in my life. I expected in the morning to find my house overflowed; but find not one drop of rain in my house, nor any news of hurt done.'

After the troubles of the previous year Pepys was now in a period of calm with his servants: a fact he open-heartedly acknowledged. 'Never since I was a housekeeper, I ever lived so quietly without any noise, or one angry word almost, as I have done since my present maids Besse, Jane and Susan come, and were together. Now I have taken a boy, and am taking a woman, I pray God, we may not be worse!' Already the new boy had endeared himself to his master: 'pretty it is to see how our boy carries himself so innocently clownish as would make one laugh'. Tom Edwards had been a member of the Chapel Royal, and it was Pepys's intention to make a clerk of him. There was no doubt he was musical: one night he played his lute till twelve, and then started again at four in the morning for another hour or two.

Nothing daunted by the violent irruption into the household of Mary Ashwell, Elizabeth was to have a new companion. She was Mary Mercer, 'a decay'd merchant's daughter', recommended by Will Hewer, who now boarded with her family. For Elizabeth it was a third time lucky, while Pepys was entering on a period of domestic calm. After a pleasant dinner, with Will and Anthony Joyce, their wives and other relations, Pepys recorded: 'I was as merry as I could, giving them a good dinner; but W. Joyce did so talk, that he made everybody else dumb, but only to laugh at him.' About Will's tongue he added: 'a cunning, crafty fellow he is, and dangerous to displease, for his tongue spares nobody'. For him there was greater contentment to be found in his own household after the guests had departed. That evening he, Elizabeth, Mercer (who played the harpsichord) and the boy Tom, sang and fiddled till eleven o'clock. 'My boy, a brave boy, sings finely, and is the most pleasant boy at present, while his ignorant boy's tricks last, that ever I saw.' After his experience with the other lads, Pepys had no illusions: boys, like puppies and kittens, would grow up. He had a great fear of thieves, and now that he was a man of property that fear had increased. 'About eleven o'clock, knowing what money I have in the house, and hearing a noise, I begun to sweat worse and worse, till I melted almost to water. I rung, and could not in half an hour make either of the wenches hear me; and this made me fear the more, lest they might be gag'd. . . . At last, Jane rose, and then I understood it was only the dog wants a lodging, and so made a noise.' He had reason to worry, since he was unwilling to place his money at a rate of interest even with someone as reputable as Alderman Backwell, and there was a considerable sum at home.

Perhaps as a result of the hot summer he suffered particular discomfort: his skin on occasion would itch almost unbearably: 'I thought myself to be mightily bit with fleas, and in the morning she [Elizabeth] chid her maids for not looking for the fleas a' days.' His eyes continued to give trouble, and for a crown he bought a frame of oiled paper, as was used by an engraver, to reduce the glare of a table light. Despite the domestic harmony Pepys's thoughts continued to wander, as when he was sitting in the next pew in Clerkenwell Church to 'the fair Butler, who indeed is a most perfect beauty still; and one I do very much admire myself for my choice of her, for a beauty, having the best lower part of her face that ever I saw all the days of my life'. He was still laying siege to Mrs Bagwell, the carpenter's wife at Deptford: 'but very modestly she denied me, which I was glad to see and shall value her the better for it, and I hope never tempt her to any evil more'. At least, not until the next time. But life at home really was harmonious. 'With my wife within doors, and getting a speech out of *Hamlet*, "to be or not to be", without book. In the evening to sing, psalms, and so to prayers and to bed.' But all the while two of the Horsemen of the Apocalypse were riding nearer and nearer: '22nd June. To the 'Change and Coffee House, where great talk of the Dutch preparing of sixty sail of ships. The plague mightily among them, both at sea and land.' '25th August. No news, only the plague is very hot still, and increases among the Dutch.' '25th September. We were told today of a Dutch ship of 3 or 400 tons, where all the men were dead of the plague, and the ship cast ashore at Gothenburg.'

That October a new warship, the *Royal Catharine*, was launched at Woolwich. It was an important occasion and Pepys, who was bringing a silver flagon to be presented to the ship's designer, Pett, invited his household to see the spectacle: Elizabeth, Mary Mercer, Jane, Sarah, Will Hewer and Tom. The King was there, as well as the Duke of York, the Court, and even the Queen and her Maids of Honour. 'One whereof, Mrs Boyton, and the Duchess of Buckingham had been very sick coming by water in the barge, the water being very rough; but what silly sport they made with them in very common terms, methought, was very poor, and below what people think these great people say and do.'

Pepys was really busy now, setting off between two and three on a November morning to go by water to the Hope (below Tilbury), where he found the seamen stepping the mast of the great warship he knew so well, the *Royal Charles*. One bright spot, if war were inevitable, was that Parliament had voted the King no less than £2,500,000 for its prosecution. Rumour had it that the Dutch were cruising up and down the coast off Ostend with twenty-two sail, and looking for trouble, while Charles asked laughingly what he should tell the Dutch Ambassador when the latter heard that the English had expelled them from several of their forts. That was not all: Colonel Richard Nicolls had headed a commission to settle part of the Atlantic coast of North America, taken the stockaded town of New Amsterdam on Manhatten Island from the Dutch, and re-christened it after his friend and patron, the Duke of York. New York had become a name on the map. If the Dutch had inflicted pin-pricks on the English, the English had retaliated with quite hard blows. Now Prince Rupert, regarded by many as a man dogged by ill luck, had sailed for Guinea.

Could it be that Pepys was jealous of Penn? '10th October. Sir W. Penn do grow every day more and more regarded by the Duke, because of his service heretofore in the Dutch war, which I am sure is by some strong obligations he hath laid upon Mr Coventry; for Mr Coventry must needs know he is a man of very mean parts, but only a bred seaman.' Penn was going to sea with the Duke of York, and so was William Coventry, and on 3 November Pepys heard a rumour that Lord Sandwich was to be sent to Tangier as governor. While such an appointment would keep him from harm in the coming war, Pepys considered that his honour would suffer, and that it was not in his interest to be so far from Court. But it was flattering to be told by Coventry that the main burden of running the Navy Office could be Pepys's responsibility. Batten was corrupt and inefficient, while old Sir John Minnes was past it: 'the latter of whom, he most aptly said, was like a lapwing, that all he did was to keep a flutter, to keep others from the nest that they would find'.

War was only one step away when news came that a cargo of masts for Sir William Warren, being brought over in a Swedish ship, had been stopped by the Dutch, in spite of Sir George Downing's demands for them to be let through. On Monday, 21 November, the months of growing tension were resolved. 'Thursday for certain, news is come that Teddiman hath brought in eighteen or twenty

Dutchmen, merchants, their Bordeaux fleet, and two men of war to Portsmouth. And I have letters this afternoon, that three are brought into the Downs and Dover; so that the war is begun; God give a good end to it!'

News was slow, and often inaccurate. While the Duke of York was at sea news came of a victory, and that the Dutch had been forced back into their harbours. But the temporary disappearance was in fact due to bad weather. As always the merchants at the Exchange were the first with news from far afield. 'Thence to the 'Change; and there, among the merchants, I hear fully the news of our being beaten to dirt at Guinea, by De Ruyter with his fleet.' Pepys was all for laying the blame for trouble-seeking in that part of the world on the merchants of the Royal Company: a view which was supported by Sir George Carteret, who talked 'with great displeasure at the loss of our honour there, and do now confess that the trade brought all these troubles upon us between the Dutch and us'. In Guinea the English had acquitted themselves badly in the first clash, and now there was yet another portent for the superstitious, which if not blazing forth the death of princes, could well foretell disasters to come. All England was coming out of doors in the cold of December to stare at the silent wonder of a great comet in the night sky. In a few evocative lines Pepys made his record. '24th. Having sat up all night to past two o'clock this morning, our porter, being appointed, comes and tells us that the bellman tells him that the Star is seen upon Tower Hill; so I, that had been all night setting in order all my old papers in my chamber, did leave off all, and my boy and I to Tower Hill, it being a most fine, bright, moonshine night, and a great frost, but no Comet seen.' The same evening— Christmas Day—he was fortunate enough to see Halley's Comet. 'I saw the Comet, which now, whether worn away or no I know not, appears not with a tail, but only is larger and duller than any other star, and is come to rise betimes, and to make a great arch, and is gone quite to a new place in the heavens than it was before; but I hope, in a clearer night, something more will be seen.'

Pepys was too busy and too preoccupied to enter fully into the Christmas and New Year festivities in his household (which included blind man's buff) and was in fact not a little vexed when on one occasion Elizabeth came to bed at eight o'clock in the morning: 'but I believe there was no hurt in it at all, but only mirth'. For him at least the year was ending with all his accounts squared, and £6

JAMES, DUKE OF YORK; LATER JAMES II

by Kneller

THE FOUR DAYS' BATTLE, 1666

paid to his bookseller, and £22 18s. to the goldsmith for spoons, forks and a sugar box. His health was better both in hot weather and in cold (despite the itching) than it had been for ten years, and he was in a contented frame of mind. On the ninth anniversary of his wedding he had thanked God for their long lives, and loves and health together, and now he could write that 'as pretty and loving quiet a family I have as any man in England. My credit in the world and my office grows daily, and I am in good esteem with everybody, I think.' Without realising it, in his thirty-second year, Pepys had become a mature and responsible man of the world, who could think of death with equanimity. 'This Christmas I judged it fit to look over all my papers and books, and to tear all that I found either boyish, or not worth keeping, or fit to be seen, if it should please God to take me away suddenly.'

Chapter 9

War and Plague
1665

ENGLAND was at war with Holland, and plague raging in
continental sea ports, but in Seething Lane Pepys could write:
'everything else is in a state of quiet, blessed be God'. And so it was
in his household as the old year ended with bitter cold and frost.
'I kissed my wife in the kitchen by the fireside, wishing her a merry
new year.' On Twelfth Night he left Elizabeth to celebrate the
revels with her own relations, preferring to play his viol by himself,
before going to bed. At Whitehall there was praise from the new
Governor of Tangier, Lord Bellasis; but soon it was followed by
bad news that two ships had gone aground and been lost in the
Straits of Gibraltar, while three more were likely to fall prey to a
Dutch fleet. At home there was more bad news. 'I was much
troubled to hear my poor canary-bird, that I have kept these three
or four years, was dead.' But the Tangier Commission was a continuing source of profit and satisfaction. With something approaching complacency Pepys watched the ineffable Povy sinking deeper
and deeper into muddle and inaccuracies with his accounts: in
fact none of the other members of the Committee could make up
their minds whether the man was a fool or a knave. Later that year,
when going about the Tangier Committee's business at the
Exchequer Office, Pepys would muse on the days when he had himself worked there as 'a mean clerk', and consider thoughtfully how
fortune had raised him above one of his old superiors. 'Here it was
mighty strange to find myself sit here in committee with my hat on,
while Mr Sherwin stood bare as a clerk, with his hat off to his Lord
Ashley and the rest; but I thank God I think myself never a whit
better man for all that.'

Pepys had come far in the world in five years, but with position
and prosperity came worry over the money he kept in the house.
Working late at the office he was interrupted by Mercer, who came

to say that Elizabeth—long since in bed—could hear strange noises on the roof over her head. In fear Pepys hurried home. 'So, at almost two o'clock, I home to my house, and, in great fear, to bed, thinking every running mouse really a thief; and so to sleep, very brokenly, all night long, and found all safe in the morning.' But at least he was not plagued with as many aches and pains as in his youth; in part, he felt, this must be due to the hare's foot he always kept in his pocket. Was it not known to be an unfailing remedy for colic? But if he had a cold in January he knew where that had started: 'by sitting too long with my head bare, for Mercer to comb and wash my ears'. Personal washing was a serious undertaking and not to be embarked on lightly or often, at least not in winter, but how justified Samuel was in being superior about Elizabeth is an open question. 'My wife busy in going with her woman to the hot-house to bathe herself, after her long being within doors in the dirt, so that she now pretends to a resolution of being hereafter very clean. How long it will hold I can guess.'

As in all marriages there were the ups and downs, and once when Pepys forgot himself so far as to give Elizabeth a black eye in a silly quarrel (she retaliated by biting and scratching), he was truly contrite afterwards: 'vexed at heart to think what I had done, for she was forced to lay a poultice or something to her eye all day, and is black, and the people of the house observed it'. But at least Elizabeth was no longer bored while he was at the Office or about his business at Whitehall or visiting the dockyards, often till late at night. Now she had Mary Mercer, who was proving herself a most pleasant young woman.

In the past Pepys had spent more on his own clothes than he allowed Elizabeth for her wardrobe, but in the spring of 1665 he gave her £24 for new clothes to wear at Easter. At the same time he allowed himself an equal sum for one suit: 'the best that ever I wore in my life'. Elizabeth was having drawing lessons, which gave her pleasure and him satisfaction. 'I think she will do very fine things, and I shall take great delight in it.' Also, he decided, she should be painted by the Dutch artist Huysman. But in the long run the drawing lessons were not all delight, at least for Pepys. More than once he admitted in the Diary that he was of a jealous nature, and perhaps with memories of Pembleton in mind, he now became suspicious of Browne, the drawing-master.

Pepys's material world was growing more and more to his liking every month; and the apple of his eye was his study, where he kept his books, nearly all of them re-bound in leather. 'Up and down to my chamber, among my new books, which is now a pleasant sight to me to see my whole study almost of one binding.' He had equal reason for satisfaction when he descended to his cellar. 'Two tierces of claret, two quarter casks of Canary, and a smaller vessel of sack: a vessel of Tent [a Spanish red wine], another of Malaga, and another of White Wine, all in my wine-cellar together.' He confesses disarmingly in his Diary to a simple delight in the new acquisitions, such as the watch given him by a solicitor friend of his Uncle Wright. 'But, Lord, to see how much of my old folly and childishness hangs upon me still, that I cannot forbear carrying my watch in my hand, in the coach, all this afternoon, and seeing what o'clock it is one hundred times.' That year he even mellowed towards Balty, when the feckless young man came asking if he could get him a job. Pepys agreed, chiefly for the sake of his wife: 'a pretty discreet young thing, and humble, and he, above all things, telling me sad stories of what she endured in Holland'. At about the same time Pepys's mother came on a visit from Brampton, and it was something of a trial to hear how she repeated herself, telling the same stories again and again.

But in the background of Pepys's life—and in the life of everyone else in and around London for that matter—was the plague. At the end of April he wrote: 'Great fears of the sickness here in the City, it being said that two or three houses are already shut up. God preserve us all!'

In the middle of January, Dutch men-of-war had been reported off Margate, and on the 15th of that month Pepys was present at a meeting with the King and the Lord Chancellor (the latter lying on a couch, stricken with gout). With him were several members of the Navy Board, as well as Privy Councillors. Charles wanted to have 130 vessels ready to put to sea by the spring, but it was pointed out to him that such a number would need 30,000 sailors to man them, while only 16,000 were available. If he wanted 130 ships, the best thing would be to stop the Turkey Fleet from sailing to the Mediterranean. If the City merchants objected, the King could suspend the Navigation Act by which goods to and from the country had to be carried in English vessels, which in itself would release seamen for the Fleet—in Holland all trading had already been suspended for eighteen months, so that nothing should interfere with the conduct of the war. What little news there was from the Fleet spoke of the Duke of York, Prince Rupert and Lord Sandwich acquitting themselves well.

It was Pepys's custom to seek out those merchants who were prepared to supply the Navy with goods at competitive prices, and now he found he had done well both for the King and for himself in the matter of flags. He gained £50 by the transaction, and at the same time saved his sovereign £100. Yet while he would take his profit where he found it, quite equally he was prepared to act in a completely disinterested fashion for the Navy's good: as for instance when he encouraged two Dutchmen to tell the secrets of 'stoving' (the method of heating ropes in a kiln to make them pliant) and when he had found out all he could, wrote a memorandum on the subject for the perusal of Mr Coventry.

The unsolicited presents he received from time to time continued to gladden his heart: like the token of esteem and gratitude from Mr Harris the sail-maker. '16th March. Mr Harris, the sail-maker, sent me a noble present of two large silver candlesticks and snuffers, and a slice to keep them upon, which is indeed very handsome.' The previous month his income had suddenly increased by £100. Old consumptive Barlow, his predecessor at the Navy Office, had died, so cancelling the sum Pepys had agreed to pay him annually from his salary. 'For which, God knows my heart, I could be as sorry as possible for one to be for a stranger, by whose death he gets £100 per annum.'

In August 1662 Pepys had resigned from the Office of the Privy Seal (though evidently still making use of the privilege of a place in the Chapel Royal at Whitehall), and only two days after had been appointed to the more lucrative Tangier Commission. Another commission on which he served, thanks to his nomination by Lord Sandwich, was that of the Royal Fisheries, but compared with the fair flower of Tangier this was not even in bud. His position on the Tangier Commission gave him a place at meetings of the Privy Council, which on 27 February discussed the necessity of the press-gang to obtain men for the Fleet: 'But, Lord! how they meet! never sit down: one comes, now another goes, then comes another; one complaining that nothing is done, another swearing that he hath been there these two hours, and nobody come. At last Lord Anglesey says, "I think we must be forced to get the King to come to every Committee for I do not see that we do anything at any time, but when he is here." '

More and more Pepys was coming to the notice of the Duke of Albemarle, who in the absence at sea of the Duke of York had become Deputy Admiral. 'And I find him a quiet heavy man, that will help business when he can, and hinder nothing. I did afterwards alone give him thanks for his favour to me about my Tangier business, which he did receive kindly, and did speak much of his esteem to me.'

The 'Tangier business' represented another step upwards. Povy, the inept treasurer, had got himself into such a complete muddle with his accounts, that he offered the job to Pepys—providing he would still have half the profits. Pepys was interested, and asked if he would obtain permission for him to take over. Permission was given: 'so that I am already confirmed their Treasurer, and put into a condition of striking of tallies: and all without one harsh word of dislike, but quite the contrary; which is good fortune beyond all imagination'.

If Pepys were the mainstay of the Navy Office, at least the Duke of Albemarle, for all his slowness of mind, had noticed the fact, and was willing to give credit where credit was due. A few days after the Council meeting he told Pepys of his good opinion. 'Thence to the Cockpit, and there walked an hour with my Lord Duke of Albemarle alone in his garden, where he expressed in great words his opinion of me; that I was the right hand of the Navy here, nobody but I taking any care of anything therein; so that he should not know what could be done without me.' What was more, the new Treasurer to the Tangier Commission was even patted on the head by the Lord Chancellor as the great man passed by in the Council Chamber. And, just before leaving to join the Fleet, Lord Sandwich had told Pepys of the Duke of York's good opinion, too. But golden opinions did not disguise the fact that the Navy was desperately short of money. Debts for the six months to April 1665 amounted to £500,000, and as a result of the war those for the next half year would amount to no less than £1 million. At the Treasury Sir William Warwick had told Pepys outright that unless the King could raise a loan from some rich nobleman or 'money-gentleman', there would be none. And therein lay the root of all the troubles that would plague the Navy during the Second Dutch War. Had the Navy been the responsibility of Parliament, money might have been voted in sufficient sums, but it was within the King's own responsibility, and was he—the son of Charles I—to be trusted? There were many in the Commons who thought not. No one was willing to lend the King money, as Pepys explained to the Privy Council. 'Says my Lord Treasurer; "Why, what means all this, Mr Pepys? This is all true, you say; but what would you have me do? I have given all I can for my life. Why will not people lend their money? Why will they not trust the King as well as Oliver?" ' There was indeed more behind the perpetual shortage of money for the Navy than incompetence or indifference: though what the obstruction was would never be clear to Pepys.

The very fact that Pepys had been spoken of as the one who did all the work at the Navy Office was the quickest way to ensure the ill-will of at least some of his colleagues, and before long it reached his ears that Sir John Minnes and Sir William Batten were complaining about his absence from the Office on other than naval business. What was unforgivable was that there might be a grain of truth in the accusation. Pepys had been a little too preoccupied with his own private affairs, and had even neglected to write to Mr Coventry, away at sea: 'which I must not do, though this night I minded it so little as to sleep in the middle of my letter to him, and committed forty blots and blurs, but of this I hope never more to be guilty'. And affairs was the right word to describe Pepys's distractions. At last Mrs Bagwell had surrendered, in a mean little ale-house in Moorfields. 'And many hard looks and sooth the poor wretch did give me, and I think verily was troubled for what I did, but at last after many protestings by degrees did arrive at what I would, with great pleasure.' Other occasions followed, and Mrs Bagwell, feeling that since she had lost her virtue she might as well turn the situation to the advantage of her cuckolded husband, asked her seducer to obtain a better ship for him. An easier conquest was Betty Lane, who probably merited his adjective of slut. She was a linen-seller in Westminster Hall, and their intermittent association did not end with her marriage to a Mr Martin (who eventually became a ship's purser, thanks to Pepys). During Elizabeth's summer visits to Brampton, Betty occasionally consoled Pepys during her own husband's absence in the daytime. There were other episodes, like those with Jane, the barber's assistant, though usually they went no further than furtive fumbling and kissing, for at times he was curiously inhibited, perhaps by the ingrained Puritanism of his childhood. From time to time he tried to reform himself, commenting: 'thereby, I may follow my business, which and my honour lies bleeding'.

The war news for several months had consisted of little more than rumours concerning the whereabouts of the Dutch fleet, but at home Pepys continued about his work among the City merchants as self-appointed watch-dog of the King's interests. Inevitably the price of necessary items such as timber and hemp for rope-making had risen; the latter now costing as much as £55 a ton. Pepys and Sir William Warren had much to be grateful to one another for, but it did not stop the Clerk of the Acts from warning the timber merchant not to become involved in price-rigging, or he would look elsewhere for wood. The older man took it well, and gave Pepys some sound advice. 'Sir William Warren did give me several good hints and principles not to do anything suddenly, but consult my pillow upon my Treasurership of Tangier, and every great thing in my life, before I resolve anything in it.'

And then at last, in early summer, the rider on a pale horse reached London, and on 7 June Pepys recorded: 'This day, much against my will, I did in Drury Lane see two or three houses marked with a red cross upon the doors, and "Lord have mercy upon us!" writ there; which was a sad sight to see, being the first of the kind that, to my remembrance, I ever saw. It put me in an ill conception of myself and my smell, so that I was forced to buy some roll-tobacco to smell and chew, which took away the apprehension.' The weather was oppressively hot, with the night sky torn with lightning. Already in the narrow streets and alleys the plague was starting to spread, and on 10 June it was in the City and all too near Seething Lane, in the house of Dr Burnett, Pepys's doctor and friend. A few days later Pepys visited Woolwich to ask his old acquaintance, Mr Sheldon, Clerk of the Cheque, if he would let Elizabeth stay at his house for a month or two, till the worst of the plague was over. Sheldon agreed, and with an easier mind Pepys returned to hear that the previous week 112 had died of the plague, while the week before it had been only forty-three. Soon after he had a bad fright while driving along Holborn. 'The coachman I found to drive easily and easily [slower and slower], at last stood still, and come down hardly able to stand, and told me that he was suddenly struck very sick, and almost blind—he could not see; so I 'light, and went into another coach, with a sad heart for the poor man and for myself also, lest he should have been struck with the plague.'

Although he was loth to see her go, Pepys decided his mother should return to Brampton at once. 'She was to the last unwilling to go, but would not say so, but put it off till she lost her place in the coach, and was fain to ride in the waggon part.' Next it was Elizabeth's turn. Her bedding and possessions were sent in advance to Woolwich, and the same day (5 August) she, Mary Mercer and one of the maids followed out of the stricken city. 'Very prettily accommodated they will be; and I left them going to supper, grieved in my heart to part with my wife, though some trouble there is in having the care of a family at home this plague time.' His own attitude was one of resignation. If he escaped it would be with God's blessing; if he succumbed he hoped he would have the courage to bear it.

At Whitehall the laughter was silenced, the search for amusement ended, and the cynical witticisms remained unuttered. Only a few weeks before Pepys had gone with Mr Povy in his carriage to join the *beau monde* circulating in Hyde Park, and had seen 'many brave ladies; among others, Castlemaine lay impudently upon her back in her coach asleep, with her mouth open'. Whilst at the theatre all had been as usual. 'All the pleasure of the play was, the King and my Lady Castlemaine were there; and pretty witty Nell Gwynn.' But by the beginning of the month, all had gone to the safety of Hampton Court, leaving the Duke of Albemarle almost alone in his apartments in the Cockpit.

It was at sea that Lord Sandwich discovered that being high in the King's favour could bring enmity in its wake. When he returned with the Fleet in March Pepys heard from Will Howe (whom he thought had grown 'a discreet but very conceited fellow') the way the Earl had been treated at sea by Sir William Penn on board the Duke of York's ship, and also by Captain Minnes, who had Prince Rupert's favour. Both men had shown him little respect, and this was to prove only the tip of the iceberg of trouble which would in the end bring about his downfall. Confidentially Lord Sandwich told Pepys when they met that whilst he thought he had the good opinion of the Duke of York and Mr Coventry, that Prince Rupert was no friend to him, and that in printed accounts of their activities the Prince took all the credit, and gave him none.

Now, in June, the Fleet was at sea again, with every likelihood of an encounter with the Dutch. Pepys had worries of his own. Tom Hayter, his head clerk, had been committed to the Gatehouse prison at Westminster by the Council because, unknown to him, someone had used his name to buy a quantity of gunpowder. It took a visit to the King and Sir George Carteret to get Hayter released on bail of £100.

For several days at the beginning of June there had been rumours of a great fight in the North Sea, and even of a victory for the English; but nothing was certain till news came while Pepys was with the Lord Treasurer. The Dutch had been routed, and the Duke of York, Prince Rupert, Lord Sandwich and Mr Coventry were all safe and uninjured: 'which did put me into such joy that I forgot almost all other thoughts. With great joy to the Cockpit—where the Duke of Albemarle, like a man out of himself with content, new-told me all.' The Battle of Lowestoft was a famous victory, though unfortunately one claimed by both sides, and Pepys's illustrious acquaintances had been in the thick of it. 'The Earl of Falmouth, Muskerry, and Mr Richard Boyle killed on board the Duke's ship the *Royal Charles*, with one shot: their blood and brains flying in the Duke's face; and the head of Mr Boyle striking down the Duke, as some say.' Admiral Sir John Lawson was among the casualties, injured in the leg. A few days later he was brought ashore. 'It seems his wound is not very bad; but he hath a fever, a thrush and a hickup, all three together which are, it seems, very bad symptoms.' Soon after the Admiral died, presumably from gangrene. Pepys was puzzled that there had been no mention of Lord Sandwich's part in the action, but the next day he heard that 'the King said "my Lord Sandwich had done nobly and worthily"'.

Pepys's head was in a whirl: in his opinion there never had been a greater victory known in the world. Back he went from Whitehall to Seething Lane. 'Then to my Lady Penn's, where they are all joyed, and not a little puffed up, at the good success of their father; and good service indeed is said to have been done by him. Had a great bonfire at the gate; and I, with my Lady Penn's people and others, to Mrs Turner's great room, and there down into the street. I did give the boys 4s. among them, and mighty merry.'

But still there was this undeniable silence about Lord Sandwich. 'I met with Mr Cooling [the Lord Chamberlain's secretary], who observed to me that he finds everybody silent in praise of my Lord Sandwich, to set up the Duke and the Prince; but that the Duke did, both to the King and my Lord Chancellor, write abundantly of my Lord's courage and service.' Then on 16 June all were back at Whitehall: 'where the Court is full of the Duke and the courtiers returned from sea. All fat and lusty, and ruddy from being in the sun'. Not all the English captains had acquitted themselves well in the face of the enemy. Captain Holmes had had a fit of pique in the midst of battle when he was not promoted Admiral to replace one of those killed in action, and returned his commission to the Duke of York, who tore it up. 'Holmes would do it, like a rash, proud coxcomb,' commented Pepys in his Diary. If people spoke slightingly of Lord Sandwich, the Earl was prepared to do the same of others when he met Pepys at a meeting of the Tangier Committee on 23 June. 'My Lord Sandwich did take me aside in the robe-chamber, telling me how much the Duke and Mr Coventry did, both in the Fleet and here, make of him, and that in some opposition to the Prince's; and as a more private passage, he told me that he hath been with them when they have made sport of the Prince, and laughed at him: yet that all the discourse of the town, and the printed relation, should not give him one word of honour, my Lord thinks very strange.' Lord Sandwich went on to declare that at the start of the engagement Prince Rupert was—quite by accident—in the van, but for the rest of the day it was he, Lord Sandwich, who was in the thick of the fight. What was more, he complained, the Prince had hardly a shot in his hull, while he had more than thirty in his, had lost most of his masts and yards, and in fact had the second highest casualty rate of any ship in the Fleet. The air was thick with grievance. Then he turned to a more personal and agreeable topic. Would Pepys like to act as intermediary between himself and Sir George Carteret in a proposed marriage between Lady Jemimah and the knight's eldest son Philip? Pepys was delighted, and quite the courtier, visited Sir George: 'and in the best manner I could, moved the business'. The proposal was received with grave interest, and he 'promised to do what he possibly could for his son, to render him fit for my Lord's daughter, and showed great kindness to me, and sense of my kindness to him herein'. Lord Sandwich was prepared to make generous provision for 'Lady Jem': a dowry of £5,000 and an annual jointure of £800.

Pepys could rejoice at a knighthood for William Coventry, considering he would 'ever find him a noble friend'. But from Portsmouth there was disquieting news. The unpaid workmen at the dockyard had gone off haymaking in order to earn enough money to buy food for themselves and their families. Also, the breach between Prince Rupert and Lord Sandwich had become wider and more public. A suggestion by the King that the Fleet should be commanded jointly by the two men had been flatly rejected by the Prince, and so Lord Sandwich remained an Admiral with Sir George Ascue and Sir T. Teddiman under him. By the middle of July the Fleet was at sea again.

'Our Fleet, under my Lord Sandwich, being about the latitude 55½, which is a great secret, to the Northward of the Texel.' Despite the presence of the Fleet off the Dutch coast, De Ruyter managed to slip through the blockade on his way back from the East Indies. The talk in London was all admiration for his feat, and criticism of the English commanders. Pepys's time was now divided between the Navy Office in the City, visiting the Duke of Albemarle at deserted Whitehall Palace, and overseeing work at the Deptford and Woolwich dockyards, interspersed with flying visits to Elizabeth. 'In the morning up, and my wife showed me several things of her doing, especially one fine woman's Persian head, mighty fine done; beyond what I could expect of her, and so away by water, having ordered in the yard six or eight bargemen to be whipped, who had last night stolen some of the King's cordage from out of the yard.'

The exodus from London had been going on since the middle of June, when Pepys had observed 'all the town almost going out of town, the coaches and wagons all being full of people going into the country'. Now, apart from those who dared not leave their businesses or were too poor to move, the capital was silent and almost deserted; save for the clanging of the bells of the parish churches, as yet more deaths were reported. On one journey from the Navy Office to Whitehall, Pepys did not pass a single coach, either coming or going. Soon the plague was in his own vicinity. 'Sad news of the death of so many in the parish of the plague, forty last night. The bell always going.' Plans were set in motion to move the Navy Office to Deptford, and on 29 July Pepys received a bad fright. Will Hewer was returning to stay in the house in Seething Lane. 'At noon to dinner, where I hear that my Will is come in thither, and laid down upon my bed, ill of the headache, which put me into extraordinary fear; and I studied all I could to get him out of the house, and set my people to work to do it without discouraging him.' Then he took a coach to visit his cousin Kate Joyce, to talk her husband into letting her go to safety at Brampton. In the end Anthony Joyce agreed she should go to friends at Windsor. 'So I took my leave of them, believing it great odds that we ever all see one another again; for I dare not go any more to that end of the town. Will is gone to his lodging, and is likely to be well, it being only the headache.'

Now, every parting could be the last, and even Pepys's natural optimism was turned to depression and apprehension. '30th July. Up, and in my night-gown, cap, and neckcloth, undressed, all day long—lost not a minute, but in my chamber, setting my Tangier accounts to rights. Will is very well again. It was a sad noise to hear our bell to toll and ring so often today, either for deaths or burials; I think, five or six times.' It was a strange paradox: in the City death was everywhere, and Pepys was almost resigned to becoming a victim himself, while at the same time he could write: 'Thus, I ended this month with the greatest joy that ever I did in my life, because I have spent the greatest part of it with abundance of joy, and honour, and pleasant journeys, and brave entertainments, and without cost of money; and at last live to see the business ended with great content on all sides.' The business was of course the marriage of Philip Carteret and Lady Jemimah.

Sir George and Lady Carteret had moved to the Treasurer's House, their official residence at Deptford, and there Pepys talked for an hour or so with Lady Sandwich, before she went on to stay at Dagenhams (Dagenham), the country house of her sister, Lady Wright. Philip Carteret had yet to face the ordeal of meeting his future in-laws for the first time, for it was truly a case of a marriage having been arranged, and he had not even set eyes on any of them. Since Lord Sandwich had to be away at sea he had requested Pepys to act as his deputy in all matters concerned with the marriage, and his kinsman filled his role most conscientiously. He suggested he should accompany Philip Carteret to Dagenhams, and the young man accepted gratefully. The next morning it took an hour to get their coach and horses across the river at Greenwich ferry before they were really on their way. 'But, Lord! what silly discourse we had as to love-matters, he being the most awkward man ever I met with in my life as to that business.'

At Dagenhams the tongue-tied young man was amiably received, but was too shy even to speak to Lady Jemimah. Lady Wright and Lord Crewe (her father) were perplexed what to do for the best, and asked Pepys if they should leave the young couple alone together, 'to begin their amours'. In Pepys's expert opinion that would be unwise, 'lest the lady might be too much surprised', and Philip Carteret was sent off up to bed. Soon he was followed by

Pepys, anxious to discover what he thought of Lady Jemimah. The young man said he liked her well enough: 'but, Lord! in the dullest insipid manner that ever lover did'. Pepys, who never wasted a moment in the pursuit of love, was almost exasperated beyond endurance at his indifference. The next day Philip showed hardly any more ardour, so Pepys gave him a lesson in gallantry in the gallery of the old house. 'Here I taught him what to do: to take the lady always by the hand to lead her, and telling him that I would find opportunity to leave them together, he should make these and these compliments. After I had instructed him, which he thanked me for, owning that he needed my teaching him.' But it was no good: Philip Carteret just had not the courage to take the girl's hand in the family coach either going to church or on the return journey. After dinner they were all seated in the gallery. First Lady Wright and Pepys went out, then Lord Crewe, leaving the young couple almost alone. 'And a pretty little daughter of my Lady Wright's most innocently come out afterwards, and shut the door to, as if she had done it, poor child, by inspiration: which made us without have good sport to laugh at.' The ice had been broken at last.

Before leaving the next morning Pepys took Lady Jem aside and asked how she liked Philip Carteret. The answer was diplomatic. 'She blushed, and hid her face awhile; but at last I forced her to tell me. She answered, that she could readily obey what her father and mother had done; which was all she could say or I expect.' Back at Deptford Pepys recounted all that had passed at Dagenhams: 'but the young man could not be got to say one word before me or my Lady Sandwich of his adventures, but, by what he afterwards related to his father and mother and sisters, he gives an account that pleases them mightily.' For his part in forwarding the match Pepys now found himself the guest of honour in the Treasurer's House, and he was invited to stay the night: 'which I did most nobly, better than ever I did in my life'. Back in the outside world once again Pepys found that the plague was increasing in severity: that week alone, 1,089 victims had died, and a visit to the Duke of Albemarle brought the observation: 'I by coach home, not meeting with but two coaches and but two carts from Whitehall to my own house, that I could observe, and the streets mighty thin of people.'

Before the great day of the wedding there was another visit to Dagenhams, which ended late at night with the occupants of the coach spending the night where they were by the ferry on the Isle of Dogs: 'a frolic [whim], being mighty merry, took us, and there we would sleep all night in the coach in the Isle of Dogs; so we did, there now being with us my Lady Scott [younger daughter of Sir George Carteret]; and with great pleasure drew up the glasses, and slept till daylight, and then some victuals and wine being brought us, we ate a bit, and so up and took boat, merry as might be; and, when come to Sir G. Carteret's, there all to bed.'

When 31 August came, there was nearly no wedding. Sir George Carteret, Lady Sandwich and Pepys set out from Deptford soon after six in the morning, but because the tide was out the horse-ferry could not cross at the same time as the coach. 'So we were fain to stay there in the unlucky Isle of Dogs, in a chill place, the morning cool, and wind fresh, above two, if not three hours, to our great discontent.' Because of the delay there was a mix-up at Dagenhams, and the marriage ceremony was nearly called off. But in the end it went ahead. 'The young Lady mighty sad, which troubled me; but yet I think it was only her gravity in a little greater degree than usual.' It was all conducted most decorously: to Pepys's wonder the young couple were even present at evening prayers. It was all so restrained, with none of the bawdy horse-play to which he was accustomed. 'I kissed the bride in bed, and so the curtains were drawn with the greatest gravity that could be, and so good night. But the modesty and gravity of this business was so decent, that it was to me indeed ten times more delightful than if it had been twenty times more jolly and jovial.' The next morning he was back in the bridal chamber where he found the flushed couple more satisfied with the state of matrimony than Philip Carteret's lack of enthusiasm had led him to expect.

Pepys had acquitted himself admirably as Lord Sandwich's deputy in the arranging of his daughter's marriage, hastened along as it had been, because of fear of the plague and the untimely death of either bride or groom. And death was everywhere: in London that week 2,020 had been carried off, and the plague was even reaching out into the country, to a near neighbour at Dagenhams in fact. The episode in question had almost the quality of a medieval Morality play. A group of young men in a coach in a narrow lane encountered another, which had its curtains drawn. Thinking they might conceal a beautiful young woman one of the gallants, full of life, leant out of his coach and thrust his head through the curtains.

Within was not Death, but a maidservant: 'in a silk dress, and stunk mightily'. It was the coach from the local pest-house collecting yet another victim.

The plague was now beginning to touch Pepys's acquaintances at Westminster. 'And poor Will, that used to sell us ale at the Hall-door, his wife and three children, died, all, I think, in a day.' By the 10 August the death-rate had passed the 3,000 mark for the previous week. 'Home, to draw over anew my will, which I had bound myself by oath to dispatch by tomorrow night; the town growing so un-healthy, that a man cannot depend upon living two days.' As a result of setting his affairs in order Pepys found he was now the possessor of £2,164: in the midst of so much misery and uncertainty he had never been more prosperous.

Now the Exchequer was moving out of London, to the mustiness of Nonsuch House near Epsom, long shut-up, and on 19 August letters from the King and Lord Arlington ordered the removal of the Navy Office to Greenwich. Pepys would not have been human had he not been relieved to go to comparative safety outside London. And not before time: for its part the Court had moved from Hampton Court, first to Salisbury, and then on to Wilton House. In the City the victims were dying in such numbers that now they were being taken for burial in plague-pits by daylight and not at night, as had previously been the custom, and Pepys even found a corpse lying in a narrow alley as he made his way home from the riverside.

Plague at home and mismanagement of affairs abroad was the situation in the middle of August. A fleet of Dutch East Indiamen had tried to return to Holland by a route round Scotland, but been forced to seek refuge in the neutral harbour of Bergen, at that time held by the Danes. Lord Sandwich sent in a small fleet under Teddiman, but because of a failure of communications with Copen-hagen, the Danish guns opened fire, inflicting casualties and forcing the English to leave the harbour. What was more, the English Fleet was already running short of provisions, and before long would have to return home, while De Ruyter was sailing to the rescue of the heavily laden merchantmen. On 23 August Pepys received a letter from Lord Sandwich announcing that he was with the Fleet in Sole Bay off Southwold, and that as far as his own affairs were concerned, he was delighted that Lady Jem was safely married. There was some public criticism of the Earl: he was blamed for the failure to capture the East India fleet. But on 4 September he was again at sea, with fresh provisions: 'in want of nothing but a certainty of meeting the enemy'.

On 10 September Pepys received word from William Coventry that Lord Sandwich had vindicated himself. With the loss of only one vessel he had located the convoy and captured two East Indiamen, as well as six or seven other merchantmen, all laden with goods from the East. Lord Sandwich would be the hero of the hour when he returned—or so it seemed. Quickly Pepys took the news to colleagues at Greenwich, among them Lord Brouncker and Sir John Minnes. With them was that other great diarist, John Evelyn. 'The receipt of this news did put us all into such an ecstacy of joy, that it inspired in Sir J. Minnes and Mr Evelyn such a spirit of mirth that in all my life I never met with so merry a two hours as our company this night was.'

But apart from the successful encounter with the Dutch convoy there was little enough reason for cheerfulness. Each week the Bills of Mortality showed a rise in the number of plague victims: 6,102 dead at the end of August, and the next week 6,978. Also the plague was disturbingly near Greenwich and Deptford. At Croome Farm close by, twenty-one had died: there the dead were as yet unburied because no order had come from the parish council: 'this disease making us more cruel to one another than we are to dogs'.

In the past Pepys had known his fellow member of the Tangier Committee Lord Brouncker only slightly, but now at Greenwich they became better acquainted. Lord Brouncker was President of the Royal Society, where Pepys was a member and, until the advent of the plague, had attended lectures and observed experiments at Gresham College. One such demonstration had showed that when fire was deprived of air, it went out. On another occasion he witnessed poison from the dreaded upas tree being administered to a dog, but there was no reaction, at least not before he went home. On another occasion he visited Gresham College with the incompetent Povy: 'where we saw some experiments upon a hen, a dog, and a cat, of the Florentine poison. The first it made for a time drunk, but it come to itself again quickly; the second it made vomit mightily, but no other hurt. The third I did not stay to see the effect of it.' Now Lord Brouncker was among the little group of refugees from Whitehall and the Navy Office at Greenwich. Together with Captain Cocke, the Paymaster, and Sir John Minnes, Pepys was a guest at a dinner party. 'None else, saving some painted lady that dined there: I know not who she was.' Pepys was soon to discover her identity, however. She was Mrs Williams, the mistress of Lord Brouncker. Another acquaintanceship which grew was with John Evelyn, who lived at Sayes Court, near Deptford. Pepys was to admire his garden, his house and library, and perhaps above all his cultivated mind.

One rainy evening, Pepys, Evelyn and Captain Cocke were discussing the situation: the indifference of their superiors, and how they would manage for money, especially as they now had thousands of prisoners, mostly taken from the Dutch convoy when the merchantmen were captured. Captain Cocke put his finger on the trouble when he declared: 'My Lord Treasurer, he minds his ease, and lets things go how they will: £800 per annum, and a game of Ombre, he is well. My Lord Chancellor, he minds getting of money and nothing else; and my Lord Ashley [the future Earl of Shaftesbury and founder of the Whig party] will rob the Devil and the Altar, but he will get money if it is to be got.'

Just as it was setting out for the safety of Salisbury Pepys saw the royal circle at Hampton Court, and for the first time kissed hands with the Duchess of York: 'and it was a fine white and fat hand'. He was growing slightly disillusioned with the divinity of kings: 'the more a man considers and observes them, the less he finds of difference between them and other men.'

Before following the Navy Office from Seething Lane to the comparative safety of Greenwich, the plague had carried off Pepys's own physician, a month or more after his servant had succumbed. 'So home, sooner than ordinary, and, after supper, to read melancholy alone, and then to bed.' He was starting to become morbid. '30th August. I went forth, and walked towards Moorfields to see, God forgive my presumption! whether I could see any dead corpse going to the grave; but, as God would have it, did not. But, Lord! how everybody's looks, and discourse in the street, is of death, and nothing else; and few people going up and down, that the town is like a place distressed and forsaken.' But even at such a time the man of mode could worry about fashion. '3rd September. Up, and put on my coloured silk suit very fine, and my new periwig, bought a good while since, but durst not wear, because the plague was in Westminster when I bought it; and it is a wonder what will be the fashion after the plague is done, as to periwigs, for nobody will dare to buy any hair, for fear of infection, that it had been cut off the heads of people dead of the plague.' As he packed up, prior to removal of the Navy Office to Greenwich, he saw the pathetic attempts to combat the plague. 'There I saw fires burning in the street, as it is through the whole City, by the Lord Mayor's order.'

On a further visit to the Duke of Albemarle, Pepys learnt the contents of a letter from Lord Sandwich, back once again in Sole Bay. Together with what had been taken previously the Fleet had now captured about thirty-five Dutch vessels, most of them rich merchantmen. That at least was wonderful news: 'I away towards the 'Change, the plague being all thereabouts. Here my news was highly welcome, and I did wonder to see the 'Change so full, I believe 200 people; but not a man or merchant of any fashion, but plain men all. And, Lord! to see how I did endeavour all I could to talk with as few as I could, there being no observation of shutting up of houses infected, that to be sure we do converse and meet with people that have the plague upon them.'

Now the dead were to be seen more and more openly: 'My meeting dead corpses of the plague, carried to be buried close to me at noon-day through the City in Fenchurch Street. To see a person, sick of the sores, carried close by me by Gracechurch in a hackney coach. My finding the Angel Tavern, at the lower end of Tower Hill, shut up; and more than that, the alehouse at Tower Stairs; and more than that, that the person was then dying of the plague when I was last there, a little while ago, at night. To hear that poor Payne, my waiter, hath buried a child, and is dying himself. To hear that a labourer I sent but the other day to Dagenhams, to know how they did there, is dead of the plague; and that one of my own watermen, that carried me daily, fell sick as soon as he had landed me on Friday morning last, when I had been all night on the water, and is now dead of the plague. To hear that Captain Lambert [whom Pepys had first known as the musical Lieutenant on the *Royal Charles*] and Cuttle are killed in the taking of these ships, and that Mr Sidney Montagu is sick of a desperate fever at my Lady Carteret's, at Scott's Hall. And lastly, that both my servants, W. Hewer, and Tom Edwards, have lost their fathers, both in St Sepulchre's parish, of the plague this week, do put me into great apprehensions of melancholy, and with good reason.' He was indeed walking in the valley of the shadow of death.

Now came news that the Fleet was sailing down the east coast to anchor at the Nore. Pepys set sail to meet them, and at dawn on 18 September there they all were, riding at anchor. Lord Sandwich was aboard the *Prince*: still in his nightgown he greeted Pepys, and recounted all that had happened since they had parted. The spoils, he told his kinsman, were very rich, and would form a handsome windfall for the King. Then it was time to speed back to London, and together with Lord Brouncker, Batten and Minnes they went to report to the Duke of Albemarle at the Cockpit. 'But, Lord! what a sad time it is to see no boats upon the river; and grass grows all up and down Whitehall Court, and nobody but poor wretches in the streets!' And the Bills of Mortality showed that the plague was claiming more victims than ever: the previous week there had been 7,165 deaths, the highest number yet.

At the Nore, Lord Sandwich and his fellow senior officers were storing up trouble for themselves. By right they would be entitled to a share of the cargo from the captured merchantmen, just as much as the seamen were entitled to goods not actually stowed in the holds. But like greedy children they had not waited for the King's authority to 'break bulk'. The flag officers had met in Lord Sandwich's cabin while they were still at sea, and egged on by Sir William Penn the Earl had agreed to an immediate share-out. The cargoes of the Dutch East Indiamen included spices, at any time a valuable commodity, and before long the sailors were swarming ashore to offer bags of cloves and nutmegs at ridiculous prices. Later Pepys and Captain Cocke bought 37 lbs. of cloves at 5s. 6d. a pound and 10 lbs. of nutmegs at 4s. a pound from 'a couple of wretched dirty seamen' in an ale-house in Gravesend. By then Pepys had gleefully joined in 'breaking bulk' with my Lord and the other admirals. Lord Sandwich and Vice-Admiral Penn had each appropriated goods worth £4,000, while the share for the remaining admirals was set at £2,000 a head. Pepys borrowed £500 from Will Howe, now Lord Sandwich's Deputy Treasurer, and together with Captain Cocke, who put up an equal sum, they bought £1,000 of spices from his old friend of the *Royal Charles*, Captain Cuttance. Later Pepys tried to obtain another £1,000 worth of goods. In Lord Sandwich's eyes it was a good way 'to get money, and afterwards to get the King's allowance thereof, it being easier, he observes, to keep money when got of the King than to get it when it is too late'. While anxious to take all he could lay his hands on for himself, Pepys also saw the prize as a means of paying for the victualling of the Fleet, and for the sick and wounded seamen, as well as helping towards the maintenance of prisoners. The sum he suggested was £10,000.

On 1 October Pepys was again with the Fleet: 'My Lord received me most kindly; and, among other things, to my great joy, he did assure that he had wrote to the King and Duke about these prize goods, and told me that they did approve of what he had done, and would have me tell all the world so, and did, under his hand, give Cocke and me his certificate of our bargains, and giving us full power of disposal of what we have so bought.' But they were all reckoning without either the due processes of law, and public opinion. On a later visit Pepys saw for himself what had been going on in the merchantmen when he was shown over one. 'And there did show me the greatest wealth lie in confusion that a man can see in the world. Pepper scattered through every chink, you trod upon it; and in cloves and nutmegs I walked above the knees: whole rooms full. And silk in bales, and boxes of copper-plate, one of which I opened.'

Although by the end of September the plague was beginning to abate slightly, it was still serious enough, and in the midst of personal gain Pepys was beset with his usual financial worries at the Navy Office. '30th September. The great burden we have upon us at this time at the office, in the providing for prisoners and sick men, that are recovered, they lying before our office doors all night and day, poor wretches. Having been on shore, the Captains won't let them on, nor money to pay them off, or provide for them. God remove this difficulty! Was set upon by the poor wretches, whom I did give good words and some little money to, and the poor people went away like lambs, and, in good earnest, are not to be censured, if their necessities drive them to bad courses.' A few days later the situation was worse than ever. '7th October. Did business, though not much, at the office, because of the horrible crowd and lamentable moan of the poor seamen, that lie starving in the streets for lack of money, which do trouble and perplex me to the heart, and more at noon. When we were to go through them, for then above a whole hundred of them followed us; some cursing, some swearing, and some praying to us.'

That same night two waggon-loads of loot arrived from Rochester, but so also did two Customs officials. 'But I showed them my *Transire*. However, after some angry words, we locked them up, and sealed up the key, and did give it to the Constable to keep till Monday and so parted. But, Lord! to think how the poor Constable come to me in the dark, going home; "Sir", says he, "I have the key, and, if you would have me do any service for you, send for me betimes tomorrow morning, and I will do what you would have me." Whether the fellow do this out of kindness or knavery, I cannot tell.'

Preoccupation with his own affairs—together with worry about the plague—had not been sufficient to stop Pepys ferreting out why the Fleet was unable to remain at sea for more than a few weeks. The trouble was that the Victuallers were just not a large enough concern to provide supplies for the vastly enlarged wartime Navy. There was talk of setting up a commission, and of a group of merchants coming together to take over from Gauden, who now had the contract. Would it not be possible, asked Pepys, to appoint a surveyor at each port to see the ships there were properly and adequately provisioned? With commendable lack of false modesty he suggested himself as Surveyor General for His Majesty's Dockyards, for which he would receive £300 per annum. Also, he presented detailed accounts of the cost of the Navy since the war began, which was now past the million pound mark. Certainly Parliament voted £1,250,000 for the Navy, but failed to say where the money would come from. In the past merchants had let bills for supplies to the Navy remain unpaid, but there was a limit to their patriotism or credit. There was no money to pay off old debts, and if the merchants did not extend their credit the Fleet would not be able to put to sea the next year—and then God help England at the hands of the Dutch. In the end goods were bought on credit on the promise that the merchants would receive interest on the value of the materials supplied, or on money lent to the government for the Navy.

After initial doubts about the scheme for raising money, Pepys decided it was, in the circumstances, the only course open for the present, and sought the co-operation of the City merchants and financiers. The first to react was Sir William Warren who supplied timber to the value of £3,600. At one time work in the dockyards was at a standstill, for like the seamen the workers were unpaid. All this was public knowledge, and as a result feelings ran high when it was reported that the Commanders of the Fleet had been pillaging merchantmen, the sale of whose cargoes would go a considerable way towards settling the Navy's debts. Lord Sandwich received the brunt of the criticism, and it was even said he had not pursued the remainder of the Dutch fleet and convoy when he could have done so because he was anxious to return to England with his loot. And now the Dutch fleet was reported to be in Sole Bay. Lord Sandwich had gone to Oxford, where the Court was, to justify himself to the King, while the Duke of Albemarle was talking of taking command of the Fleet himself, and asking Pepys to have ready at least twenty ships. All he could muster was seven. Finally, a gale forced the Dutch to retire back across the North Sea, but now Parliament wanted blood, preferably Lord Sandwich's. Pepys could count himself lucky that when he said he had acted in good faith in entering into partnership with Captain Cocke to buy goods his statement had been accepted, and that the Customs had records of what had been removed. In all he made about £500 profit out of the transaction.

At Oxford a bill was brought in to make it a felony to 'break bulk', and Sir George Carteret told Pepys 'it was proposed by some hot-heads in the House of Commons, at the same time when they voted a present to the Duke of York, to have voted £10,000 to the Prince, and half-a-crown to my Lord of Sandwich; but nothing come of it'. While the King was prepared to defend Lord Sandwich, the Duke of York maintained a damning silence, saying neither good nor bad about him. In the end he was pardoned by the King, and made Ambassador Extraordinary to Spain. Pepys was fortunate that the Duke of Albemarle had a high opinion of him: between them they were about the only officials of any consequence to remain in London during the worse of the plague, and when the Duke visited Oxford he spoke highly of the conduct of the Clerk of the Acts to the Duke of York. He was more fortunate than Will Howe, my Lord's Treasurer. 'Captain Cuttance tells me how Will Howe is laid by the heels, and confined to the *Royal Catharine*, and his things seized.'

'My own proper accounts are in great disorder, having been neglected about a month. This, and the fear of the sickness, and providing for my family, do fill my head very full, besides the infinite business of the office, and nobody here to look after it but myself.' The anger of the unpaid seamen had reached the point of violence. '4th November. After dinner to the office, and much troubled to have 100 seamen all the afternoon there, swearing below, and cursing us, and breaking the glass windows, and swear they will pull the house down on Tuesday next. I sent word of this to Court, but nothing will help it but money and a rope.' Again he was lucky: Sir William Batten had his cloak torn off his back, and Mingo, his African servant, was beaten up in the street.

At last the plague was abating. 'I walked to the Tower; but, Lord! how empty the streets are, and melancholy, so many poor, sick people in the streets full of sores; and so many sad stories overheard as I walk, everybody talking of this dead, and that man sick, and so many in this place, so many in that. And they tell me that, in Westminster, there is never a physician and but one apothecary left, all being dead; but that there are great hopes of a decrease this week; God send it!'

For six years Lord Sandwich had been a friend and patron to Pepys, and now that he had fallen there were those ready to be spiteful towards the Clerk of the Acts. One such was the Duchess of Albemarle, no doubt remembering how Lord Sandwich had deprived her of what she considered her rightful commission when he insisted on nominating Pepys as Clerk of the Acts. 'At table, the Duchess, a very ill-looked woman, complaining of her Lord's going to sea the next year, said these cursed words: "If my Lord had been a coward, he had gone to sea no more. It may be then he might have been excused, and made an Ambassador," meaning my Lord Sandwich.' Some even chose to remember that in the past both Pepys and Lord Sandwich had been Parliamentarians: like one elderly Royalist who remarked: 'This is the time for you, that were for Oliver heretofore; you are full of employment, and we, poor Cavaliers, sit still and get nothing.' But at least the frost had come and there was ice on the Thames, and week by week the Bills of Mortality showed a decrease in the number of plague deaths. Elizabeth returned to London, first to rooms Pepys had rented, and then to their own house in Seething Lane.

Slowly, as more and more people returned to the capital, Samuel and Elizabeth picked up the threads of their former life, though there were many of their friends and acquaintances they would never see again. Pepys even found time for a little composition, setting lines beginning 'Beauty Retire', from *The Siege of Rhodes*, which he must have seen half a dozen times. At the beginning of December he spent an ecstatic musical evening at the house of Mr Pierce the surgeon. Everything was delightful: the company and the music. 'Here the best company for music I ever was in, in my life, and wish I could live and die in it, both for music and the face of Mrs Pierce, and my wife, and Knipp, who is pretty enough. I spent the night in an ecstasy almost, and, having invited them to my house a day or two hence, we broke up.'

There was one appetite Pepys had never lost, even during the worst weeks of the plague, as Mrs Bagwell, among others, knew only too well. Even the maid Susan did not escape from his loving hands, as he recorded in a multi-lingual entry in the Diary. At times the Puritan refused to be still, with curious results: 'nuper ponendo mes mains in su des choses de son breast, mais, il faut que je leave it lest it bring me to alcun major inconvenience'. That was after Elizabeth's departure for Woolwich. Now his eyes were wandering round the parish: 'Mr Lethulier, I like, for a pretty, civil, understanding merchant; and the more by much, because he happens to be husband to our noble, fat, brave lady in our parish, that I and my wife admire so.' On Christmas Day he wrote: 'To Church in the morning, and there saw a wedding in the church, which I have not seen many a day; and the young people so merry one with another! and strange to see what a delight we married people have to see these poor folks decoyed into our condition, every man and woman gazing and smiling at them. Here I saw again my beauty Lethulier.' And back home he went to straighten out his accounts, as well as those for Tangier, for he felt that if he died no one else could have put them in order. When he came to make his annual assessment of his and the nation's affairs he was delighted to find he was now worth more than £4,000: 'and [it] is principally occasioned by my getting £500 of Cocke, forming profit in his bargains of prize goods, and from Mr Gauden's making me a present of £500 more, when I paid him £800 for Tangier'.

Were it not for the plague and Lord Sandwich's fall from favour, 1665 would have rated one of the best years Pepys had known. It must have taken great courage to remain in Seething Lane with the plague all around, and even when he did move to Woolwich to join Elizabeth, to keep returning to report to the Duke of Albemarle. Compared with many, Samuel and Elizabeth had been lucky. 'My whole family hath been well all this while, and all my friends I know of, saving my Aunt Bell, who is dead, and some children of my cousin Sarah's, of the plague. But many of such as I know very well, dead; yet, to my great joy, the town fills apace, and shops begin to be open again. Pray God continue the plague's decrease! for that keeps the Court away from the place of business, and so all goes to rack as to public matters, they at this distance not thinking of it.'

Chapter 10

'A most horrid, malicious, bloody flame'
1666

NEW YEAR'S DAY, 1666, was for Pepys an occasion for exceptionally hard work. At 5 a.m. he started to dictate a memorandum for Sir William Coventry: a distillation of all he had found out and taught himself about the business of being a ship's purser. Having control of a ship's finances was wide open to abuse, as the Clerk of the Acts very soon discovered. His findings, which still survive, covered nineteen pages, and bear the superscription: 'A letter from Mr Pepys, dated at Greenwich, 1st January 1665-6, which he calls his New Year's Gift to his hon. friend, Sir William Coventry, wherein he lays down a Method of securing his Majesty in husbandly execution of the Victualling Part of the Naval Expense.' Tooker, the Navy Office messenger, acted as secretary: 'while I dictated to him, my business of the Pursers; and so, without eating or drinking, till three in the afternoon, to my great content, finished it'. Although Pepys was working as hard as ever he had done in his life, he also threw himself into social gatherings with all his old enthusiasm for pleasure: though still being strict with himself about drinking too much. Perhaps the nearness of death had made him acutely aware of the transitoriness of life, which in twenty-four hours could be snuffed out, but he now revelled in congenial company more than ever. He even softened towards Sir John Minnes: from having regarded him as a toothless, prating old fool, he could now write 'the most excellent pleasant company he is, and certainly would have made an excellent actor, and now would be an excellent teacher of actors'.

Quite apart from relief at the decrease in the number of fatalities from the plague there was another reason for his high spirits: he was smitten by the little actress Mrs Knipp, also known as Bab Allen, who was admitted to the circle of Lord Brouncker and Mrs Williams. What was more, her surly husband, a jockey, did not appreciate her: 'and I fear she leads a sad life with that ill-natured fellow her husband'. Later, when he knew her better, Pepys confided that Elizabeth didn't really understand him either. It was a classic situation, and perhaps the only surprising thing about it was that it did not end in at least one broken marriage. What completed Mrs Knipp's conquest of Pepys was the fact she was an accomplished singer. 'And in perfect pleasure I was to hear her sing, and especially her little Scotch song of "Barbary Allen".' Those long winter evenings at the beginning of January were gloriously happy for Pepys, filled with laughter and music, and some of what was sung was by Samuel Pepys, composer. 'And good music we had, and among other things, Mr Coleman sang my words I set, of "Beauty Retire", and they praise it mightily. Then to dancing and supper, and mighty merry till Mr Rolt come in, whose pain of the toothache made him no company, and spoilt ours. So he away, and then my wife's teeth fell to aching, and she to bed. So forced to break up all with a good song, and so to bed.'

Within a day or two Pepys and Mrs Knipp were exchanging little notes, signed 'Dapper Dicky' (the title of a popular song) and 'Barbary Allen'. It may have been due to lack of opportunity but the whole affair was remarkably innocent.

Now it was felt safe for the Navy Board to resume its meetings at the office in Seething Lane, and on Twelfth Night the return of Pepys's household to his old home was almost complete. 'My wife to fetch away my things from Woolwich, and I back to cards, and after cards to choose King and Queen, and a good cake there was, but no marks found: but I privately found the clove, the mark of the knave, and privately put it into Captain Cocke's piece, which made some mirth.'

Getting the house straight was a major operation. Pepys lent a hand, and could write of Elizabeth: 'My poor wife, who works all day at home like a horse, at the making of her hangings for our chamber and the bed.' As the figures recorded in the Bills of Mortality continued to decrease, so life returned to the City; though Covent Garden and Westminster remained still very empty, largely because the Court had not yet returned. But there was one danger which worried Pepys very much: 'It frighted me indeed to go through the church more than I thought it could have done, to see so many graves lie so high upon the churchyards, where people have been buried of the plague. I was much troubled at it, and do not think to go through it again a good while.' He was not the only one anxious on that score: there were others who wanted to see the City churchyards covered with quicklime.

At the onset of the plague one of the first to leave the parish of St Olave's had been the Rector, Mr Mills. Now he had returned, and Samuel and Elizabeth went to hear what he had to say for himself: 'expecting a great excuse for his leaving the parish before anybody went, and now staying till all are come home, but he made but a very poor and short excuse, and a bad sermon'. The Rector was not the only one to make a poor showing during the plague: many of the fashionable doctors also fled into the country, declaring that it was the sensible thing to do, as that was where all their patients were living.

Once before, to Pepys's great satisfaction, Elizabeth had had her portrait painted. Now she was sitting again, this time for the artist Hales. That first sitting must have had something of the quality of a musical comedy. 'Mr Hales begun my wife's portrait in the posture we saw one of my Lady Peters [Lady Petre, whom Pepys's cousin Will Joyce was once unwise enough to attempt to have arrested for debt], like a St Catharine. While he painted, Knipp, and Mercer, and I, sang; and by and by comes Mrs Pierce, with my name in her bosom for her Valentine, which will cost me money.' As on a previous occasion Pepys turned art critic; now he doubted whether the portrait of Lady Petre as St Catharine (a fashionable tribute to Catharine of Braganza), was by Hales at all. But he was satisfied with the work, especially when he returned to find Elizabeth together with Mercer, Mrs Pierce and Mrs Knipp. 'There sung, and was mighty merry, and I joyed myself in it.' The chief reason for his joy was of course Mrs Knipp, and what was more Elizabeth liked her. 'Comes Mrs Knipp to see my wife, and I spend all the night talking with this baggage, and teaching her my song of "Beauty Retire", which she sung and makes go most rarely, and a very fine song it seems to be.' If Pepys was inclined to quibble about the portrait, for his part the artist complained that Elizabeth's nose 'had given him as much work as another's whole face'. But in the end Pepys considered it well worth the £14, plus £1 5s. for the frame, and at once sat for his own portrait. 'He promises it shall be as good as my wife's, and I to sit to have it full of shadows, and do almost break my neck looking over my shoulder to make the posture for him to work by. Home, having a great cold; so to bed, drinking butter-ale.'

Pepys was not too dazzled by Mrs Knipp (and on one occasion she sat on his knees in Lord Brouncker's coach) not to go in search of easier conquests. When she had been Betty Lane, the linen-seller in Westminster Hall had never said no to him, nor did she do so now simply because she was Mrs Martin. 'I did what I tenais a mind pour ferais con her,' wrote Pepys in his inhibited bastard French, but was a little taken aback when she promptly asked for a loan of £5. Obviously she was going to the dogs, but even so from time to time he stalked her beneath the great hammer-beam roof of Westminster Hall. At the end of the year she hinted he was the real father of Mr Martin's child, but even that did not act as a deterrent. More often than not, at least with his other adventures, his inhibitions were so deep-rooted that his love-making went no further than a little indelicate fumbling. Even Mary Mercer's breasts were not to escape Pepys's enfolding hands. At this time he very much had the attitude of 'gather ye rosebuds', intending it seems to have a past to look back on in the winter of his old age: 'The truth is, I do indulge myself a little more in pleasure, knowing that this is the proper age of my life to do it; and, out of my observation that most men that do thrive in the world do forget to take pleasure during the time they are getting their estate, but reserve that till they have got one, and then it is too late for them to enjoy it.'

A few days before delivering himself of that philosophical judgement, Pepys had discovered he was now worth £4,600; and only a few years earlier he had lain in bed with Elizabeth building castles in the air about what they could do when he possessed £2,000: obtain a knighthood and keep a coach and horses. So much for dreams. Since the play-houses would remain shut up for months to come he found himself deprived of a diversion second only to music, and Pepys was reduced to reading plays as he rode in a carriage to and from the dockyards or travelled along the Thames. Thanks to Mrs Knipp and her theatrical friends he could go back-stage at the King's play-house, though it proved rather a disillusioning experience. 'But to see their clothes, and the various sorts, and what a mixture of things there was; here a hobby-horse, there a crown, but make a man split himself to see with laughing; and particularly Lacy's wardrobe, and Shotrell's. But then again to think how fine they show on the stage by candle-light, and how poor things they are to look on too near hand, is not pleasant at all. The machines are fine, and the paintings very pretty.'

Pepys had been as good as his word to Balty, and obtained him the position with the Fleet of Muster Master to a squadron. Later that year he would be gratified at the way his brother-in-law acquitted himself during a series of battles with the Dutch, when the war flared up once again. There was little he could do for his perpetually hard-up father-in-law, short of having him to live in Seething Lane, which he obviously had no intention of doing. But Pepys put a little money in the old man's way by letting him rule paper for use in the Office.

Although from time to time Samuel and Elizabeth chastised their servants—and on one occasion Pepys boxed the ears of young Tom Edwards so hard 'that I do hurt my thumb so much, that I was not able to stir all the day after, and in great pain'—they could not have been bad employers, for after an absence of about two years Jane Wayneman returned to work for them. 'This day, poor Jane, my old, little Jane, come to us again, to my wife's and my great content, and we hope to take mighty pleasure in her, she having all the marks and qualities of a good and loving and honest servant.' But all this was incidental to work at the Navy Office, which still occupied Pepys from early in the morning until, on occasions, late at night. The Navy Board resumed its meetings in London early in January, yet another indication of returning normality.

The news brought from Court by Mr Pierce was not particularly encouraging so far as Lord Sandwich and Sir George Carteret were concerned. My Lord was still blamed for the failure to take the Dutch vessels sheltering in Bergen harbour, and for the premature seizure of prizes, while 'Sir George Carteret is neglected, and hath great enemies at work against him'. Also, it was openly said that the King would not leave Oxford until Lady Castlemaine was up and about again, after being delivered of the future Duke of Northumberland, in a Fellow's chamber at Merton College.

Lord Crewe, father-in-law of Lord Sandwich, sought out Pepys to ask whether he thought the unfortunate Earl would be wise to sue for a pardon for his errors of judgement while at sea (nothing to do with the episode of the prizes taken from the Dutch East Indiamen), before taking up his new post as Ambassador Extraordinary to Spain. Pepys considered the idea favourably, and at the end of the month he went to Hampton Court: 'I found my Lord Sandwich there, poor man! I see with a melancholy face, and suffers his beard to grow on his upper lip more than usual.' Now, Pepys found he would have to use his powers of diplomacy to keep in with all factions. If he walked and talked with Sir William Coventry, who took the Duke of York's side against his patron, it could antagonise both Lord Sandwich and Sir George Carteret; while Sir William might turn against him if he seemed over-friendly with the two who were almost ostracised at Court. But at least he had the good opinion of the Duke of York, who said he had read and approved of Pepys's memorandum on Pursery. As for the King, he said: 'Mr Pepys, I do give you thanks for your good service all this year, and I assure you I am very sensible of it.'

An anxious onlooker to the war was France, who, fearing England's supremacy on the sea if she defeated Holland, sided with the Republic and declared war. This meant that Pepys would be busier than ever in the coming months, and always with the nagging worry of debts. Even if £1½ million were made available, debts now totalled £2,300,000. Getting money for the Navy was like putting water in a bottomless bucket. Not only had accounts been somewhat neglected in the upheavals of moving the Navy Office to and from Greenwich, but Pepys's conscience was pricking him for the way he had neglected to write to his most influential superiors. 'Made a visit to the Duke of Albemarle, and, to my great joy, find him the same man to me he has been heretofore, which I was in great doubt of, through my negligence in not visiting of him a great while; and now having set all to rights there, I shall never suffer matters to run so far backwards again as I have done of late, with reference to my neglecting him and Sir W. Coventry.' But it really was a struggle to keep his mind on his work, as he candidly admitted in the privacy of the Diary: '17th May. To the office, but, Lord! What a conflict I had with myself, my heart tempting me 1000 times to go abroad about some pleasure or other, notwithstanding the weather foul. However, I did not budge; and, to my great content, did a great deal of business.'

Preparations went on for the inevitable renewal of the conflict with the Dutch, and from time to time a pleasant windfall came the way of Pepys, like £200 from merchants named Houblon, five brothers and all in business in the City; or the contract put in his way by Captain Cocke, who 'proposes another proposition of serving us with a thousand tons of hemp, and tells me it shall bring me £500 if the bargain go forward, which is a good word'. June saw the Dutch in the Straits of Dover under their commander De Ruyter, while

Prince Rupert was following up a rumour that the French were also out, further down the Channel. On 2 June it was reported that the Duke of Albemarle was preparing to engage the Dutch off the Thames Estuary. 'Besides, several do aver that they heard the guns yesterday in the afternoon. This put us at the Board in a toss. Presently come orders for our sending away to the fleet a recruit of 200 soldiers.' Pepys went to Greenwich, and there in the park could hear the guns for himself. Out to sea the English and Dutch were locked together in what would become known as the Four Days' Fight. 'Down to Blackwall, and there saw the soldiers, who were by this time gotten most of them drunk, shipped off. But, Lord! to see how the poor fellows kissed their wives and sweethearts in that simple manner at their going off, and shouted, and let off their guns, was strange sport.' As soon as the troops were safely on board Pepys returned to London. On Sunday the news at Whitehall was that three of the largest Dutch men-of-war had been sunk or set on fire, and that the tobacco-chewing Duke of Albemarle had been joined by Prince Rupert's squadron. Later news was contradictory: the Prince had returned to Dover unaware there was a battle taking place a few miles away. Next came a report that the *Henry*, on which Balty was serving as Muster Master, had been surrounded by Dutchmen, and set upon by three fire-ships, but thanks to the bravery of her captain, Harman, she had fought off her assailants, put out a fire and limped home to safety. 'God knows what is become of Balty,' wrote Pepys. On Monday, 4 June, the crash of guns could be heard in London itself, and people flocked into St James's Park to listen. No sooner had Pepys returned to Seething Lane: 'but news is brought me of a couple of men come to speak with me from the Fleet, so I down, and who should it be but Mr Daniel, all muffled up, and his face as black as the chimney, and covered with dirt, pitch, tar, and powder, and muffled in dirty clouts, and his right eye stopped with oakum'. The officer had come ashore at Harwich from the *Royal Charles*. At once Pepys bundled him and his companion into a coach, as far as Somerset House Stairs, where they continued to Whitehall by boat: 'all the world gazing upon us, and concluding it to be news from the Fleet, and everybody's face appeared expecting of news'. At Whitehall they found the King in the park: the news was that the Duke of Albemarle was still un-injured the previous evening, and had been joined by Prince Rupert. Then the two seamen were sent for to tell their own account of the

THE HEART OF THE CITY BEFORE AND AFTER THE GREAT FIRE

by Hollar

Left: St Mary le Bow. *Right*: background, the Guildhall

THE GREAT FIRE AT ITS HEIGHT, 4 SEPTEMBER 1666, *Anon*

In the centre is Old St Paul's immediately before its destruction, while in the foreground Tower Wharf is crowded with the homeless

battle. Next day there was no further real news, but on 6 June came reports that the English had had the best of the fight, though the excellent Captain, Sir Christopher Mings, had been wounded. Of one hundred Dutch ships, not more than fifty would return home. Off Pepys went as fast as he could to spread the good news. 'Away I go by coach to the New Exchange [in the Strand], and there did spread this good news a little, though I find it had broke out before. And so home to our own church, it being a common fast-day [for the plague]. But, Lord! how all the people in the church stared upon me to see me whisper to Sir John Minnes and my Lady Penn.' Soon the news was being passed from pew to pew. Pepys found his own was empty, and decided to take a coach and run his family to earth, wherever they might happen to be. At last he found them all at Will Hewer's lodgings. All the City was celebrating, and the Clerk of the Acts joined his family, friends and acquaintances letting off fireworks in the street. 'By and by comes in our fair neighbour, Mrs Turner, and two neighbour's daughters, Mrs Tite—the eldest of which, a long red-nosed silly jade; the other a pretty black [haired] girl, and the merriest sprightly jade that ever I saw. Idled away the whole night, till twelve at night, at the bonfire in the streets.'

But the next day came disillusionment: it had been no victory for the English. The truth of it was, Albemarle and his old-style captains (referred to as 'tarpaulins') who were seamen through-and-through had been replaced by gentlemen-captains who tried to fight as though engaged in a land battle between Cavaliers and Roundheads. Also, by now, the Duke's tactics were sadly out of date. Ten or twelve years before he had acquitted himself well during the First Dutch War, but now he was limping home with the loss of twenty ships and no less than 8,000 men. According to the seamen, who knew what they were talking about, the Duke of York's tactics had been hopeless, and the only real hero had been Harman of the *Henry*, who had in fact doubted the wisdom of attacking the Dutch in the first place. Sir William Penn, a Bristol sailor all his life, pointed out that ships should fight in line, and not break off in the middle of an engagement to return to port for a refit. The necessity for overall control was one lesson learnt by the English as a result of the Four Days' Fight.

Pepys redoubled his efforts to get the shattered Fleet into a condition when it could set sail again for another confrontation with the Dutch. Money had been obtained from City merchants, and supplies and ammunition sent to the Fleet. At least Balty was safe. '8th June. To my very great joy, I find Balty come home without any hurt, after the utmost imaginable danger he hath gone through in the *Henry*, being upon the quarter-deck with Harman all the time; and for which service, Harman I heard this day commended most seriously and most eminently by the Duke of York.' A few days later Pepys went with Lady Penn and her daughter to see Harman, in bed with a broken ankle, but otherwise recovering well from the fight: 'and a fine person, by his discourse, he seems to be'.

Less fortunate among the Commanders was Sir Christopher Mings, shot in the face and shoulder, for he died from his wounds, and Pepys was invited to his funeral. Afterwards there came a remarkable example of the loyalty and devotion that some commanders could engender in those who served under them, right down to Nelson's time, and beyond. 'There happened this extraordinary case—one of the most romantic that ever I heard of in my life, and could not have believed, but that I did see it; which was this:—About a dozen able, lusty, proper men come to the coach-side with tears in their eyes, and one of them that spoke for the rest begun, and said to Sir W. Coventry, "We are here a dozen of us, that have long known and loved, and served our dead commander, Sir Christopher Mings, and have now done the last office of laying him in the ground. We would be glad we had any other to offer after him, and in revenge of him. All we have is our lives; if you will please to get His Royal Highness to give us a fire-ship among us all, here are a dozen of us, out of all which, choose you one to be commander; and the rest of us, whoever he is, will serve him; and, if possible, do that which shall show our memory of our dead commander, and our revenge." ' Both Pepys and Sir William Coventry were moved to tears, and the latter took their names, promising to do what he could for the men who had served under the shoemaker's son who had been 'a very stout man, and a man of great parts'.

Soon Pepys was to see for himself with what harshness and injustice men such as these were pressed into service, even though he endorsed the system of press-gangs. Men had been taken in the City, pounced on in the open streets, and confined in the Bridewell Prison by the Fleet Ditch. But the Lord Mayor—'a silly man'— lacked even the money to pay them what was their right: an equivalent of 'the Queen's Shilling'. It was Pepys himself who came to the rescue. 'I did out of my own purse disburse £15 to pay for their pressing, and diet last night and this morning.' The next day, 1 July, he was about the business of shipping the men down-river to the Fleet. 'But, Lord! how some poor women did cry; and in my life I never did see such natural expression of passion as I did here, in some women bewailing themselves, and running to every parcel of men that were brought, one after another, to look for their husbands, and wept over every vessel that went off, thinking they might be there, and looking after the ship as far as ever they could by moon-light, that it grieved me to the heart to hear them. Besides, to see poor, patient labouring men and housekeepers, leaving poor wives and families, taken up on a sudden by strangers, was very hard, and that without press-money, but forced against all law to be gone. It is a great tyranny.'

The result of the press-gangs roaming the streets was that within a few days there was hardly an able-bodied man to be seen in the City, though there were plenty of women about. And it was not only the relatives of those caught up by the press-gang who were in need, as Pepys found out. '10th July. To the office; the yard being very full of women, I believe above 300, coming to get money for their husbands and friends that are prisoners in Holland; and they lay clamouring, and swearing, and cursing us, that my wife and I were afraid to send a venison-pasty that we have for supper tonight to the cook's to be baked, for fear of their offering violence to it: but it went, and no hurt done. To the Tower, to speak with Sir John Robinson about the bad condition of the pressed men for want of clothes.' Still he was writing to the Duke of York about the Navy's desperate need for money, and also forwarding Captain Cocke's tender for hemp—for which he would receive £500. That done, he visited Thames Street, to buy five tons of cork to make barricades for the ships, which was immediately dispatched to the Fleet. For one reason or another Pepys's health was affected, and he suffered from the early stages of an ulcer, though he had his own theories as to the possible cause. 'In mighty pain all night long, which I impute to the milk I drank upon so much beer, and the cold, to my washing my feet the night before.'

Back went Balty to rejoin his ship, and Pepys was sure that he would be in the thick of another engagement before he was two days older. For himself, he could only look to the future with fore-boding: the morale of the sailors was at a very low ebb. The captains

were ready to blame anyone except themselves, and especially the
Navy Board, while the gentlemen-captains were a thoroughly
undisciplined group. Since they were for the most part friends of
the King and his circle they were prepared to take orders from no
one except possibly the Duke of York. But at least, thanks to Pepys,
when the Fleet set sail it would have sufficient provisions to remain
at sea for more than a short while. In his opinion they should be the
best provisioned vessels that had ever left harbour, and that thought
encouraged him to think about asking for his own salary. It was not
only the seamen who were behind with their pay.

In fact a week elapsed after Balty's departure before the guns
were heard once again in the park and over Whitehall Palace as the
two fleets again fought it out in the North Sea. News came when
everyone was at church on Sunday, 29 July, telling of a victory:
two large Dutch merchantmen captured and burnt, for the loss of
the *Resolution*. 'This is all, only we keep the sea, which denotes a
victory, or, at least, that we are not beaten; but no great matters to
brag of, God knows.' Perhaps the best news for England was the
fact that in Holland De Ruyter's popularity had waned, for losing
the battle and for the deaths in action of some 5,000 men. It was
even said he dared not come ashore at Flushing, so great was the
hostility. The victory was sufficient in England for public and private
celebration: after attending a service of thanksgiving in the Chapel
Royal, Pepys took Elizabeth and Mercer to the Bear Garden in
Southwark. 'Where I had not been, I think, of many years, and
saw some good sport of the bull's tossing the dogs—one into the
very boxes. But it is a very rude and nasty pleasure.' In the evening
they all went to the house owned by Mary Mercer's mother (near
the modern Fenchurch Street station) where there would be fireworks and a bonfire: 'till about twelve at night, flinging our fireworks, and burning one another, and the people over the way'.
Then, after blacking up each other's faces with soot and candle-
grease to look like devils, the whole party, including Lady Penn
and her daughter Peg, returned to Pepys's house to drink and dance
till four in the morning. Pepys slept late, until after eight o'clock,
and was wakened to receive a letter from Sir William Coventry.
That hot-headed coxcomb Captain Holmes had burnt 160 ships on
the island of Vlieland, landed with about 1,000 men and burnt a
town, before putting to sea again. 'The service is very great, and our
joys as great for it. The guns of the Tower going off, and their being

bonfires also in the street for this late good success.' In June the following year the Dutch had their own humiliating revenge, when 'Holmes' Bonfire' could not have seemed quite such a splendid adventure.

Pepys's preoccupation with the question of whether purple might prove too sombre a colour for 'that melancholy room', his closet, came to a sudden end when the Fleet returned to English waters, and the Admirals complained to the King that when they had asked for provisions all they had received from Pepys were invoices. But he could prove that it was the Admirals who were at fault for not keeping him informed as to their whereabouts or exactly what it was they required. In the end all the Admirals did was to pinpoint their own inefficiency.

Although as loyal as ever to the institution of monarchy, Pepys had few illusions now about the reality of a King and his idle courtiers. These, since there was a war in progress, had at last exhibited some qualms about spending their lives in an endless round of gaming and other amusements. But not knowing what else to do they stayed abed. 'Creed tells me, he finds all things mighty dull at Court; and that they now begin to lie long in bed . . . though there be work enough for their thoughts and councils and pains, they keep long in bed.' Yet while he might in his heart of hearts despise the Court, Pepys also feared its power. Had it not broken his patron Lord Sandwich? And if a scapegoat were wanted for any failings, real or imaginary at the Navy Office, who was more likely to be the victim than his protégé? 'It being a mighty fine cool evening, my wife and I spent an hour in the garden talking of our living in the country, when I shall be turned out of the Office, as I fear the Parliament may find faults enough to remove us all.'

During 1661, when Pepys had been burning the candle at both ends, there had been friction in his marriage; and again in 1666 there were more differences with Elizabeth than there had been in the intervening years. Certainly he gave her cause for jealousy with the attentions paid to such as Mrs Knipp and Mrs Pierce. 'My wife mightily vexed at my being abroad with these women; and, when they had gone, called them I know not what, which vexed me, having been so innocent with them.' Had she but known, the ones Elizabeth should have worried about were Betty Martin and Mrs Bagwell. The latter's grateful husband overtook Pepys walking from Deptford to Redriffe one day, and told him how he fared in his new ship the

185

Providence (obtained for him by the Clerk of the Acts) during the Four Days' Fight. Mary Mercer was another object of jealousy: Pepys had taken to giving her singing lessons, which he never bothered to do with Elizabeth: 'which I acknowledge; but it is because that girl do take music mighty readily, and she [Elizabeth] do not, and music is the thing of the world that I love most'. In Mrs Knipp he found an all-too sympathetic listener when he took her to dine at the very tavern on Fish Street Hill where he and Elizabeth had celebrated their wedding breakfast in 1655. 'And here we talked of the ill-humour of my wife, which I did excuse as much as I could.' Poor misunderstood Pepys, being so understanding about his wife's shortcomings, and wallowing in the sympathy of *la belle* Pierce and Barbary Allen. On one occasion a quarrel with Elizabeth ended with Samuel pulling her nose, which not altogether unexpectedly 'vexed her mightily'.

It seems that at this time Pepys was not in a pacifying frame of mind. 'I and my wife up to her closet, to examine her kitchen accounts, and there I took occasion to fall out with her, for buying a laced handkerchief and pinner without my leave. From this we began both to be angry, and so continued till bed.' But they were only passing squalls, and from time to time that hot dry summer Pepys, Elizabeth and Mercer would go for drives in the evening in a hired coach: to such places as Newington and Islington, to stop and refresh themselves with cakes and ale (a phrase common to Shakespeare, Beaumont and Fletcher and Pepys himself). Though even such outings, when accompanied by the ubiquitous Mrs Knipp and Mrs Pierce, could end in less than perfect harmony. Elizabeth's preferred reading were interminable French romances, which she would then retell in elaborate detail, and in a coach she had a captive audience. 'I find my wife troubled at my checking her last night in the coach, in her long stories out of *Grand Cyrus*, which she would tell, though nothing to the purpose, nor in any good manner. This she took unkindly, and I think I was to blame indeed; but she do find with reason, that, in the company of Pierce, Knipp, or other women, that I love, I do not value her, or mind her as I ought.' But in the pages of the Diary Pepys can always be relied on to provide some little vignette to erase the impression of less than admirable conduct: like the entry for 5 May. 'It being a very fine moonshine, my wife and Mercer come into the garden, and, my business being done, we sang till about twelve at night, with mighty pleasure to ourselves and neighbours, by their casements opening.'

Also, in 1666 Pepys seemed to draw closer to his father, now a frail old man, who came with Pall to stay for a while in Seething Lane. 'Word is brought me that my father and my sister are come: he, poor man, looks very well, and hath rode up this journey on horseback very well, only his eyesight and hearing is very bad.' He was still not over-attached to his sister, and while admitting her figure was better than he had expected, he found her face full of freckles and not handsome. But at meals the table was enlivened by a pet sparrow of Mercer's which she had had for three weeks, and was now so tame 'that it flies up and down, and upon the table, and eats and pecks, and do everything so pleasantly, that we are mightily pleased with it'. While John Pepys was in London, Samuel took him to Hales to have his portrait painted, and in the Diary paid him a generous tribute. 'It joys my very heart to think that I should have his picture so well done; who, besides that he is my father, and a man that loves me, and hath ever done so, is also, at this day, one of the most careful and innocent men in the world.' When the time came for their return to the country, Pepys again recorded how glad he was to be of comfort to him: 'he is such innocent company'. Perhaps without even being aware of it he had been comparing the old man with some of the bugs with gilded wings at Whitehall.

Ever-curious, Pepys now literally widened his horizons when Mr Reeve, who specialised in optical instruments, set up a large telescope on the leads of his house: 'and there we endeavoured to see the moon, and Saturn and Jupiter, but the heavens proved cloudy, and so we lost our labour, having taken pains to get things together, in order to the managing of our new glass'. The next night he was more fortunate: 'though very sleepy, till one in the morning, looking on the moon and Jupiter. So to bed mighty sleepy, but with much pleasure, Reeves lying at my house; and mighty proud I am, and ought to be thankful to God almighty that I am able to have a spare bed for my friends.' A few days later back came Mr Reeves: 'bringing me a lanthorn, with pictures in glass, to make strange things appear on a wall, very pretty. We did also at night see Jupiter and his girdle of satellites, very fine, with my twelve-foot glass, but could not see Saturn, he being very dark.'

Pepys's inquiring mind also took him to hear more Royal Society lectures at Gresham College. One lecture he found particularly pleasing was delivered by the President of the College of Physicians on the subject of respiration: 'that it is not to this day known, or concluded on, among physicians, how the action is managed by nature, or for what use it is'. Near the end of the year Pepys would witness a truly remarkable experiment, almost three hundred years ahead of its time: 'There was a pretty experiment of the blood of one dog let out, till he died, into the body of another on one side, while all his own run out on the other side. The first died upon the place, and the other is very well, and likely to do well . . . as Dr Croune says, may, if it takes, be of mighty use to man's health, for the mending of bad blood by borrowing from a better body.' A fortnight later the dog was still well.

The second of England's three great disasters of the 1660s began on 2 September. '(Lord's Day) Some of our maids sitting up late last night to get things ready against our feast today, Jane called us up about three in the morning, to tell us of a great fire they saw in the City.' Pepys got up, put on his nightgown and went up to look out of the girl's window. It seemed to be somewhere on the far side of Mark Lane, but there had been fires before, so he went back to bed and to sleep. When he looked out at seven in the morning in the daylight it seemed smaller and further off, so he set about tidying up his study which had been cleaned the day before. Then Jane came to him with the news that 300 houses had been burnt in the night and that the fire was spreading down Fish Street Hill towards London Bridge. Obviously it was serious, and off Pepys went to the Tower: 'and there got up upon one of the high places, Sir J. Robinson's little son going up with me; and there I did see the houses at that end of the bridge all on fire, and an infinite great fire on this and the other side of the end of the bridge; which, among other people, did trouble me for poor little Michell and our Sarah [a one-time maid] on the bridge.'

According to Sir John Robinson, it had all started in a baker's shop in Pudding Lane, and already Fish Street and St Magnus Martyr at the end of London Bridge had been destroyed. To make matters worse there had been no rain for weeks and a strong wind, which would reach gale force, was driving the fire westwards along the Thames-side and also into the very heart of the City. Pepys took a boat, shot London Bridge, and on the upstream side surveyed the conflagration. It was burning westwards at an alarming rate, and while he watched it reached the Steelyard, the headquarters of the Hanse merchants. 'Everybody endeavouring to remove their goods, and flinging into the river, or bringing them into lighters that lay off: poor people staying in their houses as long as till the very fire touched them, and then running into boats, or clambering from one pair of stairs, by the waterside, to another. And among other things, the poor pigeons, I perceive, were loth to leave their houses, but hovered about the windows and balconies, till they burned their wings, and fell down.' During that first day there was no organised fire-fighting, though the Lord Mayor had been called to the outbreak in the small hours. Not only did he underestimate the seriousness, commenting that a woman might piss it out, but as a leader he proved worse than useless. When someone suggested making firebreaks by blowing up houses, he promptly pointed out that under a City ordinance anyone who destroyed his neighbour's property was responsible for its rebuilding; and with that he left the scene.

Pepys watched for an hour, noting that everybody was too busy trying to save their own possessions to think about fire-fighting, and then decided it was his duty to go to Whitehall. There he found that no one seemed aware of what was happening only a few miles away, and he was taken at once to the King. He told Charles and the Duke of York that unless orders were given to blow up houses nothing could check the fire. Go to the Lord Mayor, and give him that order, was the gist of the King's reply. Captain Cocke lent him his coach, and together with Creed Pepys drove back into the City as far as St Paul's, whence he continued on foot along Watling Street, against a mounting tide of humanity fleeing from the fire, and among them sick people being borne along on their beds.

'At last met My Lord Mayor in Cannon Street, like a man spent, with a handkercher about his neck. To the King's message, he cried, like a fainting woman, "Lord! What can I do? I am spent: people will not obey me. I have been pulling down houses; but the fire overtakes us faster than we can do it." That he needed no more soldiers; and that, for himself, he must go and refresh himself, having been up all night.'

Only on the Wednesday, when the worst of the fire was over, did Sir Thomas Bludworth reappear on the scene. Had he acted decisively in the first few hours, blown up houses and organised fire-fighting, it is just possible there would have been no Great Fire of London.

First Sarah and her shoemaker husband had been **burnt out on**

the bridge; next Pepys saw St Lawrence Pountney go up in flames—
it had been the church of his old school-fellow Elborough. Now as
he walked back through the City he saw one of the Houblon
brothers quietly awaiting the inevitable near where Cannon Street
Station now stands. 'Here I saw Mr Isaac Houblon, the handsome
man, prettily dressed and dirty at his door at Dowgate, receiving
some of his brothers' things, whose houses were now on fire; and
as he says, have been removed twice already; and he doubts, as it
soon proved, that they must be, in a little time, removed from his
house also, which was a sad consideration.' Pepys returned home
about midday to greet the guests against whose coming the maids
had been up so late the night before. After dinner Pepys and one of
his guests walked back into the City: 'the streets full of nothing but
people; and horses and carts loaden with goods, ready to run over
one another, and removing goods from one burned house to
another.' Only a few hours before people had been moving their
possessions to safety in Cannon Street: already that was threatened,
and another exodus was under way.

Back to the river Pepys went to view the scene from there, and
met the King and the Duke of York, supervising the fire-fighting.
By pulling down houses at the Three Cranes they caused a temporary check: 'but the wind carries it into the City, so as we know
not, by the water-side, what it do there. River full of lighters and
boats taking in goods, and good goods swimming in the water; and
only I observed that hardly one lighter or boat in three that had the
goods of a house in, but there was a pair of virginals in it.' Pepys,
who missed nothing, noticed how the wind was carrying burning
particles ahead of the main blaze: 'With one's face to the wind, you
were almost burned with a shower of fire-drops. This is very true:
so as houses were burned by these drops and flakes of fire, three,
four, nay, five or six houses, one after another.'

Of all contemporary accounts of the fire, perhaps the few lines
which followed were the most vivid of all. Samuel, Elizabeth, Creed,
Wood the mast-maker and his wife, took to a boat to see the disaster
from the Thames. 'When we could endure no more upon the water,
we to a little alehouse on Bankside, over against the Three Cranes,
and there stayed till it was dark almost, and saw the fire grow; and
as it grew darker, appeared more and more; and in corners and upon
steeples, and between churches and houses, as far as we could see
up the hill of the City, in a most horrid, malicious, bloody flame, not

like the fine flame of an ordinary fire. We stayed till, it being darkish, we saw the fire as only one entire arch of fire from this to the other side of the bridge, and in a bow up the hill for an arch of above a mile long: it made me weep to see it. The churches, houses, and all on fire, and flaming at once; and a horrid noise the flames made, and the crackling of the houses at their ruin.'

When they returned to Seething Lane it was to find that poor Tom Hayter, Pepys's Head Clerk, had come to them with the few possessions he could save before his home had been engulfed on Fish Street Hill.

The destruction of the City took about four days and nights, and at no time was the whole area ablaze at once. The fire burnt on a long but narrow front, rather like a field of stubble, as the timber houses were destroyed in a matter of minutes, though the brick hearths and chimneys were usually left intact. In the wake of the destruction were the shells of stone buildings, and scores of burnt-out parish churches, and everywhere the ash, ankle deep, from houses that had been totally consumed.

That evening, a fine moon-lit one it was too, Pepys became anxious for his own house, as news came that the fire was even creeping slowly backwards against the wind: 'and Mr Hayter and I did remove my money and iron chests into my cellar, as thinking that the safest place. And got my bags of gold into my office, ready to carry away, and my chief papers of accounts also there, and my tallies in a box by themselves. So great was our fear, as Sir W. Batten hath carts come out of the country to fetch away his goods this night. We did put Mr Hayter, poor man! to bed a little: but he got but very little rest, so much noise being in my house, taking down of goods.'

In this time of stress Pepys's old adversary, Lady Batten, showed great kindness, lending him a cart to remove his valuables to the house of Sir William Rider (a member of the Tangier Commission) at Bethnal Green. Among the items he took to safety, riding in the cart in his nightgown, was the Diary. When daylight came on Monday morning Pepys set about securing a lighter, and the whole household carried goods over Tower Hill to where it was moored by Tower Dock. Later the Duke of York came to the Navy Office: the direction of the fire-fighting had been entirely entrusted to him. Mary Mercer had gone to help her own mother, which Elizabeth considered unreasonable, and in the ensuing argument with Mrs

Mercer she dismissed the girl on the spot, whereupon her irate mother said she was not a 'prentice girl, to ask leave every time she went abroad. Wearily Pepys recounted (at a later date): 'At night, lay down a little upon a quilt of W. Hewer's in the office, all my own things being packed up or gone; and, after me, my poor wife did the like, we having fed upon the remains of yesterday's dinner, having no fire nor dishes, nor any opportunity of dressing anything.'

To the west of Seething Lane the fire had already burnt the heart out of the City: Sir Thomas Gresham's handsome Royal Exchange was in ruins; Cornhill and Lombard Street were no more, while such churches as St Stephen Walbrook and St Mary Woolnoth were among at least twenty-five destroyed in an area between Thames Street, Billingsgate and as far north as Leadenhall Street. Pepys was lucky to have got his best possessions away on Sunday night. In an attempt to lessen the confusion, on Monday afternoon carts were banned from entry into the City. The congestion near the City gates must have been unbelievable, with carts either over-turned where the streets had been dug up to get at the water-pipes, or else with their wheels wedged together completely blocking the way. People with anything on wheels had started flocking into the City, demanding up to £20 or £30 to remove goods. And all the while England was a country at war, and from time to time rumours swept the City that not only was the fire the work of the Dutch or the French, but that armies had landed and were marching on the capital. In the half-crazed atmosphere indiscriminate, often bestial, attacks took place on almost anyone suspected of being a foreigner.

Pepys was up again at dawn: first busy at the Navy Office, and then getting the remainder of what could be removed from his own house to the lighter still waiting at the quayside. Now the fire was in Tower Street: 'The fire coming on in that narrow street, on both sides, with infinite fury. Sir W. Batten not knowing how to remove his wine, did dig a pit in the garden, and laid it in there; and I took the opportunity of laying all the papers of my office that I could not otherwise dispose of. And in the evening Sir W. Penn and I did dig another, and put our wine in it; and I my parmezan cheese, as well as my wine and some other things.'

In the afternoon he and Sir William Penn were sitting in Pepys's garden, feeling depressed and helpless, when the Clerk of the Acts had an inspiration. Why not send for men from the Woolwich and Deptford dockyards to pull down houses about the Navy Office, so isolating it: 'rather than lose this office, which would much hinder the King's business'. Straightway Pepys wrote to Sir William Coventry, but received no reply. It was in fact the worst day of all for magnitude of destruction (4 September): 'Only now and then, walking into the garden, saw how horribly the sky looks, all on fire in the night, was enough to put us out of our wits; and, indeed, it extremely dreadful, for it looks just as if it was at us, and the whole heaven on fire.' In that wall of fire the Guildhall was burning like 'a great building of Burnished Brass', and would continue to do so for twenty-four hours. Earlier in the day, the fire had swept past Old St Paul's at a terrifying rate, jumped the Fleet Ditch and swept up Fleet Street as far as the Temple, carried forward by the wind which was now at gale force. Then, at about eight o'clock scaffolding set about the cathedral tower for repair work caught fire, and before long the whole vast structure was blazing from end to end: the heat causing the stonework to explode like grenades, and the molten lead from the roofs to cascade inexorably down Ludgate in a glowing all-consuming stream.

At last, when it was almost too late, orders were given for the destruction of timber houses nearest the Tower. Had the fire leapt the walls of the fortress the disaster would have been incalculable. Not only did the White Tower contain the nation's archives, but during the war it had become an arsenal, and was filled with gunpowder. 'Now begins the practice of blowing up of houses in Tower Street, those next the Tower, which at first did frighten people more than anything; but it stopped the fire where it was done.' Will Hewer went to see how his mother was faring, and had to move her out to Islington, for the fire had reached Pie Corner (where it was checked, but where it did *not* end). Again Pepys slept in the Office, to be awakened at about 2 a.m. by Elizabeth with the news that the fire had reached All Hallows Barking, at the end of Seething Lane. Pepys decided it was time to evacuate his own household. Disposing £2,350 in gold about himself, he, Will Hewer and Jane went by boat to Woolwich and to the house of Mr Shelden, the Clerk of the Cheque: 'where I have locked up my gold, and charged my wife and W. Hewer never to leave the room without one of them in it, night or day'. Then he returned to London, expecting to find his house on fire, and not daring to inquire about it as he drew near, till he caught sight of it, intact. As a result of blowing up houses and organised fire-fighting by men from the dockyards, the blaze had actually stopped at Barking Church, burning only the dial of the clock and part of the porch. 'I up to the top of Barking steeple, and there saw the saddest sight of desolation that I ever saw; everywhere great fires, oil-cellars, and brimstone, and other things burning. To Sir W. Penn's, and there eat a piece of cold meat, having eaten nothing since Sunday, but the remains of Sunday's dinner.'

With two flag-makers Pepys walked into the still smouldering City: 'and find Fenchurch Street all in dust. The Exchange a sad sight, nothing standing there, of all the statues or pillars; but Sir Thomas Gresham's picture [statue] in the corner.' Then they trudged on through the ash to Moorfields, where many of the homeless were camping under the stars: 'and find that full of people, and the poor wretches carrying their goods there, and everybody keeping his goods together by themselves; and a great blessing it is to them that it is a fair weather for them to be abroad night and day'. The price of a loaf, they found, had already risen to twopence. Back they went by way of Newgate Market, which like Cheapside no longer existed: nor for that matter did the tavern of which Anthony Joyce had been the landlord. At the Mercers' Hall Pepys stopped to pick up a piece of glass from the once so-beautiful chapel, which had been buckled by the heat. 'I did also see a poor cat taken out of a hole in a chimney, joining to the wall of the Exchange, with the hair all burnt off the body, and yet alive.'

A most remarkable aspect of the Great Fire was that in spite of the speed with which it spread only four deaths could be directly attributed to the disaster. But there was still the risk of it flaring up again, as it did the following morning (6 September), when Pepys went with the men from the dockyard to Bishopsgate to extinguish an isolated outbreak. The men were billeted in the Navy Office itself, and given drink, bread and cheese. There was a further outbreak at the Temple, and in Shoe Lane, but to all intents and purposes the Great Fire of London had burnt itself out, and that Thursday Pepys felt it was safe to go to Westminster: 'thinking to shift for myself, being all in dirt from top to bottom, but could not there find any place to buy a shirt or a pair of gloves, Westminster Hall being full of people's goods'. Later in the day he went downriver to Deptford and unloaded his possessions from the lighter he had hired, stowing them at Sir George Carteret's house until they could be returned to London.

Back he hurried to the City, to spend another night at the Office, but because of all the coming and going by the labourers, sleep was almost impossible. By five o'clock he was up and about again, walking through the City: 'and saw all the town burned, and a miserable sight of Paul's Church, with all the roofs fallen, and the body of the choir fallen into St Faith's; Paul's School also, Ludgate, and Fleet Street. My father's house [in Salisbury Court], and the church [St Bride's], and a good part of the Temple the like.' Then he made his way to Creed's house, where he washed and rested before going on to Sir William Coventry at St James's.

In the midst of fire, war had continued; the news was that the opposing fleets had sighted one another, but then been driven apart by the same wind that had ensured the destruction of the City.

Only five days after the outbreak the City was returning to normal: already the merchants were meeting at Gresham College. But rents were soaring, and Pepys heard of a house that before the fire had brought in £40 a year, and was now fetching £150. Already the King had arranged for £500 to be provided for bread for the homeless, of which there were 100,000 (13,200 houses having been burnt). The magistrates of Middlesex, Surrey and Essex were ordered to open churches, chapels and schools for the storage of goods, while in the immediate area of the fire the churches were to be opened as temporary accommodation for the homeless.

When Pepys returned to Seething Lane it was Sir William Penn who gave him a night's lodging. 'So here I went the first time into a naked bed, only my drawers on; and did sleep pretty well: but still both sleeping and waking had a fear of fire in my heart, that I took little rest.'

While there had been many acts of unselfishness and heroism during the fire, Pepys did not fail also to record displays of meanness and self-centredness, such as that of Alderman Starling who also lived in Seething Lane: 'a very rich man, without children, the fire at next door to him in our lane, after our men had saved his house, did give 2s. 6d. among thirty of them'. Now Pepys was joined by his brother John, who had hurried to London to discover how Samuel had fared. It was Sunday, exactly a week since it all began. Pepys sent his brother to Woolwich to see Elizabeth, while he went to St Olave's, where Mr Mills preached a suitable but melancholy sermon which made everyone cry. In the afternoon he sat in the Office entering up the Diary, committing his account of the fire to loose sheets of paper, till it could be copied out at leisure.

When John returned from Woolwich, where there was nowhere for him to stay, Samuel suggested he should go back to Cambridge. 'But I was very kind to him, and do take very well of him his journey. I did give him 40s. for his pocket, and so, he being gone, and it presently raining, I was troubled for him, though it is good for the fire. Anon to Sir W. Penn's to bed, and make my boy Tom to read me asleep.'

Now Pepys could think about bringing back his possessions from Sir William Rider's house at Bethnal Green, to store them in safety at the Office. But there was a very real risk from thieves, and before going to Woolwich he set Balty—just back from sea—Tooker the Navy Office messenger, and Tom Edwards to watch there all night. At Woolwich all was well, and late the following evening Pepys could relax, in the knowledge that his chests and money were safely stored in the more remote of his cellars. 'So very late and weary to bed.' Elizabeth was back, and also staying in the house were Balty and his wife. But in the midst of getting the house straight and setting up beds, Pepys had to go about his official business. Despite his 'infinite joy' at finding his house once again clean, and lying in his chamber with Elizabeth by his side, his sleep was far from peaceful. 'But much terrified in the nights, now-a-days, with dreams of fire, and falling down of houses.' His was a resilient nature though, and only two days later he could write: 'Up betimes, and shaved myself after a week's growth: but, Lord! how ugly I was yesterday, and how fine today!'

'By water, seeing the City all the way—a sad sight indeed: much fire still being in.' Business had taken him back to Whitehall, to Sir William Coventry. The Dutch fleet had sailed north, and there was anxiety for the convoy bringing timber from Gothenburg, while at the same time there were fears that the English might miss the French fleet, reported to be somewhere in the Channel, altogether. But for him and for the other members of the Navy Board the enemy was very near at hand. Parliament wanted to know where no less than £2 million had gone which it declared had been given to the King, but which now could not be accounted for. The members of the Navy Board would have to appear before a committee at the beginning of October, and Pepys set about preparing detailed accounts. Whether the £2 million had ever existed was open to question, but now the populace was prepared to think the worst of the King, and the story was widely believed. The officers of the King's Navy were responsible for all their actions to Parliament, and now that body was prepared to make them aware of the fact. Like two office messengers Pepys and Sir George Carteret went to Westminster, where the former was to hand in a letter to Sir Philip Warwick, signed by all his colleagues, detailing where money received for the war had gone. Meanwhile, Sir George, his account-book under his arm, had gone to present it to the House itself.

Everything had to be itemised, and lists drawn up for presentation to a sub-committee, and Pepys would have to be there in person when they were handed over. As if there were not trouble enough, highly confidential documents went astray: 'When come home, I to Sir W. Penn's, to his boy, for my book and there find he hath it not; but delivered it to the doorkeeper of the committee for me. This, added to my former disquiet, made me stark mad, considering all the nakedness of the office lay open, in papers within those covers. But . . . I found they had [been] found [by] the housekeeper, and the book simply locked up in the Court.'

October 3 was the day which might have seen the end of Pepys's career: 'Waked betimes, mightily troubled in mind, and in the most true trouble that I ever was in my life, saving in the business last year of the East India prizes.' Sir W. Batten, Sir W. Penn, Lord Brouncker and Sir John Minnes were all called briefly to appear before the Committee. Then it was Pepys's turn. '. . . and left me all the morning with them alone to stand or fall. After dinner to work again, only the Committee and I, till dark night; and it ended with good peace and much seeming satisfaction.' But even at such a time Pepys, together with Penn, Batten and Sir Richard Ford (the merchant), could not resist a little free enterprise. They had in fact begged and borrowed a small vessel, the *Flying Greyhound*, from the King, intending to fit her out and send her to sea as a privateer licenced to prey on enemy merchantmen in time of war. But not all was going smoothly. It had to be made very clear to Anthony Deane at Harwich that they were doing it at their own and not at the nation's expense; while 'W. Penn told me W. Batten swears he will have nothing to do with the Privateer, if his son do not go Lieutenant, which angers me and him; but we will be even with him, one way or another'.

Shortly after the Committee had ended its inquiry, Parliament voted another £1,800,000 for the war, and if credit were given it should have been extended to Pepys for the answers he gave, for it was he who bore the greater part of the interrogation, and he who had prepared the accounts. But what was the use of £1,800,000 even, when most of it would vanish if existing debts were paid? An equal sum was required for future outlay, not merely to settle past expenditure. Unless the Fleet were made ready, England would be open to attack by the Dutch the following summer. Anxiety took Pepys to Whitehall where in front of the King, the Duke of York, Prince Rupert, the Duke of Albemarle, Lord Clarendon and others he spoke up. 'Nobody beginning, I did, and made a current, and I thought, a good speech, laying open the ill state of the Navy: by the greatness of the debt; greatness of the work to do against next year; the time and materials it would take; and our incapacity, through a total want of money.' Prince Rupert, ever a touchy individual, thought Pepys was making a personal attack on him: 'I had no sooner done, but Prince Rupert rose up, and told the King, in a heat, that whatever the gentleman had said, he had brought home his fleet in as good a condition as ever any fleet was brought home, that twenty boats would be as many as the fleet would want.'

Pepys stood his ground, saying that what he had said was based on reports received from the Surveyors. There was a long silence, but nobody backed Prince Rupert, and Pepys withdrew. Later Sir William Coventry told him that the King was prepared to hand over £5,000 or £6,000, a drop in the ocean of the Navy's requirements. 'This is every day a greater and greater omen of ruin,' recorded Pepys prophetically. It was a hopeless situation: the Duke of York was now completely taken up with his mistress, Lady Denham, while the King was so little oppressed by state business that he could find time to declare at a meeting of the Council that he would set a new fashion in simplified clothing, by wearing a long vest-like tunic in the Persian style, and he hoped that in the name of economy that the Court would do likewise. But the scheme misfired: when Louis XIV heard how his English rivals were dressing themselves he promptly put his footmen in a similar rig-out.

What was more, there seemed to be dissension everywhere: the Duke of York was at loggerheads with the Duke of Albemarle, who in his turn was less than in agreement with Prince Rupert; Lord Sandwich was out of the service altogether, disgraced and abroad; and with a Navy to all intents and purposes bankrupt, Pepys's despondency deepened. 'Time spending, and no money to set anything in hand with; the end thereof must be speedy ruin.' He was even thinking of resigning and going to live at Brampton: he who had done more for the Navy in the last five years than anyone was almost defeated.

Before long the Commons slashed the Parliamentary grant by £150,000, which was to be saved by laying up the Fleet. Discipline was bad in the ships, and everything seemed enmeshed in a web of intrigue, spite and professional jealousy. The account Pepys received from one Captain Guy about the sea-fights in June and July made them sound a great deal less creditable and valorous than the man in the street had been led to believe. 'He assures me we were beaten home the last July fight, and that the whole fleet was ashamed to hear of our bonfires.'

Pepys decided to write to the Duke of York. '17th November. In the afternoon shut myself up in my chamber, and there till twelve at night finishing my great letter to the Duke of York, which do lay the ill condition of the Navy so open to him, that, it is impossible if the King and he minds anything of their business, but will operate upon them to set all matters right, and get money to carry on the war, before it be too late, or else lay out for a peace upon any terms.' After obtaining the signatures of several of his colleagues Pepys took his 'great letter', which he considered 'is as good a letter in the manner, and believe it is the worst in the matter of it, as ever come from any office to a prince', to Whitehall to be laid before the King and Council. Although it did not concern Pepys directly, Parliament still wanted an answer about the monies it claimed were unaccounted for by the sovereign.

'8th December. The Great Proviso passed the House of Parliament yesterday: which makes the King and Court mad, the King having given order to my Lord Chamberlain to send to the playhouses and brothels, to bid all the Parliament-men that were there to go to the Parliament presently. This is true, it seems; but it was carried against the Court by thirty or forty voices. It is a Proviso to the Poll Bill [to raise taxes], that there shall be a Committee of nine persons that shall have the inspection upon oath, and power of giving others, of all the accounts of the money given and spent for this war.'

By now Pepys felt so dispirited that he went through all his old letters of the last four or five years, tearing up and burning: 'Which I intend to do quite through all my papers, that I may have nothing by me but what is worth keeping, and fit to be seen, if I should miscarry.'

It was becoming painfully obvious that Charles II's financial and sexual morality were on the same plane. Whilst he had been prepared to offer only £5,000 for the Navy, in the middle of December he cleared Lady Castlemaine's debts, which amounted to £300,000. Pepys also heard that '£400,000 hath gone into the Privy-purse since this war; and that it is that hath consumed so much of our money, and makes the King and Court so mad to be brought to discover it'.

Because of the lack of money, work at the Navy Office had slowed almost to a stop, and Pepys concerned himself more and more with his own affairs, and leading a full social life. His brother John had come down from Cambridge, and was going into the Church, though Samuel had reservations in his heart about the young man's suitability. '7th October. I made my brother, in his cassock, to say his grace this day; but I like his voice ill, that I begin to be sorry he hath taken orders.' He was disconcerted to discover that John had only preached twice in his life. At least he seemed serious-minded, however, so 'I did give him some advice to study pronunciation, but I do fear he will never make a good speaker, nor, I fear, any general good scholar'.

Shortly before the outbreak of the Great Fire, Pepys had been delighted to hear from Orange Moll at the King's Playhouse that the theatres were re-opening, and now with time on his hands he felt justified in enjoying himself with a clear conscience. The new play-house at Whitehall was something of a disappointment when Samuel, Elizabeth, Mr and Mrs Pierce and the inevitable Mrs Knipp went to see *Love in a Tub*—'a silly play'. Not even the presence of the King and Queen, the Duke and Duchess of York and 'all the great ladies of the Court' could make up for the poor acoustics. More to his liking was *The English Monsieur*, at the King's Playhouse. 'And the women do very well; but, above all, little Nelly.' Thanks to Mr and Mrs Pierce, who had received invitations, Pepys managed to smuggle himself into the ball given to celebrate the Queen's birthday, watching the proceedings from a loft or gallery. 'Anon the house grew full, and the candles light, and the King and Queen and all the ladies sat: and it was, indeed, a glorious sight to see Mrs Stuart in black and white lace, and her head and shoulders dressed with diamonds, and the like many great ladies more.' Pepys, the conscience of the Navy, had once again been seduced by the splendour and glitter of the Court and those who were either directly or indirectly responsible for its dangerous condition.

Not only were unpaid seamen from time to time in an ugly mood outside the Navy Office, but in the middle of December Pepys saw about 300 or 400 of them holding a meeting on Tower Hill. 'This made me afraid: so I got home as fast as I could.'

Writing up the Diary in cypher was a strain to Pepys's over-tired eyes, and on Christmas Eve he bought a pair of green spectacles, to see if they would bring any relief. The following day provided an excuse to lie long in bed, while Elizabeth who had been up till four in the morning making mince pies lay longer. After being dismissed by Elizabeth while the fire was at its height, Mary Mercer never came back to Seething Lane as an employee, but the relationship remained friendly, and on a number of occasions she was a guest either at parties or on excursions around London. In her place as companion to Elizabeth was a girl Pepys found adequate, if nothing more. 'I to church, where our parson Mills made a good sermon. Then home, and dined well on some good ribs of beef roasted, and mince pies, only my wife, brother and Barker [the girl], plenty of good wine of my own, and my heart full of true joy; and thanks to God Almighty for the goodness of my condition at this day.' For Pepys, if not for the country as a whole, 1666 had ended well. 'Blessed be to God! and I pray God make me thankful for it, I do find myself worth in money, all good, above £6,200; which is above £1,800 more than I was the last year.' Blessed be to God indeed.

Chapter 11

Shame and Disaster
1667

O F all the years since the end of the Civil War, 1667 was to prove the most disastrous for the nation, and for Pepys the most fraught with trouble of his public life. Scapegoats would be demanded to answer for the humiliation by the Dutch, culminating in the impeachment of Clarendon, the Lord Chancellor.

Since the Restoration, Clarendon had towered over all others politically, and he was equally hated by the frivolous Court, which regarded him not only as out of date, but more particularly as out of sympathy with their code of behaviour; and by the Dissenters who felt his heavy hand while at the same time seeing the open tolerance of Papists at Court. Even the unpaid seamen blamed him for their lot, though that was in fact the fault of a Parliament which was loth to loose the purse-strings for a monarch who could not account for what he had already received. The upshot was that for the nation Clarendon might have been described as a devil everyone knew. His rivals were the close circle of Charles's advisers and policy makers, whom Pepys was very soon referring to as the Cabal; the word formed a convenient mnemonic for the original five members: Clifford, Arlington, Buckingham, Ashley and Lauderdale. The first two were Roman Catholics in all but open profession, while the remainder were to a greater or lesser degree political adventurers of whom the most outstanding was Ashley. He would beget the Whig party—a crystallisation of the discontent of the Dissenters, while the future Tory party would come to stand for High Church and the established order.

Charles II, beneath the wit and self-indulgence, was no mere playboy on the threshold of middle age. His was a complex character, formed surely both by ancestry and the experiences of early life. He may have been King of England, but he was not an English king. The last all-English ancestor he could claim was Elizabeth of York, five generations back. His father was half Scottish and half Danish, while his mother (Henrietta Maria) was the daughter of Henri IV of France, and had Medici blood in her veins. Further back was another Frenchwoman, Mary of Guise, the mother of Mary Stuart. And the treatment of his family in England, culminating in the execution of his father, can have given him no cause to love his fellow-countrymen. Further, up to the age of thirty he had had to live as a poor man in Europe, surviving by his wits and other people's charity. Then suddenly came wealth and a crown.

Never before having had money of his own, he now proceeded to make it fly, and had he not been a king he would undoubtedly, and deservedly, soon have been dunned by his creditors. Consequent on all these things, when Parliament kept him short of gold, he had few scruples about selling out to the French. Theirs was a religion he subscribed to, and a political system he admired. Voltaire may have put the words '*L'état c'est moi*' into the mouth of Louis XIV, but it was a sentiment the Sun King lived up to, and one which his impecunious English cousin would dearly have loved to emulate. Louis for his part was only too willing to allow Charles to become dependent on him financially, since he knew only too well how to manipulate that dependence for his own political ends.

Money was in fact the root of very nearly all evils in England as January 1667 came in: 'being a bitter, cold, frosty day', and nowhere was the result of its shortage more evident than in the Navy. Before the year was over the members of the Navy Board would have to answer for failures which Pepys—at any rate—had long foreseen, and in his repeated requests to the Duke of York for funds had tried to stave off.

The year began in Seething Lane with dinner parties: first at Sir William Penn's house, and then on 4 January at Pepys's, who acted as host to his neighbours and to Lord Brouncker. Among the guests was Peg Penn and her fiancé: 'Mr Lowther, a pretty gentleman, too good for Peg.' Pepys was entertaining in style and revelling in it. 'I did make them all gaze to see themselves served so nobly in plate, and a neat dinner, indeed, though but of seven dishes. At night to sup, and then to cards; and, last of all, to have a flagon of ale and apples, drunk out of a wooden cup, as a Christmas draught, which made all merry; and they full of admiration at my plate.' Accepting someone's hospitality has never stopped people from making derogatory remarks afterwards (an offence Pepys was himself guilty of in a number of entries in the Diary), and a few days later Sir William Warren repeated a remark made by Lord Brouncker about the two very fine flagons given by Mr Gauden the Victualler. 'Sir W. Warren told me, how my Lord Brouncker should take notice of the two flagons he saw at my house at dinner, at my late feast, and merrily, and yet I know enviously, said, I could not come honestly by them. This I am glad to hear, though vexed to see his ignoble soul, but I shall beware of him, and yet it is fit he should see I am no mean fellow, but can live in the world, and have something.'

Consequently, it was with pleasure that Pepys heard in March how his guest's father had come by his peerage: 'with Sir G. Carteret and Sir J. Minnes; and they did talk of my Lord Brouncker, whose father, it seems did give Mr Ashburnham and the present Lord Bristol £1,200 to be made an Irish Lord, and swore the same day that he had not 12d left to pay for his dinner: they made great mirth at this, my Lord Brouncker having lately given great offence both to them and us all, that we are at present mightily displeased with him.'

But passing displeasure with the President of the Royal Society was nothing to Pepys's abiding dislike of Penn and Batten. He had more to say on the subject of Peg's marriage. The ceremony had been private, which in his opinion was to avoid buying new clothes before Easter when the new fashions would be out. Also he wrote: 'Borrowed many things of my kitchen for dressing their dinner.' Later Sir William celebrated the occasion with a dinner. 'It is instead of a wedding dinner for his daughter, whom I saw in paltry clothes, nothing new but a bracelet that her servant [fiancé] had given her, and ugly she is, as heart can wish. A sorry dinner, not anything handsome or clean, but some silver plates they borrowed of me.' Nine months later he was feeling as uncharitable as ever when Peg came to dine. '11th September . . . and Mrs Lowther, who is grown, either through pride or want of manners, a fool, having not a word to say; and as a further mark of a beggarly, proud fool, hath a bracelet of diamonds and rubies about her wrist, and a sixpenny necklace about her neck, and not one good rag of clothes upon her back.'

In 1661, when he was first introduced to Dr Clerke's household at Whitehall, he had been quite disconcerted by Mrs Clerke, who seemed a very *grande dame* indeed. Perhaps she had been unwise

enough to patronise the little Clerk of the Acts, who retaliated by
ensuring her a dubious immortality in the Diary. '. . . so that we had,
with my wife and I, twelve at table, and very good and pleasant
company and a most neat and excellent, but dear dinner; but,
Lord! to see with what way they looked upon all my fine plate was
pleasant; for I made the best show I could, to let them understand
me and my condition, to take down the pride of Mrs Clerke, who
thinks herself very great.'

But that revenge was nothing to the sweetness of the gossip he
received from Mrs Turner. What she told Pepys must have had him
sitting on the edge of his chair, being detrimental to Lord
Brouncker as well as to Sir William and Lady Penn. Details about
the former had come from Mrs Turner at second hand from a maid
in the peer's employment. According to this unimpeachable source
he was extremely hard-up, and Mrs Williams, his mistress, had had
to pawn a jewel: 'and that he do not keep Mrs Williams now for
love, but need, he having another mistress that he keeps in Covent
Garden'. What was to come about Sir William and Lady Penn was
even more interesting to Pepys. At the outset of his career Penn was
a pitiful fellow in the eyes of Mrs Turner, while his first wife
was one of the sourest, dirty women, that ever she saw; that they
took two chambers; one over another, for themselves and child, in
Tower Hill; that for many years together they eat more meals at her
house than at her own'. As for Lady Penn: 'she was a dirty slattern,
with her stockings hanging about her heels, so that afterwards the
people of the whole Hill did say that Mrs Turner had made Mrs
Penn a gentlewoman'.

Sir William's rise in the world had been equally unedifying:
realising that William Coventry was a man to be courted he had
asked Mr Turner to copy out all useful material about the Navy,
giving him £5 for his pains, which he then presented to the Duke of
York's secretary as being all his own work. It was through Penn that
Mr Falconer became Clerk of the Ropeyard at Woolwich, on his
advice giving Coventry £200, and, for his part in the transaction,
settling £80 a year on his daughter Peg. How he came by his estate
was nothing to be proud of either. 'That he was in the late war a
most devilish plunderer, and that got his estate, which he hath in
Ireland, and nothing else.' Pepys's considered opinion of Sir W.
Penn was that he was the most false fellow ever born of woman.

Although Pepys gloried in his acquaintances seeing how he

prospered in the world there were times when Elizabeth's desire to keep abreast of the latest fashions (seen at the theatre) only irritated him. 'Mrs Stuart, very fine, with her locks done up with puffs, as my wife calls them: and several other great ladies had their hair so, though I do not like it; but my wife do mightily—but it is only because she sees it is the fashion.' Later Elizabeth adopted the fashion of wearing fair hair, to her husband's real anger. 'My wife being dressed this day in fair hair did make me so mad, that I spoke not one word to her, though I was ready to burst with anger.' Later he did say what it was that annoyed him: 'swearing several times, which I pray God forgive me for, and bending my fist, that I would not endure it. She, poor wretch, was surprised with it, and made no answer all the way home; but there we parted, and I to the office late, and then home, and without supper to bed, vexed.'

Clothes as well as hair-styles could bring out the worst in Pepys, especially on an empty stomach. 'My wife having dressed herself in a silk dress of a blue petticoat uppermost, and a white satin waistcoat and white hood, though I think she did it because her gown is gone to the tailor's, did, together with my being hungry, which always makes me peevish, made me angry.' But such occurrences were only passing squalls. One morning at the end of February Elizabeth and Samuel lay long in bed, talking about old times: 'how she used to make coal fires, and wash my foul clothes with her own hand for me, poor wretch! in our little room at My Lord Sandwich's; for which I ought for ever to love and admire her, and do'.

In the past Elizabeth had with good reason reproached her husband for giving Mercer music lessons, while not bothering to instruct her. Now he made amends by arranging for one Greeting to teach her the flageolet, while another by the name of Goodgroome was employed to give singing lessons. But Pepys's musical ear was offended by her voice. 'Poor wretch! her ear is so bad that it made me angry, till the poor wretch cried to see me so vexed at her, that I think I will not discourage her so much again.' Later he came to the conclusion that one day she would sing admirably: 'and to trill in time, which pleases me well'. But progress was slow, and eventually he struck a bargain with Goodgroome, that he should be paid 10s. for each song she really learned to sing. Her progress on the flageolet was better, and even gave pleasure to her exacting husband.

Though the King preferred French music, it was already the

Italian style that was beginning to dominate—a domination which would last for a century and a quarter. Tom Killigrew had visited Rome eight or ten times, to hear the new music, and now he was introducing it to London, especially at Lord Brouncker's house, where both Pepys and Dr Wren were among the privileged audience. Pepys was fascinated, considering that the Italian musicians kept better time than their English counterparts; but their compositions were inferior to the native growth, and much as he enjoyed Mrs Knipp's singing he preferred to reserve judgement since he could not compare the relationship between words and music. But the two castrati he found most curious: 'two eunuchs, so tall, that Sir T. Harvey said well that he believes that they do grow large as our oxen do, and one woman very well dressed and handsome enough, but would not be kissed, as Mr Killigrew, who brought the company in, did acquaint us'. The musicians, lured 'from several courts in Christendom', were expensive, with salaries of £200 a year each (paid by the King), who came in place of 'four ridiculous gundilows [gondolas given by the Doge of Venice], he [Killigrew] having got the King to put them away, lay out this money; and indeed I do commend him for it, for I think it is a very noble undertaking'. When it came to music Pepys was human enough to let his own preferences override disapproval of the King's undoubted extravagance.

Of all musical instruments there can be few less likely to leave a museum than the Marine Trumpet: an outlandish name for an outlandish looking and sounding instrument. It resembled a seventeenth-century wooden speaking trumpet as used in the Fleet, and had one string, played with a bow in the manner of a double bass. The coarse and limited sound produced was thought to be not unlike that of a trumpet, and it was seen and heard by the ubiquitous Pepys at the house where his father-in-law had once lodged. 'We went in to see ... one Monsieur Prin, play on the trump-marine, which he do beyond belief; and, the truth is, it do so far outdo a trumpet as nothing more, and he do play anything very true. The instrument is open at the end, I discovered, but he would not let me look into it.'

Pepys's old enthusiasm for the theatre returned in 1667 with greater force than ever: one week he would visit the play-house no less than six times. Part of the enjoyment sprang from watching little Mrs Knipp, whether acting, dancing, or listening to her singing in

Italian or English. His judgement was already biased in her favour, and Tom Killigrew told him that in his opinion she was likely to be one of the best actresses on the stage, and he was in fact increasing her salary by £30 a year. Through Mrs Knipp, Pepys came to know several of the actors at the Duke's Playhouse, and invited them to Seething Lane. The party started at his house, but soon they—and four fiddlers—all moved to the Office, continuing singing and dancing until three in the morning. Mercer as well as Mrs Knipp and *la belle* Pierce were there, to Pepys's delight. Towards the end of the party Mrs Knipp felt slightly unwell, and was taken to lie down on Elizabeth's bed, which gave Pepys the opportunity for a little quick fondling. The only thing to mar the evening's pleasure were the four fiddlers: 'they not being contented with less than 30s'.

The Merry Wives of Windsor failed to please. But this was more than made up for by *Macbeth*, which Pepys saw twice within a few days: 'a most excellent play in all respects, but especially in divertisment, though it be a deep tragedy; which is a strange perfection in a tragedy, it being most proper here, and suitable'. Evidently, Pepys's vow of not visiting the theatre without Elizabeth still held good, which robbed him of the opportunity of telling how he was present at a first night which developed into a scandal. A new play was being given at the King's Theatre: *The Change of Crowns* by Edward Howard. All the Court was present and the house packed. Pepys was lucky, even though he had to stand by a draughty door: many others were turned away. It was about a country gentleman who comes to London and to Court, 'who do abuse them with all imaginable wit and plainness about selling of places, and doing everything for money'. Back he went the next day with Elizabeth, only to find the play had been changed to Ben Jonson's *The Silent Woman*. It was Mrs Knipp who told him all the details. The King was not amused by *The Change of Crowns*, and sent for the leading actor 'to abuse him to his face, and forbad them to give the play again. The King mighty angry; and it was bitter indeed, but very fine and witty. Pretty to hear them talk of yesterday's play, and I durst not own to my wife that I had seen it.'

That same week Pepys saw a further four plays, excusing his indulgence in the Diary with the comment: 'The Duke of York and W. Coventry gone to Portsmouth, makes me thus go to plays.' But his behaviour was not passing unnoticed, and Elizabeth repeated Will Hewer's advice that the clerks in the Office were talking:

'which I confess, and am ashamed of, and so from this day take upon me to leave it till Whit Sunday'. He was in fact back at the play-house ten days later.

Pepys frequently had the good fortune to meet people who were either famous or about to become so: and so it was with 'pretty witty Nell', whom he met while he was playing the admirer to Mrs Knipp. The little actress brought her friend to meet Samuel and Elizabeth in a box at the King's Playhouse. 'And Knipp took us all in, and brought to us Nelly, a most pretty woman, who acted the great part of Coelia today very fine [in *The Humerous Lieutenant*], and did it pretty well: I kissed her, and so did my wife; and a mighty pretty soul she is.' Soon after he saw her in Dryden's *The Maiden Queen*, first as a mad girl and then in a travesty role as a young gallant. 'It makes me, I confess, admire her.' He again saw her on May Day. 'To Westminster; and in the way meeting many milk-maids with their garlands upon their pails, dancing with a fiddler before them; and saw pretty Nelly standing at her lodgings door in Drury Lane in her smock sleeves and bodice, looking upon me: she seemed a mighty pretty creature.' Indeed, she would capture not only the heart of a King, but those of many generations to come.

Thanks to Mrs Knipp, Pepys had the pleasure of being admitted into the women's dressing-rooms, 'where Nell was dressing herself, and was all unready, and is very pretty, prettier than I thought'. Then they went into the scene room where Pepys was plied with fruit by Nell, and then took Mrs Knipp through her lines in the play *Flora's Vagaries*. But something in him was revolted by their make-up and by their male companions who drifted in and out. 'How lewdly they talk! and how poor the men are in clothes and yet what a show they make on the stage by candle-light, is very observable. But to see how Nell cursed, for having so few people in the pit, was pretty; the other house carrying away all the people at the new play, and is said, nowadays, to have generally most company, as being better players.' To his concern Nell Gwynn had become the mistress of Lord Buckhurst, receiving £100 a year, but contrary to rumour it had not meant her retirement from the stage. The little Cockney, better in comedy than as a straight actress, was seldom at a loss for words, as when she fell out with Beck Marshall, who had called her Lord Buckhurst's mistress. 'Nell answered her, "I was but one man's mistress, though I was brought up in a brothel to fill strong waters to the gentlemen; and you are a mistress to three or four, though a Presbyter's praying daughter!" ' By the time Pepys made her acquaintance Nell Gwynn had graduated from selling oranges in the play-house to actress, but there was at that time at the King's Playhouse one who must have been an archetypal Restoration doxy: Orange Moll. On one occasion, Pepys was at a performance of *Henry IV*—the only part he liked was Falstaff's speech on honour—'and it was observable how a gentleman of good habit, sitting just before us, eating of some fruit in the midst of the play, did drop down as dead, being choked; but with much ado Orange Moll did thrust her finger down his throat, and brought him to life again'.

A play which improved on further acquaintance was *The Tempest*. After a first visit Pepys considered it the most innocent play he had ever seen, and though having 'no great wit, but yet good, above ordinary plays'. After a second visit he considered it very pleasant, and full of good variety, that apart from the tediousness of the seaman's part, he could not have been more pleased by a comedy. But now, in the middle of November, his conscience was beginning to prick and he vowed he would only go to the theatre every other week until after Christmas, or give £10 as a forfeit to the poor. He kept his vow, and then saw three plays before the year's end.

There were other pleasures to be enjoyed besides theatre-going, including a visit to a prize-fight at the Bear Garden in Southwark, between a waterman and a butcher. The place was so crowded he had to go into the bear-pit itself to watch the contest, standing on a stool. It was a fight with swords, and when the waterman dropped his weapon the butcher gave him a quick slash across the wrist, so ending the contest. 'But, Lord! to see how in a minute the whole stage was full of watermen to revenge the foul play, and the butchers to defend their fellow, though most blamed him; and there they all fell to it knocking down and cutting many on each side.' There were other less violent pleasures, like buying a hundred pieces of sparrow-grass (asparagus) in Fenchurch Street for 18*d*. on the way home. 'We had them and a little bit of salmon, which my wife had a mind to, cost 3s. So to supper.' As in other years Pepys, the patriarch, would take Elizabeth and his household for outings, to Islington or Newington, or across the water to Vauxhall and Spring Garden, where a man could spend little or nothing, and still enjoy himself. 'To hear the nightingale, and other birds, and hear fiddles, and there a harp, and here a Jew's trump, and here laughing, and there fine people walking, is mighty diverting.' When Pepys saw two pretty unaccompanied women being pestered by 'some idle gentlemen' he was relieved when they took to a boat to escape their unwelcome attentions. 'I was troubled to see them abused so; and could have found it in my heart, as little desire of fighting as I have, to have protected the ladies.'

Perhaps Pepys's greatest pleasure, and one for which posterity should be grateful, was simply that of observing the passing scene, and all the infinite variations that go to make up the human race. This he did in no uncertain manner one Sunday afternoon in May in St Margaret's, Westminster. Evidently he had a small telescope with him. 'After dinner I by water alone to Westminster to the parish church, and there did entertain myself with my perspective glass up and down the church, by which I had the great pleasure of seeing and gazing at a great many very fine women; and what with that, and sleeping, I passed away the time till sermon was done.'

In March his life had been shadowed first by the news of the illness of his mother at Brampton, and then, on 27th of the same month, another letter came from his brother John. 'Received from my brother the news of my mother's dying on Monday, about five or six o'clock in the afternoon, and that the last time she spoke of her children was on Friday last, and her last words were, "God bless my poor Sam!" ' Pepys wept heartily, and then ever practical, went with Elizabeth to buy mourning clothes to send to his family in the country. He also decided his whole household should go into mourning, including Will Hewer, Tom Edwards, and even the two under-maids. 'So to my tailor's, and up and down, and then home, and to bed, my heart sad, though my judgement at ease.'

But everything in that year of 1667 was incidental in Pepys's life to the war with Holland, which reached its climax—as far as he was concerned—in June, though the repercussions would continue rumbling on well into 1668. For months he had been predicting disaster if more money were not forthcoming for the Navy, and soon he would be proved right. What could he do though when such as Lord Ashley refused to let the Navy have timber and hemp taken as a prize of war, but insisted that it must be sold so he could claim part of the profit for himself: 'at which I am astonished, and will never wonder at the ruin of the King's affairs, if this be suffered'.

In Parliament, the Lords and Commons were at odds, and all was not harmonious in the Navy Office. In his heart-of-hearts Pepys now considered old Sir John Minnes as incompetent as he was toothless, and of course he had no illusions about 'both Sir Williams'. His opinion of Lord Brouncker was no higher: a rotten-hearted false man of whom he must beware. In particular with the Commissioner of the Navy Board it was on Pepys's part a case of hostile neutrality, summed up in an entry in the Diary for 29 January. 'To the office where Sir W. Penn and I look much askew one upon another, though afterward business made us speak friendly enough, but yet we hate one another.' There was comfort, however, to be drawn from his position of Surveyor-General of the Navy, as well as the fruits from Tangier, which continued to swell Pepys's money-chests. On 4 February Denis Gauden the Victualler parted with £500 as a thank-you for the continuance of his contract to victual the Navy, together with another £100 for supplying the garrison at Tangier. But only a few days later instinct told Pepys actually to refuse a bribe. 'There come to me Mr Young and Whistler, flag-makers, and with a mighty earnestness did present me with, and press me to take a box, wherein I could not guess there was less than £100 in gold; but I did wholly refuse it. The truth is, not thinking them safe men to receive such a gratuity from . . . but desirous to keep myself free from their reports, and to have it in my power to say I had refused their offer.'

Private gain did not lessen Pepys's concern for the Navy's penury, and he took pains to point out to the Duke of York that its debts now passed the million mark, while all the King would allow from the provisions of the Poll Bill was a paltry £35,000, and that was meant to be enough to prepare the Fleet for active service. Now more seamen and dockyard workers were to be paid off (just when their services were likely to be needed) and there was not enough to pay the men in cash, with the inevitable result. 'There was a very great disorder this day [13 February] at the Ticket Office, to the beating and bruising of the face of Carcasse [Clerk of the Ticket Office, later proved to be dishonest] very much. 14th. To the office, where Carcasse comes with his plastered face, and called himself Sir W. Batten's martyr, which made W. Batten mad almost, and mighty quarrelling there was.'

There was talk of a treaty with Holland and it was said the Dutch were in great straits, and would not be able to put a fleet to sea during the coming summer. If ever there were a case of wishful thinking, that was it. In March the King announced his plans for the Fleet. As an economy the battle fleet, which included great warships such

HOWLAND GREAT DOCK, NEAR DEPTFORD

by J. Kip, after Bastide

FUNERAL EFFIGY OF KING CHARLES II, IN WAX

as the *Royal Charles*, would be laid up, and only a few squadrons of small vessels maintained to prey on the Dutch merchantmen. For defence England would rely on the fortifying and strengthening of Sheerness and Portsmouth to resist a possible invasion. And with that the King returned to matters of greater moment, such as maintaining the peace between Lady Castlemaine and Mrs Stuart. Pepys left a mordant thumb-nail sketch of his sovereign at a meeting of the Council: 'all I observed there is the sillyness of the King, playing with his dog all the while, and not minding the business; and what he said was mighty weak'. But then he did not see the reality of his policy as it affected his own seamen: 'This day a poor seaman, almost starved for want of food, lay in our yard a-dying. I sent him half-a-crown, and we ordered his ticket to be paid.'

Both the King and the Duke of York visited Harwich and Sheerness to supervise the preparations for defence, which infuriated Pepys, who considered the Lord High Admiral's place was at sea, especially after all the defiance that had been hurled at the Dutch. It fell to Sir William Penn to decide what should be done at Chatham to fortify the Medway, where the main part of the Fleet lay, disarmed and even dismasted: a sitting target if ever there was one. In Penn's opinion a chain should be stretched across the river to prevent the Dutch sailing right up to the Fleet, which should retain at least some guns to defend itself from fire-ships.

Since the Fleet was immobilised, all the English could do was wait for the Dutch to make the first move, which they did when the weather improved. On 8 June, eighty Dutch ships were reported off Harwich, and gunfire could be heard at Bethnal Green. The King ordered the eastern counties to be put on a war footing, and sent several of his Court to lead the defenders, which drew a cynical comment from Pepys: 'but to little purpose, I fear, but to debauch the country women thereabouts'. The next day the seriousness of the situation was borne home: the Dutch had sailed up the Thames Estuary as far as the Nore, and an order had come to the Navy Office for fire-ships. That day old Sir John Minnes had gone down-river with money to pay some of the crews of the ships at the Hope (between Gravesend and Canvey Island), but because of the proximity of the Dutch, he returned it undistributed. Pepys hurried to Gravesend, where already the inhabitants were starting to evacuate their possessions. 'Where I find the Duke of Albemarle just come, with a great many idle lords and gentlemen, with their pistols and fooleries; and the bulwark [blockhouse] not able to have stood half an hour had they [the Dutch] come up.' The next morning, 11 June, word came from Commissioner Pett that after a half-hearted fight of two or three hours' duration Sheerness had been captured by a Dutch landing-party of about 800 men. The garrison had, in fact, run like rabbits. Presumably the money which Sir John Minnes should have paid out to the sailors had been taken to the Navy Office, for on Will Hewer's advice, Pepys chose this of all moments to claim his unpaid salary, amounting to £400, which Hewer received for him. Whilst public-spirited to a degree quite unknown to most of his colleagues, Pepys also had a strong instinct for self-protection.

Later that day Pepys received orders from the Council giving him powers to commandeer any vessels he chose to be used as fire-ships: while in the City the drums were beating up and down the streets to call out the Train Bands (Defence Volunteers) 'upon pain of death to appear in arms tomorrow morning, with bullet and powder, and money to supply themselves with victuals for a fortnight'. The next day the Dutch did nothing but lie at anchor: 'and the Duke of Albemarle writes that all is safe as to the great ships fortified against any assault, the boom and chain being so fortified; which put my heart into great joy'. But Pepys's joy was short-lived: soon came news that the Dutch had burst through the boom, and at Court everyone was in tears, or so it seemed.

Without seeing anyone of consequence Pepys—in his own words —slunk out of Whitehall and took a coach back to the City. Hourly the news was growing worse. 'Home, where all our hearts do now ache; for the news is true, that the Dutch have broke the chain and burned our ships, and particularly the *Royal Charles*.' Of all vessels in the Fleet, the *Charles* meant most to Pepys. He had made his rendezvous with the future Lord Sandwich on the *Naseby*, as she then was, in Danish waters. Later he had crossed and recrossed the North Sea in her during those exhilarating weeks culminating in the Restoration. But in fact the *Royal Charles* had not been burnt: her fate was, if possible, even more humiliating, for eventually she was towed out of the river and taken back to Holland as a prize of war.

Pepys was filled with foreboding. He had grown up during a civil war, and now he feared revolution. His father was in London at this time. 'I took him and my wife up to her chamber, and shut the door, and there told them the sad state of the times, how we are like all to be undone; that I do fear some violence will be offered to this office, where all I have in the world is, and resolved upon sending it away.'

As soon as he was up the following morning, Pepys heard what had actually happened at Chatham. Instead of having vessels such as the *Royal Charles* towed further up the Medway out of harm's way, Commissioner Pett had busied himself going from one ship to another removing his own models from them. Certainly the beautifully constructed models were valuable, being like three-dimensional blueprints, but he had bungled badly, and in Pepys's opinion deserved to hang for it. More than ever he felt it was a case of *sauve qui peut*, and at two hours' notice packed off his father and Elizabeth to Brampton by coach, with £1,300 in gold in their night-bag. Then he sent reliable Will Hewer to Alderman Backwell, the goldsmith, to draw out £500 deposited with him: 'but they are so called upon that they will all be broke, hundreds coming to them for money'. Soon Gibson, an office clerk, was riding after Elizabeth and John Pepys with 1,000 gold pieces, 'under colour of an express to Sir Jeremy Smith; who is, as I hear, with some ships at Newcastle'. For a while Pepys even considered throwing his silver into the privy, but then had second thoughts: 'how shall I come by it, if we are made to leave the office?'

That evening Pepys sent for Sarah Gyles, his cousin, to come to Seething Lane. He handed over for safe keeping papers relating to the estate and Brampton, and even his Diary, 'which I value much'. His two handsome silver flagons, given by Denis Gauden, were sent to Kate Joyce, and he even had a belt made: 'by which, with some trouble, I do carry about me £300 in gold about my body, that I may not be without something in case I should be surprised.'

The mood of the City bordered on panic. Everywhere people were removing themselves and their goods to safety; talking of treachery and blaming the Papists. Those at Court refused to believe the disaster was the result of their sovereign's short-sighted policy, and looked for scapegoats in the Ordinance Office for not having supplied gunpowder for Chatham's defence, and for allowing Upnor Castle to have been dismantled. Now there was talk of an invasion by the French, who were supposed to be massing an army at Dunkirk (itself recently sold back to the French by Charles II), while another Dutch fleet was reported in the Thames Estuary.

'Holmes's Bonfire' of the previous summer was coming home to roost in terrible fashion, and the very real fear was that the Dutch would sail right up the Thames and make a second bonfire of what remained of the City below London Bridge. Orders were given to sink vessels in the fairway at Woolwich, but in the confusion supply ships meant for defenders at Gravesend were scuttled, with munitions worth £80,000 on board. It was as disastrous a week as England had ever known.

On 14 June Pepys received an eye-witness account of the happenings at Chatham when the *Royal James*, the *Royal Oak* and the *London* were burnt. 'They all lying dry, and boats going from the men-of-war to fire them. But that, that he [Mr Hudson, a cooper] tells me of worst consequence is, that he himself, I think he said, did hear many Englishmen on board the Dutch ships speaking to one another in English; and that they did cry and say: "We did heretofore fight for tickets; now we fight for dollars." ' What was more seamen were now holding the nation to ransom at the Navy Office. Several came to Pepys and told him outright that if their tickets were not changed into money they would go and fight the Dutch, otherwise they were not prepared to risk their lives: 'so that I was forced to try what I could do to get them paid'. Also, there was open disaffection at Wapping. There the seamen's wives roamed the streets shouting: 'This comes of your not paying our husbands; and now your work is undone, or done by the hands that understand it not.' Sir William Batten was abused by one such woman on Tower Hill, and at the Navy Office a man was set to guard the door lest anyone should slip in and set fire to the building.

While ashamed that he had heard nothing from his colleagues at Chatham that he could pass on to inquirers who called at the Office, Pepys was honest enough to admit he was glad to be out of danger and near his own home: 'yet in a place of doing the King good service'. Everybody was blaming everyone else, but one bright spot for Pepys was the return from Brampton of the clerk Gibson: the money was safe in the country, whatever might happen in the capital. For the moment there was nothing he could do: if he were removed from office, so be it. 'Home and to my flageolet. Played with pleasure, but with a heavy heart, only it pleased me to think how it may please God I may live and spend my time in the country with plainness and pleasure, though but with little glory.'

Pepys had to wait only another forty-eight hours before he, and

the rest of the country, knew who the scapegoat was to be. '18th
June. To the office, and by and by word was brought me that Commissioner Pett is brought to the Tower, and there laid up close
prisoner; which put me into a fright, lest they may do the same with
us as they do with him.' The following day an order came from the
Council telling him to attend with all the books and papers which
were relevant to the Medway. The thought crossed Pepys's mind
that he would be the target for their wrath, but then reasoned it
must be in connection with Peter Pett. Among those he had to face
was the Duke of Albemarle and all members of the Cabal.'Then
was Peter Pett called in, with the Lieutenant of the Tower. He is
in his old clothes, and looked most sillily.' What was more his
answers were foolish to the charge concerning the removal of his
models. Several of the Council commented that they wished the
Dutch had the models but not the King's ships. At that Pett
answered 'he did believe the Dutch would have made more advantage of the models than of the ships, and that the King had had
(and would have had) the greater loss thereby: this they all laughed
at'.

That he was not in disgrace must have been brought home to
Pepys when Lord Arlington instructed Sir Richard Browne, the
Clerk of the Council, to hand over his own minutes to him: 'to put
into form, I being more acquainted with such business: and they
were so. So I away back to my books and papers; and when I got
out into the Court it was pretty to see how people gazed upon me,
that I thought myself obliged to salute people and to smile, lest they
should think I was a prisoner too: but afterwards I found that most
did take me to be there to bear evidence against P. Pett.' However,
he knew only too well how quickly a man's fortunes could change,
and gave Tom Hayter the key of his study, telling him where to
discover more than £500 in gold and silver should he too find
himself in the Tower. Soon his wife returned: to complete the
undermining of his peace of mind, by telling him how she and his
father had disposed of his gold. 'My father and she did it on Sunday,
when they [other people] were gone to church, in open daylight, in
the midst of the garden; where, for aught they knew, many eyes might
have seen them.' What a world he lived in: at any moment he
might lose his job; the Dutch were blockading the Thames; thieves
might be digging up his gold, and as for the King—the night the
Dutch burnt the Fleet and the dockyard 'the King did sup with my

Lady Castlemaine, at the Duchess of Monmouth's, and them were all mad the hunting of a poor moth'. That piece of gossip was passed on by Sir Hugh Chomley of the Tangier Commission. Captain Cocke's account of the Court was little more reassuring: 'He tells me, speaking of the horrid effeminacy of the King, that the King hath ten times more care and pains in making friends between my Lady Castlemaine and Mrs Stuart, when they have fallen out, than ever he did to save his kingdom.'

At three in the morning of 30 June, he and John Creed took coach for Chatham. Such was Pepys's nature that even at such a time he could enjoy the ride in the cool of a fine summer morning. At Chatham he climbed the hill above the dockyard to look across to Sheerness and to where the Dutch fleet had lain, but now all that remained was one solitary vessel. The weather had changed: 'it raining hard, down to the chain; and in our way did see the sad wrecks of the poor *Royal Oak*, *James*, and *London*; and several other of our ships by us sunk, and several of the enemy's, where three men-of-war that they could not get off, and so burned. I went on shore on Upnor side to look upon the end of the chain; and caused the link to be measured, and it was six inches and one-fourth in circumference.' That the Dutch had been able to break through the chain was in part due to the fact that as they came up the Medway on a high spring tide they also had a strong wind astern of them. With regret Pepys also noted in the Diary that when the enemy had landed their men had behaved in an exemplary fashion, killing no one, and neither looting nor burning private houses, which was more than could be said for the English soldiers sent to defend the area. 'They plundered and took all away; and the watermen that carried us did further tell us, that our own soldiers are far more terrible to those people of the country-towns than the Dutch themselves. Our great ships that were run aground and sunk are all well raised but the *Vanguard*, which they go about to raise tomorrow. The *Henry*, being let loose to drive up the river of herself, did run up as high as the bridge, and so back again with the tide, and up again, and then berthed herself so well as no pilot could ever have done better.'

Later Pepys was to have an eye-witness account of the débâcle from Balty's wife, who at the time was at Leigh, in Essex. 'My sister Michell [St Michel] come from Lee to see us; but do tattle so much of the late business of the Dutch coming thither that I am weary of it. Yet it is worth remembering what she says, that she hath heard both seamen and soldiers swear they would rather serve the Dutch than the King, for they should be better used. She saw the *Royal Charles* brought into the river by them; and how they shot off their great guns for joy, when they got her out of Chatham River.'

After a conversation in a tavern at Lord Brouncker's bedside ('and find him a very weak man for this business that he is upon; and do pity the King's service') Pepys and Creed went by coach— dozing on the way—to inspect the defences at Gravesend. There Pepys was embarrassed by the outspoken criticism of the way ships laded with much needed munitions and supplies had been sunk in the fairway in mistake for empty vessels: all the actions of the Navy Board's officers were being openly questioned, and 'the meanest people do begin to see through them, and condemn them'.

In spite of the body-blow administered by the Dutch to both the Fleet and to English prestige, the plans for a peace between the two countries were still going ahead. On 8 July, Sir William Coventry returned from Breda, bringing the terms, which included revision of the contentious Navigation Act; a definition of what constituted contraband goods; and freedom from further persecution for refugees who might flee to Holland.

After all the storm and stress of the previous few weeks, Pepys decided a day on Epsom Downs would make a pleasant change for himself, Elizabeth and Mrs Turner. With them went Will Hewer on horseback. The evening before Pepys had arranged for a coach to be ready to make an early start: at 5 a.m., in spite of being delayed by Elizabeth taking so long to dress. With them they took wine, beer and cold chicken, and despite the way being dusty they enjoyed the drive: 'talking all the way pleasantly, and particularly of the pride and ignorance of Mrs Lowther [Sir William Penn's daughter]'. At Epsom, Pepys drank no less than four pints of the water, and was fascinated to learn that Lord Buckhurst and Nell Gwynn were lodging at the house next to the King's Head. 'Poor girl! I pity her: but more the loss of her at the King's [play-] house.' But the loss to the theatrical world was only very temporary; Nell was soon back on the stage.

After dinner the whole party lay down in the inn, it being an extremely hot day, and slept for a while. Then Samuel showed them the house which used to belong to his cousin, and where as a small boy he had stayed, playing in the garden and stuffing himself with mulberries. As is so often the case, the house seemed much smaller than it had done all those summers ago, when Cavalier was preparing to fight Roundhead. Then came an interlude—an English pastoral scene, which in its way is as evocative as anything he wrote of the Plague or the Great Fire. The party walked on the Downs.

'We found a shepherd and his little boy reading, far from any houses or sight of people, the Bible to him; so I made the boy read to me, which he did, with the forced tone that children usually do read, that was mighty pretty, and then I did give him something, and went to the father. He did content himself mightily in my liking of his boy's reading, and did bless God for him, the most like one of the old patriarchs that ever I saw in my life, and it brought those thoughts of the old age of the world in my mind for two or three days after. We took notice of his woolen knit stockings of two colours mixed, and of his shoes shod with iron, both at the toe and heels, and with great nails in the soles of his feet, which was mighty pretty; and, taking notice of them, why, says the poor man, the downs, you see, are full of stones, and we are fain to shoe ourselves thus; and these, says he, will make the stones fly till they ring before me. I did give the poor man something, for which he was mighty thankful, and I tried to cast stones with his horn crook. He values his dog mightily, that would turn a sheep any way which he would have him, when he goes to fold them: told me that there was about eighteen score sheep in his flock, and that he hath four shillings a week the year round for keeping of them: and Mrs Turner, in the common fields here, did gather one of the prettiest nosegays that ever I saw in my life . . .'

Back they went to rejoin their coach, 'and through Epsom town to our inn, in the way stopping a poor woman with her milk-pail, and in one of my gilt tumblers, did drink our bellyfuls of milk, better than any cream'. At seven they set out on the return journey, passing families taking the air on this beautiful Sunday evening, and quietly retelling to each other of the day's pleasures. Mrs Turner was particularly pleased when Pepys decided not to buy a house in the country, but to acquire a coach and horses of his own, and make visits into the peace and quiet of rural England at the weekends, such as they had just enjoyed. There would be more variety, he decided, and at no greater cost than if he had a place in the country. On the walk on the Downs Pepys had sprained his right ankle jumping down a bank. 'Anon it grew dark, and we had the pleasure to see several glow-worms, which was mighty pretty, but my foot begins more and more to pain me, which Mrs Turner, by keeping her warm hand upon it, did much ease.'

Time and again Pepys had the good fortune to be on the spot when events, great or small, actually happened. On 29 July he obviously saw the original of the character Solomon Eagle in Harrison Ainsworth's *Old St Paul's*, as he passed through Westminster Hall. 'This day a man, a Quaker, came naked through the Hall, only very civilly tied about the loins to avoid scandal, and with a chafing-dish of fire and brimstone burning upon his head, did pass through the Hall, crying, "Repent! Repent!" '

Perhaps it was because the tension of waiting for the inevitable disaster at the hands of the Dutch had come and gone, and without his own disgrace, but at home he was probably easier to live with than he had been for some time. 'Howe to supper: a pullet, with good sauce, to my liking, and then to play on the flageolet with my wife, which she now does very prettily, and so to bed.' Also, Tangier continued to justify his opinion that it was the fairest bloom in his garden. On 2 August he received no less than £400 from Mr Gauden as his share in the profits, together with the promise that even if he gave up the office of Victualler the merchant would not forget him. Little wonder Pepys considered him 'a most noble-minded man as ever I met with'. But a great deal of work and worry lay ahead still: there was the Commission to be faced which would inquire into failures on the part of the Navy Board during the Dutch incursion up the Medway. Pepys drew up what he called his great account. 'Busy at my office from morning till night, in writing with my own fair hand our large general account of the expense and debt of the Navy, which lasted me till midnight to do so, that I was almost blind.' Before the disaster the debt of the Navy was past the £950,000 mark, and considering the scale of the King's personal debts it was unlikely it would be paid off for months or even years to come. And just how humiliating those debts were Pepys saw and overheard for himself in a row when one of the Grooms of the Bedchamber slated Townsend (responsible for the King's wardrobe) about the lack of linen. 'The King having this day no handkerchers, and but three bands to his neck, he swore. Mr Townsend pleaded want of money and the owing of the linen-draper £5,000; and that he hath of late got many rich things made—beds, and sheets, and saddles, without money, and that he can go no further.'

Peace, when it came on 24 August, brought little joy either to Pepys or his fellow-citizens. Bells were rung, but at least to his knowledge no bonfires were lit, and he was more taken up with his own affairs—like not being able to look at Mrs Knipp, 'for fear of angering Elizabeth'. Some time before they had concluded their own peace treaty when he promised to give her a sum equal to whatever he spent on Mrs Pierce and Mrs Knipp. 'Most of my discourse is about our keeping a coach the next year, which pleases my wife mightily; and if I continue as able as now, it will save us money.'

If Pepys did remain in office, he could count himself lucky. Sir George Carteret had resigned as Treasurer in June; in his place was Lord Anglesey; while at the beginning of September Sir William Coventry (who had resigned from the Navy Board earlier in the year) advised Pepys that he was also resigning as secretary to the Duke of York: 'which I was amazed at'. The parting was most friendly, and due to Sir William's desire to devote more time to his duties at the Treasury. In his place would be Matthew Wren, cousin to Dr Wren, who was already preparing plans for the re-building of London. It was an appointment which met with Pepys's approval: 'he being a very ingenious man'.

Another change, although it did not affect Pepys personally, was a momentous alteration on the political scene. At last his enemies had succeeded in overthrowing that mighty oak, the Lord Chancellor. At last Lord Clarendon was down, with his enemies triumphant, and they included nearly all the younger generation at Court, who looked on the formidable and gouty old man as a reactionary of the worst kind. As much as anyone it was Sir William Coventry himself who had ensured his eclipse, but when Pepys heard the Great Seal had been taken from him and returned to the King it put him, in his own words, into a great horror.

On 3 October Pepys heard his old rival Sir William Batten was ill and in bed. Two days later Batten was dead, to Pepys's surprise, if nothing more. At once he and Sir William Penn wrote to Sir William Coventry, suggesting one Colonel Middleton should take his place: 'who we think a most honest and understanding man, and fit for that place'.

It looks as though Pepys deliberately avoided having to go to Batten's funeral by taking a few days off from the office to go to Brampton with Elizabeth, her maid Deb Willet and Will Hewer, as well as an old naval acquaintance, Captain Murford. At the Reindeer at Bishop Stortford Pepys nearly renewed an acquaintance first made when he was a Cambridge undergraduate at Magdalene. The acquaintance was Mrs Aynsworth, a notorious procuress: 'and whom I knew better than they think for, I do live. It was the woman that, among other things, was great with my cousin Barnston of Cottenham, and did use to sing with him, and did teach me "Full Forty Times Over", a very lewd song: and is here what she was at Cambridge, and all the good fellows of the county come hither. But there was so much taring company in the house, that we could not see the landlady; so I had no opportunity of renewing my old acquaintance with her.'

Pepys also revisited Audley End; though now having seen other great houses he did not consider it quite as fine as he had done some seven years before. As on that earlier visit he and Elizabeth found their way to the cellars: 'where we went down and drank of much good liquor; and indeed the cellars are fine: and there my wife and I did sing to my great content'. With pride and pleasure Pepys showed his companions some of the sights of Cambridge, and when they left the Rose Inn next morning he must indeed have felt a person of consequence: '9th October. Up, and got ready, and eat our breakfast; and then took coach: and the poor, as they did yesterday, did stand at the coach to have something given them, as they do to all great persons; and I give them something: and the town music [the waits] did also come and play: but, Lord! what sad music they made.'

All was well with his father and with Pall at Brampton. After dinner he walked across to Hinchingbrooke to see Lady Sandwich and the children: now nearly all grown up. What with Lord Sandwich being in Spain and his family in the country, during the last few months Pepys had rather neglected his eminent relations, and felt ashamed he had not written to his patron. Just before the débâcle at Chatham he had briefly seen Lady Jemimah when she was about to leave for the country to await the birth of a son. Lady Sandwich was as charming as ever: 'the same most excellent, good, discreet lady that ever she was; and, among other things, is mightily pleased with the lady that is like to be her son Hinchingbrooke's wife. But I do find, by my Lady, that they are reduced to great straits for money, having been forced to sell her plate, £8 or £9,000 worth; and she is now going to sell a suit of her best hangings, of which I could almost wish to buy a piece or two, if the pieces will be broke.'

The next day the whole Pepys family, including John and Pall, were invited to dinner: 'where we had a good plain country dinner, but most kindly used'. After dinner Pepys saw more of the family: Oliver and John Montagu. 'And anon the two twins were sent for from school, at Mr Taylor's, to come and see me, and I took them into the garden, and there, in one of the summer-houses, did examine them, and do find them so well advanced in their learning, that I am amazed at it.' To his surprise and pleasure they could repeat a whole ode of Horace, while their Greek grammar was excellent, and in his opinion they would be ready for Cambridge in two years at the latest. It was gratifying to realise that Lady Sandwich looked on him as one of her own family. While she had her problems, Pepys had his: chiefly his brother and sister. He and his father decided that John should stay on at Brampton for the winter; the last had been spent at Seething Lane, and Samuel said he would see if he could find a living for him, 'or send him to sea as a chaplain, where he may study, and earn his living'.

Pall was a greater worry, for her future. In the past attempts to find her a husband had failed: 'but we must endeavour to find one now, for she grows old and ugly'. The next year would prove to be her *annus mirabilus*, when she would make a prosperous and contented marriage.

Apart perhaps from avoiding having to attend Sir William Batten's funeral, it was something very personal that had brought Pepys to Brampton: to retrieve the greater part of his wealth which Elizabeth and his father had so incautiously buried in the garden that Sunday morning when fear of the Dutch was at its height. Out into the garden father, son and Elizabeth went that night with a dark lantern. To Pepys's worry at first they could not agree exactly where it was that the coins had been buried. When they finally located the spot, he was horrified. 'But, Good God! to see how sillily they did it, not half a foot under ground, and in the sight of the world from a hundred paces, if anybody by accident were near at hand, and within sight of a neighbour's window. I was out of my wits almost, and the more from that, upon my lifting up the earth with the spade, I did discover that I had scattered the pieces of gold round about the ground among the grass and loose earth.' Already the bags had rotted in the wet earth. In a temper Pepys gathered up what he could find and after supper (and of his own admission he was always inclined to be peevish when hungry): 'Will Hewer and I did all alone, with several pails of water and besoms, at last wash the dirt off of the pieces; and do find that there was short above a hundred pieces; which did make me mad.' Pepys's father was deaf, and when searching in the garden Samuel had had to shout to make the old man hear. Now he feared his neighbours might have heard, and come looking for treasure before the night was out.

It was nearly midnight, but out went Pepys and Will Hewer, and with the aid of candles found another forty-five pieces. It was 2 a.m. before the Clerk of the Acts got to bed, but not to sleep: 'and lay there in some disquiet all night, telling of the clock till it was daylight'. Back he and Will Hewer went early in the morning: 'and there gather all the earth about the place into pails, and then sift those pails in one of the summer-houses, just as they do for diamonds in other parts of the world; and there, to our great content, did by nine o'clock make the last night's forty-five up to seventy-nine.' If only twenty or thirty coins were missing, Pepys was thankful, and it put him into a philosophical frame of mind, contemplating how painful the getting and keeping of money could be. Now there was the anxious task of getting it all safely back to London. In a fit of generosity Samuel gave Pall 20s.: 'but, God forgive me! I take her to be so cunning and ill-natured, that I have no great love for her; but only [she] is my sister, and must be provided for'.

Good, kindly Lady Sandwich knew what Pepys had been up to in the middle of the night—what had brought him to Brampton in fact, and without saying why, sent Mr Shepley the steward and John Bowles, another of her household, to accompany the coach on part of its journey. 'But, before we went out, the Huntingdon music come to me and played, and it was better than that of Cambridge.' The gold was in a basket stowed under one of the seats, and every quarter of an hour Pepys checked to see all was well, and when they stopped for the night at Stevenage, the treasure was cached under a bed: 'and then sat down to talk, and were very pleasant, satisfying myself, among other things, from John Bowles, in some terms of hunting, and about deer, bucks and does'. By five the next afternoon they were all back in Seething Lane: 'where I find all well; and did bring my gold, to my heart's content, very safe, having not this day carried it in a basket, but in our hands: the girl took care of one, and my wife another bag, and I the rest, I being afraid of the bottom of the coach, lest it should break'.

If the visit had been timed to coincide with the funeral of his old enemy Batten, it was successful. 'At home we find that Sir W. Batten's body was today carried from hence, with a hundred or two of coaches, to Walthamstow, and there buried.' Later, Lady Batten returned from the funeral, to a family which was already starting to quarrel among itself. 'With Sir W. Penn to my Lady Batten, whom I had not seen since she was a widow, which she took unkindly, but I did excuse it; and the house being full of company, and of several factions, she against the children, and they against one another and her, I away.'

At the end of the previous year, Penn and Batten—with extra financial assistance from Sir Richard Ford—had gone shares in the privateer the *Flying Greyhound*, borrowing the vessel from the King. Not only Dutch merchantmen but even Swedish vessels fell prey to the licensed pirate ship: a most dubious undertaking for senior members of the Navy Board, one might assume, but by seventeenth-century standards not in any way improper. When it transpired on the other hand that the Captain of the *Flying Greyhound* had been defrauding his employers, it was Pepys who was scandalised, branding him as a rogue and an embezzler. But this particular venture had had to end with the Peace of Breda, so the three colleagues had the idea of asking the King outright if in return for their services to their country they could have the *Flying Greyhound* on what amounted to permanent loan, to indulge in a little lawful trading. Then Pepys discovered Penn was trying to cut out his two partners. Wrathfully he rounded on the 'base rogue', and Penn quickly suggested that he should use his own influence with the Duke of York to obtain a vessel for Pepys's exclusive use. He did so; the vessel was a galliot, the *Maybolt*, and the whole transaction was legitimised with a warrant. But it was to be a troublesome venture, and at the year's end Pepys considered selling the *Maybolt*: 'though my employing her to Newcastle this winter, and the next spring for coals, will be a gainful trade, but yet makes me great trouble'. Since by December his salary was £500 in arrears, and he was forced to petition for its payment, perhaps Pepys was justified in finding his money where he could.

When Pepys considered his fortunes, he could have told himself that the fact that at the end of the disastrous year of 1667 he was still Clerk of the Acts was due to the years of hard work and loyal service he had given. Although he had had less to fear than most, facing the Committee of Inquiry had been a nerve-racking experience, which cost him several sleepless nights. Not only were he, Lord Brouncker, Sir William Penn and Tom Hayter cross-examined before the whole House of Commons about the state of the defences at Chatham, but they were also questioned about the system of payment with tickets, the cause of so many seamen deserting to the Dutch. Pepys's examination went on until an hour after dark: 'I had a chair brought me to lean my books upon; and so did give them such an account, in a series of the whole business that had passed the office touching the matter, and so answered all questions given me about it, that I did not perceive but they were fully satisfied with me and the business as to our office.' Commissioner Pett made the worst possible showing when questioned, and in particular made a bad impression when he tried to blame the Duke of Albemarle for not moving the *Royal Charles* to a safer mooring higher up the Medway.

In the midst of the inquiry into all that concerned the running of the Navy Office the Duke of York fell ill with smallpox, and as if that were not enough Parliament was engaged in an attempt to impeach Lord Clarendon, chiefly on a charge of betraying the King's councils to his enemies. As a result it would not be until February that Pepys's ordeal would be over. What was more, Pepys had personal worries of his own. 'To the office, where about my letters, and so home to supper, and to bed, my eyes being bad again, and by this means, the nights, nowadays, do become very long to me, longer than I can sleep out.'

During the year, servants had come and gone in bewildering numbers, among them Luce, a poor ugly lump of a girl, who frightened Pepys nearly out of his wits when she fell down the upper flight of stairs and lay groaning so much he thought she must be dying. The truth was she had a failing: 'Vexed with our maid Luce, our cook-maid, who is a good drudging servant in everything else, and pleases us, but that she will be drunk, and hath been so last night and all this day, that she could not make clean the house. My fear is only fire.' On another occasion Pepys encountered her when drunk at the back entrance to the house, and so far forgot himself as to give her a hearty kick: his only regret afterwards was that he had been observed by Penn's boy, and he knew perfectly well that the young wretch would tell what he had just seen to his master and mistress.

At the end of September yet another young girl, just out of school and as innocent and endearing as could be imagined, came to live in Seething Lane as companion to Elizabeth. Her name was Deb Willet, and from the outset Pepys was enchanted, though even before she joined the household he was fearful lest he should show her too much attention: 'to the discontent of my wife'. On the last day of September, Pepys returned home 'and there find our pretty girl Willet come, and she is very pretty, and so grave as I never saw a little thing in my life. I wish my wife may use her well.' It was his own conduct about which he should have been concerned. Almost at once Pepys started to show too much interest in her, with the inevitable effect on Elizabeth. 'I perceive she is already jealous of my kindness to her, so that I begin to fear this girl is not likely to stay long.' Before she departed the following year, Pepys, by his indiscreet behaviour had nearly wrecked his own marriage, and caused a great deal of suffering to Elizabeth. But at the end of 1667 he could record that he had 'great happiness to myself and family as to health and good condition in the world, blessed be to God for it!' Serious trouble at home was still ten months away.

Chapter 12

Honourable Acquittal
1668

As the New Year came in there was the thought at the back of Pepys's mind that before long he would have to face the Committee inquiring into the part played by the Navy in the recent disastrous conflict with Holland. But he was too much of an optimist to let it completely dampen his life, and so the year began with a visit to what must have been his favourite comedy, *Sir Martin Mar-all*: 'which I have seen so often, and yet am mightily pleased with it, and think it mighty witty; and the fullest of proper matter for mirth that ever was writ'. Twelfth Night was an even happier occasion: among the party at the Duke of York's theatre to see *The Tempest* were Elizabeth, Mrs Pierce and her cousin, Mrs Knipp and 'little James', presumably a friend of the last named. 'And the house being full, was forced to carry them to a box, which did cost me 20s, besides oranges, which troubled me, though their company did please me.' Together with Harris the actor they all returned to Seething Lane, where fires were burning and candles lighted, both in the house and at the more spacious Office. There were more guests than those at the theatre: Mary Mercer and his sister, Betty Turner (daughter of their neighbours the Turners), Will Batalier the merchant, and even Pembleton, the dancing-master. Presumably the latter was included at Elizabeth's insistence.

The music for dancing that Twelfth Night was the best in town—usually employed by the Duke of Buckingham—consisting of two violins, a bass viol and a theorbo: the last being a large and obsolete form of two-necked lute. As the evening wore on more guests arrived, uninvited, but nonetheless welcome. Mrs Turner and a friend, as well as other neighbours, until there were twenty dancing, singing, drinking sack posset and eating the traditional Twelfth Night cake, till after two o'clock in the morning. 'They being gone, I paid the fiddlers £3 among the four, and so away to bed, wearily and mightily pleased.' There Pepys reflected that such occasions, and also visits to the theatre, were among life's greatest pleasures. In the back of his mind was the fear that changing fortunes or poor health might put a stop to such diversions, and perhaps already he was haunted by the thought that one day he might lose his sight altogether.

Someone for whom life became too much was his cousin-by-marriage Anthony Joyce, whose tavern had been burnt in the Great Fire, and who was greatly worried about money. For some months he had been in a depressed state and on 21 January Pepys received word from Kate Joyce that if he wished to see Anthony alive he had better hurry. A few days previously he had attempted to drown himself in a pond at Islington, and although dragged out alive was now dying. By law a suicide's possessions were forfeit to the Crown, which added to Kate's distress. 'My cousin did endeavour to remove what she could of plate out of the house, and desired me to take my flagons [deposited there during the scare the previous summer], which I did.' Soon after, Anthony Joyce died, and Kate begged her cousin's help, which he gave to the full. Straightway he went to Sir William Coventry at Whitehall, who took him in to the King and the Duke of York, and explained the situation. 'And the King, without more ado, granted that, if it was found, the estate should go to the widow and children.' Next day was the inquest, which was promptly adjourned until Shrove Tuesday. The jury departed, leaving Pepys to console his cousin: 'though I can find she can, as all other women, cry and yet talk of other things all in a breath'.

Whilst doing all he could to help Kate Joyce, Pepys was hardly grief-stricken at Anthony's death. The funeral was two days later. On his way Pepys dropped Elizabeth off at the King's Playhouse, while he went to the 'Quest House in Holborn where the mourners were gathering: 'a very great rabble of four or five hundred people of mean condition, but left again on the pretext of not having a cloak'. Back he went to the King's Playhouse; and there saw the best part of *The Maiden Queen*, another favourite play.

Kate Joyce's troubles were not yet over, however. The inquest on Shrove Tuesday was again adjourned, chiefly because of the sermon preached at the funeral. 'He [Dr Stillingfleet, who later became a noted Divine] declaring, like a fool, in his pulpit, that he did confess that his losses in the world did make him do what he did.' In other words, it was suicide and not an accident, as the family wished the world to believe. But a fortnight later a verdict was returned that Anthony Joyce had died from a fever, which meant his estate passed to his widow without any further delay or difficulties. She now became the landlady of the tavern, and within a few weeks Pepys received a letter informing him that Kate Joyce was likely to ruin herself with a bad marriage. He invited her to dine on the following Sunday, and the matter was discussed openly. If she did remarry it would be to a tobacconist called Holinshed: 'a plain, sober man, and in good condition', which relieved Pepys's mind, for he did not like the idea of the tavern being run by a good-looking young widow. In May he was surprised, and not a little nettled, to hear that without a word to him, Kate had married Holinshed. 'I do fear, by her doing this without my advice, it is not as it ought to be; but, as she brews, let her bake.' And with that variant on the proverb about sowing and reaping Kate Joyce disappeared from the pages of the Diary.

For some years Pepys had intermittently worried about finding a husband for his sister Pall; one attempted match had failed, and he had even hoped to yoke her to his old schoolfriend Dick Cumberland (who later became Bishop of Peterborough). But now he felt success was in sight. Pall was engaged to John Jackson, a grazier. Between the pages of the Diary Pepys really could be devastatingly candid, as he was about his future brother-in-law: 'a plain young man, handsome enough for Pall, one of no education or discourse, but of few words, and one altogether that, I think, will please me well enough . . . my mind pretty well satisfied with this plain fellow for my sister; though I shall, I see, have no pleasure or content in him, as if he had been a man of ready parts like Cumberland.' But he was generous nonetheless: by Deed of Settlement Pall would have £600, and an annual jointure of £60. Originally it had been Elizabeth's idea to have the marriage in London, with Will Hewer and Will Batelier as bridesmen, and Mary Mercer and Deb Willett as bridesmaids. But in the end Pall was married in the country. '2nd March. This day I have the news that my sister was married on Thursday last to Mr Jackson; so that work is, I hope, well over.' Just over a year later he made a curious entry concerning his sister, which reflected his ambivalent attitude towards children. 'He [his brother John] tells me the first news that my sister Jackson is with child, and far gone, which I know not whether it did more trouble or please me, having no great care for my friends to have children, though I love other people's. So, glad to see him, we to supper, and so to bed.'

Pepys was in touch with gossip at Court not only through friends such as Mr Pierce, the Duke of York's physician, but also through his theatrical contacts. Now the King had taken a new mistress, Moll Davis, the actress who in Mrs Pierce's opinion was 'a most impertinent slut'. She was reputed to be the illegitimate daughter of Lord Berkshire, and now she was showing everyone a ring worth £700, and occupying a house in Suffolk Street: 'and my Lady Castlemaine being melancholy and out of humour'. Not only that, but Charles was starting to show interest in Nell Gwynn. 'The King did send several times for Nelly, and she was with him; and I am sorry for it, and I can hope for no good to the State from having a Prince so devoted to his pleasure.' The point was rapidly being reached when the most tolerant were becoming exasperated with the licence those at Court allowed themselves. The waylaying and beating-up of actors by hirelings of aggrieved noblemen who felt they had been ridiculed on stage were becoming almost common-place. Tom Killigrew, boon companion of the King and moving spirit behind the King's Playhouse, was a particular offender, and it reached Pepys's ears 'that Tom Killigrew hath a fee out of the Wardrobe for cap and bells, under the title of the King's Fool or Jester, and may revile or jeer anybody, the greatest person, without offence, by the privilege of his place'.

The following year, in February 1669, Killigrew received his deserts, though not as might have been expected from a staid courtier, but from the hardly adult Earl of Rochester. Both were among the guests, along with the King, at the Dutch Ambassador's, when Killigrew angered Rochester so much 'that he did give Tom Killigrew a box on the ears in the King's presence, which do give much offence to the people here at Court, to see how cheap the King do make himself'.

But the one person above all others who still fascinated Pepys was the incomparable Lady Castlemaine. '14th February. I was told tonight that my Lady Castlemaine is so great a gamester as to have won £15,000 in one night, and lost £25,000 in another night, at play, and hath played £1,000 and £1,500 at a cast.' Then something happened worthy of a comedy by Aristophanes, which must have made even her pause and reflect.

By tradition the City 'prentices had always been Puritan in

outlook: from time to time the theatres were their target—slashing clothes and tearing up play-books, especially during Lent. But most often it was the brothels that suffered, and in March 1668 they literally caused a riot in the Moorfields area. Such behaviour threw the Court into a state bordering on panic. Mounted and foot soldiers were called out, trumpets and drums sounded the alarm in Westminster, and in Pepys's opinion it was as though the French had landed. Off he went with Creed to see what there was to observe in Lincoln's Inn Fields, which were full of soldiers: 'and my Lord Craven commanding of them, and riding up and down to give orders, like a madman'. Public opinion was on the side of the 'prentices, and against the soldiers for interfering, and scuffling went on all night. 'Some blood hath been spilt, but a great many houses pulled down; and, among others, the Duke of York was mighty merry at that of Dagman Page's, the great bawd of the seamen; and the Duke of York complained merrily that he hath lost two tenants, by their houses being pulled down, who paid him for their wine-licences £15 a year. But these idle fellows have the confidence to say that they did ill in contenting themselves in pulling down the little brothels, and did not go and pull down the great one at Whitehall.' That was not the end of the affair. If someone wished to send a barbed shaft in the direction of the Court, what better than in the shape of a petition (or libel) from the unhoused whores of London addressed to Lady Castlemaine? My Lady 'was horribly vexed', and Pepys had the good fortune to lay hands on a copy of the offending broadsheet. 'I have got one of them, and it is not very witty, but devilish severe against her and the King: and I wonder how it durst be printed and spread abroad, which shows that the times are loose, and come to a great disregard of the King or Court or Government.' Of course, another pamphleteer had to reply: 'The Gracious Answer of the Most Illustrious Lady of Pleasure, the Countess of Castle . . . to the Poor Whores' Petition.' Pepys may have laughed, but already Nemesis had marked him down for a day of reckoning for his own infidelities.

For some time there had been romance in the air in the house in Seething Lane. Jane Birch, the maid, was in love with Tom Edwards, and now they wanted to get married. First the young couple told Elizabeth (who advised Tom to be true to Jane), and she in her turn told Samuel. He was glad for Jane's sake, though he had reservations about how Tom might turn out: 'I think she will have no good bargain of it. But if I do stand [keep in office], I do intend to give her £50 in money, and do them all the good I can in my way.' Perhaps he was right about Tom: in August the young man was trying to cry off, but Jane was not prepared to make things easy, and evidently had a fit, either real or simulated. 'It was beyond four or five of our strength, to keep her down; and, when all come to all, a fit of jealousy about Tom, with whom she is in love . . . and he is now cold in it, so that I must rid my hands of them, which troubles me.'

A few hundred yards away, at the end of Seething Lane, a new City of London was starting to arise: by law all the houses had to be of brick, and while a few of the streets were widened, most buildings were going up on the old sites. The plans produced by John Evelyn and Dr Wren to make London the handsomest capital in Europe had proved nothing more than grandiose dreams. For six months after the disaster, fires had kept breaking out again, especially when cellars filled with coals or combustible materials were opened. Other cellars had become the refuge of vagabonds and robbers. Few cared to enter the City after dark, and on one occasion, when Pepys crossed it in a coach, he sat with his sword drawn. St Paul's, the Londoner's church since 1087, was beyond repair, and the whole site was to be cleared by a decree signed in July 1668 by the King. '26th August. It is strange to say with what speed the people employed to pull down Paul's steeple [tower: the word was used indiscriminately in the sixteenth and seventeenth centuries], and with what ease: it is said that it, and the choir are to be taken down this year, and another church begun in the room thereof, the next.' But three weeks later the workmen were still chipping at the great tower (it was not until six years later that it was finally demolished with the aid of gunpowder) and fascinated Pepys stopped to stare: 'where strange how the very sight of the stones falling from the top of the steeple do make me sea-sick!'

If Pepys had hoped to make a pleasant profit by the galliot *Maybolt*, he was disappointed. It turned out to be one of his less successful financial ventures, and early in 1668 he decided to sell, having already lost £100 by her. At the Navy Office there were still the unpleasant hours to be faced when he and his colleagues would have to appear before the Committee of Miscarriages, and even before the assembled House of Commons. Matters were not made easier by the differences of opinion between the Duke of York, the

Duke of Albemarle and Prince Rupert: the latter's attitude being that even if some of the captains were known to drink heavily, what of it if they fought well in battle? Meanwhile on the last day of January Pepys and Will Griffin, the doorkeeper at the Navy Office, took the Contract Books to Durham Yard, to the Commissioners for Accounts. Pepys found them less formidable to deal with than he had feared, and explained the running of the Navy Office and what duties were expected of various officials: in his opinion these Commissioners were men of understanding.

Quite apart from the impending inquiry it was a singularly busy time for Pepys. '1st February. Home, my head mighty full of business now on my hands: viz. of finishing my Tangier Accounts; of auditing my last year's Accounts; of preparing answers to the Commissioners of Accounts; of drawing up several important letters to the Duke of York and the Commissioners of the Treasury . . . and the setting of many things in the Office right; and the drawing up of a new form of Contract with the Victualler of the Navy, and several other things, which pains, however, will go through with.'

The ordeal really began before the Commissioners of Accounts on 5 February with some probing questions about his part in the episode of the prize-goods taken from the captured Dutch merchantmen in 1665. Although anxious, Pepys trod a careful path, and did not incriminate himself. Next to be questioned was his business associate in the venture, Captain Cocke. Pepys feared he might make foolish answers, confiding ungallantly to the Diary: 'but I hope to preserve myself, and let him shift for himself as well as he can'. A few days later he was summoned before the Committee of Miscarriages, which made him really angry. Had he lived three centuries later he would probably have commented that the others at the Navy Office had left him to 'carry the can'; as it was he wrote: 'it makes me mad, that I should by my place become the hackney of this office, in perpetual trouble and vexation that need it least. Here I brought a book to the Committee, and do find them, and particularly Sir Thomas Clarges, mighty hot in the business of tickets, which makes me mad to see them bite at the stone, and not at the hand that flings it.'

A few days later he was back before the Commissioners of Accounts, with his written statement concerning dealings in the prize-goods. Since he had acted on Lord Sandwich's assurance that he (the Earl) had the King's approval in 'breaking bulk', he could not really be blamed: if blame were to be apportioned, it should have been for Lord Sandwich's confident assumption that the King would countenance his actions. In the Report which went to the Commissioners of Miscarriages (and eventually before the Commons), it was Lord Brouncker who was blamed for all the trouble caused by issuing the seamen with tickets: but since there was no money to pay wages he hardly deserved censure. Little wonder that Sir William Coventry, the one-time secretary to the Duke of York, commented that if there were another Dutch war the powers-that-be would not find a Secretary (in him). Pepys's reply was: 'Nor a Clerk of the Acts, for I see the reward of it: and, thank God! I have enough of my own to buy me a good book and a good fiddle, and I have a good wife.'

At a time when he had most need of a good reputation, Lord Sandwich did much to restore his name by his diplomacy in Spain, where he succeeded in bringing about a peace between that country and Portugal: 'which is mighty great news, and, above all, to my Lord's honour, more than anything he ever did; and yet I do fear it will not prevail to secure him in Parliament against incivilities there'. When the question of tickets was debated, the opinion was arrived at that there had been a miscarriage, though no one was singled out by name for censure. In the midst of all this at least some of the business of maintaining the Navy continued: by a narrow margin the King was voted £300,000; based on Matthew Wren's estimation that the maintenance of the Fleet would come to £270,000, but in Pepys's opinion at least £200,000 of that sum would be needed for fitting out alone. But still there was the question of responsibility for the issuing of the tickets, and on 28 February the members of the Navy Board were chilled to hear they must all appear 'at the bar of the House upon the business on Thursday next. This did mightily trouble me and us all; but me particularly, who am least able to bear these troubles, though I have the least cause to be concerned in it.'

Armed with all the relevant notes and papers, Pepys went to Sir William Coventry to prepare their defence for the coming Thursday. Sir William had his own particular worries: he would rather not have to give straight answers to straight questions about the selling of places. While Pepys thought they could make a good defence he feared that in the end they would all be turned out of office. The next few days were agonising. '4th [Wednesday].

Vexed and sickish to bed, and there slept about three hours, but then waked, and never in so much trouble in all my mind, thinking of the task I have upon me.'

'5th [Thursday]. With these thoughts I lay troubling myself till six o'clock, restless, and at last getting my wife to talk to me to comfort me, which she at last did, and made me resolve to quit my hands of this office, and endure the trouble no longer than till I can clear myself of it.'

Never could Pepys have set out more unwillingly towards Westminster than on that March morning, accompanied by the faithful Will Hewer. He arrived with time to spare and 'to comfort myself, did go to the Dog and drink half-a-pint of mulled sack, and in the Hall did drink a dram of brandy at Mrs Hewlett's; and with the warmth of this did find myself in better order as to courage, truly.'

He and his colleagues waited in the lobby, and between eleven and twelve o'clock were called into the House, which was crowded. There they stood at the bar: Lord Brouncker, Sir John Minnes, Pepys and another Navy Office colleague, Sir Thomas Harvey. The only reason Sir William Penn was not ranged alongside them was that, as a sitting member, he was among those who made up the House. But his turn would come later. First the Speaker informed the four officials of the dissatisfaction of the House, and then read the Report of the Committee of Miscarriages. It was Pepys, junior to two of his colleagues, who would make the defence for the Navy Board. Whether it was his natural genius rising to a crisis, or the half pint of mulled sack topped up with a dram of brandy, but something loosed his tongue, and he spoke with great clarity and eloquence.

Standing at the bar of the House he spoke for about three hours: 'as if it had been at my own table, from that time till past three in the afternoon; and so ended, without any interruption from the Speaker'. His colleagues were delighted with Pepys's speech, as well they should have been, and they were all only recalled to the House to answer one question regarding the handling of tickets. But the length of his speech, however eloquent, had its disadvantage. 'My speech, being so long, many had gone out to dinner and come in again, half drunk.' So, in view of 'other business', voting (on a motion of censure) would be put off for a week; and then postponed again, until the matter was no longer a heated issue. In a much happier state of mind Pepys returned home. 'I betimes to bed, having had no quiet rest a good while.'

Early the following morning Pepys returned to Westminster, and to Sir William Coventry, who greeted him with the words: 'Good-morrow Mr Pepys, that must be Speaker of the Parliament-house,' adding that another had said if he 'would put on a gown and plead at the Chancery-bar' he could make £1,000 a year. The Solicitor General had added his praises to the speech in defence of the actions of the Navy Office by its Clerk of the Acts. Even the King exclaimed: 'Mr Pepys, I am very glad of your success yesterday.' All that day people came up to him to offer their congratulations. It was his finest hour, and even at such a time he could note in his Diary: 'God make me thankful! and that I may make use of it, not to pride and vainglory, but that, now I have this esteem, I may do nothing to lessen it.'

The trials were not yet over: on a number of occasions Pepys and his colleagues would have to return to Westminster to answer further questioning. 'To fit myself for attending the Parliament again, not to make any more speech, which, while my fame is good, I will avoid, for fear of losing it; but only to answer to what objections will be made against us.'

Now the Clerk of the Acts knew what it was like to be at the beck and call of Parliament, and it gave him a feeling of sympathy towards the royal brothers. He encountered the King and the Duke of York by the Privy Stairs at Whitehall: 'and the Duke of York called to me whither was I going? and I answered aloud "To wait on our masters at Westminster"; and he and all the company laughed; but I was sorry and troubled for it afterwards, for fear any Parliament-men should have been there; and it will be a caution to me for time to come.'

Though Pepys was out of trouble, Sir William Coventry had much to worry him, including a story circulating that he would have to repay money which he had received for places given to various people. 'A wicked design,' was Pepys's scandalised comment. Another to suffer was Sir William Penn. On 27 April he had to appear before the House of Lords to hear his impeachment read. Whether it was due to the presence of the Duke of York or not he was treated with consideration, and given two days in which to prepare his answer to the indictment. In his Diary Pepys could be so scornful or cutting about those he disliked, but in time of trouble compassion—or just innate kindness—over-rode old prejudices, and realising what distress of mind Penn must be in, he went to his neighbour. 'To Sir W. Penn's, where I supped, and sat all the evening; and being lighted homeward by Mrs Markham [Sir William's maid] I blew out the candle and kissed her.' Later he took Lady Penn, her daughter Peg Lowther and her old mother-in-law for a Sunday trip on the river as far as Chelsea and to the Spring Garden at Vauxhall: all of them sheltering from the rain under his cloak in the boat on the return journey.

At the end of April Pepys paused to take stock of the situation, both in his own affairs and those of the nation. For himself there was both good and bad in the scales. 'Thus ends this month; my wife in the country, myself full of pleasure and expense; in some trouble for my friends, and my Lord Sandwich, by the Parliament, and more for my eyes, which are daily worse and worse, that I dare not write or read almost anything. The kingdom in an ill state through poverty: a fleet going out, and no money to maintain it, or set it out; seamen yet unpaid, and mutinous when pressed to go out again; our office able to do little, not any trusting us, nor we desiring any to trust us, and yet have not money for anything, but only what particularly belongs to this fleet going out, and that but lamely too.'

With so much work that could be neither avoided nor delegated the strain on Pepys's eyes was increasing, until it was now causing acute physical discomfort. '2nd May. And so home to the Office, ended my letters, and, to spare my eyes, home, and played on my pipes, and so to bed.' For recreation there was music, and Pepys wrote another song, 'It is Decreed', and continued his visits to the theatre. Perhaps an even greater pleasure than the plays themselves was going into the dressing-rooms, especially when Mrs Knipp was there. At the King's Playhouse he could not help noting 'how strange they are all, one to another, after the play is done'. After thinking that perhaps she might be past the first flush of her beauty, Pepys had once again been captivated by Lady Castlemaine, and what was more one evening at the Duke of York's Playhouse the theatre was so crowded that he and John Creed found themselves actually sharing the box she occupied. 'Here I sat by her fine woman, Willson, who indeed is very handsome, but, they say, with child by the King. One thing of familiarity I observed in my Lady Castlemaine: she called to one of her women, another that sat by this

[Willson], for a little patch off of her face, and put it into her mouth and wetted it, and so clapped it upon her own by the side of her mouth, I suppose she feeling a pimple rising there.'

Life for Pepys certainly had its pleasant diversions during Elizabeth's absence: like inviting Mrs Pierce and her young daughter, one Mrs Foster—and of course Mrs Knipp—to dinner at Seething Lane and then taking them to see the Tower, like any modern tourist, including the Regalia which at that time would have been kept in the Martin Tower. 'And [showed them] among other things, the Crown and Sceptres and rich plate, which I myself never saw before, and indeed is noble, and I mightily pleased with it.' That was in April 1668; had Pepys been there on another April morning three years later he would have witnessed Colonel Blood's celebrated attempt to steal the Crown Jewels.

Since work at the Navy Office was now slack, Pepys felt justified in going to visit Elizabeth, still at Brampton, and off he went to Bishopsgate Street to book places for himself and Tom Edwards on the coach going to Cambridge. All was well at Brampton, and there was quite a family reunion. 'Here I saw my brother and sister [Mrs] Jackson, she growing fat, and, since being married, I think looks comlier than before: but a mighty pert woman she is.' But at least Pall and her husband were fond of one another, and before long would be moving to the village of Ellington: 'and will keep malting, and grazing of cattle'. That afternoon Pepys walked across to Hinchingbrooke, where he found the family listening to a sermon by their own chaplain. Of course he was happy to see Lady Sandwich again, but there was the slightest stiltedness between them. A few days before Pepys had been warned by old Shipley the steward what to expect: Lady Sandwich would ask to borrow £100. Pepys would lend the sum, though in his heart-of-hearts he doubted if he would see the money again.

After a happy day revisiting old haunts in and around Cambridge, he and Tom Edwards returned to London; departing at 6 a.m. and reaching the coach office in Bishopsgate Street before eight in the evening, despite the way being bad because of heavy rains. To his other worries Sir William Penn had now added gout, as Pepys found when he visited his neighbour: 'sitting in his great chair, made on purpose for persons sick of that disease, for their ease; and this very chair, he tells me, was made for my Lady Lambert [wife of the Parliamentarian general]'.

So wonderfully detailed is the Diary that it is only on the rarest of occasions that Pepys makes the reader feel an outsider in his world of more than three hundred years ago. One such occasion comes at the end of an entry when he had taken Mary Mercer and a friend of hers for an outing into the countryside—to Bow and Mile End, and bought cherries costing 2*s*. After that he went his own way, by water to Deptford, and then home: 'taking into my boat, for company, a man that desired a passage . . . with whom I had good sport, talking of the old woman of Woolwich, and telling him the whole story'. Like Shakespeare's poor cat in the adage, or the ape in the basket, the old woman of Woolwich is one of those jokes that means exactly nothing to later generations.

The visit to Brampton had been only a flying one, and after presenting the Duke of York with an account of the expenses of the Fleet, he requested five or six days' leave of absence: 'which he did give me, saying, that my diligence in the King's business was such, that I ought not to be denied when my own business called me any whither'. It turned out to be longer than the inside of a week, for he, Elizabeth, Deb Willett, his cousin Betty Turner (complete with a pet sparrow), Will Hewer and Captain Murford set out, on what must have been a most happy visit, towards the West Country. But Pepys did not take the Diary: on his return he inserted five sheets, but most of the entries between 5 and 17 June were more in the nature of brief notes intended for expansion at a later date. That, however, was never done.

'9th Tuesday. We came to Oxford, a very sweet place; paid our guide £1 2s 6d [presumably for the coach]; barber 2s 6d; book [about] Stonehenge, 4s; boy that showed me the colleges before dinner, 1s.' And so on: from Oxford they journeyed on through Abingdon to Hungerford, where despite 'very good trouts, eels, and crayfish (dinner 12s)' he found it a mean town. Then on, guided as all travellers have been since the late Middle Ages: 'So all over the Plain by the sight of the steeple, the Plain high and low, to Salisbury, by night; but before I come to the town I saw a great fortification, and there 'light, and to it and in it: and find it prodigious, so as to fright me to be in it all alone at that time of night, it being dark. I understand, since, it to be that that is called Old Sarum. Come to the George Inn, where lay in a silk bed; and very good diet. To supper; then to bed.' Pepys loved Salisbury: 'a very brave place', and in his opinion the cathedral was handsomer even than Westminster Abbey. Then they went sight-seeing, on horse-back this time. The women of the party rode behind Will Hewer, Captain Murford and their guide, while Pepys rode alone. 'To Stonehenge, over the Plain and some great hills, even to fright us. Come thither, and find them as prodigious as any tales I ever heard of them, and worth going this journey to see. God knows what their use was! they are hard to tell, but yet may be known.' Back they went to Salisbury, though this time not to the George Inn. 'This day from Salisbury I wrote by post my excuse for not coming home, which I hope will do, for I am resolved to see Bath, and, it may be, Bristol. 12th [Friday]. Up, finding our beds good but lousy, which made us merry. We set out, the reckoning and servants coming to 9s 6d; coachmen advanced 10s.' In addition to frequently giving money for the poor, from time to time as they journeyed along Pepys would give sixpence or a shilling to the roadmenders they passed.

On they went, into Somerset: 'where my wife and Deb, mightily joyed thereat'. Both could claim Somerset as their home county. At Bath the town Pepys and his companions saw was small, medieval and compact, and dominated by its great Abbey Church. Whilst famous from Roman times for its therapeutic hot waters, its Roman remains were as yet un-rediscovered, and its great crescents and squares unbuilt. Up at 4 a.m. the morning after their arrival, the travellers were taken to the baths. 'Much company come; very fine ladies; and the manner pretty enough, only methinks it cannot be clean to go so many bodies together in the same water. Strange to see how hot the water is; and in some places, though this is the most temperate bath, the springs so hot as the feet not able to endure. Carried back, wrapped in a sheet, and in a chair home; and there one after another thus carried, I stayed above two hours in the water, home to bed, sweating for an hour; and by and by comes music to play to me, extraordinary good as ever I heard at London, almost, or anywhere: 5s.'

Although up at 4 a.m. the travellers were on their way again by 11, this time for Bristol: 'In every respect another London.' Even at that date Bristol was the centre of the wine trade, and above all for sherry. Pepys observed a curious fact about the life of the city. 'No carts, it standing generally on vaults, only dog-carts.' Even the horses' hooves and the mettle-rimmed wheels would have been sufficient to disturb the sherry maturing in the cellars beneath the city streets. After a quick look at the docks in the heart of the city with Deb Willett's uncle: 'a sober merchant, very good company, and so like one of our sober, wealthy, London merchants, as pleased me mightily', they returned to the uncle's house, by way of the street where Deb was born: 'But, Lord! the joy that was among the old poor people of the place to see Mrs Willett's daughter, it seemed her mother being a brave woman and mightily beloved!' At the merchant's house Pepys and his companions were handsomely entertained: 'strawberries, a whole venison pasty, cold, and plenty of brave wine, and above all Bristol milk'. At that date Bristol milk was not the name of a world-famous sherry, but a milk punch with a rum basis. It was a happy encounter for all, and then by moonlight the party returned to Bath. After another day in the resort, seeing the sights and 'walking round the walls of the city, which are good, and the battlements all whole', it really was time for the return journey. *En route* they stopped at Avebury, to marvel and speculate at the circle and 'the mount cast [up] hard by it called Silbury', being told by a local man who showed them the prehistoric remains 'that most people of learning, coming by, do come and view them, and that the King did so'.

The rest of the way back to London was without incident: only Pepys was now reflecting to himself that the more liberty Elizabeth had, as when she was at Brampton, the more she was inclined afterwards to be out of hand—not to say impertinent. But there were two sides to that particular coin, as Pepys began to discover from the moment of their return. 'Home, and there with my people to supper, all in a pretty good humour, though I find my wife hath something in her gizzard, that only waits an opportunity of being provoked to bring up; but I will not, for my content sake, give it.' The next day, when Pepys returned for dinner, the storm began to break. 'My wife still in a melancholy, fusty humour, and crying and do not tell me plainly what it is: but I by little words find that she hath heard of my going to plays and carrying people abroad every day in her absence; and that I cannot help but the storm will break out in a little time.' And so she continued for the rest of the day: even refusing to go to a new play, and blighting a supper-party with the Turners, Mary Mercer and Mr Pelling, an apothecary.

That night in bed, Elizabeth cried, and Pepys, probably wondering exactly what she had found out, was becoming unnerved. 'I then rose, and would have sat up all night, but she would have me come to bed again; and being pretty well pacified, we to sleep.' But not for long: there was an alarum caused by a fire in Mark Lane, and after they were once again in bed it all came out in a flood of tears. Elizabeth wanted to go and live in France because she felt all Samuel thought about was his own pleasure; and also she had been quarrelling with his father at Brampton: 'whom, for ever hereafter, I must keep asunder, for they cannot possibly agree'. Wisely Pepys said as little as possible, and soon the storm blew itself out: 'till we begun to be very quiet, and I think all will be over, and friends'. By now there was enough trouble in Pepys's life, due to the condition of his eyes, without the undermining of his marriage.

On 23 June he went to see Dr Turberville, who discoursed learnedly about his eyes, but wanted time to think before deciding exactly what to prescribe. A few days later, Pepys returned, and was given eye-drops, and encouraged to think that all might yet be well. Seventeenth-century medicine being what it was, he was even bled, losing 14 ounces, 'towards curing my eyes'. But still work had to go on, 'till I was almost blind, which makes my heart sad'. Much of the trouble was undoubtedly due to the use of Shelton's short-hand for the Diary, and ruefully he commented: 'God knows! I have paid dear for it, in my eyes.' Now he had seen an account, in a learned journal, of spectacles, like two tubes, which he was anxious to try out for himself. 'At office all the afternoon till night, being mightily pleased with a trial I have made of the use of a tube-spectacle of paper, tried with my right eye.' At least the peculiar device made it possible for him to continue reading and writing without too great discomfort, so Elizabeth and Deb set about making a pair for his use.

More than ever Pepys turned to music for recreation and con-solation, and bought a spinet, costing £5. Soon, even his other great love, the theatre, became painful to him because the candles in front of the stage hurt his eyes. Not that it stopped him, Elizabeth and Deb from going. On one occasion at the Duke of York's Play-house they again beheld Gosnell: 'who is become very homely, and sings meanly, I think, to what I thought she did'. But there were outdoor pleasures which could be enjoyed without discomfort, such as Bartholomew Fair. There one of the attractions was a knowing horse which could count, 'and among others, come to me, when she was bid to go to him of the company, that most loved a pretty wench in a corner'. Unfortunately it did not make him more circumspect

WHITEHALL PALACE, ABOUT 1645, *by Hollar*

On the left are the royal apartments: in the background
Inigo Jones's Banqueting House and the roof of the Great Hall

LADY CASTLEMAINE, LATER DUCHESS OF CLEVELAND, AS THE MADONNA
after Lely

where Elizabeth was concerned: though her accusation that he thought only of himself was less than just, he was paying more attention to *la belle* Pierce and Mrs Knipp than was wise or necessary.

Earlier that year Elizabeth herself had reckoned she possessed more than £150 of jewellery, as well as being abreast the latest fashions. But best of all Pepys had commissioned Cooper, one of the greatest of all English miniaturists, to paint Elizabeth's portrait, although it would cost £30. The miniature was finished on 10 August, though Pepys was just a little disappointed: 'but it is most certainly a most rare piece of work, as to the painting'. Unfortunately, it seems to have disappeared without trace. Nor did Pepys neglect his own appearance: 'Up, and put on a new summer black bombazine suit; being now come to an agreement with my barber, to keep my periwig in good order at 20s a year, I am like to go very spruce, more than I used to do.'

Soon after, disaster came to one of his periwigs in most distinguished surroundings. At the end of September, Lord Sandwich was due to return to England, and Pepys had gone to receive news at Lord Burlington's house (Burlington House, Piccadilly—though much altered since) from Edward, the Earl's eldest son, now Lord Hinchingbrooke. Also, there was a delicate matter to be discussed. Lord Sandwich would need £2,000; and Pepys—troubled by his conscience in that he had hardly written to his cousin and one-time patron while he was in Spain—was himself prepared to lend £500. 'Which I am sorry for, to see in what a condition my Lord is for money, that I dare swear he do not know where to take up £500 of any man in England at this time, upon his word, but of myself.' Also, there was the news that Mrs Pickering (Lord Sandwich's niece) was about to marry John Creed, who would therefore at several removes become a cousin-by-marriage of Pepys. It was at this point that Pepys nearly immolated himself. 'Here I also, standing by a candle that was brought for sealing a letter, do set my periwig afire, which made such an odd noise, nobody could tell what it was till they saw the flame, my back being to the candle.'

Eventually, on 23 October 1668, Pepys once again saw Lord Sandwich, and talked with him for more than an hour: 'he, taking physic and keeping to his chamber'. Or to put it another way, the Earl was waiting for a dose to work. Over the years Pepys had on occasions missed going to church on Sunday mornings for the self-same reason. And there was the occasion when Lady Sandwich had been invited to dine at Seething Lane, when Pepys had entered the dining-room without warning, to their mutual confusion and embarrassment, for that was where the chamber-pot had been placed for the distinguished guest's convenience.

Those who knew and loved Lord and Lady Sandwich were deeply concerned for their future well-being. Pepys heard the details from his old friend of the days at the Exchequer Office: 'Mr Moore tells me of the sad condition my Lord is in, in his estate and debts; and the way he now lives in, so high, and so many vain servants about him, that he must be ruined, if he do not take up [borrow money].' And it was Pepys who now helped his kinsman over a difficult period.

High honour, if not success, had not brought Lord Sandwich happiness or prosperity, and Pepys was saddened to observe the change in him. He found the Earl 'moped, or reserved rather, I think, with his own business, that he bids welcome to no man, I think, to his satisfaction. I bear with it . . . wishing only that I had my money in my purse, that I have lent him; but, however, I show no discontent at all.'

The members of the Navy Board had escaped without being publicly disgraced for their failures during the late Dutch War, but there was little cause for complacency, and Captain Cocke told Pepys of a rumour that they were all likely to be turned out of the Navy Office. Ever practical, he wrote to his father at Brampton, telling him not to part with the furniture to Pall when she set up house with her husband James Jackson: 'because I think I may have occasion to come thither; and so I do, by our being put out of the Office, which do not at all trouble me to think of'.

Even if he were indifferent for himself Pepys was still anxious for the well-being of the Navy, and he resolved to write the Duke of York a letter setting forth the shortcomings in the Navy Office, and if necessary, sparing no one. Aided by Tom Hayter, Will Hewer and Richard Gibson (a clerk), Pepys drew up another of his 'grand letters'. He took it in person to the Duke of York at St James's Palace. There the Duke read it through most carefully, and then thanked Pepys both generously and sincerely, realising that he at least had the welfare of the Navy Office at heart. Pepys reported that the Duke 'with the utmost confidence desires my further advice on all occasions: and he resolves to have my letter transcribed, and sent forthwith to the office'. Although it did not appear with Pepys's signature, his colleagues knew perfectly well who was the only one with the ability, and the brains, to have written such a letter. Not that he cared now what any of them thought. 'I met Lord Brouncker, who, I perceive, and the rest, do smell that it comes from me, but dare not find fault with it; and I am glad of it, it being my glory and defence that I did occasion and write it.'

The manner of doing business was truly remarkable. In due course Lord Brouncker, Sir William Penn and Sir John Minnes wrote answering the statements about the management of the Navy Office. Matthew Wren, the Duke of York's secretary, was particularly busy at that time, and handed them unread to Pepys: 'which do give me great opportunity of altering my answer, if there was cause. After supper, made my wife to read them all over [to save his poor tired eyes], wherein she is mighty useful to me; and I find them all evasions, and in many things false, and in a few, to the full purpose.' After deciding to take copies before returning them to Matthew Wren, Pepys retired to bed, contented. The one who tried to hit back was Lord Anglesey (who a few months before had implied that Pepys had overstayed his leave when he visited the West Country). He now asked the Duke of York's secretary to inspect all Pepys's books, in the hope of finding inaccuracies or irregularities. But he had picked on the wrong member of the Navy Board if he wished to expose incompetence.

Whether he meant to or not, Pepys had raked his colleagues with a deadly broadside: at the end of October old Sir John Minnes resigned as Comptroller of the Navy, though retaining the office of a Commissioner. A few days later it was Lord Anglesey's turn: he was suspended as Treasurer of the Navy, and Sir Thomas Littleton and Sir Thomas Osborne appointed jointly in his place. But for two of Pepys's colleagues at the Navy Office there was deserved promotion. Tom Hayter, his Head Clerk, was promoted on the Duke of York's orders to become Petty Purveyor of petty missions, while Mr Turner became Storekeeper at Deptford: 'which contents me mightily', Pepys could note in his Diary.

Now nearly all the old faces had gone from the Navy Board. On 5 November it was Sir William Penn who left the Office, to go into the victualling business with Denis Gauden. Only Lord Brouncker, Sir John Minnes (now hardly still in this world), the comparative newcomer Colonel Middleton—another Commissioner—and of course Pepys, were left. Although he might stand well in the opinion of the Duke of York, Pepys was not sanguine about his own future, almost hoping he might be turned out of office before his eyes forced him to resign.

In 1660, when Pepys was starting to furnish the house as he wished, he had bought gilded leather hangings for the walls of the dining-room. Now he and Elizabeth were considering buying tapestries: a set of the Apostles costing £83, and a day later the parcel arrived at the house.

Meanwhile there was a larger and more impressive purchase under consideration. Perhaps more than anything in the way of worldly possession (except for his library) that Pepys wanted was a coach and horses of his own. For years he had admired—and coveted— my Lord's 'noble, rich coach'. The idea had come a step nearer reality after Samuel and Elizabeth enjoyed the pleasure of driving to Epsom Downs, and in October Pepys was seriously looking about him for a coach, and made an offer of £50 for one which caught his eye, 'which do please me mightily'. Mr Povy, one-time Treasurer of the Tangier Committee, may have been a fool in some matters, but he knew more about coaches than Pepys did. 'I got him to go and see it, but where he finds most infinite fault with it, both as to being out of fashion and heavy, with so good reason that I am mightily glad of his having corrected me in it; and so I do resolve to have one of his built, and with his advice, both in coach and horses, he being the fittest man in the world for it.' Povy recommended him to a good coach-maker, but the model he wanted had been sold that very morning.

A few days later, Pepys and Povy spent a whole afternoon going up and down among the coach-makers in Cow Lane, and finally settled for a small chariot, which was not quite finished. 'It being light, and will be very genteel and sober: to be covered with leather, but yet will hold four.' Then there was the question of where he was going to keep it: his own yard not being large enough. But the next-door neighbour to the Navy Office was Sir Richard Ford, and to Pepys's great content the merchant said he could let it stand in his yard. A few days later, on 28 November, it arrived. 'All morning at the Office, where, while I was sitting, one comes and tells me that my coach is come . . . and so I ordered it [to be put in Sir Richard's yard], to my great content, it being mighty pretty, only the horses do not please me, and, therefore, resolve to have better.' A coach and horses meant a coachman (or boy), and now his new clothes were being delivered, which also pleased Pepys mightily. When Sir William Warren first saw the coach the hope crossed his mind that it would not be a cause of jealousy and spite (which much later proved to be the case), but Pepys felt that it was hard if after eight years' work he could not afford such a luxury. It was Elizabeth who first went out in the coach, to call on relations: Roger Pepys the Member of Parliament; the new Mrs Creed; and lastly to Pepys's cousin Mrs Turner, who before the Great Fire used to live in Salisbury Court.

If Mr Povy came to his aid over choosing the coach, it was Ned Pickering and a jockey friend of Will Hewer's who went with him to Smithfield to choose new coach-horses. '. . . here I do see instances of a piece of craft and cunning that I never dreamed of: concerning the buying and choosing of horses.' As it was late in the afternoon no purchase was made. A week later Pepys and Will Hewer returned to Smithfield, where Ned Pickering was waiting. Pepys's education in the world of horse-coping continued: 'and up and down all the afternoon about horses, and did see the knaveries and tricks of jockeys'. Even Mrs Knipp's husband, himself a jockey, was there to give advice, to the embarrassment of Pepys, in view of the domestic crisis at home. In the end—on Ned Pickering's advice—he finally chose a fine pair of black horses, costing £50, and on 12 December he wrote: 'This day was brought home my pair of black coach-horses, the first I ever was master of, a fine pair!'

To the outside world Pepys was going about his business as usual, still discussed with praise for his eloquent speech in defence of the Navy Board at the bar of the House, and obviously prospering; with beautiful new furnishings for his house, and a smart new coach and pair. But behind closed doors it was a very different story. Pepys's marriage was nearly breaking up, and his private life one of misery. After thirteen years of marriage, during which time Elizabeth had had some reason to doubt her husband's fidelity, the inevitable day came when she entered a room unexpectedly, not to discover Samuel quite *in flagrante*, but behaving in a way in which no wife would wish to discover her husband. In the seventeenth and eighteenth centuries, ladies' underwear was unknown. '25th October (Lord's Day). At night W. Batelier comes and sups with us; and after supper to have my head combed by Deb, which occasioned the greatest sorrow to me that ever I knew in this world, for my wife coming up suddenly did find me embracing the girl con my hand sub su coats.' Such shared intimacies had in fact been going on since August, and not only with Deb Willett; and now Elizabeth had the evidence of her own eyes. There was no scene. Elizabeth became angry, but then quiet. For his part Pepys said little, and slipped off to bed as soon as possible. At 2 a.m. he was awakened by Elizabeth who told him she was a Roman Catholic who had received the Holy Sacrament. Samuel was upset, but not sure whether she was merely saying it in order to hurt him. Then the tears and the reproaches came, and there was no sleep for the erring husband.

The next day, Pepys went about his business as usual: discussing with the Duke of York the letter he had written concerning the shortcomings of the Navy Office. At home 'my wife mighty discontented', but it was not until they were abed that the storm broke for the second night running. Pepys knew he was in a situation where he could not defend himself: not only over his conduct with Deb, but the way he had occupied so much of his time with Mrs Knipp and Mrs Pierce. The situation being what it was the only course open was to make concessions. 'I did offer to give her under my hand [in writing] that I would never see Mrs Pierce more nor Knipp, but did promise her particular demonstrations of my true love to her, owning some indiscretions in what I did, but that there was no harm in it.'

For a week there was an uneasy peace in the house; but during that time Elizabeth was making up her mind. Deb's aunt was asked to come to Seething Lane, and with unexpected diplomacy Elizabeth suggested that the girl should leave her present employment. Samuel was sorry, but hardly surprised. In the past it had been the custom for either Elizabeth's companion or one of the maids to assist him to dress in the morning. But not now: if he wanted help Elizabeth was at hand to provide it. In fact he hardly dare so much as look at Deb, knowing Elizabeth was watching his eyes whenever the girl was present. It was a miserable existence for both of them; then on Friday, 13 November, Pepys came home to hear that Deb had found a new employer, and would be leaving the next day. 'My wife told me she would not have me to see her or give her her wages; and so I did give my wife £10 for her year and half and quarter's wages. And so to bed, and there, blessed be God! we did sleep well and with peace, which I had not done in now almost twenty nights together.' But the next morning Elizabeth would not even allow Samuel to go through the kitchen where Deb was (he wanted to slip her some money screwed up in a piece of paper): '. . . and I vexed at it, answered her a little angrily, upon which she flew into a rage, calling me dog and rogue, and that I had a rotten heart.' Pepys knew he deserved her anger, and soon Deb and her possessions were trundling out of Seething Lane in a coach, without so much as a goodbye from him. With a heavy heart he went to the Office reflecting that from now on Elizabeth had the upper hand, and 'that I shall ever be a slave to her'. Even at such a time he could admit that for her part Elizabeth would labour to be a good wife. But contrition had nothing to do with repentance, and even before Deb was out of the house Pepys could write: 'I have a great mind for to have the maidenhead of this girl,' and within a few days he was seeking his wife's ex-companion.

By Wednesday Pepys had found her new address, near Holborn, where she was employed by an impecunious doctor. In the dark she climbed into his hired coach, and once again Pepys's hand strayed beneath her petticoat. 'I did nevertheless, give her the best council I could, to have a care for her honour and to fear God, and to suffer no man para avoir to do con her as je have just done, which she promised.' A particularly fine example of—'but it's different in my case'. Returning home Pepys told Elizabeth 'a fair tale': a variation on the theme of working late at the office.

The next day when Pepys returned home at noon he raced up-stairs to see how the upholsterers were getting on, setting up a new and somehow symbolic bed, only to find Elizabeth 'sitting sad in the dining-room'. She charged him with having been with Deb the day before. At first Pepys denied it, but then: 'I did confess all, and I did endure the sorrow of her threats and vows and curses all the afternoon.' Next she threatened to walk out then and there, but changed her mind and demanded three or four hundred pounds: 'to buy my peace, or else protested that she would make all the world know of it'. Pepys spent an agonising afternoon, not knowing what to do. Finally he sent for Will Hewer. 'Who I was forced to privy now to all: and the poor fellow did cry like a child and obtained what I could not, that she would be pacified upon condition that I would give it under my hand never to see or speak to Deb while I live, as I did before with Pierce and Knipp.' Even now Pepys had the honesty to admit in the Diary that he had obtained a durable peace which was more than he deserved. If he had been a moth about a candle flame he had suffered a terrible singeing, and that night began 'to pray to God upon my knees alone in my chamber, which God knows I cannot yet do heartily; but I hope God will give me the grace more and more every day to fear Him and to be true to my poor wife'.

If there were to be peace, there was a condition Elizabeth insisted must be strictly observed. In her present frame of mind she was not prepared to go out and about with Samuel, so, wherever he went Will Hewer must go, acting as a chaperone to his master. And so it was: wherever Pepys went, Will Hewer was sure to follow. But if anyone saved the marriage it was Hewer. Whether it was the truth or only said in a fit of pique, Elizabeth told Will Hewer that on a number of occasions she had had temptation put in her way, but had resisted it.

Even now all was not well at home. 'Hoping for a further degree of peace and quiet, I found my wife upon her bed in a horrible rage afresh, calling me all the bitter names; and, rising, did fall to revile me in the bitterest manner in the world, and could not refrain to strike me and pull my hair, which I resolved to bear with, and had good reason to bear it.' Now it was he who was in tears, and in the end Will Hewer came upstairs to them. While Pepys threw himself down on a bed in a state of abject misery, Will Hewer tried to reason with Elizabeth in the adjoining room. In the end he succeeded in pacifying her by suggesting that her husband should write Deb an offensive letter, calling her a whore and saying he never wanted to see her again. Pepys did so, and Will Hewer promised to see it delivered, but somehow it never reached its destination. But at least Elizabeth was satisfied. 'So from that minute my wife begun to be kind to me, and we to kiss and be friends, and so continued all the evening, and fell to talk of other matters with great comfort.'

By Sunday, 22 November, the storm was beginning to blow itself out, to be succeeded by an empty calm. 'And so to the Office, to set down my journal, for some days leaving it imperfect, the matter being mighty grievous to me, and my mind, from the nature of it; and so in, to solace myself with my wife, whom I got to read to me, and so W. Hewer, and the boy; and so, after supper, to bed.'

It was an extraordinary situation. Will Hewer, who was ten years Pepys's junior, now accompanied his master like his shadow: to Whitehall, to my Lord's—everywhere. 'With Will Hewer, who goes up and down with me like a gaoler, but yet with great love and to my great good liking, it being my desire above all things to please my wife therein.' Such was the state Elizabeth had reduced Samuel to that when they did resume visits to the theatre he dare not even look round, for fear of displeasing her, and the presence of Mrs Pierce with her husband at dinner brought him little joy. Every night he prayed on his knees in his chamber, hoping that before long Elizabeth would join him: 'though I cannot yet get my mind off from thinking now and then of Deb'.

At the end of November he briefly assessed the situation, and could find that whilst it had been most sad to his heart, and expensive to his purse (furnishings and the new coach), and that he was in 'the greatest condition of outward state that ever I was in, or hoped ever to be, or desired; and this at a time when we do daily expect great changes in this Office; and by all reports we must all of us, turn out. But my eyes are come to that condition that I am not able to work; and therefore that, and my wife's desire, make me have no manner of trouble in my thoughts about it.' One bright spot in all the gloom was the fact that after telling Samuel she was a Roman Catholic, Elizabeth was still prepared to accompany him to St Olave's on Sunday at the beginning of December: 'which pleases me mightily'.

Life was beginning to return to normal, with visits to the theatre, though Pepys had to be careful to keep his eyes on the stage still; and visitors were coming to dine in Seething Lane, such as his cousin Will Joyce: 'as troublesome a talking coxcomb as ever he was, and yet once in a year I like him well enough'. But still Pepys was under strict surveillance, and if Will Hewer could not accompany him wherever he went, then it must be Tom Edwards, even if the young man was unaware why Pepys requested the pleasure of his company. 'My own coach carrying me and my boy Tom (who goes with me in the room of W. Hewer, who could not, and I dare not go alone), to the Temple, the first time my fine horses ever carried me, and I mighty proud of them.' That same evening Elizabeth, Samuel and Will Hewer went to the Duke's Playhouse to see *Macbeth*. What thoughts, if any, crossed the Clerk of the Act's mind as he watched a husband driven to ultimate destruction by a relentless wife? All the Court was there, seated in a box just over their heads, and in Pepys's mind Elizabeth appeared as pretty as any lady present. At least on this occasion he had the courage to look round and up at the comedy going on in the auditorium. 'The King and Duke of York minded me, and smiled upon me; but it vexed me to see Moll Davis, in the box over the King's and my Lady Castlemaine's, look down upon the King, and he up to her; and so did my Lady Castlemaine once, to see who it was; but when she saw Moll Davis, she looked like fire; which troubled me.' Life was returning to normal for Pepys.

Christmas Day had come round again, and while Elizabeth stayed at home altering and putting lace on a petticoat, Samuel went to church: 'where Alderman Backwell coming in late, I beckoned to his lady, to come up to us, who did, with another lady, and after sermon, I led her down through the church to her husband and coach, a noble, fine woman, and a goodly one, and one my wife shall be acquainted with'. That evening as Elizabeth busied herself with needle and thread, the new boy Pepys had taken into his household read to his master, first from a life of Julius Caesar, and later from Descartes's book on music, which even Pepys admitted he could not understand. 'Then after supper, I made the boy play upon his lute, which I have not done before, since he came to me; and so, my mind in mighty content, we to bed.'

The year was ending in calm and companionship, and a few days later he wrote: 'Blessed be God! the year ends, after some late very great sorrow with my wife by my folly; yet ends, I say, with great mutual peace and content, and likely to last so by my care, who am resolved to enjoy the sweet of it which I now possess by never giving her like cause to trouble.' But it would be the last Christmas and New Year's Eve they would have together. For Elizabeth, death was only ten months away.

Chapter 13

'My eyes mighty weary'
1669

THE worst of the crisis might be over, but at the beginning of 1669 Will Hewer was still playing gaoler to Pepys, who for his part was either very anxious to placate Elizabeth, or genuinely wishing to make amends for his past conduct. On New Year's Day he bought her a cabinet of walnut, costing £11, and took her to see *The Maiden Queen* at the King's Playhouse, where they were seen by Mrs Knipp; Pepys dare not acknowledge the presence of the little actress. 'I found my wife uneasy there, poor wretch! therefore, I shall avoid the house as soon as I can.' In the circumstances safer company were the five Houblon brothers, some of whom had been encountered a few hours earlier at the Exchange. The year before Pepys had seen the whole close-knit family together. 'Here it was a mighty pretty sight to see old Mr Houblon, whom I never saw before, and all his sons about him, all good merchants.' One of the brothers—he did not record which—had a wife 'mighty like Elizabeth', a thought which troubled him at the time. Not only had Elizabeth forced her husband back on to the straight and narrow path, but now she had won yet another concession: instead of having to ask for money for clothes and the like she would have an allowance of £30: 'which she was mightily pleased with, it being more than ever she asked or expected'. Even so, Elizabeth wanted it in writing, and when the agreement had been drawn up it was given to Will Hewer for safe keeping.

One by one the characters, whether famous or obscure, who had crossed and recrossed the pages of the Diary were making their last appearances; at least as seen through the over-strained eyes of Pepys. Thus 'pretty witty Nell', last recorded at a visit to the King's Playhouse: 'We sat in an upper box, and the jade Nell came and sat in the next box: a bold merry slut, who lay laughing there upon people, and with a comrade of hers of the Duke's House, that came in to see the play.'

But at home good days alternated with bad ones. Pepys could play the perfect host to such guests at dinner as Lord Brouncker, Matthew Wren, Captain Cocke and the Lieutenant of the Tower, and then spend the remainder of the day amid the pleasures of his books. Quite equally, if Elizabeth were again tormented with suspicions there was misery enough for both of them: like the night when she brought fresh candles and more wood for the fire, while Pepys unsuccessfully beseeched her to come to bed. But no, there was another stormy and protracted scene, when he was called rogue and faithless. 'I did, as I might truly, deny it, and was mightily troubled, but all would not serve. At last, about one o'clock, she came to my side of the bed and drew my curtain open, and with tongs red hot at the end made as if she did design to pinch me with them: at which, in dismay, I rose up, and with a few words she laid them down, and did by little and little, very sillily, let all the discourse fall; and about two, but with much seeming difficulty came to bed, and there lay well all night, and long in bed talking together with much pleasure.' The cause of all the trouble turned out to have been nothing more than that the day before he had gone to the Treasury from the Navy Office without telling her. Before long the evening came when Elizabeth answered him shortly, and at which Pepys took to his bed in tears: 'weeping to myself for grief, which she discovering, come to bed, and mighty kind'.

Although for months, years almost, Pepys had been expecting to be turned out of office, he still continued to embellish his house. At different times he had added a new upper storey, put in a staircase, decorated fireplaces; as well as purchasing movable adornments, like his hangings and tapestries. On 22 January he bought a new looking-glass for the dining-room at a cost of £6 7s. 6d., and arranged with Henry Dankers, the Dutch landscape painter, to provide four panels for the dining-room depicting Whitehall, Hampton Court, Greenwich and Windsor.

Now he was preparing for the grandest dinner he had ever given in Seething Lane. Though hiring a servant or servants especially for a party was itself no innovation—'Mightily pleased with the fellow that came to lay the cloth, and fold the napkins, which I like so well, as that I am resolved to give him 40s to teach my wife to do it'—perhaps that 23 January 1669 was to be the highwater mark of Pepys's prosperity as a married man, the peak of a long ascent, from that windy, sun-filled summer of 1660 when Sir Edward Montagu, future Earl of Sandwich and Garter Knight, had told Pepys that if they had a little patience they would rise together. Pepys's rise had been less spectacular than that of his patron, but more soundly based on hard work, unswerving loyalty to the Navy Office—and no aversion from accepting 'tokens of esteem' from merchants and the like. Now it was the son of a tailor from East Anglia who could talk if not familiarly, at least with honesty and freedom to the King and the Duke of York; claim such as John Evelyn as a friend; discourse intelligently on the rapidly expanding world of science and medicine; in music hold his own with professionals as an executant, and above all show guests a library containing books and prints the most discerning would be proud to possess. Those who accepted his hospitality that night were Lord Sandwich, Lord Peterborough (one-time Governor of Tangier), Sir Charles Harbord (future Paymaster for Tangier), Sir William Godolphin (secretary to Lord Arlington), and Lord Sandwich's two sons, Edward (Lord Hinchingbrooke) and Sidney Montagu. What was more it was one of those rare occasions when everything went without a hitch, 'And after greeting them, and some time spent in talk, dinner was brought up, one dish after another, but a dish at a time, but all so good; but, above all things, the variety of wines, and excellent of their kind . . . a dinner of about six or eight dishes, as noble as any man need to have, I think; at least, all was done in the noblest manner that ever I had any, and I have rarely seen in my life better anywhere else, even at Court. After dinner my Lords to cards, and the rest of us sitting about them and talking, and looking on my books and pictures and my wife's drawings, which they commended mightily; and mighty merry all day long, with exceeding great content; and so till seven at night, and so took their leaves. Thus was this entertainment over, the best of its kind and the fullest of honour and content to me that ever I had in my life; and I shall not easily have so good again.'

Domestic contentment had returned to the house in Seething Lane, and at the end of January Pepys could write that it had contained 'many different days of sadness and mirth, from differences between me and my wife; but this night we are at present very kind'. Even so, there could have been little peace of mind for Pepys. Will Batelier had returned from a visit to France, bringing with him books for Pepys, including two books of songs: 'but my eyes are now too much out of time to look upon them, with any pleasure'. More and more frequently the references come: 'W. Batelier and Balty dined with us, and I spent all afternoon with my wife and W. Batelier talking, and then making them read. After supper, my wife begun another book I lately bought, called *The State of England*, which promises well, and is worth reading.' The next evening Elizabeth and the boy again read to him, one after the other.

Work continued with the Tangier Committee, and Pepys had the satisfaction of learning that the Duke of York would not let certain business go forward in his absence. When he expressed his thanks, the Duke replied that he should 'have a care for him [Pepys] that do the King's business in the manner that I do, and words of more force than that'. It was now as though the Duke of York and not Lord Sandwich was Pepys's patron. When the Earl suggested that Sir Charles Harbord should become paymaster in Tangier, the Duke firmly said it was 'fit to have Mr Pepys satisfied therein first, and that it was not good to make places for persons'. My Lord took the snub remarkably well, and did not hold it against his kinsman. As for Navy business, the Surveyor had told the King and cabinet that it would take two years to get the Fleet battle-worthy once again. 'I did give them hopes that, with supplies of money suitable, we might have them all fit for sea, some part of the summer after this.' Then he was asked how long it would take to get forty ships ready: given the money, said Pepys, they could be at sea by May. But at the back of his mind the Clerk of the Acts felt sure that at the end of the year all there would be to show would be a small fleet of hired merchantmen. It was all very discouraging, and with renewed pleasure Pepys returned to his own affairs, which included having a cast made of his face at a plasterer's near Charing Cross: 'but I was vexed first to be forced to daub all my face over with pomatum: but it was pretty to feel how soft and easily it is done on to the face, and by and by, by degrees, how hard it becomes, that you cannot break it'. A few days later he returned: 'To the plasterer's, and there saw the figure of my face taken from the mould: and it is most admirable like, and I will have another made, before I take it away.'

But the laborious shorthand used for the Diary was causing increasing discomfort, especially if he had been working too near candles: 'and [that] do teach me, by a manifest experiment, that it is only too much light that do make my eyes sore. Never the less, with the help of my tube, and being desirous of easing my mind of five or six days journal, I did venture to write it down from ever since this day se'nnight, and I think without hurting my eyes any more than they were before, which was very much, and so home to supper and to bed.'

Pepys may have learnt his lesson, but where an attractive woman was concerned he was incorrigible: even if she had been dead for some two hundred years. He had gone sightseeing in Westminster Abbey, where the building of the Henry VII Chapel had necessitated the demolition of the chapel in which Katherine de Valois—Henry V's queen, and later maternal ancestor of the Tudors—had been buried, and until 1776 she lay disinterred in an open coffin. 'And here we did see,' recorded Pepys on 23 February 1669, 'by particular favour, the body of Queen Katherine of Valois; and I had the upper part of her body in my hands, and I did kiss her mouth, reflecting upon it that I did kiss a Queen, and that this was my birthday, thirty-six years old, that I did kiss a Queen.'

Of the daughters of Lord Sandwich it had always been Lady Jemimah who had been Pepys's favourite, but now he heard that her sister Paulina was 'desperately sick'. Always a nervous girl she was now dying at Chelsea. On 1 March he heard she was dead and went to condole with Lord Sandwich at Whitehall. 'But he is so shut up with sorrow, and so not to be spoken with.' Later he heard from Mr and Mrs Creed of her last days. 'They do here talk mightily of my Lady Paulina making a good end, and being mightily religious in her lifetime; and she hath left many good notes of sermons and religion, wrote with her own hand, which nobody ever knew of; which I am glad of: but she was always a peevish lady.'

Whilst at this time Pepys might congratulate himself that he had the Duke of York's favour, he could by no means feel secure. There were hostile factions at Court, notably that of the Duke of Buckingham, who now had the same powerful—not to say malign—influence over Charles II that his father had exercised over James I and then Charles I. Now there came a bombshell that must have shaken Pepys to the foundations of his world. Sir William Coventry had been sent to the Tower. If it sounded unbelievable the reason was just that, and reflected no credit on the King or his circle. Little love was lost between Coventry and Buckingham: the latter fancied himself as a playwright, and had proposed to ridicule the Duke of York's ex-secretary in a play. Coventry retaliated by threatening to slit the nose of any actor who impersonated him, and sent Buckingham a challenge to a duel through Henry Saville, a member of the

Duke of York's household. As a result Coventry found himself in
the Tower, while Saville was confined in the Gatehouse prison at
Westminster. At this the Duke of York complained that if the Tower
was good enough for Coventry, why wasn't it also good enough for
Saville, a member of his own household? Obligingly Charles had
him moved to the fortress, where he remained for a fortnight.

'4th March. Being very much troubled at this, I away by coach
homewards, and, directly to the Tower, where I find him in the
Brick Tower.' There Pepys greeted Sir William, offered his service,
and left. Then Pepys went on to the Treasurer's House at Deptford,
where he found the Duke and Duchess of York, the Duchess of
Monmouth, Lady Castlemaine and others of the anti-Buckingham
faction. To his satisfaction Pepys was invited to dine with the Maids
of Honour, and afterwards saw the Duke and Duchess 'with all the
great ladies sitting upon a carpet, on the ground, there being no
chairs, playing at "I love my love with an A, because he is so and so:
and I hate him with an A, because of this and that", and some of
them, but particularly the Duchess herself and my Lady Castlemaine, were very witty.'

From watching royalty at play, Pepys 'slunk out to Bagwell's;
and there saw her, and her mother, and, our late maid Nell, who
cried for joy to see me'. After a meeting soon after in a tavern on
Moorfields the humble carpenter's wife, who was perhaps the
most likeable-sounding of Pepys's conquests, disappears from the
Diary.

Nearly every day now Pepys walked to the Tower to see Sir
William Coventry in his not too rigorous confinement, and together
they paced up and down Northumberland Walk, named after the
'Wizard Earl' imprisoned in the aftermath of the Gunpowder Plot.
Visiting Sir William became a way of showing disapproval of the
Duke of Buckingham. 'Whilst I was there [7 March], came in; so
that I do hear that there was not less than sixty coaches there
yesterday, and the other day; which I hear also that there is great
exception taken at, by the King and the Duke of Buckingham, but
it cannot be helped.' Two days later he was back again, and for the
first time told another person of the existence of the Diary. 'Up, and
to the Tower; and there find Sir W. Coventry alone, writing down
his Journal, which, he tells me, he now keeps of the material things;
upon which I told him, and he is the only man I ever told it to, I
think, that I kept it most strictly these eight or ten years, and I am

sorry almost that I told him, it not being necessary, nor may be convenient, to have it known.'

On 22 March, Sir William Coventry was released from the Tower, though not given permission to return to Whitehall. Not that he wished to: after years of loyal service he had had enough of the Court and its foolish ways. What was more, while in the fortress his name had been removed from the Privy Council, and if the King wanted nothing of him, he for his part wanted nothing of his sovereign. He would be glad to retire into the country, and at least metaphorically cultivate his garden.

For Pepys work at the Navy Office went on, and with the departure in March of Penn he was the last one left of those who had gathered round the table in the boardroom in the morning of the Restoration. As Clerk of the Acts his was, technically, the most junior post on the Navy Board, but more and more he noticed that others—especially the Duke of York—looked to him for advice, or at least for his opinion on all matters concerning the Navy and Tangier. 'I see that on all these occasions they seem to rely most on me,' he could note as far back as January 1669. And that included listening carefully to his suggestions for maintaining the Fleet within the budget allowed of £200,000 a year.

One by one the characters who had helped fill the Diary for so long appear for the last time. When Navy business took him to the Privy Seal Office on 8 March, Pepys ran into his one-time fellow-clerk at the Exchequer Office a decade before. 'Met Mr Moore, and I find him the same discontented poor man as ever.' Discontented or not, Henry Moore had news of an old mutual acquaintance: Edward Shepley, the steward at Hinchingbrooke, whose book about St Paul's Pepys and Lord Sandwich had referred to to settle a wager whether the cliffs at Dover or the tower of St Paul's was the higher, during those heady days of excitement and anticipation while awaiting my Lord's summons to join his newly returned master at Whitehall. 'He tells me that Mr Shepley is upon being put away from my Lord's family, and another sent down, which I am sorry for; but his age and good fellowship have almost made him fit for nothing.'

Another Pepys saw from time to time who had set sail for Holland on the *Naseby* beneath the Commonwealth flag, and returned on the *Charles* with the royal cypher fluttering in that easterly wind, was Will Howe. He was among the guests when Pepys entertained,

among others, his cousin Mrs Turner and her daughter 'The.'
(Theophela), the other Turners, once Pepys's neighbours but now
at Deptford, and Will Batelier. A few weeks earlier he had entertained his noble acquaintances in handsome style; now it was the
turn of his own circle to share his hospitality. What was more he
again employed the best music in town for their pleasure: 'We fell
to dancing, and continued, only with intermission for a good supper,
till two in the morning . . . and so with mighty mirth and pleased
with their dancing and jigs . . . and then to a country dance again,
and so broke up with extraordinary pleasure, as being one of the
days and nights of my life spent with the greatest content, and that
which I can but hope to repeat again a few times in my whole
life.'

Business took Pepys to the Privy Seal Office, and also to the
Patent Office: after dining with Will Howe at a cook's shop in
Gray's Inn and seeing the room where he lived: 'Where I never
was before; and it is very pretty, and little, and neat as he was
always.' Will Howe was working in the Patent Office, deputising
for his brother Jack, 'an idle rogue', who was hiding from his
creditors. Still Pepys was accompanied everywhere he went by
Will Hewer, for even now Elizabeth had her suspicions about her
husband. That evening (12 March) he returned home expecting
to find her well satisfied with the hard day's work he had put in, but
that was not the case. 'I find her in her closet, alone in the dark, in a
hot fit of railing against me, upon some news she has this day heard
of Deb's living very fine, and with black spots, and speaking very
ill of her mistress . . . but God knows, I know nothing of her, nor
what she do.' Recently Elizabeth had hired a new girl, but now she
decided she was too attractive to keep in the same house as Samuel,
and she must go. In her place she hired a young woman scarred with
smallpox, 'which vexed me all night', though wisely Pepys said
nothing. However, he was not too disappointed in the appearance of
the new girl: she had a pleasant voice, 'but hath most great hands,
and I believe ugly; but very well dressed, and good clothes, and
that otherwise I believe will please me well enough'.

At last Jane Birch and Tom Edwards were to be married. A licence
was obtained for the marriage to take place during Lent, as it happened on the date Pepys always kept as a feast day to celebrate the
anniversary of the day on which he was cut for the stone. But when
26 March came he was not there to see the young couple married:

Navy business had taken him to Chatham. All went well, as he heard from Elizabeth on the following day. 'They being married, it seems, very handsomely at Islington; and dined at the old house, and lay in our blue chamber, with much company, and wonderful merry. "The." Turner and Mary Batelier bridesmaids, and Talbot Pepys [son of Roger Pepys the MP], and Will Hewer bridesmen.' It was not until the next morning after his return that Pepys saw the young couple. 'To the office with Tom, who looks mighty smug upon his marriage, as Jane also do, both of whom I did give joy.' And so two more of Pepys's circle take their leave of the Diary and their place in Restoration England, with the exception of a reference at the end of April when Pepys gave Tom a sword costing 12*s*., and a belt of his own.

The duty that had taken Pepys to Chatham was to attend a court martial inquiry into the loss of *The Defiance*; for to his amusement (and satisfaction) he had been given a commission as a captain by the Duke of York. Among those with whom he travelled on that bitter cold March day was his colleague from the Navy Office, Commissioner Middleton. Before the court martial Pepys visited Maidstone, a town he had never seen, but which he now viewed from the top of the tower of the parish church. Everything in life still interested Pepys: 'and in the town did see an old man beating flax, and did step into the barn and give him money, and saw that piece of husbandry which I never saw, and it is very pretty'. After that, on his way back to Chatham, he stopped the coach to get out and view Kit Coty's Cottage, the prehistoric grave not far from Hoo. 'Which is of three stones standing upright, and a great round one lying on them, of great bigness, although not so big as those on Salisbury Plain, but certainly it is a thing of great antiquity, and I am mighty glad to see it.'

At Chatham there were old acquaintances to be renewed, with Captain Allen and his attractive daughter Rebecca; first encountered on that happy visit nine years before. In anticipation of re-meeting Becky, Pepys had himself spruced up by a barber in Maidstone. Now she was Mrs Jewkes, having married a lieutenant, and delighted to talk with the Clerk of the Acts. There were other guests, neighbours of Captain Allen, and while they talked and drank Becky and Samuel reminisced about old times. 'Mrs Jewkes and I to talk and there had all our old stories up, and there I had the liberty to salute her often and pull off her glove, where her hand mighty moist, and she mighty free in kindness to me, and je do not at all doubt but I might have had that that I would have desired de elle had I had time to have carried her to Cobham as she, upon my proposing it, was willing to go, for elle is a whore, that is certain, but a very brave and comely one. Here stayed till almost twelve at night, and then with a lanthorn from thence walked over the fields, as dark as pitch, and mighty cold and snow, to Chatham.'

The next morning he was up by 8 a.m., and together with Rear-Admiral Kempthorne, seven other captains and Commissioner Middleton boarded the *Charles*, launched in March the previous year to replace her namesake towed away by the Dutch. Evidently, a careless gunner had caused *The Defiance* to be burnt at her moorings. The court martial—presided over by Pepys and Middleton—lasted till seven at night. It fell to the other members of the court to decide the punishment, during which time Pepys and his colleague were dined on hot salt beef, brown bread and brandy: 'So good as I never would desire to eat better meat while I live, only I would have cleaner dishes.' Considering the severity of sentences which could be meted out in the Navy, the gunner was lucky. 'They do sentence that the gunner of *The Defiance* should stand upon the *Charles* three hours, with his fault writ upon his breast and with a halter about his neck, and so be made incapable of any service. The truth is, the man do seem, and is, I believe, a good man; but his neglect, in trusting a girl to carry fire into his cabin, is not to be pardoned.'

As soon as the verdict had been given, the other captains were away, to catch the tide to take them back to London that night, despite it having been 'a great snowy and mighty cold, foul day'. Pepys spent another day at Chatham, visiting the dock, and looking over the storehouses, and the house once occupied by Commissioner Pett, but soon to be lived in by his successor in office, Captain Cox. Whilst the new Commissioner had complained that it would need a great deal of money to set the house in order before he moved in, in Pepys's opinion £10 would cover all necessary expenses, but then 'so free everybody is of the King's money!' That evening Pepys went to bed at Hill House overlooking Chatham, and thinking that after all his colleague Middleton was not so dour when you got to know him. Also he thought how merry they must all be at home in Seething Lane, celebrating Tom and Jane's wedding.

The usual round of work continued: to the Navy Office, and to

Whitehall to recount at first hand to the Duke of York what happened at the court martial. More than ever Pepys had learnt to be circumspect, as when Sir Thomas Clifford, one of the joint treasurers for Tangier, commented that he thought both Commissioner Middleton and Sir John Minnes were too old for their jobs, and that Lord Brouncker spent too much time thinking about his beloved mathematics.

And now it was Pepys's turn to be slightly jealous of Elizabeth. One who had come into their circle was Henry Sheres, the engineer responsible for the mole at Tangier. Years later he would sail with Pepys to Tangier to destroy that same mole when that most expensive colony on the North African coast was abandoned.

By chance Samuel and Elizabeth met Henry Sheres at the King's Playhouse. 'Yet I could not but be troubled because my wife do so delight to talk of him, and to see him. Nevertheless, we took him with us to our mercer's, and to the Exchange, and he helped me choose a summer suit of coloured camlot, coat and breeches, and a flowered tabby coat [watered silk] very rich; and so home.' The next day there was more fuel for his suspicions. Henry Sheres had been invited to dinner, and Elizabeth did nothing by half measure. 'Yet I see no reason to be troubled at it, he being a very civil and worthy man, I think; but only it do seem to imply some little neglect of me.' Had the situation been reversed and the guest been Mrs Knipp or Mrs Pierce, both of whom had already ceased to figure in the Diary, he would no doubt have considered Elizabeth's attitude unfounded and unreasoning. The worst of it was that Pepys, who admitted his own jealous nature, enjoyed Henry Sheres's company as much as did Elizabeth—such as the occasion when he took them to Mulberry Garden (now covered by the grounds of Buckingham Palace) to sample a Spanish dish prepared by a cook who had been in Lord Sandwich's employment in Spain. 'And the Olio was indeed a very noble dish, such as I never saw better, or any more of. This, and the discourse he did give us of Spain, and the description of the Escorial, was a fine treat.' But the suspicions remained; they flared up, for instance, when he went to the theatre, and there saw Elizabeth and Will Hewer in the pit, and who should come up to them but Henry Sheres.

References to the discomfort of his eyes come with greater and greater frequency. '25th April. W. Howe came and dined with us; and then I to my office, he being gone, to write down my journal

for the last twelve days: and did it with the help of my vizard [mask]
and tube fixed to it, and do find it mighty manageable, but how help-
ful to my eyes this trial will show me.' At least there was the pleasure
of their coach and as the weather improved he and Elizabeth went
for drives to the neighbouring villages or to Hyde Park: 'to the
Lodge, the first time this year, and there in our coach eat a cheese-
cake and drank a tankard of milk.'

May Day was approaching, and for the first time Pepys would be
able to join the fashionable world in his own coach as it circulated
round Hyde Park. For that the coach must be looking its best. Some
time before he had had to pay 40s. for new glass fitted to one of the
doors. How it had got broken he could not think, unless he had
caught it with his knee. But now he would have the coach varnished,
and that too cost 40s. On 30 April he hurried to the coach-maker's
to ensure all would be finished in time, and there saw a curious sight:
'I do find a great many ladies sitting in the body of a coach that must
be ended by tomorrow: they were my Lady Marquiss of Winchester, Bellassis, and other great ladies, eating of bread and butter
and drinking ale.' He feared the workmen were not getting on with
silvering and varnishing his own coach: 'so I put it in a way of
doing'. Then off he went to see Sir William Coventry, and to visit
an old woman—in a hat—who had a water which he hoped would be
good for his eyes. It certainly made them smart most horribly, and
he left with a phial of the stuff. Back he went at three in the afternoon to the coach-makers, and stood over the workmen till eight at
night, to make sure the work was finished in time, though he did
buy the painters a drink.

It was May Day, but there was rain in the air. Samuel put on his
best suit, with gold lace cuffs, while Elizabeth looked exceedingly
fine in her flowered tabby gown. 'And so anon we went alone through
the town with our new liveries of serge [for the coachman], and the
horses' manes and tails tied with red ribbons, and the standards
gilt with varnish, and all clean, and green reins, that people did
mightily look upon us; and, the truth is, I did not see any coach
more pretty, though more gay, than ours all the day.' But there was
a snake in that particular paradise, in the form of the unwitting
Henry Sheres. They met him in Pall Mall, and Samuel had to invite
him into the coach, and then sulked for the rest of the day. The park
proved to be dusty, windy, cold and with intermittent drizzle:
'and, what made it worse, there was so many hackney coaches as

spoiled the sight of the gentlemen's; and so we had little pleasure'. But Pepys need not have been so annoyed by the meeting: that same evening Henry Sheres was leaving for Portsmouth, the first stage of the journey back to Tangier, to Elizabeth's obvious sorrow. Both of them were out of humour when they got home.

The best suit with its gold trimmings might have delighted Pepys's heart, but it brought a well-meaning warning from Creed not to overdo things. He had heard how the fine coach and horses had been observed, and advised Pepys not to make himself too conspicuous. Pepys made up his mind never to appear at Court wearing his gold-laced sleeves: 'but presently to have them taken off, as it is fit I should, and so called at my tailor's for that purpose'. Since the Duke of Buckingham and his circle had become all-powerful at Court, any who did not belong to it, such as Pepys, had to tread carefully if they wished to remain in office.

On 17 May Pepys took his paper dealing with the administration of the Navy to the Duke of York, and the next day he, Commissioner Middleton and Sir John Minnes, were present when it was read over to the King, the Duke of York and Prince Rupert. After it had been read no comment was made, and the day's business passed on to the old question of money for the Navy. Later the Duke of York told Pepys the letter would be made available for those in authority to make their comments, and there the matter rested.

All the while his eyes were causing him more and more discomfort. Now he had two tubes, fixed to a mask, with glasses which could be inserted or removed at will, at a cost of 15s. But not only did the light in the theatre cause pain, but Pepys even moved his seat at the Office, so that he no longer had the light from the windows in his eyes: 'and I did sit with much more content than I had done on the other side for a great while, and in winter the fire will not trouble my back'.

Soon it would be time for Parliament's summer recess, and Pepys decided that for the sake of his eyes he must give them a really long rest, and perhaps travel abroad, so this seemed as good a time as any to ask leave of absence. '16th May. I all the afternoon drawing up a foul [rough] draft of my petition to the Duke of York, about my eyes, for leave to spend three or four months out of the office, drawing it so as to give occasion to a voyage abroad, which I did, to my pretty good liking.' Elizabeth was delighted at the prospect of a visit to France, and together they discussed taking a French-speaking maid with them. For his part, the Duke was genuinely concerned for Pepys's misfortune. 'By and by the Duke of York comes, and readily took me to his closet, and pitied me, and with much kindness did give me his consent to be absent, and approved my proposition to go into Holland to observe things there, of the Navy; but would first ask the King's leave, which he anon did, and did tell me that the King would be a good master to me (these were his very words) about my eyes, and do like of my going into Holland.'

A few days later Pepys was back once again at Whitehall: 'where I attended the Duke of York, and was led by him to the King, who expressed great sense of my misfortune in my eyes, and concernment for their recovery . . . and commanded me to give them rest this summer, according to my late petition to the Duke of York'. There were still duties to be carried out, including a visit to the Commissioners of Accounts about his Treasurership for Tangier.

Once again it was the anniversary of the Restoration. Exactly nine years before to the day Charles II had crossed London Bridge in a great glittering procession: 300 gentlemen in cloth of silver, 300 soldiers in velvet, trumpeters and drummers, his own Life Guards, the two Sheriffs, the Aldermen, the Lord Mayor carrying the Sword of London unsheathed before the returning sovereign. How much had happened in those intervening years. But now it was all ending for Pepys the diarist. Everything would be set in order quietly and methodically, and then there would be nothing left to do but close the Diary, and blow out the candle.

'And thus ends all that I doubt I shall ever be able to do with my own eyes in the keeping of my journal. I being not able to do it any longer, having done now so long as to undo my eyes almost every time that I take a pen in my hand; and therefore, whatever comes of it, I must forbear; and therefore resolve from this time forward to have it kept by my people in long-hand, and must be contented to set down no more than is fit for them and all the world to know, or, if there be anything, which cannot be much now my amours are past and my eyes hindering me in almost all other pleasures, I must endeavour to keep a margin in my book open, to add, here and there, a note in shorthand with my own hand.

'And so I betake myself to that course, which is almost as much as to see myself go into my grave: for which, and for all the discomforts that will accompany my being blind, the good God prepare me!

'May 31 1669   S.P.'

Chapter 14

The End of the Story
1669–1703

THE fear that had haunted Pepys for months, even years, was not realised. Although he had obviously strained his eyes very seriously, he did not go blind. For nine and a half years he had kept his Diary in cypher, but now he put it away, set his affairs in order and prepared for the holiday he had promised himself and Elizabeth. They set out first for Holland, then to what is now Belgium, and finally on to Paris. There, with introductions from John Evelyn, the couple made new friends, and it must have been a time of great happiness for both of them. But on the return journey Elizabeth fell ill in Brussels. At the end of October they were home again in Seething Lane, where Elizabeth developed a high fever, and on 10 November she died, not yet thirty. Impetuous, scolding, loving and in some ways so child-like, she was gone, leaving Pepys alone and desolate on the threshold of middle age.

Elizabeth was buried in St Olave, Hart Street, which, though it survived the Great Fire unharmed, was to be reduced to a shell by fire-bombs during the Second World War. But the charming portrait bust of 1669 by John Bushnell survives, together with most of the church's fittings, which were moved to a place of safety before the holocaust.

Samuel Pepys remained a widower. He prospered, and did much towards reorganising the Navy along practical lines. Honours and public offices came his way, beginning with Trinity House of which he became first a Warden and then the Master. In 1673 he became Secretary to the Admiralty, and six years later one of the Members of Parliament for Harwich. His later career was not free from trouble. He found himself involved in Titus Oates's monstrous Popish Plot, and had considerable difficulty clearing his name, and in fact was sent for a while to the Tower of London. In 1683 he went as confidential adviser to Lord Dartmouth to Tangier after it had been decided that the little colony was too expensive to maintain. There he helped settle the claims of the merchants and residents before the harbour and mole were destroyed, along with much of the town.

After the overthrow of James II in 1688 Pepys was offered the opportunity of remaining in office by William and Mary, but since his loyalty was to the deposed monarch, he declined the offer.

The last years were ones of peace, but not of total inactivity. He performed many acts of generosity, especially towards the young, and worked on his *Memoirs of the Navy*. It was at Will Hewer's house at Clapham, on 26 May 1703, that his old enemy the stone killed Samuel Pepys, sometime Clerk of the Acts and later Secretary for Admiralty Affairs. Thirty-four years after her death he was buried alongside Elizabeth in St Olave, Hart Street. In his work for the Navy he performed a service to his own generation and those who came after, but in keeping his Diary he gave something unique to the world.

The Diary is contained in six calf-bound volumes of unequal size (totalling about a million and a quarter words), of which about seventy per cent was published in the version most readily available. The Diary was first transcribed in 1825 by the Rev. J. Smith, and then much more fully by Mynars Bright in 1875–9: the latter with notes by H. B. Wheatley having been used for most modern editions. The complete and unexpurgated Diary is now in course of publication in a definitive and scholarly edition.

As early as 1666 Pepys had the first bookcases specially made for his library, which continued to grow over the years, and by the terms of his will it was left to his nephew and executor John Jackson, and on the latter's death to Magdalene College, Cambridge, where it remains.

When Pepys died another diarist, his friend John Evelyn, paid a tribute that was as generous and truthful as any man could desire.

'This day died Mr Samuel Pepys, a very worthy, industrious and curious person, none in England exceeding him in the knowledge of the navy, in which he passed through all the most considerable offices—Clerk of the Acts, and Secretary to the Admiralty—all which he performed with great integrity. When King James II went out of England he laid down his office and would serve no more. But, withdrawing himself from all public affairs, he lived at Clapham with his partner—formerly his clerk—

Mr Hewer, in a very noble house and sweet place where he enjoyed the fruit of his labours in great prosperity, and was universally beloved. He was hospitable, generous, learned in many things, skilled in music, a very great cherisher of learned men, of whom he had the conversation.'

Table of Events

1633 Samuel Pepys born, 23 February.
1642 Outbreak of Civil War.
     Pepys at Grammar School, Huntingdon.
1646 Attends St Paul's School, London.
1649 Witnesses execution of Charles I.
     Roundhead in sympathy.
1651 Undergraduate at Magdalene College, Cambridge.
     (1 January) Charles II crowned at Scone.
     (3 September) Defeated at Worcester.
1652 Start of First Dutch War.
1654 Pepys graduates as a B.A.
     Probably works in his father's shop.
     End of First Dutch War.
1655 Marries Elizabeth le Marchant de St Michel.
1658 Becomes a Clerk in the Exchequer Office.
     Death of Cromwell.
1659 On Mission to Sir Edward Montagu in Danish waters.
     Becomes a Royalist.
     (May) Richard Cromwell forced from office.
1660 (1 January) General Monk marches from Scotland with Army.
     Pepys begins the Diary on same date.
     (April) Parliament invites Charles II to return to England.
     (May) Pepys accompanies Edward Montagu on mission to bring back the King.
     (July) Pepys becomes Clerk of the Acts at the Navy Office.
1661 (April) Visits Chatham on Navy business.
     Witnesses Coronation Procession. Attends Coronation and banquet. Visits Portsmouth on Navy business.
1662 Pepys becomes immersed in work at the Navy Office.

(April) Again visits Portsmouth. Attacks corruption among merchants and contractors.

(August) Becomes a member of the Tangier Commission.

1663 His diligence appreciated by the Duke of York.

(September) Rebukes Lord Sandwich for his private life.

1664 (February) Death of brother Tom.

Helps prepare Navy for possible war with Holland, though hindered by lack of money.

(July) He incurs Lord Clarendon's wrath.

His eyes start to give discomfort.

(November) War with Holland (Second Dutch War).

1665 (June) Start of the Plague. Court leaves London.

Pepys celebrates Battle of Lowestoft.

(August) Household sent for safety to Woolwich.

Navy Office moved to Greenwich.

Pepys arranges marriage between daughter of Lord Sandwich and son of Sir Philip Carteret.

Lord Sandwich captures Dutch merchantmen: anticipates prize-goods by 'breaking bulk', and is himself disgraced in the ensuing scandal.

(September) Pepys also involved with prize-goods, but cleared of improper conduct.

(November) Rioting by unpaid sailors.

1666 (January) Family returns from Woolwich, and the Navy Office from Greenwich.

(February) Court returns to London.

Lord Sandwich becomes Ambassador Extraordinary to Spain.

(June) Celebrations for Four Days' Fight. The press-gangs

(September) The Great Fire of London.

(October) Inquiry into possible miscarriages by the Navy Board. Pepys gives evidence, and later writes letter to Duke of York setting out failings of the Navy Office.

1667 (March) Death of Pepys's mother.

Plans to lay up the Fleet.

(June) Dutch sail up Medway and burn Fleet and Dockyard. Pepys fears revolution. He visits Chatham.

(July) Peace of Breda ends Second Dutch War.

(August) Lord Clarendon falls from power.

(October) Death of Sir William Batten of the Navy Office.

(December) Officers of the Navy Board, including Pepys,

cross-examined before the Commons. Pepys acquits himself well. Troubled by eyesight.

1668 (March) Pepys appears at the bar of the House of Commons, and defends the Navy Office in an excellent three-hour speech.
(June) Visits the West Country.
(October) Indiscreet behaviour with his wife's companion leads to great domestic trouble for several months.

1669 Growing discomfort with his eyes.
(31 May) Pepys abandons the Diary because of eye-strain.
(November) Elizabeth dies.

1673 The Navy Office, scene of so much of Pepys's labours, was destroyed by fire.

1703 Pepys dies, 26 May 1703.

Principal Personages Mentioned
in Young Mr Pepys

Albemarle, Duke of (George Monk, or Monck). 1608–1670. Made his career in the Army from an early age, and fought in the Dutch army against the Spanish at the siege of Breda (1637). Later he saw service against the Scots and Irish before the outbreak of the Civil War. He then fought for Charles I until captured, and after two years in the Tower sided with the Parliamentarians. In 1652 he was made a General at Sea, and twice defeated the Dutch during the First Dutch War. After Richard Cromwell's removal from power he set the movement in motion which culminated in the Restoration of 1660, chiefly by bringing the armed forces over to his side. Immediately following Charles II's return, he became the Duke of Albemarle. Later, during the Plague, he showed courage by remaining at Whitehall when nearly everyone else had sought safety in the country. His wife, a strong-minded woman, was the daughter of an Army farrier.

Allen, Rebecca (Becky). Daughter of Captain Allen of Chatham, admired by Pepys.

Anglesey, Earl of (Arthur Annesley). 1614–1686. Concerned with affairs in his native Ireland during and after the Civil War on behalf of the Parliamentarians, but shifted his sympathies to the Royalists prior to the Restoration, and in June 1660 he became a member of the Privy Council. When revenge was in the air his was a moderating influence, and in 1661 he became Earl of Anglesey. In 1667 he was appointed a Treasurer of the Navy, and in 1672 received the office of Lord Privy Seal. Ten years later he fell from favour and retired from public life.

Arlington, Earl of (Henry Bennett). 1618–1685. Supported Charles I during the Civil War, and after the Restoration came to Court through the influence of Lady Castlemaine, and on her behalf became an active opponent of Lord Clarendon. He was a leading member of Charles II's Cabal, but in 1674 his enemies tried to have him impeached as 'a promoter of evil councils'. The attempt failed, but he retired from public life.

Ashwell, Mary. Companion to Elizabeth Pepys.

Backwell, Alderman Edward. Died 1683. Prominent London goldsmith, regarded as the father of modern banking: in return for money deposited clients were given 'goldsmiths' notes', the earliest form of banknotes. Frequently it was he who advanced the sums voted to Charles II by Parliament. After the Treaty of Dover in 1670 he acted as intermediary in financial transactions between Charles II and Louis XIV.

Bagwell, Mrs. Wife of a ship's carpenter at Deptford: seduced by Pepys.

Barkstead, Sir John. Executed 1662. A Parliamentarian soldier, and judge at the trial of Charles I. In 1652 he was appointed Governor of the Tower, and before fleeing was reputed to have buried treasure in the fortress. He took refuge in Germany, but upon venturing into Holland was arrested by Sir George Downing, brought to London, tried as a regicide, and executed in 1662.

Barlow, Thomas. Clerk of the Acts prior to Pepys's appointment.

Batelier, Will. City merchant and friend of Pepys.

Batten, Sir William. Died 1667. Appointed Surveyor of the Navy in 1638, and fought for Charles I during the Civil War, but saw action during the First Dutch War as a Parliamentarian. However, at the Restoration he was reinstated as Surveyor of the Navy. In 1661 he became MP for Rochester, and in June 1663 Master of Trinity House. He was twice married, with a son and daughter (Martha). For seven years he was the colleague, neighbour, rival and enemy of Pepys.

Becke, (Mrs) Betty. A London merchant's daughter living at Chelsea: the mistress of Lord Sandwich.

Bellassis, Lord. Governor of Tangier.

Berkenshaw, Mr. Music-master to Pepys.

Betterton, Thomas. 1635–1710. The leading actor in the years following the Restoration. His career started with Sir William Davenant in 1656-7, but he came into his own, acting with his wife, when the theatres reopened after the Restoration. He joined Davenant in the Duke's Company at Lincoln's Inn Fields (the Duke's Playhouse) in 1661. His leading roles included Hamlet, Mercutio, Sir Toby Belch, Bosola (*Duchess of Malfi*), Macbeth and in Davenant's *The Siege of Rhodes*. In 1671 the Duke's Company moved to Salisbury Court, the Dorset Garden Theatre.

Birch, Jane. Maidservant to Pepys. Married Tom Edwards, the young clerk employed by Pepys.

Blackburne, Robert. Secretary to the Admiralty, and uncle of Will Hewer.

Bludworth, Sir Thomas. Incompetent Lord Mayor during the Great Fire of London.

Bohemia, Queen of (the Winter Queen). Daughter of James I.

Bowyer, William. Clerk in the Exchequer Office and friend of Samuel and Elizabeth Pepys.

Brouncker, Viscount (William). 1620?-1684. Became a Doctor of Medicine at Oxford, 1647. He lived quietly during the Commonwealth, and translated a number of books, including Descartes's *Musical Compendium*. As well as being a good linguist he was a serious mathematician. Following the Restoration he took part in the meetings of students of the sciences, from which grew the Royal Society, which was incorporated by Royal Charters of 1662-3. He was its first president until 1677, being elected annually. From 1644 till 1667 he was also President of Gresham College (where the Royal Society met), as well as serving on the Commission for Tangier and later becoming Commissioner for the execution of the Office of Lord High Admiral. In 1681 he became Master of St Catharine's Hospital.

Buckingham, Duke of (George Villiers). 1627-1687. Son of the first Duke, the favourite of James I assassinated in 1628, and after his father's death he was brought up with the King's children. During the Civil War he went with Prince (later King) Charles to Scotland, and after the Royalist defeat at the Battle of Worcester in 1651 made an even more dramatic escape abroad than his master. At the Restoration his estates were restored, and he continued as a boon companion of the King, encouraging his excesses. Later he

became a member of the Cabal, and a mortal enemy of Lord Clarendon, whose downfall he eventually brought about. His decline from
royal favour began after the secret Treaty of Dover with Louis XIV,
of which he was unaware. He was related by blood to Lady Castlemaine.

Burnett, Dr. Pepys's physician.

Carcass, James. Clerk of the Ticket Office, later accused of fraud.

Carteret, Sir George. *c.* 1612–1680. Served in the Navy, becoming
its Comptroller in 1639. He supported Charles I during the Civil
War, and became Lieutenant-Governor of Jersey in 1643. When
Prince Charles took refuge on the island in 1646 he was knighted,
and later granted what became New Jersey. He went into exile in
France, and in 1660 became a member of the Privy Council, and
Vice-Chamberlain of the Royal Household. In 1661 he exchanged
his office with Lord Anglesey as Deputy Treasurer of Ireland.
During and after the Second Dutch War he was censured by Parlia-
ment for gross mismanagement and carelessness in keeping accounts.
By a vote of the Commons in December he was suspended from
sitting in the House. However, in 1673 he was appointed a Com-
missioner of the new Admiralty. It was Pepys who acted as intermediary when his son Philip married Lord Sandwich's daughter
Jemimah in 1665. Sir Philip Carteret was killed in action at the
Battle of Sole Bay (Third Dutch War) in May 1672.

Castlemaine, Countess (Barbara Villiers, Mrs Palmer, and later
Duchess of Cleveland). 1641–1709. Her grandfather was a half-
brother of the 1st Duke of Buckingham, and she was reputed to be
promiscuous from an early age. In 1659 she married Roger Palmer,
but seems to have become the mistress *en titre* of Charles II literally
from the day of his return to Whitehall. Her first child, Anne, was
claimed both by her husband and by the King, though others
nominated Lord Chesterfield. In shameful circumstances she was
forced into the household of the new Queen, Catharine of Braganza,
and in 1662 her first son, Charles, was born. Since Lady Castlemaine
had become a Roman Catholic the child received a double baptism.
A year later a third child, Henry, was born, but Charles II denied
paternity. Next followed Charlotte, born 1664. By that date Lady
Castlemaine had a rival in Frances Stuart, future Duchess of
Richmond. However in 1667 she threatened Charles II that she

would dash out the brains of the child she was then expecting if he again denied paternity, and the King literally begged her pardon on his knees. (Little wonder Pepys and all England was avid for the latest Court gossip.) Her greatest enemy was Lord Clarendon, who disapproved of everything about her, and she as much as anyone was responsible for his downfall. Extravagant and luxury loving, voluptuous and sensual, she was the embodiment of the Restoration. After 1669 she received £4,700 a year from the revenues of the Post Office, quite apart from her other numerous and improper sources of income. On one occasion it was estimated she was wearing £40,000 worth of jewellery at the theatre, and she travelled abroad in a carriage-and-eight. Her hold over Charles II declined after 1670, and by 1674 she had been quite supplanted by Louise de Quérouáille, Duchess of Portsmouth. Among her later lovers were John Churchill, the future Duke of Marlborough, and reputed father of her daughter Barbara. John Hall, the rope-dancer from Bartholomew Fair, received a salary as a member of her household, while among others to enjoy her favours was the playwright William Wycherley, and as late as 1685 she gave birth to a son by the actor Cardonnell Goodman. The three royally recognised sons, Charles, George and Henry (Fitzroy), all received Dukedoms; while the King also recognised two daughters, Anne and Charlotte Fitzroy. On Roger Palmer's death in 1705 she remarried, but since her new husband was committing bigamy the union was short-lived. She died of dropsy at Chiswick in 1709.

Catharine of Braganza, Queen. 1638-1705. Daughter of King John of Portugal, while her mother was a member of the powerful Spanish family of Medina Sidonia. As early as 1642 her father had proposed Catharine as the future wife of Prince Charles, to cement Anglo-Portuguese relations. Immediately after the Restoration, negotiations were started for the marriage. As part of her dowry England would receive Tangier, Bombay and full trading rights in the Indies. Both Spain and Holland were against the marriage, and in November 1660 the Dowager Queen Henrietta Maria came to London from France to try to dissuade her son from the union. But in May 1662 Catharine of Braganza came to England, and was married in two ceremonies, Roman Catholic and Anglican. Quiet and pious, she was at first only able to communicate with her husband in Spanish. Soon she came to enjoy the pleasures and frivolous entertainments of the English Court, vastly different to her upbringing in Portugal, but she was never touched by scandal. Lady Castlemaine in particular did much to make her life miserable, though in his curious way Charles II was fond of her, and she devoted to him. Catharine of Braganza enjoyed music, while her addiction to tea helped make the beverage fashionable in England. She was not, as was widely rumoured, barren: but miscarried or gave birth to stillborn children on several occasions. At the height of the Popish Plot there were moves to have her banished (Titus Oates even accused her of treason at the bar of the House), but Charles II defended her against all attacks. At his death she was genuinely distressed, and retired to live either at Somerset House or at Hammersmith, and even interceded with James II for the life of the Duke of Monmouth. After the revolution she fell foul of Queen Mary, and finally left England in 1692. Back in Portugal, she lived quietly, being loved and respected, and it was while acting as regent for her brother Pedro that she died in 1705.

Charles II. 1630–1685. Eldest son of Charles I and Queen Henrietta Maria. When only twelve he and his brother James (Duke of York) were nearly captured at the Battle of Edgehill. In 1645 he was ordered to leave England for France by his father, but went first to the Scilly Isles and then to Jersey, before going to France for two years. From Holland he tried to save his father, and is reputed to have sent the Parliamentarians a sheet of paper blank save for his signature, for whatever terms they chose to demand for his father's life. In June 1650 he landed in the Firth of Cromarty, but on 3 September 1650 was defeated at Dunbar. On New Year's Day 1651 he was crowned at Scone, and later marched south, only to be defeated on 3 September that year at Worcester. After his escape he wandered Europe as an exile. It was in April 1660 at Breda that he received the letter that was the prelude to the Restoration. General Monk was responsible for his return, but it was Lord Clarendon, his companion in exile, who was the dominant influence over the King for the first few years of his reign. Clarendon had a particular enemy in Lord Bristol, who even tried to have him impeached, and also Lady Castlemaine, who hated all she thought he stood for. In 1662 Charles II married Catharine of Braganza, a political anti-French move. It was in that same year, however, that he started to receive secret payments of gold from Louis XIV, intended to make him independent of Parliament; also Dunkirk (captured during the Commonwealth) was sold back, an unpopular move at home. The King's attempt to issue a Declaration of Indulgence for freedom of religious beliefs was brought to nothing by Clarendon: instead the Act of Uniformity was forced on the King, a Catholic at heart. The Second Dutch War, another trade war, began in 1665, which resulted in the disgrace of Lord Sandwich and the eventual breaking of Clarendon's power. In the years 1667–74 the Cabal, Charles II's slightly sinister cabinet, was all powerful so far as the ruling of the country was concerned. By the secret Treaty of Dover (1670) England was drawn well into the power of France, leading to the Third Dutch War, which as much as anything was brought about by France's desire to break the power of her maritime rival (1672–4). Now the Duke of Buckingham was forced out of office, and Lord Danby became his successor. In 1675 Charles II was in debt to the tune of £4 million, and he and Louis XIV concluded an agreement that in return for an annual subsidy of £100,000 Charles II would not enter into any foreign agreements without the French King's approval. The anti-French Danby arranged the marriage of Princess Mary (James, Duke of York's elder daughter) to her Dutch cousin, William of Orange, and they were married in 1677. The following year saw the start of the Popish Plot, designed to ensure the exclusion of the Catholic Duke of York from the succession. Many were in favour of the Duke of Monmouth as the next king, and there was a rumour that he was not illegitimate, but that Charles II had been married to his mother. In 1683 came the Rye House Plot, in which Monmouth was involved, to kill Charles and his brother James, and set up the young Duke. Monmouth was banished, but others were executed for their part. At the end of the reign of a quarter of a century Parliament tried to bring in the Exclusion Bill to bar James, and forced through the Test Act, banning Catholics from public office.

Cholmely, Sir Hugh. Member of the Tangier Commission.

Clarendon, Earl of (Edward Hyde). Lord Chancellor. 1608–1674. As a young man he studied law, and entered Parliament in 1640. He tried to defend Charles I not only from the Parliamentarians but also from the more irresponsible elements at Court, including the Queen. In 1648 he was appointed Chancellor of the Exchequer, and after that year he acted on behalf of Prince Charles. It was he who drew up the Declaration of Breda (April 1660) which paved the way for the King's return. He was created Earl of Clarendon in 1661, and remained the King's chief minister until 1667. Whilst a staunch monarchist, he was not particularly severe in his dealings with Dissenters, and the 'Clarendon Code' of religious restrictions was not to any great extent his work. In 1667 the younger elements at Court made him the chief scapegoat for the disaster when the Dutch sailed up the Medway and burnt or towed away much of the Fleet. On his fall he fled to France, and spent the rest of his life in exile, dying at Rouen. His daughter Anne became Duchess of York, first wife of the future James II.

Clerke, Dr. Physician first in the Navy and then at Court. A friend of Pepys.

Cocke, Captain. Paymaster to the Navy, and Steward for sick and wounded seamen. Friend of Pepys.

Cooper, Samuel. 1609–1672. Miniaturist. Resided in Henrietta Street, Covent Garden. Pepys called him 'the greatest limner in little'. He painted Elizabeth Pepys, and was also an excellent amateur musician. During the Commonwealth he painted Cromwell and his relations, and later most of the royal family as well as many of the famous people of the day.

Coventry, Sir William. 1628?–1686. The fourth son of Lord Coventry. Shortly before the Restoration he travelled to The Hague to offer his services to James, Duke of York, who appointed him his private secretary. In 1661 he became MP for Great Yarmouth, and in 1662 a Commissioner for the Navy, in which capacity he quarrelled frequently with Sir George Carteret. In October 1662 he was made a Commissioner for Tangier, and knighted three years later. He became an enemy of Lord Clarendon, and almost a protégé of Lord Arlington, one of the Cabal. In 1667 he was made a Commissioner of the Treasury, and resigned as the Duke of York's secretary soon after. In 1668 he challenged the all-powerful Duke of Buckingham to a duel, for which he was deprived of his seat on the Privy Council and sent to the Tower. On his release after several weeks he retired to the country, where for the remainder of his life he lived quietly.

Creed, John. Secretary to Lord Sandwich, and later Deputy-Treasurer to the Fleet. A friend of Pepys.

Crewe, Mr (afterwards Lord), father of Lady Sandwich.

Cuttance, Captain (later Sir) Roger. fl. 1650–1669. Captain of the *Royal Charles*, friend of Pepys, and a member of the Tangier Commission. Transferred with Lord Sandwich to the *Royal James* in 1661, and then in 1665 to the *Prince*, in which Lord Sandwich hoisted his flag as admiral of the Blue Squadron. He was knighted in 1665, but nothing is known of him after Pepys gave up the Diary.

Davis, Mr. Storekeeper at Deptford, and sometime neighbour of Pepys.

Davis, Moll. Actress (fl. 1663–1669). A member of Sir William Davenant's company, and for a while the leading actress immediately after the Restoration. She was reputed to be the illegitimate daughter of Lord Berkshire. She appeared at the Duke's Playhouse in Lincoln's Inn Fields, in particular in Dryden's *Sir Martin Mar-all*. In 1668 she attracted the King's attention, and gave up the stage. According to legend when Nell Gwynn heard that Moll Davis was to visit the King she invited her to supper, plying her with sweet-meats liberally dosed with jalup. However, she remained in favour with Charles II for at least several months, presenting him with a daughter, who in due course became the grandmother of James, Earl of Derwentwater, the only English peer executed for his part in the Jacobite rising of the 'Fifteen'.

Deane, Sir Anthony. 1638?–1721. A sailor from early life, after 1660 he was Master Shipwright at Woolwich, when he became friendly with Pepys. In 1664 he was Master Shipwright at Harwich, and in 1668 held the same post at Portsmouth. Later (1675) he became Comptroller of Victualling and Commissioner of the Navy, and at about that time he received his knighthood. On the King's orders he built two yachts for Louis XIV, which were taken over-land to be launched on the Grand Canal at Versailles. He found himself dragged into the involved plot which was also designed to discredit Pepys, and in 1679 they were both committed to the Tower, but discharged the following year. He resigned as a Commissioner of the Navy and ceased to play any part in public life.

Downing, Sir George. 1623?–1684. Partly educated at Harvard College (his uncle being Governor of Massachusetts). He became a chaplain after 1650, serving with Cromwell's army in Scotland, and became an MP. Later he conveyed Cromwell's disapproval to Louis XIV for the massacre of the Vaudois in 1655. Two years after he became Resident at The Hague, and early in 1660 shifted his allegiance to Charles II. After the Restoration he was made a Teller of the Exchequer (and so Pepys's employer), and at about that time received a grant of land near Whitehall—the future Downing Street. When the regicides Okey, Corbet and Barkstead met at Delft, Downing arrested them, and had them brought to London for trial and execution in 1662. In 1663 he was knighted, and in 1667 when the Treasury was reorganised he became its Secretary. Also he sat as MP for Morpeth. Later he was employed by Charles II deliberately to antagonise the Dutch as a prelude to the Third Dutch War, which he did with such success that he had to flee from The Hague, and for his pains was imprisoned in the Tower for a while for leaving his post without royal permission.

Edwards, Tom. A boy from the Chapel Royal, employed by Pepys to make himself useful, and be trained as a clerk. Later he married Jane Birch, the maid.

Evelyn, John. 1620–1706. Diarist and man of taste. He drifted through adolescence, and spent much of the Civil War travelling in France and Italy, finally returning to England in 1650. He settled at Sayes Court, Deptford. There he lived quietly until the Restoration. In 1659 he suggested founding a college for a few men of science, and from that grew the idea of the Royal Society. In 1664 he became a Commissioner for the care of sick and wounded and prisoners during the Second Dutch War. In later years, though a staunch Anglican, he was in favour with James II. John Evelyn was a connoisseur of art, architecture and of gardening, and it was he who discovered the talents of Grinling Gibbons. In 1694 he left Sayes Court (visited by Pepys) which was sublet to Peter the Great while on his visit to England, who all but ruined the beautiful gardens. Evelyn's Diary was first published in 1818, and more fully in 1827.

Fairfax, Thomas (Lord). Parliamentarian General.

Falconer, Mr. Chief Clerk of the Rope-yard at Woolwich.

Fenner, Mr. Uncle of Samuel Pepys. Second marriage to a midwife. By his first marriage a daughter, Peg.

Ferrers, Captain. Employed in the household of Lord Sandwich. Something of a turbulent character, with whom Pepys was friendly.

Ford, Sir Richard. City merchant and a member of the Tangier Commission, also a near neighbour of Pepys.

Fox, Sir Stephen. Treasurer of the Army and friend of Pepys.

Gauden, Sir Denis. Victualler of the Navy and to the Tangier garrison. Business associate and friend of Pepys.

Gloucester, Duke of. Youngest brother of Charles II. Died of smallpox shortly after the Restoration.

Gosnell, Mrs. Briefly a companion of Elizabeth Pepys, and then an actress.

Gwynn (or Gwyn or Gwynne), Nell. 1650–1687. According to one account born at Hereford, but more probably in Coal Yard, Drury Lane, London. In her early years she was employed in a brothel run by one Mother Ross, and later as an orange-seller at the Theatre Royal (King's Playhouse). Her admirers assisted her to become an actress, and she first appeared in Dryden's *The Indian Emperor* in 1665, as well as in *Flora's Vagaries* by Richard Rhodes. Between 1670 and 1677 she left the stage; after that date she returned to acting until the King's and the Duke's companies merged in 1682. Her speciality was speaking the prologue and the epilogue, and it was after seeing her deliver one of the latter (in a hat as large as a cartwheel), that Charles II first took her home in his coach. Nell Gwynn endeared herself to the English public as a rival to the hated French spy, Louise de Quérouáille, Duchess of Portsmouth. Such was the hatred for Charles II's French love that when Nell Gwynn in her coach was mobbed by a hostile crowd by mistake, she thrust her head out of the window exclaiming: 'Pray, good people, be civil: I am the Protestant whore.' 'Pretty witty Nell', who was never at a loss for an answer, was in fact illiterate, and could only sign 'E. G.' (Eleanor Gwynn) to letters written for her. Had Charles II not died when he did she would probably have become Countess of Greenwich, and his dying remark to his brother James of 'Let not poor Nelly starve' does seem to be genuine, having been recorded by both Evelyn and Bishop Burnet. Her debts were settled by James II, paid with money meant for the secret service, and she was given Bestwood Park, Nottingham. Unlike Lady Castlemaine, she ended her days quietly.

Hales (or Hayls), John. Died 1679. Portrait painter and rival of Lely. He painted what is perhaps the finest portrait of Pepys, and also Elizabeth Pepys as St Catharine, but the latter has long since vanished.

Henrietta Maria, Queen. 1609–1669. The daughter of Henri IV of France and wife of Charles I. Her surviving children were Charles (II); Mary, Princess of Orange; James (II); Henry (Duke of Gloucester); Elizabeth; and Henrietta (Duchess of Orleans). Henrietta Maria was strong willed and pleasure-loving, and before the outbreak of the Civil War interfered in politics, as well as giving her husband the King a great deal of unsound advice. In 1642 she left England, taking with her part of the Crown Jewels, which were pawned in Amsterdam to buy munitions. In 1644 she visited France to attempt to enlist aid, and after the execution of her husband remained in that country, where she turned to religion for consolation. There was almost a breach between herself and Charles II over her attempts to convert his youngest brother Henry, Duke of Gloucester, to Catholicism. In November 1660 she returned to England, hoping to break the proposed union between Charles II and Catharine of Braganza, which was not in the interest of the French, but failed. Henrietta Maria had her own household at Somerset House, where she was seen by Pepys, who also attended services in her Catholic chapel. In 1661 she returned to France, where her youngest daughter Henrietta was married to the King's brother, the Duke of Orleans. Later she again made England her home, but left for good in 1665, dying near Paris in 1669.

Hewer, Will. Born 1643. Nephew of Robert Blackburne, Secretary of the Admiralty. He originally entered Pepy's service as clerk in 1660, and became a lifelong friend. It was at his house that Pepy's died in 1703.

Holmes, Sir Robert or Robin (sometimes described as Major or Captain) 1622–1692. Of Irish parentage, he served in the Royalist Army during the Civil War, and during the Commonwealth saw action with James, Duke of York. In October 1660 he was appointed Captain and Governor of Sandown Castle, Isle of Wight, and sailed for the Guinea coast to protect trade routes. It was his being charged with letting a Swedish vessel sail past him without striking her flag which set Pepys delving into the history of the English Navy. In

1663 Holmes was again in West Africa (Gambia), supporting English traders against their Dutch rivals. Then he crossed the Atlantic and forced the Dutch from the New Netherlands, for which he was sent to the Tower on his return. But with the start of the Second Dutch War a few months later he returned to royal favour, and saw action in the *Revenge* at the Battle of Lowestoft in June 1665. The following year he was knighted, and acquitted himself well aboard the *Defiance* during the Four Days' Fight (June 1666), and later in the St James's Day Fight (25 July 1666). On 8 August he attacked the islands of Vlieland and Terschelling, and burnt between 150 and 160 merchantmen, as well as causing havoc ashore. At home the event was referred to as 'Holmes' Bonfire'. In June the following year the Dutch had their revenge when they sailed up the Medway and burnt or towed away much of the English Fleet. Early in 1667 Holmes became an Admiral at Portsmouth, and MP for Winchester. During the Third Dutch War he made an unwise and unsuccessful attack on a Dutch convoy coming up the Channel, and after that time his active career at sea ended. Later he became Governor of the Isle of Wight, dying in 1692.

Howe, Will. First employed by Lord Sandwich, he became acquainted with Pepys during the mission to bring Charles II to England for the Restoration. Later he rose in importance in Lord Sandwich's household. On a number of occasions he and Pepys made music together.

James, Duke of York (later James II). 1633–1701. The second surviving son of Charles I, he escaped abroad shortly before his father's execution, going to Holland. During much of the Commonwealth he was in France, serving with Marshal Turenne in the Wars of the Fronde, and later with the Spaniards in Flanders. At the Restoration his brother appointed him Lord High Admiral, with command of the Navy (his secretary being Sir William Coventry). In that capacity he took an active part in the Second Dutch War, particularly in the sea fights of 1665. In 1659 he had married (in secret) Anne Hyde, daughter of the Lord Chancellor, Lord Clarendon. By this marriage he had two daughters, Mary and Anne, both of whom became Queen. In 1670 he became a Roman Catholic, and after Anne Hyde's death married Mary of Modena (1673). It was the birth of their son James (the Old Pretender) which touched off the revolution which drove him from the throne in 1688.

The Test Act of 1673 forced James, as a Catholic, to resign from all public offices, and between 1679–81 the Exclusion Bills were laid before Parliament in an attempt to exclude him from the succession. But on his brother's death in 1685 he did become King, which led to Monmouth's Rebellion. James II, as he now was, appointed Roman Catholics to high office, and in 1687 he was responsible for the Declaration of Indulgence, which resulted in the trial of the Seven Bishops, ending in their acquittal amid public rejoicing. In 1688 Prince William (a descendant of James I) landed from Holland, and James II's own daughter Mary went over to his side. The Glorious Revolution had come about, and James II went into exile. Despite campaigns in Ireland, fought with the aid of French troops supplied by Louis XIV, which culminated in his defeat by King William at the Battle of the Boyne in 1690, he never returned to England, and died in exile at St Germain in 1701.

Joyce, Anthony. Cousin by marriage of Pepys and landlord of a tavern in Holborn. He suffered financial loss as a result of the Great Fire, and later committed suicide. His wife Kate (Pepys's cousin on his mother's side) remarried.

Joyce, William. Brother of Anthony, and friendly with Pepys, who however feared his tongue.

Killigrew, Tom. 1612–1683. Son of Sir Robert Killigrew. As a small boy he used to offer to play the parts of devils or boys at the Red Bull Playhouse, so he could see the performance for nothing. Later he became a page to Charles I, and after 1647 became the inseparable companion of the future Charles II. In exile he visited Italy, becoming the English Resident in Venice, but his removal was requested because of his scandalous and irresponsible conduct. After the Restoration he was appointed a Groom of the Bedchamber, and in 1662 he and Davenant were granted patents to erect two new play-houses. Killigrew built the Theatre Royal, later to be called the Drury Lane Theatre, which opened in 1663. In 1668 Killigrew became the King's Jester, so making him immune from the justifiable wrath of those who suffered from his buffoonery. He was in fact one of the most rakish of the Restoration wits.

Kite, Mrs. Aunt of Pepys.

Knipp, Mrs (Bab Allen). An actress, much admired by Pepys.

Lambert, Lieutenant (later Captain). Naval officer and friend of Pepys, killed during the Second Dutch War.

Lane, Betty (later Mrs Martin). A linen-seller in Westminster Hall, and one of Pepys's conquests.

Lely, Sir Peter. 1618–1680. Court painter of Dutch origin, who came to England in 1641 at the same time as Prince William of Orange (not to be confused with the future King William). He painted Charles I when the King was held at Hampton Court in 1647, and during the Commonwealth Cromwell was among his sitters. He came into his own at the Restoration, becoming the most fashionable painter in England. On the Duke of York's instructions he painted the Admirals who had taken part in the Battle of Lowestoft (1665), including Lord Sandwich.

Locke, Matthew. 1630?–1677. Composer. At an early age he became a chorister of Exeter Cathedral (where he scratched his name on the organ screen). By 1651 he was composing, and part of the *Siege of Rhodes* (1656) was from his pen. Three years later he met Pepys, who sang some of his vocal pieces. Locke composed music 'for the king's sagbutts and cornets' used in the procession of recognition across London the day before Charles II's Coronation. Later he became 'Composer in Ordinary to His Majesty', and composed a number of anthems, and a setting (tried over by Pepys) of the Ten Commandments. In addition to composing, particularly for viols, he also wrote on the theory of music.

Mercer, Mary. Companion to Elizabeth Pepys, who left during the Great Fire, but remained on friendly terms with the family.

Mills, Daniel. Rector of St Olave, Hart Street.

Mings, Sir Christopher. A particularly gallant sea captain beloved by his men. Pepys attended his funeral during the Second Dutch War.

Minnes (or Mennes), Sir John. 1599–1671. Admiral and Comptroller of the Navy. He made the Navy his career, and by 1640 he was Captain of the *Victory*. At the outbreak of the Civil War he was knighted, and in 1644 became Governor of North Wales. Later he served at sea with Prince Rupert, and was in the squadron finally destroyed by Blake in 1650. At the Restoration he returned from exile, and in October 1661 was appointed Comptroller of the Navy in succession to Sir Robert Slingsby. A year later he was elected Master of Trinity House. At the Navy Office he came into frequent contact with Pepys, who summed him up as 'a very good, honest gentleman, though not fit for business'; though there were occasions when he thought him a prating fool. Sir John was buried, like Pepys, in St Olave, Hart Street.

Monmouth, Duke of (James Crofts, later took his wife's surname of Scott). 1649–1685. Illegitimate son of Charles II and Lucy Waters. He was brought up first by Lord Crofts, and later in France by Queen Henrietta Maria. He was called to England to take his place at Court soon after the Restoration, where he became something of a spoilt darling, and while still adolescent was married to Anne Scott (of Buccleuch). His sympathies were Protestant, and those of that faction saw him as a figurehead and even as a future king, and the rumour started that his parents were in fact married. Lord Shaftesbury went so far as to urge Charles II to legitimise him, but after the failure of the Rye House Plot (for the assassination of Charles II and James, Duke of York) he fled abroad, but was pardoned. After the accession of James II he invaded the West Country in Monmouth's Rebellion, but was defeated and captured at Sedgemoor, and later executed.

Montagu, Edward (1st Earl of Sandwich). 1625–1672. Son of Sir Sidney Montagu and Paulina, daughter of John Pepys of Cottenham (and great-aunt of Samuel Pepys). As a young man he was Parliamentarian in sympathy, and in fact related to Oliver Cromwell, with whom he had close and personal contact. In 1642 he married Jemimah, daughter of John (later Lord) Crewe. Edward Montagu took part in the Battle of Marston Moor (1644) and later commanded a regiment of the New Model Army. In 1653 he was nominated a member of the Council of State, and a year later became a Commissioner of the Treasury. In 1656 he became joint commander of the Fleet with Robert Blake. The same year he was present in Spanish waters when their West India Treasure Fleet was captured. In 1657–8 he commanded the Fleet in the Downs. After the Protector's death he remained loyal to Richard Cromwell, and assumed command of the Fleet ordered to the Ore Sund to arrange a peace between Sweden and Denmark. It was on that mission that he was visited by Pepys, acting on behalf of the government at home. For a while Pepys had already been Edward Montagu's secretary, transacting business for him from lodgings in Whitehall. As much as anything it was private information that Pepys brought him that changed his sympathies to the Royalists and he entered into correspondence with Charles II. On his return to England he resigned his command and retired to his estate at Hinchingbrooke. In February 1660 he was reappointed General of the Fleet (jointly with General Monk), and in April he read the King's letter from Breda to the assembled officers of the Fleet, and less than a month later the Restoration was an accomplished fact. For his part in it Edward Montagu became a Knight of the Garter and Earl of Sandwich. Also he was appointed Master of the Wardrobe, Admiral of the Narrow Seas, and Lieutenant-Admiral to the Duke of York. In the second capacity it was his duty to escort Queen Henrietta Maria to and from England, and to bring Catharine of Braganza from Portugal to become the wife of Charles II (1662). During 1665, after the outbreak of the Second Dutch War, Lord Sandwich had his flag on the *Prince*, as Admiral of the Blue Squadron, acquitting himself well during the Battle of Lowestoft. In July he sailed towards Bergen to intercept a convoy of Dutch merchantmen. When he pursued them into harbour as a result of a misunderstanding he was fired on by the Danes (then holding what is now a Norwegian port). In September he had better luck, when he captured nine large merchantmen with cargo from the East Indies. Unwisely he 'broke bulk', seizing part of the cargo for himself and his fellow Admirals. The result was a scandal, made worse by his enemies, which broke him, and there was even talk of impeachment. But he retained the King's favour, and was made Ambassador Extraordinary to Spain, where he remained from 1666 until 1668. There he negotiated treaties between England and Spain as well as between Spain and Portugal. At the outbreak of the Third Dutch War in 1672 he was second in command of the Fleet, under the Duke of York. This time France was an ally against the Netherlands. At the Battle of Sole Bay (28 May 1672) Lord Sandwich led the Blue Squadron. He was outnumbered, but fought gallantly; then the *Royal James* was grappled by a Dutch fire-ship, and it blew up. Lord Sandwich's body was found off Harwich nearly a fortnight later, and in due course he was given a hero's funeral, being buried in the Henry VII Chapel in Westminster Abbey. Also killed at the Battle of Sole Bay was his son-in-law Sir Philip Carteret. Lady Sandwich was particularly kind to Pepys, who advised on many matters during her husband's absence at sea or abroad in Spain. Pepys was also very friendly with the children: Edward (later Lord Hinchingbrooke); Sidney; Oliver and George; and the two daughters, Jemimah and Paulina.

Moore, Henry. Clerk at the Exchequer Office, and friend of Pepys.

Pembleton, Mr. A dancing-master of whom Pepys was jealous.

Penn, Sir William. Died 1670. He came from a West Country seafaring family, and after 1644 served in the Parliamentarian Navy, and in 1648 became a Vice-Admiral. His duties took him to the Azores, searching for Prince Rupert. He saw service under Blake in the First Dutch War, with Monk as a fellow commander. In 1654 he changed his allegiance, but was advised by the Royalists to sail for the West Indies, which he did. On his return he and Venables, also a commander on the expedition, were committed to the Tower for a reason which has remained obscure. After a few weeks of imprisonment Penn returned to estates in Ireland, granted in 1653, where he remained until sailing in the *Naseby* to bring over Charles II in 1660. He was knighted on the spot by the King, and later appointed a Commissioner of the Navy. In March 1665 he served as second in command to the Duke of York on the *Charles* during the Battle of Lowestoft. But his tactics were criticised, and after that time he was not employed afloat. In 1667, after the disaster at Chatham, he resigned as a Commissioner of the Navy. He married about 1639 and had two sons: the elder, also William, was the founder of Pennsylvania, and there was a daughter Margaret (Peg). For seven years he was Pepys's colleague, neighbour and sometime friend.

Pepys, Elizabeth. 1640–1669. Wife of Samuel. Born Elizabeth Le Marchant de St Michel, she was the daughter of a French émigré who came to England at the same time as Queen Henrietta Maria, and the daughter of an Anglo-Irish knight. Only fifteen when she married Samuel Pepys in 1655, her early death was a tragic blow for Pepys. There were no children.

Pepys, John. 1601–1680. Father of Samuel Pepys. Originally from Cambridgeshire, he came to London to become a tailor, and married Margaret Kite. They had four surviving children: Samuel, Tom, Paulina (Pall) and John. He retired from tailoring in 1661, going to live at Brampton in Huntingdonshire, where his wife died in 1667.

Pepys, John. 1641–1677. Brother of Samuel. Educated at St Paul's School, and Christ's College, Cambridge. He entered the Church, and died a bachelor.

Pepys, Paulina (Pall). 1640–1680. Sister of Samuel. Moved to the country when their father gave up business, and eventually married John Jackson, a prosperous grazier. Their son, of the same name, became a particular favourite of Pepys in his last years and one of the executors of his will.

Pepys, Robert. Uncle to Samuel (and half-brother to his father), from whom he inherited property at Brampton, Huntingdonshire.

Pepys, Roger. Son of Talbot Pepys, and cousin of Samuel, MP for Cambridge.

Pepys, Thomas. Uncle of Samuel, and father of Thomas Pepys the Turner, a cousin who had an ironmonger's business near Old St Paul's, which was burnt in the Great Fire.

Pepys, Thomas (Tom). 1634–1664. Brother of Samuel. He took over the tailor's shop in Salisbury Court on the retirement of their father, but failed to make a success of the business. He died from tuberculosis.

Pett, Peter (Sir). 1610–1670? Commissioner for the Navy, and a member of a distinguished family of shipbuilders at Deptford and Woolwich. During the Civil War he built ships for the Parliamentarians and during the Commonwealth became a Commissioner of the Navy at Chatham (responsible for the maintenance of the dockyard), where he had a house. He was reappointed at the Restoration, and remained in office until September 1667, when he was suspended during the inquiry following the Dutch incursion up the Medway. Earlier, in June, he had been committed for a while to the Tower, and examined before the Council, and even threatened with impeachment. After that date he disappeared from public life and even the date of his death is uncertain.

Pickering, Edward (Ned). Related by marriage to Lady Sandwich, he was a great retailer of Court and family gossip to Pepys.

Pierce, James. Originally the surgeon on the *Naseby*, and later surgeon to James, Duke of York. He and his wife, *la belle* Pierce, were personal friends of Samuel and Elizabeth Pepys.

Pierce, Mr. Purser of the *Naseby* (later *Royal Charles*).

Povy, Thomas. Member of the Tangier Commission. Pepys admired his life-style, but found him a fool who was defeated by his duties as Treasurer of the Tangier Commission, which he took over from him. It was Povy who introduced Pepys to Lord Brouncker and later proposed him for membership of the Royal Society.

Rider, Sir William. A member of the Tangier Commission, who took care of Pepys's most treasured possessions (including the Diary) during the Great Fire.

Robinson, Sir John. Lieutenant of the Tower, and later Lord Mayor of London. Although a friend of Pepys, the diarist had no very high opinion of his intelligence.

Rochester, Earl of (John Wilmot). 1647–1680. An individual whose reputation as a poet has not altogether surprisingly been eclipsed by his sensational career at Court as a rake, seducer and wit.

Rupert, Prince. 1619–1682. Son of Elizabeth, Queen of Bohemia (the Winter Queen, and a daughter of James I) and Frederick V, Elector Palatine. He accompanied his parents as an infant when they fled from Prague in 1620 after the Battle of the White Mountain, going with his mother to live in Holland. As a young man he saw action during the Thirty Years War. In the Civil War he was the victor at Cirencester, Birmingham, Lichfield and Chalgrove Field; as well as capturing Bristol and relieving Newark, but his campaigning in the north was ended at Marston Moor in 1644. During the Commonwealth he headed the Royalist exiles in France, and commanded a Royalist fleet, but was defeated by Blake in 1650. He returned to England with Charles II, and served at sea during the Second Dutch War. In 1673 he was made an Admiral of the Fleet. His last years were devoted to art and science.

St Michel, Balthazar (Balty). Brother of Elizabeth Pepys, and regarded for several years by the diarist as something of a ne'er-do-well, who however acquitted himself admirably during the Second Dutch War. Years later Pepys obtained a post for him at Tangier.

Sarah. Maid to Mr and Mrs Pepys.

Sarah, Mrs. Housekeeper to Lord and Lady Sandwich.

Savill, Mr. Artist residing in Cheapside who painted both Samuel and Elizabeth Pepys.

Shaftesbury, Earl of (Anthony Ashley Cooper). 1621–1683. MP for Tewkesbury in 1640, he was at first a Royalist, and then a Parliamentarian, becoming a member of the Privy Council. But he supported the Restoration, and was one of the twelve who went to Holland to invite the King to return. In 1661 he became Baron Ashley, Chancellor of the Exchequer and a Lord of the Treasury. Later he became a member of the Cabal, and in 1672 received the title of Earl of Shaftesbury, as well as becoming Lord Chancellor (and founder of the Whig Party). He was opposed to the Duke of York, and sided with the Duke of Monmouth, which resulted in his being sent to the Tower. After his acquittal he went to live in Holland, where he died.

Shepley, William. Steward to Lord Sandwich at Hinchingbrooke. He showed a kindly interest in Pepys during his early years.

Slingsby, Colonel (Sir) Robert. Comptroller of the Navy. An honest and zealous man much admired by Pepys who regretted his death in 1661.

Stuart, Frances (later Duchess of Richmond). 1648–1702. Her father was a member of the household of Queen Henrietta Maria, and she spent her earliest years in exile in France. In 1663 she was appointed a Lady-in-Waiting to Catharine of Braganza, when she first attracted Charles II's attention. Although all her life 'a bright young thing', addicted to blind man's buff, hunt the slipper and building houses with cards, she was not promiscuous. Finally Charles II struck a bargain with her, if she wanted to be the first to ride out in a calèche—newly arrived from France—she could do so, at a price. To the fury of the tempestuous Lady Castlemaine the King became more and more enamoured of her, but in 1667 Frances Stuart ran away from Court to become the third wife of the Duke of Richmond. Charles II was furious, having even considered divorcing the Queen in order to marry her. But the Queen considered her less harmful than others in the royal circle, mediated in the quarrel, and even had her appointed a Lady of the Bedchamber. The Duke, however, was sent abroad as Ambassador to Denmark. It was her profile that first appeared on the halfpennies as Britannia in 1672, and was later transferred to the pennies.

Turner, Mrs Jane. Cousin of Pepys, resident in Salisbury Court until the Great Fire. She had a daughter Theophila, referred to in the Diary as The.

Turner, Mr. Employed at the Navy Office (in 1669 made Store-keeper at Deptford) and neighbour of Pepys (who found his wife particularly attractive).

Warren, Sir William. Timber merchant, business associate and friend of Pepys.

Warwick, Sir Philip. Treasury official.

Wayneman, Jane. Serving-girl to Mr and Mrs Pepys.

Wayneman, Will. Brother of Jane, employed for a while by Pepys.

Willett, Deb. The young girl employed as a companion to Elizabeth Pepys, but who left as a result of Pepys's indiscreet conduct. Nothing is known of her subsequent life.

Williams, Mrs. Mistress of Lord Brouncker.

Wood, Mr. Mast-maker and business associate of Pepys.

Wren, Dr. Later Sir Christopher, the celebrated architect.

Wren, Matthew. Cousin of Dr Wren, and secretary to the Duke of York.

Young, Mr. Flagmaker, and business associate of Pepys.

Index